Praise for Ed Robertson

Reviews for *This is Jim Rockford/The Rockford Files*

"An important history in the entertainment world."

The Salisbury Post

"The most comprehensive episode guide ever seen in any book."

Television Chronicles

"Another great work by Robertson … He's still the standard by which TV reference should be judged."

Popocalypse World of Fun

Reviews for *The Ethics of Star Trek*

"Trekkies will want to beam this book up to their shelves."

Publishers Weekly

"The writing is non-technical and accessible, and this book, with its focus on a piece of popular culture, can be a useful introduction to the various philosophical schools of thought."

Boulder Weekly

"A fascinating use of popular culture to engender sophisticated discussions of ethical theory … One need not be a guru in the cabala of *Star Trek* to appreciate and understand the witty instruction in ethics found in this volume."

The Reading Room

"This isn't a book for the hardcore *Star Trek* canon. It's for the vast majority of us—people who are intimately familiar with *Star Trek* just because it's so darned pervasive culturally."

Netsurfer Books

Reviews for *Maverick: Legend of the West*

"This is one of those books that transcends its own parochial interest to shed light on an entire medium: the players emerge as three-dimensional, idiosyncratic characters, and when the decline of the series is delineated, one feels it profoundly as the genuine tragedy and short-sided artistic waste that it was. Mr. Robertson performed the same honors in *The Fugitive Recaptured*, and, as notable works of television journalism, both deal a straight flush."

The Nassau Herald

"A thorough documentation of the Emmy Award-winning series."

Ingram Reviews

"Ed Robertson has studied and described this entertainment phenomenon from its beginning in 1956 to its most recent return, the Warner Bros. movie in 1994. Robertson has made that history suspenseful and absorbing, and I am persuaded, after reading *Maverick: Legend of the West*, that *Maverick* is nowhere near the end of its illustrious history."

Roy Huggins
creator of *Maverick* and co-creator of *The Rockford Files*,
from his Foreword to *Maverick: Legend of the West*

Reviews for *The Fugitive Recaptured*

"The definitive book on the series."

TV Guide

"What a break for fans of the original series ... with entertaining details about and analysis of each episode."

The Los Angeles Times

"By the scrupulous research and tasteful presentation of his book, Ed Robertson has created a brilliant record of one of the outstanding achievements of television history, of which I for one am proud to have been a part. It will fascinate viewers of all generations."

Barry Morse,
"Lt. Philip Gerard" on *The Fugitive*,
from his Foreword to *The Fugitive Recaptured*

Thirty Years of
THE ROCKFORD FILES

Also by Ed Robertson

The Ethics of Star Trek

This is Jim Rockford/The Rockford Files

Maverick: Legend of the West

The Fugitive Recaptured

Original art © 2005 by Darin Bristow

Thirty Years of
THE ROCKFORD FILES

An Inside Look at America's Greatest Detective Series

Ed Robertson

ASJA Press
New York   Lincoln   Shanghai

Thirty Years of THE ROCKFORD FILES
An Inside Look at America's Greatest Detective Series

Copyright © 1995, 2005 by Ed Robertson

ASJA Press
an imprint of iUniverse, Inc.

iUniverse books may be ordered through booksellers or by contacting:

iUniverse
2021 Pine Lake Road, Suite 100
Lincoln, NE 68512
www.iuniverse.com
1-800-Authors (1-800-288-4677)

ISBN: 0-595-34244-2

Printed in the United States of America

Contents

In Memoriam

Roy Huggins
1914–2002

He was a gracious, quiet man, with a dancing quality in his eyes that made it clear that the world around him was fresh material for a new direction. If he had one particular strength, it was in creating original characters who were always just ahead of the genre in which they existed.

Stuart Kaminsky,
Author,
The Rockford Files: The Green Bottle
The Rockford Files: Devil on My Doorstep
As quoted in *January Magazine*

Roy was a giant in the television history. He was brilliant. He had a very fertile mind and was a great storyteller. I think he had a sort of natural sense of popular art at the time.

Jo Swerling, Jr.
Supervising Producer,
The Rockford Files
As quoted in *The Los Angeles Times*

He taught me everything that I used throughout my career on how to create and produce a television show. I couldn't have been luckier. Even when he was in his 80s, he was like a guy 30 years old.
He was always hip, always current. He talked the talk of young people. In his head, he wasn't an old man at all.

Stephen J. Cannell
Co-Creator, Writer, and Supervising Producer,
The Rockford Files
As quoted in *The Los Angeles Times*

Photograph by Chloe Ann Rounsley

Ed Robertson (left) and Roy Huggins. This photograph was taken in July 2001, nine months before Huggins passed away.

There's not much I can add to the eloquence of Messrs. Kaminsky, Swerling and Cannell ... except to say that Roy Huggins was a very important part of my life. He played a vital role in the success of my first three books. He was also a friend, a mentor, and in many ways a father figure.

This book is dedicated to his memory.

Ed Robertson
January 2005

Prologue with Acknowledgments

This book was originally published in July 1995 under the title *This is Jim Rockford: The Rockford Files*. Obviously much has happened since that time, not only with respect to the history of *The Rockford Files* but also in the career of James Garner.

As the 2004-2005 season marks the 30th anniversary of *Rockford's* premiere on NBC, there is no better time to commemorate the occasion than with a second edition of the book. This updated volume includes over 250 pages of new information, including additional interviews, a behind-the-scenes look at all eight CBS movies, new data about the NBC *Rockford Files,* and other interesting material that was not included in the original book due to editorial decisions or simply for reasons of space. This second edition also features new artwork and photographs, many of which have never been published before. Finally, this update allowed me to correct certain goofs that I had somehow failed to catch before the first edition went to press. In many ways, *Thirty Years of The Rockford Files* is a brand new book. I hope that you all enjoy it.

Writing, revising or even updating a book of this kind is impossible without the help of a great many people. I want to thank them all and hope I haven't overlooked anyone.

For their time, patience and professionalism in granting interviews for the first edition, I thank Frank Price, Luis Delgado, Howard Browne, Jack Garner, Jack Wilson, Gretchen Corbett, and Jo Swerling Jr.

I am particularly indebted to James Garner, Juanita Bartlett, and Charles Floyd Johnson, all of whom took time from the making of the new *Rockford Files* movies in 1995 to take part in this project; to Stephen J. Cannell, who, though under deadline at the time with regard to his first novel *King Con*, was also gracious enough to meet with me in January 1995 to take part in this project; and to Roy Huggins and Adele Mara, for their time, for answering dozens and dozens of questions, and for granting me access to their personal files regarding the series.

This history could not have been completed without the help of Grace Curcio and Christine Trepcyzk of Cannell Entertainment; Kathy Ezso, Sally Scovel, and MaryAnn Rea of *The Rockford Files*; Francis Cavanaugh, Director of Photography, CBS-TV; Colleen Lightfoot of Mike Post Productions; Kimberly Koonen of Price Entertainment; Jennifer Allen; Dave Charmatz and Judith Currin of A&E; David Martindale; and my original publishers, Kathryn Leigh Scott and Ben Martin of Pomegranate Press.

I also thank JoAnn Collins, Barry Gruber, Frank Free, Rusty Pollard, David Miller, Bob Charger, Stuart Shostak, Mary DeBoom and Jon Strauss, Jim Benson, Jim Rondeau, Bob Rubin, and Blake Delgado.

My gratitude goes to the various members of the following organizations who provided assistance and/or information along the way: the San Francisco Public Library; the University of Southern California Reference Library; Certification Section, Civil Processing Division, Los Angeles County Records Center (special thanks to Dante for service above and beyond the call of duty); the Screen Actors Guild; the Directors Guild of America; the National Academy of Television Arts and Sciences; ASCAP; Susan Chicone of Nielsen Media Research; Sherry Ceiling of DeForest Research, Inc.; the TV History Archive; and Photofest of New York.

A collective Thank You to the many readers who have sent me cards, letters and emails over the years. I appreciate your comments and suggestions, and have implemented as many as possible.

A further mention must go to Charles Floyd Johnson and MaryAnn Rea. In addition to helping me on the first edition, they also provided essential background information about the CBS movies for the second edition.

Special thanks to the following people for their invaluable contributions to the second edition:

- Darin Bristow, for designing a brand new front and back cover for this edition, and for contributing the many original sketches of James Garner and *The Rockford Files* that grace these pages;

- Rob Howe, for providing additional insight into the fifth and sixth seasons of the original series, as well as for sharing many of the rare behind-the-scenes photographs that appear in this volume;

- Frankie Montiforte, whose passion for *Rockford* (particularly when it comes to "Feeding Frenzy" and "Irving the Explainer") and understanding of television are truly unmatched;

- Steve Reich, for his insight into Rockford's Pontiac Firebird;

- Ray Claridge and Cinema Vehicle Services, for providing the photograph of the Firebird that appears in Appendix F;

- Steve Rinek, publisher of the *Wrightwood Mountaineer-Progress*, for use of the article and accompanying photo of James Garner that appears in the write-up on "Deadlock in Parma";
- Mike Altman of iUniverse Publishing Services;
- and Ronn Owens, award-winning radio talk show host and author of *Voice of Reason*, who graciously shared the microphone with me on the day James Garner appeared on his top-rated morning show on KGO-AM/San Francisco. Not everyone would have done that, Ronn, and that's what makes you the best.

Last, but not least ... my wife Chloe Rounsley, with all my heart and soul.

Photograph courtesy of Milton T. Moore Jr.
© 1974 Universal City Studios, Inc.

Introduction

He looked like Steve McGarrett. He dressed like Joe Mannix. But he acted like no other private detective prime time television had ever seen.

When he threw a punch, Jim Rockford (James Garner) was more likely to hurt his own hand than his opponent. He rarely carried a gun (he didn't have a permit), and on those occasions when he did, he was more likely to point the weapon than fire it. Rockford hated trouble, wouldn't hesitate to quit in the middle of a case if things got too rough, and had no qualms about telling you why ("You're damned right I'm afraid!"). But he did like money: he charged $200 a day, plus expenses, so he'd hang in there no matter what if he could smell a fat check down the road. "I won't kill for money, and I won't marry for it," he once said. "Other than that, I'm open to just about anything."

Most private eyes—at least, the ones we see portrayed in movies and on television—have a lieutenant friend on the police force with whom they trade information in the course of a given case. But because Rockford was an ex-con (he was unjustly convicted of armed robbery and served five years in prison before receiving a full pardon), he didn't always trust the police. For that matter, nearly everyone in the Los Angeles Police Department despised Rockford because he had a propensity for solving cases that the cops had either closed or considered unsolvable. In fact, whenever Rockford showed up at headquarters with a broken nose or a bloody lip, morale in the department automatically went up ten percent!

The one cop willing to stand up for our man Jimbo was the overworked and grossly underappreciated Sergeant Dennis Becker (Joe Santos), who genuinely liked Rockford even though he was occasionally embarrassed by their relationship, particularly whenever it interfered with his police duties.

Rockford had a lot of other characteristics that TV audiences could identify with. He had a paunch (he had a weakness for Oreo cookies). He also liked to drink beer and eat fast food (in one episode, Becker calls him "the taco king"). He preferred watching baseball and basketball games over the theater or opera. He didn't like to exert himself (if he could, he'd spend all day fishing on the beach). He didn't like going to the dentist (he once put off a root canal appointment four times). He'd go to any lengths (even asking for a note from his doctor) to avoid jury duty.

Rockford could be a rascal—he was once considered one of the finest grafters in the business. But he also had a sweetness that particularly came across in his relationship with his father, Joseph "Rocky" Rockford (Noah Beery), a retired truck driver who doesn't quite understand what his son does for a living. Rockford had a big heart (sometimes, despite himself), which explains why he occasionally worked *pro bono* for his friend and attorney Beth Davenport (Gretchen Corbett). But he also had a limited amount of patience, which was often exhausted by the exasperating antics of his former cellmate Angel Martin (Stuart Margolin).

Fueled by excellent writing, memorable characters, and the star power of James Garner, *The Rockford Files* enjoyed a solid six-season run on NBC (1974-1980), and remains one of the most beloved television programs of all time. Winner of five Emmys, including Best Actor (Garner) and Best Dramatic Series (1978), *Rockford* came back with a splash in 1994 as a series of two-hour movies on CBS. Reruns of the original NBC series have played continuously in syndication and on national cable TV over the past 25 years, while the reunion movies from CBS have been a staple of Court TV and the Hallmark Channel since early 2001.

Of course, in some ways, Jim Rockford wasn't original at all: he was Bret Maverick reincarnated, the folksy, quasi-con man who would change his mind in a minute if he thought it would get him out of trouble. Like Maverick, Rockford was a man much smarter than he let on, and who couldn't care less about being a hero.

All of which was deliberate. *The Rockford Files* first sprouted from the fertile mind of Roy Huggins, the creative force behind *The Fugitive* and *77 Sunset Strip*, as well as the man who had helped make Garner a star years before on *Maverick*. Huggins understood Garner's uncanny knack for playing wry, understated humor like few others. That Garner's greatest successes on television are tied directly to Huggins is no coincidence.

You actually could break down *The Rockford Files* into three different series: the episodes from the first year, when it was a Top Ten hit; the shows from the second year, when it lost a huge chunk of audience that it would never recover; and the episodes from the remaining four seasons, when it started winning all those Emmy Awards.

Rockford in its first season (1974-1975) was to private-eye shows what *Maverick* was to Westerns in the 1950s: fresh, irreverent, and clever. At a time when network TV was saturated with flatfoots and gumshoes, *Rockford* took all the cliches and turned them inside out. NBC programming executives may not have understood the show's sophisticated sense of humor, but the viewers certainly did, taking to Garner like a long-lost friend. *Rockford* suddenly made it cool to stay home on Friday nights.

When the first season ended, executive producer Roy Huggins left *Rockford* in the hands of his protégé Stephen J. Cannell (now the author of such bestselling crime novels as *The Plan, King Con, Final Victim, Riding the Snake, The Devil's Workshop, The Tin Collectors, The Viking Funeral, Hollywood Tough, Runaway Heart* and *Vertical Coffin*). Though Cannell understood Maverick/Rockford almost as well as his mentor, and had himself created two of the show's greatest characters (Rocky and Angel), he initially lost sight of what made *Rockford* work—and the show suffered as a result. The key to *Rockford* was that, no matter what, Jim Rockford was always smarter than anyone else. But that wasn't the case early in the second season (1975-1976) when, week after week, Jimbo found himself played like a fool, particularly by his own friends.

Both *Maverick* (and *Rockford* under Huggins) dared to invert that most sacred of TV rules: the hero always comes out on top in the end. Maverick/Rockford was occasionally done in by his own mercenary tendencies, often to hilarious effect. But Huggins also knew that the key to breaking the rules was doing so with restraint. The audience was bound to grow tired of watching if Rockford ended up with egg on his face every week.

That's exactly what happened in the second season. By Halloween, *Rockford* had lost nearly 20% of its total audience; by the end of the season, it was finishing third in a time slot it once owned. Though Cannell recognized the problem with the stories, and was able to steer the series back on track, *Rockford* would never see the Top Ten (or even the Top 20) again.

Then a funny thing happened in the third season (1976-1977). Buoyed by the addition of writer/producer David Chase *(The Sopranos)*, the stories got better, the audience numbers steadied … and the show started winning awards.

Chase's versatility breathed new life into *Rockford*. In addition to populating the series with a wide array of colorful characters, the stories began tackling everything from controversial social issues to Chase's own peculiar obsession with the mob. In the process, Jim Rockford became reinvented as a sort of Everyman, a lone voice of common sense in a world of increasing absurdity.

Rockford also survived a number of controversies that plagued the series behind the scenes. NBC was initially reluctant to finance the pilot because of its previous experience with Garner in the ill-fated Western series *Nichols*. A conflict between Garner, Huggins and executive producer Meta Rosenberg led to the departure of Huggins after the first season. Problems fomented by the show's approach to humor during the second season led to an angry confrontation between Garner and Universal Television president Frank Price. A power play between Universal Studios and Garner's production company resulted in the loss of one of the show's most popular characters, Beth Davenport. Finally, the abrupt end of *The Rockford Files* (brought on by Garner's illness in December 1979), coming on the heels of a startling report indicating that the series was nine million dollars in the red, precipitated a bitter legal battle between the actor and the studio that would last nearly ten years.

We'll explore these aspects of the show's history, and much, much more.

I also discovered, as I conducted interviews for this book, that the people who made *Rockford* all remember the series with affection. Ask anyone who has ever worked on the staff or crew of a James Garner production, and they will all characterize their experience in one word: *family*. You'll get a sense of what that environment was like through the recollections of many members of the Garner family: Juanita Bartlett, Jo Swerling, Luis Delgado, Gretchen Corbett, Charles Floyd Johnson, Jack Wilson, Jack Garner, and MaryAnn Rea. In addition, Roy Huggins, Stephen J. Cannell and Frank Price will walk us through the events leading to the premiere of the series. Plus, you'll hear from James Garner himself ... the actor, the director, the employer, and the man.

This is Jim Rockford. This is the 30-year history of *The Rockford Files*.

Author's Note

As Count Galeazzo Ciano observed in his Diary of 1942 (and which was echoed by President John F. Kennedy after the Bay of Pigs incident two decades later): "As always, Victory finds 100 fathers—but Defeat is an orphan."

There are two "fathers" to The Rockford Files, Roy Huggins and Stephen J. Cannell. Not surprisingly, each has his own version of how the series came to be.

According to Cannell, Rockford was borne out of an emergency situation brought on by the Writers Guild strike of 1973. Whereas script preparation of television series scheduled to premiere in the fall usually commenced sometime in the spring, because the writers' strike did not settle until mid-summer, the production schedules for many series (including Toma, a police drama on which Cannell worked as a writer/producer) were thrown out of whack. Cannell recalls Roy Huggins, the executive producer of Toma, determining that the series was going to have trouble meeting its airdates (and, specifically, that the fifth episode of the show was still going to be in the lab the week it was scheduled to go on the air). That being the case, according to Cannell, Huggins decided to shoot two episodes of Toma simultaneously in order to buy themselves some time. At that pont, Huggins gave Cannell a story that introduced a private investigator named Tom Rockford and told him to turn it into a teleplay as soon as possible, so that they could begin filming. Five days later, Cannell delivered the pilot script.

Huggins' account of the origin is considerably less dramatic: once he learned of James Garner's desire to return to television, he decided to reincarnate Maverick as a contemporary private eye series. He then developed a story for a proposed pilot called The Rockford Files and presented it to Frank Price, who at the time was President of Television at Universal Studios, where Huggins and Cannell were both under contract. Once Price greenlighted the project, Huggins assigned Cannell to write a teleplay based on his original story.

While Huggins' and Cannell's versions are distinctly different, they are not entirely opposite. Huggins did in fact originally intend to produce the Rockford pilot as an episode of Toma, although those plans were almost immediately abandoned. And there was a breakdown in Toma's production schedule (series star Tony Musante injured his leg in November 1973) that had an adverse impact on the show's ability to have the episodes that were scheduled for broadcast in

December filmed, processed and delivered to the network on time. While both Huggins and Price recall these circumstances, neither remember this or any other emergency having any bearing on the creation of The Rockford Files.

Cannell, as mentioned above, did not in fact enter the picture until several weeks after Huggins had developed the idea of The Rockford Files *and presented it to Price for approval. That said, there is no question that once Cannell did become involved, he made several significant contributions to the creation of* The Rockford Files. *According to Huggins, Cannell is largely responsible for the style of the pilot episode, which in turn provided the basis for the style of the series. In addition to enhancing Huggins' original concept of the Rockford character (such as originating Jimbo's peculiar preference to live and work out of a trailer), Cannell created two of the show's most memorable regular characters, Angel and Rocky. Cannell also suggested that Mike Post and Pete Carpenter compose the music for the series.*

The problem with trying to conform various accounts of a given story is that no matter how hard you try, the details will never quite mesh perfectly. However, as I reviewed the transcripts of my interviews and pored over the various documents and accounts regarding The Rockford Files *that I collected over the course of my research, it became clear to me that the creation of the series was indeed a collaboration. Therefore, a true picture of the events pertaining to its origin can be gleaned from both Huggins' and Cannell's accounts of the story. This, ultimately, is what this book attempts to provide.*

Part 1:

The Making of the Pilot

Thank You, Jane Musante

(or, "Roy, I Guess We'll Have to Do This One")

The roots of *The Rockford Files* date back to October 1972, when Roy Huggins first gave thought to a television series concerning "closed cases." The protagonist would be "a private investigator who handles only cases the cops have closed without bringing the culprit to justice," Huggins wrote at the time. "He was a cop who quit [the force] one day because, for some reason or other, they told him a case was closed. He [finally] closed the case by bringing the guy to justice, so the police don't like him at all because it was a case the police didn't want solved."

Given the nature of closed cases, Huggins believed a series of this kind would be open to many dramatic possibilities: "There is always some strong and powerful group or individual that doesn't want a closed case re-opened." Huggins initially called the project *The Clausum Files*, after the Latin word for "closed."

However, Huggins couldn't develop that idea right away because he was busy with another project: the pilot for a series based on the real-life exploits of New Jersey undercover police detective David Toma. The fact that Huggins was producing a straight police drama was somewhat unusual, considering that most of the other series created by the prolific writer/producer were the antithesis of traditional law-and-order shows. *Maverick*'s protagonist was a con artist; *The Fugitive* centered around a man escaping from an unjust murder conviction (and an obsessed police lieutenant); *The Outsider* was about an underprivileged, underpaid police investigator whose chief antagonist was the police department; the attorneys on *The Bold Ones* were always getting their clients out of jail (after they'd been put there by less-than-honest police officers); *Alias Smith and Jones* concerned two career outlaws who were seeking amnesty (while trying to avoid the numerous bounty hunters determined to turn them in); and *Cool Million* was about a detective who charged his clients one million dollars per case.

But after meeting David Toma, Huggins discovered that the detective had more in common with his television characters than he'd first imagined. The real Toma was a maverick, insofar as he was frequently in conflict with his colleagues in the police department. He was also, by his own admission, a consummate con artist who often used disguises in his work. And, like the lawyers in *The Bold Ones*, Toma had infinite compassion for those who suffered arrest and trial: he once had to seek medical treatment because the prospect of testifying against persons he would like to have seen released made him physically ill.

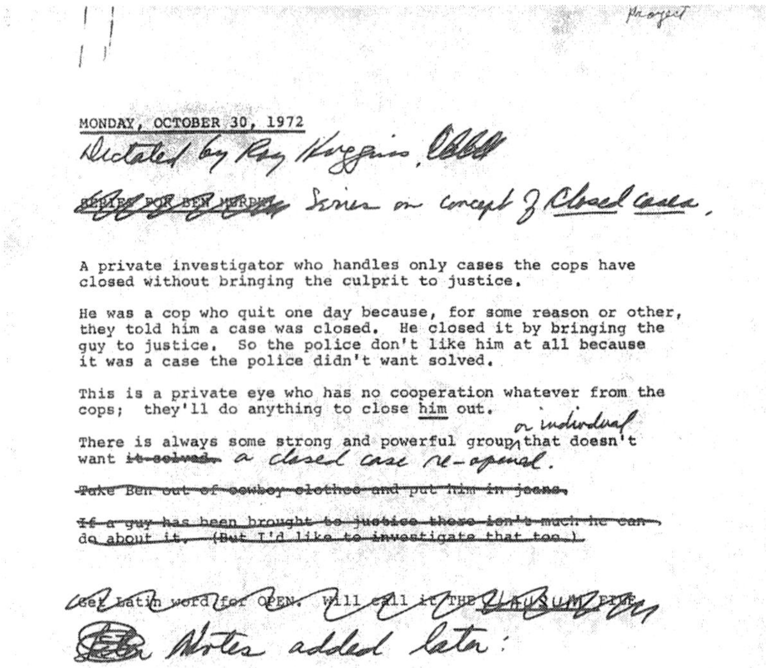

[handwritten: project]

MONDAY, OCTOBER 30, 1972

[handwritten: Dictated by Roy Huggins. ABH]

[handwritten, struck through] Series on concept of Closed Cases.

A private investigator who handles only cases the cops have closed without bringing the culprit to justice.

He was a cop who quit one day because, for some reason or other, they told him a case was closed. He closed it by bringing the guy to justice. So the police don't like him at all because it was a case the police didn't want solved.

This is a private eye who has no cooperation whatever from the cops; they'll do anything to close <u>him</u> out. *[handwritten: or individual]*

There is always some strong and powerful group, that doesn't want ~~it solved~~. *[handwritten: a closed case re-opened.]*

~~Take Ben out of cowboy clothes and put him in jeans.~~

~~If a guy has been brought to justice there isn't much he can do about it. (But I'd like to investigate that too.)~~

[handwritten: Use Latin word for OPEN. Will call it THE CLAUSUM FILES]

[handwritten: Notes added later:]

From the personal files of Roy Huggins.
Reprinted with his permission

An early draft of Roy Huggins' concept for what became *The Rockford Files*, transcribed from a tape recording dictated by the producer in October 1972 during one of his legendary "story drives." From this document we learn that (1) Huggins originally called the series *The Clausum Files*, after the Latin word for "closed," and (2) he initially considered developing the series as a vehicle for Ben Murphy, one of the stars of *Alias Smith and Jones*, which Huggins produced for ABC from late 1970 to late 1972. As it happens, *Alias Smith and Jones* was canceled by ABC shortly after these notes were dictated. Murphy went on to co-star with Lorne Greene in the detective drama *Griff* (ABC, 1973-1974), while Huggins developed the "series on concept of closed cases" into *The Rockford Files*.

What really made *Toma* peculiar, however, was the situation facing Universal Studios with regard to star Tony Musante. Prior to agreeing to do the series, the talented but intense performer had made it clear to the studio (and to Huggins) that regardless of how popular *Toma* might become, or how lucrative making the series might prove to be, he would star in the series for no more than one year.

Although Huggins believed Musante was serious when he first stated his position, he did not actually think the actor would carry it out. "I told the people in the Black Tower [the building where the executive offices of MCA, Universal's parent company, were housed] that I didn't believe we should take Tony's statement seriously," he said. "I figured that if the show was a hit—even if he *hadn't* said that business about only doing it one year—he would come to us and ask for a new contract. I wanted the people in the Tower to know what Tony had said, even though I didn't believe there would ever be a problem."

Nor did the studio think there would ever be a problem. In fact, according to Frank Price, president of Universal Television at the time, regardless of what Musante may have said, the actor was in fact contractually bound for a second season of *Toma* … provided that ABC renewed the series. "At the time we'd made the *Toma* pilot," Price recalled, "I had made a deal with Tony Musante, whereby after the first season, he would have been obligated to do only 13 shows a year [as opposed to a full season of 22 shows], each additional year that *Toma* was on, up to another four years. I made that deal because I couldn't get Tony to commit to doing every show [other than in the first year]."

In the meantime, Huggins, who was apparently unaware of these negotiations, did everything he could to accommodate Musante in order to keep him interested in doing the series. For instance, Huggins, who personally developed most of the stories for *Toma* (as was his practice on all his other television series), began meeting regularly with his star and soliciting his input on the stories that were planned for the show. On one such occasion during the summer of 1973, Huggins invited Musante and his wife Jane to his Bel Air home to discuss a story he had written for *Toma*. The story was about a woman who hires a derelict to "stand in" for her wealthy fiancé (who had died only hours before their wedding) so that she can "stage the marriage" and inherit the dead man's fortune.

Although the Musantes liked the story, they weren't convinced it was the right kind of story for *Toma*. "In fact, Jane Musante suggested that it might work better as a private eye story," Huggins said. "I thought about it, and I agreed with her. So I laid that story aside, thinking that I might come back to it later, and we continued discussing other stories for *Toma*."

James Garner and Tony Musante in a publicity still for "Charlie Harris at Large," an episode from *Rockford's* first season. Musante and his short-lived detective series *Toma* are inextricably linked to the creation of the *The Rockford Files*.

In hindsight, that proved to be one of the best things that ever happened to Huggins. "And I thank Jane Musante at least once a month for giving me another series," he chuckled.

A short while later, Huggins received a telephone call from his brother-in-law Luis Delgado, whose personal friendship and professional association with James Garner spanned nearly 40 years. Delgado informed Huggins that Garner was interested in doing another television series. "Luie, that's very good news," Huggins told Delgado. "I'll come up with something for Jim."

Huggins thought back to the story he'd first developed for *Toma* (the one that Jane Musante suggested had the makings of a private detective story) and decided to rework it as a possible vehicle for Garner. So he took to the road— literally, as part of the routine he practiced while developing stories for all his television series and movies. Huggins would embark on a three-or-four-thousand mile drive, and dictate stories into a tape recorder while he drove. Four or five days later, he'd return to the studio with several tapes' worth of stories. These stories included not only a detailed plot, but also notes pertaining to characterizations, the nature of the relationships in the story, and actual dialogue. By the time they were transcribed, Huggins' stories were often longer than the script for which they would be written.

Huggins not only reshaped his murder mystery into a private eye story, he also incorporated the character he had first sketched nearly a year earlier. By the time he was finished, Huggins had developed the "private investigator who only handled closed cases" into a character that bore a striking resemblance to his greatest television creation. "I wanted to develop the story as a pilot for Jim," Huggins recalled, "and then I decided that I ought to do *Maverick* as a private eye series."

Maverick (ABC, 1957-1962) was the revolutionary Western that made James Garner a star and launched Huggins into the upper echelon of TV producers. In an era in which prime time television was saturated with Westerns featuring traditional altruistic heroes who never hesitated to involve themselves in the plight of others, *Maverick* depicted a man who *did* think twice—and whose first thought was usually *"What's in it for me?"* He was a man who avoided trouble,

ABC Photo courtesy of Milton T. Moore Jr.
© 1957 Warner Bros Television, Inc.

James Garner as Bret Maverick

but who would tackle it head on if left with no choice; who relied on his wits more often than on his gun; and who unabashedly never lost sight of his own self-interest. Maverick's attitudes may have been socially unacceptable, but television audiences loved him: the series was a Top Ten hit during its first two years on the air.

Maverick was developed at a time when both Huggins and Garner were under contract at Warner Bros. Around the time Huggins first conceived the idea for the series, he discovered that Garner had an instinct for playing the kind of humor that made *Maverick* work: a subtle, wry, understated humor that was based on a total understanding of the character's thoughts and motivations. "I don't think there's ever been anyone like Jim Garner playing that kind of character," said Huggins. "That is a traditional role: the sly con man with a twinkle in his eye, who is willing to change his opinion *in a second*. It is the country bumpkin who is really *very* smart, who surprises you by being smarter than the city slickers, but who also is modest, and wry, and underplayed. And also, of course, a man who tries *never* to appear to be stalwart and brave.

"Some lines, like punch lines or joke lines, are almost always funny, no matter how they are read. But humor that genuinely works is the kind that comes out of character. It's funny only if the actor knows what the character is thinking as he is saying those lines. That's what Jim does so well. And to this day, I have no idea why that particular character was so clear to Jim—I'm not even sure if Jim knows. But there's no question that he was the perfect vehicle for *Maverick*."

Huggins figured that what had worked once before, could work again. "I had great faith in Jim Garner," he reasoned. "I figured that if I did a private eye series in which Jim played Maverick, it would be a tremendous success." So Huggins developed a modern-day private eye who was the spit and image of Bret Maverick: a character who would argue with a woman client over whether she would pay for his lunch; who was more likely to get hurt whenever he's in a fight, so he has to think his way out of trouble; and who absolutely does not want to be a hero.

Huggins christened his new creation Tom Rockford. "I thought it had the right sound," he said. "It was a rugged-sounding name for a character who was anything but rugged."

Because Huggins was busy producing *Toma*, he originally designed *The Rockford Files* (as he now called the pilot) as an episode of *Toma*. Huggins' original story called for a scene at the outset of the episode establishing that Detective Toma had been probing the circumstances surrounding the death of the derelict on behalf of the old man's daughter. Although Toma believed there was something strange about the case, his initial investigation led him nowhere; as a result, his superior officer Spooner (played by Simon Oakland) ordered him to put the case aside. But the conscientious Toma wouldn't let the matter rest, so he advised the girl to bring the case to his friend Tom Rockford, a private investigator who only handled closed cases.

In mid-September 1973, Huggins presented *The Rockford Files* to Frank Price. Price was well acquainted with Huggins: they had worked together years before on *The Virginian* (NBC, 1962-1970), and they were also related to each other (Price is Huggins' son-in-law). Price liked the concept and gave Huggins the go-ahead to develop *Rockford* as an episode of *Toma*.

In October 1973, Huggins gave the task of writing his story as a teleplay to Stephen J. Cannell, the talented young writer who was also a producer on *Toma*. Cannell not only completely understood Huggins' concept, he added nuances of his own, so that by the time the script was finished, private eye Rockford and the world in which he lived were the collaborative efforts of two great talents.

The inspiration for one such embellishment came out of Cannell's reactions to an episode of *Mannix*, the long-running CBS private eye series starring Mike Connors. "The day before I started writing," Cannell began, "I'd seen this episode in which a little black girl who had lost her mother comes to Mannix and says, 'Mr. Mannix, my mother's missing, and I don't know where she is. My little brother and I are alone at home. We can't find her. You're a private investigator, can you help me?' Mannix says to the little girl, 'Why, yes. I absolutely would.' The girl then asks, 'How much do you cost?' And Mannix says, 'How much have you got?' So the little girl reaches into her pockets, pulls out some lollipops and quarters, and dumps them on Mannix's desk. Mannix looks at the girl and says, 'That's just the right amount.'

"As soon as I saw that, I thought, 'Bingo! If that same little girl went up to Rockford, he'd say, 'What, are you kidding me? I've got expenses!' That locked me into that whole idea of how Rockford was this kind of guy that never did anything for free, because he had to pay his bills. In fact, that sequence [at the beginning of the pilot] where he ran the credit check on Lindsay Wagner came right from that *Mannix* episode."

The longer Cannell wrote, the quirkier Rockford became ... and the more Cannell became delighted with the character. "I was having so much fun writing it. Every time Rockford was threatened, he'd quit. It was so much fun to write something that you'd never been able to write before, where if somebody threw a gun down on him, he'd say, 'Look, I've been giving this some more thought, and I just don't think that there's much more that I can really do.' And then I would have him present Lindsay Wagner with itemized lists of his expenses: 'Now, I didn't charge you for the gas, or for the time I peeled rubber, but it's x-number of cents a mile,' and so forth and so on. And she'd look at him and say, 'What is it with you and these lists?'"

Roy Huggins

THE ROCKFORD FILES

Theory of series/idea (dictated 9/13/73) – rough for Roy

I want to go into detail on The Rockford Files. I'd like to go into detail first on how I see it as a series, and then tell you the story I've worked out to be put on paper.

You know what private eyes do: there's a murder over there, and someone comes and says, "Solve that murder!" In the first place, he would never do it. He would say, "Are you kidding? It's a murder -- the cops are on it!" There is practically nothing that a private eye can do with a case that has just occurred, that he will do a real case. He'll follow errant husbands and errant wives -- or maybe not errant -- and he will look for missing persons although there is a Missing Persons Department in every police department. But most of the jobs that private eyes do are sleazy jobs that you would never use as the basis for a series. But The Rockford Files is an area in which a private eye would indeed be called upon -- a guy man who specializes in closed cases.

The Rockford Files is about a man who may or may have not been a former policeman -- I don't think that's too important. It depends on how we cast really. If we cast a guy who looks like a former cop, then he's a former cop. But he could be anything. He could be a lawyer who got disbarred, the way F. Lee Bailey was disbarred in New Jersey just for criticizing the system of justice there. Or he could be a man with a cause. He could be anything.

But there are thousands of cases that end up being closed and unsolved -- or solved wrong in the minds of somebody. And in that area where they become closed cases, and no police department is operating on those cases any more, then there is a place for a private investigator -- and that's what The Rockford Files is. I think it's fresh and it would work.

There is a history in this business which you probably don't know about, of people trying to get a show on the air based on Erle Stanley Gardner's little group called The Court of Last Resort. Everyone likes the idea but somehow or other it never made it because there was something wrong with it. It was a little too crusading, a little too much of an accusatory finger at our system of justice. There are a lot of things wrong with it. But The Rockford Files avoids all those things and has within it all of the things that were good about that idea that people responded to over the years. It's a way of solving that problem and going beyond it, because here's a man who is in business and he takes only cases that have been closed.

From the personal files of Roy Huggins.
Reprinted with his permission

An early draft of the proposal for *The Rockford Files* that Roy Huggins put together for Universal in September 1973

Photograph by Robert Howe

Having Rockford operate out of a trailer was one idea that originated from
Stephen J. Cannell

Rockford's reluctance and unceasing self-interest, of course, were characteristics that were present in Huggins' original concept—just as they had been, years before, on *Maverick*. But Cannell, without question, understood the concept almost as well as Huggins himself. And Cannell added several facets to Huggins' story, including the creation of two of *Rockford*'s most memorable characters.

"I had originally written a very commonplace character—a semi-heavy who I had not considered to be very important," Huggins said. "Steve took that character and came up with Angel, which I thought was an absolute stroke of genius."

Just as Rockford is a modern-day version of Bret Maverick, Angel Martin is reminiscent of Dandy Jim Buckley, the character Roy Huggins had designed years before as a contrast to Maverick (both are grafters, but only Maverick has something of a conscience). Similarly, while Rockford is somewhat mercenary, he does have his principles (he'd turn down a case if he thought it would be a waste of the client's money). Angel, on the other hand, would do just about anything for a buck, including advertising himself as a hit man just to collect the front money.

Whereas Mannix had a posh downtown office, Cannell had Rockford operating out of a house trailer ("It's cheap, tax-deductible, earthquake-proof, and when I get a job out of town, I take it with me"). In Cannell's first draft, the trailer was located in a vacant downtown lot; however, by the final draft, the trailer had been relocated to the beach. While Mannix had a dedicated secretary, Rockford's "support staff" consisted of a telephone answering machine.

Cannell then made one other important change. "I'd always been amused by the fact that no character in private-eye history, that I could recall, ever had a family," he recalled. "They were always such iconoclastic, lone characters. It's like the Greek gods never had families. So I thought, 'I'm going to give this guy a family. I'm going to give him a dad.'"

Cannell decided to pattern Rockford's relationship with his father after his relationship with his own dad. "I named him after my father, Joseph Cannell," he said. "My father had an interior design business in Los Angeles [where Cannell was born and raised] which he wanted me to inherit. And when I became a writer, my dad thought I was the stupidest guy on the planet! Now, he's my best friend, but he just couldn't understand why I would want to be a writer. He would just say to me, 'Why would you want to do that, when you've got this business waiting for you?'

Photograph courtesy of TV History Archive
© 1979 Universal City Studios, Inc.

James Garner (left) and Noah Beery Jr. in their roles as Jim and Joseph Rockford.

"So I decided that I was going to write Rockford's dad like he was my dad—because my father was very embarrassed that I'd passed up the family business. His friends would ask, 'Hey, what's Steve up to these days?' And my dad would have to say, 'Well, he's walked away from my company, and he's scratching around out there with all those guys with gold chains around their necks.' He was very embarrassed."

So Rockford was going to have a father: Joseph Rockford (affectionately known as "Rocky"), who drove a truck and who had no idea of what his son did for a living. In fact, in one episode ("The Four Pound Brick," written by Leigh Brackett and Juanita Bartlett), Rocky stretched the truth by telling a friend that his son "is really a truck driver who only does private investigation on the side."

"Look at it my way," Rocky explains to Rockford later in the episode. "If I tell folks that my son's in trucking, right away they know what I'm talking about. But if I tell them my kid's in the private eye business, they just don't understand."

Because Rocky doesn't understand what his son does for a living any better than his friends do, Rockford tries to explain his job from time to time. But it isn't always easy to do. "When you're driving a rig, you know that Lancaster is ten miles down the road," he tells his dad. "But when I'm on a case, a lot of times I don't know what's down the road."

In the meantime, at some point between the time Cannell began writing the script in mid-October 1973 and the time it was completely drafted in early November 1973, a decision had been made regarding *The Rockford Files*. Instead of being developed as a spinoff of *Toma*, the pilot was now being planned as a possible 90-minute made-for-TV movie.

Huggins read the script and thought it was "beautiful." Cannell had perfectly reincarnated Bret Maverick—interestingly enough, without having any knowledge of who Huggins had in mind to play Rockford. Cannell had figured that the role would go to an actor like James Wainwright, a "leading man" type who was under contract to the studio, and therefore easily accessible. Wainwright, in fact, had recently starred in a private detective series for Universal called *Jigsaw* (ABC, 1972-1973).

In truth, Price and Huggins had begun exploring contingency plans in the event that Garner either didn't like the pilot or was somehow unavailable to do it.

"I had discussed casting with Roy," recalled Price, "and one of the things I had discussed was the idea of Robert Blake playing Rockford as a 'short' detective—because you're always looking for something that makes your show a little different. I had seen *Electra Glide in Blue* (1973), a feature starring Robert Blake, and I was very amused by it, because the makers of that film took advantage of the fact that Blake was short. I particularly thought the humor that was involved in *The Rockford Files* would work if Rockford was a short detective. There's that scene in the pilot, for example, where the big guy (William Smith) is following Rockford, and Rockford has to go into the men's room, where he puts the soap on the floor. That scene would go over very well if you had a little guy playing Rockford."

In fact, when word had spread that Price was considering a "not too tall" lead to play Tom Rockford, a casting executive at the studio sent Price a memo recommending character actor Terry Kiser (*Weekend at Bernie's*) for the role.

Today, it may sound sacrilegious to think of anyone other than James Garner in the role of Rockford. But you have to keep two factors in mind. First, not only did Price consider other actors in case Universal couldn't get Garner, Huggins himself already had an auxiliary plan in the making. "If I had ever done *Rockford* without Jim Garner," Huggins recalled, "I might not have used the Maverick character. Instead, I might have made Rockford more like the character I used in *The Outsider:* a loner who was a little put-upon, and somewhat rough around the edges."

In fact, in the notes for his September 1973 presentation to Frank Price, Huggins wrote that *The Rockford Files*

> is about a man who may or may not have been a former policeman—I don't think that's too important. It depends on how we cast, really. If we cast a guy who looks like a former cop, then he's a former cop. He could be a lawyer who got disbarred, or he could be a man with a cause. He could be anything.

Think of Rockford in those terms, and the idea of another actor playing him—be it Robert Blake, James Wainwright, or even Darren McGavin (who starred in *The Outsider*)—is not at all incongruous.

The second factor to consider is that Universal had reservations about working with Garner: reservations that stemmed from the fallout surrounding the actor and NBC over Garner's previous television venture, a short-lived series called *Nichols.* "There was a general feeling, which I believe emanated from NBC, that Garner and Meta Rosenberg [Garner's former agent, who at the time was the actor's business partner on Cherokee Productions, the production company started by Garner in 1964] could be difficult to work with," Price recalled. "NBC had worked with Jim and Meta on *Nichols,* and that proved to be a very negative experience."

An offbeat, turn-of-the-century Western, *Nichols* attracted a lot of attention when it premiered on NBC in September 1971. The series not only marked Garner's return to weekly television after a ten-year motion picture career, it was also produced by Garner's company for Warner Bros. Television—the same studio that the actor had defeated in court in 1960 after a highly-publicized breach-of-contract dispute. *Nichols* featured an immensely talented cast and crew, including Stuart Margolin (who would later join Garner as Angel on *The Rockford Files*), Margot Kidder (*Superman*), John Beck (*Dallas*), character actress Neva Patterson, award-winning writer-director Frank Pierson (*Cat Ballou, Cool Hand Luke, Dog Day Afternoon, Presumed Innocent*), and future *Rockford* writer-producer Juanita Bartlett.

Garner played a career cavalryman named Nichols who returns to the eponymous Arizona town founded by his grandfather and soon finds himself coerced into becoming sheriff by the Ketchams, the corrupt family who runs the town. Only Nichols, who's a bit rascally himself, spends more time upending the Ketchams (and pursuing his own self-interest) than he does upholding the law. The series aimed for the unconventional, character-driven humor that Garner had honed on *Maverick*, as well as in such pictures as *Support Your Local Sheriff* and *Skin Game*. Nichols didn't carry a gun unless he had to, and wouldn't think twice about avoiding trouble by sneaking out the back door. However, the humor in *Nichols* was both inconsistent (sometimes dry, sometimes broad) and erratic (sometimes it worked, sometimes it didn't), not to mention hampered by excruciatingly slow pacing.

After a few weeks on the air, *Nichols* was in serious ratings trouble. NBC gave the series a new time slot during midseason, and even retitled the show *James Garner as Nichols* in the hopes that Garner's name would attract more viewers. Garner even tried to retool the series by killing off the main character in the final episode and replacing him with a twin brother (also played by Garner), a more traditional, itinerant Western character who avenged the death and took over as sheriff (and as the focal point of the show). But none of the changes worked. Television audiences never accepted *Nichols*, and NBC canceled the series at the end of the season.

Garner took the failure of *Nichols* very hard—for many years, he railed at NBC for not supporting the show, which he proclaimed "the best TV series he'd ever done."

Universal, which had a close relationship with NBC (it supplied many hours of television for the network at the time), was well aware of the problems with *Nichols*. However, despite the studio's own qualms about possibly working with Garner, Universal did not entirely dismiss the notion. After all, Garner was still a widely recognizable personality, so the studio knew that it could market a television series around him—particularly a series produced by Huggins, who knew Garner's strengths intimately and who could bring them out like few others could.

In truth, Universal had more concerns about a promise Garner had made to Meta Rosenberg after *Nichols*: specifically, that if he ever returned to television, he would make her the executive producer of whatever series he appeared in. Rosenberg had made her reputation as a tough-negotiating agent (besides Garner, her previous clients included Robert Redford, Alan Arkin, Richard Benjamin, Ben Gazzara, and William Devane) before becoming Garner's partner in Cherokee Productions.

Rosenberg had some experience in television. She had packaged shows such as *Hogan's Heroes* and *Ben Casey*—meaning, she sold the ideas for these series, helped her clients put together the series, and assisted the network in finding sponsors. However, her track record as a producer in television was not very good. Meta Rosenberg was the executive producer of *Nichols*.

"I think we explored whether it was possible to get Jim without Meta," recalled Price. "But then Roy called me, and he said he felt he could work with both Meta and Jim."

In November 1973, Garner notified Huggins that he wanted to do *The Rockford Files*. There was still the matter of the promise Garner had made to Rosenberg, but as far as Huggins was concerned, that wasn't a problem. Although Huggins wrote most of the shows he produced, he often removed his name from those credits because he didn't like seeing it flashed onscreen more than once (if at all). If he didn't give the credit entirely to someone else, he would take it under a pseudonym such as "John Thomas James."

Huggins informed Garner that Rosenberg could have the "executive producer" title on *The Rockford Files* on one condition. "I told Jim that she wouldn't actually be the executive producer," he said. "I said that I would be running the show. Jim said, 'That'll be all right, as long as I can give Meta executive producer credit.'"

Garner also asked Huggins to make one small change in the script. "I had originally named the character 'Tom Rockford,' after one of my sons," Huggins said. "Jim asked me to change his first name to 'Jim,' and so we did."

Garner's reasoning for changing the character's name? Since most people on the set, such as the director, tend to address the star while he is filming the show by the name of the character he's playing, Garner figured he would feel more comfortable if they did so using his own name ("Okay, when Jim does this in this next scene …").

In any event, Huggins was happy to oblige: he also happened to have a son named Jim.

Apparently Garner had been considering another television series offer, but changed his mind once he read *The Rockford Files*. "I believe there was something at MGM that I was thinking about doing," the actor recalled, "but *Rockford* was much more attractive because of that character. Steve Cannell wrote a wonderful script. I don't know whether he had me in mind when he wrote it, but he might have, because when I first read it, the character was all there."

In the meantime, Frank Price saw *The Rockford Files* as a way of resolving the uncertainty hanging over *Toma* regarding the future of Tony Musante. "I had two ways to go about that," he said. "One, I had hoped to talk Tony into changing that provision [whereby he'd only have to do 13 shows a year if *Toma* was renewed]—and I believed, if he was happy with the show, there was a good chance of that happening.

"My backup plan was to do a 'wheel,' like what we had done with *The NBC Mystery Movie* [whereby two or three shows rotate with each other every week in the same time slot]. I was ready to offer *The Rockford Files* to ABC and pair it with *Toma*, and those two shows would alternate in *Toma*'s time period."

Price's scheme covered all the bases: it would have sold another series (*Rockford*) to ABC, and it probably would have kept *Toma* on the air with Musante intact. There was only one problem: ABC passed on *The Rockford Files*. "They didn't like the script," explained Price. "And they weren't interested in doing *Toma* as part of a 'wheel.' They sneered at that idea."

Given the cloudy situation regarding Musante, perhaps ABC rejected *Rockford* simply because it was down on *Toma*. That may also have been the reason why ABC ultimately canceled *Toma* at the end of the 1973-1974 season, despite the fact that the series had drawn decent audience figures throughout the year. Instead of getting two shows for the price of one pilot, ABC lost any chance of keeping Musante, while *The Rockford Files* eventually became a monster hit for another network. (However, Universal Television did not completely give up on *Toma*. After persuading ABC to reconsider its decision, Price and Huggins replaced Musante with Robert Blake and retooled the entire series. *Toma* went back on the air in January 1975 under the title *Baretta*. *Baretta* would enjoy a successful four-season run on ABC, winning two Emmys along the way—including a Best Actor award for Robert Blake.)

Meanwhile, Price began pitching *The Rockford Files* to the other networks. "I called John McMahon, who was NBC's head on the West Coast at the time," he recalled. "I sent him the pilot script, and I told him that we had interest from Garner in doing the pilot. I also told him that I felt that we wouldn't have the problems with *Rockford Files* that existed on *Nichols*, because Roy would be connected to it, and he felt he could have a good working relationship with Meta and Jim."

"Selling a series to a network is a special problem," explained Roy Huggins. "You have an idea for a series, and then you have a way of selling that idea to a network—and the two may not have any connection."

If *The Rockford Files* was going to sell, NBC had to be convinced that it was unlike any private eye series that had ever been done. Because prime time television was inundated with police and detective shows at the time, Huggins knew that the network was unlikely to purchase another private eye series unless it had something that made it stand out. That something could be expressed in terms of locale (*Hawaii Five-O*, *The Streets of San Francisco*, both of which were both filmed entirely in those respective cities), a visible characteristic (Cannon was fat, Barnaby Jones old, Kojak bald, Ironside wheelchair-bound) or some other idiosyncrasy (Columbo was disheveled, Harry O rode the buses).

Even though the concept of *Rockford* (Maverick as a private eye) would already appear to address that matter, Huggins decided that the best way to sell the series was to play off its title. "In some cases," he explained, "you could say something like 'I want to do Jim Garner as a private eye,' and the network will buy the series. But in the case of NBC and *The Rockford Files*, that wouldn't have worked, because NBC had just done *Nichols*, which was a costly failure.

"So I decided to sell *The Rockford Files* as a series about a private eye who only handles closed cases. That would make it sound 'different.' This has happened time and time again—Mannix, as an example, started as a detective who works in an agency that bases its procedures on computers. That sold the series, but that concept was quickly forgotten [once the show got on the air]."

Huggins admits that pitching Rockford as a gumshoe who "only handles closed cases" was nothing more than smoke and mirrors. "No homicide case is ever closed," he explained. "The case that Rockford took on in the pilot was never closed—the police considered it inactive and unsolvable, but they never closed it. And I knew that. But I used it as a gimmick to help sell the series. So, *The Rockford Files* were 'closed files.'" (The "closed cases" story point was also incorporated into many of the early episodes for the benefit of those viewers who may have been watching the show for the first time. However, once *Rockford* had established itself as an enormous hit, it became less of a need to remind the viewers of that particular story point.)

By this time, it was December 1973. If Price wanted to market *Rockford* as a potential Fall 1974 series, the pilot had to be completed and ready for broadcast in the spring. That meant that production of the pilot had to begin no later than February—which in turn meant that the pre-production planning had to get underway no later than the first of January. In order to get the ball rolling, Price needed to close the deal quickly. So he imposed an artificial deadline on NBC: the network had 24 hours to make up its mind on *The Rockford Files*.

Original art © 2005 by Darin Bristow

Graphic artist Darin Bristow renders his interpretation of the "closed cases" concept from which *The Rockford Files* originally developed. Dennis Becker has his arm resting his arm on a pile of "unsolved mysteries," while the sign displayed atop the other stack of files in the background is a reference to Robert Stack, longtime host of the popular NBC documentary series *Unsolved Mysteries*.

"Sometimes it helps generate enthusiasm if you tell the network, 'Hurry! Get it now, or it won't be there,'" explained Price. "That's the way we did business at Universal: we often, in general, financed our own development. That meant that the networks couldn't just sit on a script—if they turned it down, we could offer the project to someone else. However, when the network finances the development, it's a different story. You can't just pull it away in 24 hours. You can only act on it when they give you permission."

Price's strategy worked. John McMahon called the next day and told him that NBC would finance the pilot. In late December 1973, Garner and the studio agreed to terms on a one-year contract with five consecutive one-year annual options. Filming on the pilot began in February 1974.

Although NBC had commissioned the pilot of *The Rockford Files*, enough members of the brass had their doubts about its prospects as a series—assuming, of course, that the pilot tested well. (The memories of the *Nichols* fiasco were still fresh in their minds.) As per standard practice in the television industry, the network arranged for an advance screening of the pilot through ASI, a market research company based in Burbank that previews television commercials and programs before live audiences, who then record their responses to the programs via use of a dial. Oftentimes, the ASI results are the deciding factor in swaying the networks (as well as potential sponsors) into purchasing new shows. The case of NBC and *The Rockford Files* was no exception.

At this time, Don Durgin was the president of the NBC television network. Although his offices were based in New York, Durgin was in Los Angeles on business at the time *Rockford* was scheduled for screening. Durgin attended the ASI session, along with Price, Huggins, Cannell, and Jo Swerling Jr. (Huggins' right-hand man on every project the executive producer did for Universal Television). The screening took place on March 22, 1974.

ASI, as a rule, considers a series pilot or commercial to be successful if it appeals to 70% of the test audience. *Rockford* scored an 85. "We blew the needle off the ASI," recalled Cannell. "We had the highest rating of any pilot ASI had ever tested up through that time. In fact, it was so high, NBC couldn't believe the score, so they re-tested it—and it scored even *higher* on the second test." (The second screening took place on March 27, 1974, the same date the pilot was scheduled to air on NBC.)

In fact, one particular scene in the pilot was so popular with the test audience, the arrow measuring the audience's approval nearly went off the chart. "During that scene in which Rockford pours soap on the bathroom floor and he hits the guy with the roll of nickels, that needle went way into the 90s," said Cannell. "I'd never seen that needle go that high. But you could just hear the audience howling through the glass wall of the booth where we were all sitting."

NBC president Durgin was astonished. "When the screening was over," Huggins added, "and the results were in, Don Durgin just shook his head, and he said, 'Well, Roy, after *Nichols*, we never thought we'd ever do another show with Jim Garner. But I guess we're going to have to do this one.'"

NBC aired *The Rockford Files* as part of a *World Premiere Double Feature* on March 27, 1974. A few weeks later, the network announced that *Rockford* would be part of its fall lineup. Production of the series began in earnest in June 1974.

The Pilot Episode

JAMES GARNER
in

THE ROCKFORD FILES

An NBC World Premiere Movie
Production Number: 31331
Original Air Date: March 27, 1974

Additional Cast: Lindsay Wagner (Sara Butler), William Smith (Jerry Grimes), Nita Talbot (Mildred Elias), Joe Santos (Sergeant Dennis Becker), Stuart Margolin (Angel Martin), Robert Donley (Joseph "Rocky" Rockford), Bill Mumy (Nick Butler), Pat Renella (Morrie Talbot), Michael Lerner (Dr. Ruben Seelman), Ted Gehring (Norm Mitchell), Joshua Bryant (Captain Harry Dell), Bill Quinn (Harvey Butler), Robert B. Williams (Arnold Demura), Claude Johnson (Officer), Mike Steele (Danford Baker), Jack Garner (Bar Patron), Luis Delgado (Groom)

Executive Producer: Meta Rosenberg
Associate Executive Producer: Jo Swerling Jr.
Produced by: Stephen J. Cannell
Director of Photography: Lamar Boren
Teleplay by: Stephen J. Cannell
Story by: John Thomas James
Directed by: Richard T. Heffron

Art Director: Robert Luthardt
Set Decorations: Don Sullivan, Gary Moreno
Assistant Directors: Howard G. Kasanjian, Lamar Card
Film Editor: John J. Dumas
Casting by: Joe Scully
Costume Design by: Charles Waldo
Unit Production Manager: William W. Gray

Stunt Coordinator: Roydon Clark
Stunts: Nick Dmitri
Sound: John Kean
Color by: Technicolor
Titles and Optical Effects: Universal Title
Editorial Supervision: Richard Belding
Music Supervision: Hal Mooney
Costume Designer: Charles Waldo
Production Assistant: Dominic Jack Pizzo Sr.

A Public Arts/Roy Huggins Production
in association with
Cherokee Productions and **Universal—An MCA Company**

Synopsis. *Rockford reluctantly agrees to investigate the death of Harvey Butler, an elderly derelict whose body was found beneath the Santa Monica pier two months ago. (Although the police consider the case unsolvable, Butler was in fact strangled to death by a man named Jerry Grimes, a karate expert with a mean streak.) Butler's daughter Sara thinks there's a connection between her father's death and socialite Mildred Elias, who has been putting Nick Butler (Sara's brother) through medical school. Although his initial investigation leads him nowhere, Rockford becomes curious when he discovers Grimes tailing him shortly after the private eye interrogates Mildred Elias.*

The sequence in which Rockford literally upends Jerry Grimes (William Smith) not only demonstrates how Rockford will often use elemental means to work his way out of trouble, it also showcases the character's droll sense of humor. It's an important scene that encapsulizes what *The Rockford Files* is all about. As is the case with many of the other staples of the series, the development of that sequence was the collaborative effort of Roy Huggins and Stephen J. Cannell.

Cannell, who had been a fan of Huggins since *Maverick*, had worked closely with the producer on *Toma*, so he had become familiar with many of his boss' idiosyncrasies. "Roy always had this thing about how heavies or private eyes in the movies are always following people around in bright red cars, just because they're cinematic—whereas nothing like that ever happens in real life," he explained. "So I put this guy in a bright red Cadillac with a white interior, and I had him following Rockford. And I had Rockford basically saying and thinking what Roy would always say: '*What kind of an idiot tries to follow you in a frigging red Cadillac?*'"

*Photograph courtesy
of Roy Huggins*

*Photograph courtesy of
Cannell Entertainment*

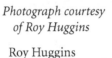

Roy Huggins   Stephen J. Cannell

In the pilot, of course, Grimes follows Rockford into a nightclub. However, in Huggins' original story, the confrontation took place in a dark alley. Grimes peers down the alley; when he isn't looking, Rockford emerges from the shadows and pounds him in the stomach. While Grimes was initially as vain and dimwitted as we ultimately see him in the pilot—Huggins' story describes him as being "so conceited, he's slow-witted; he's so attracted to women that he stopped thinking when he was about 19 [because] he found out he didn't have to think"—he was also originally oafish, and not exactly a formidable opponent. Cannell changed that by making Grimes a strongman who was also expert in karate. Rockford's only chance against this man is through trickery: first he distracts Grimes, then he nails him with a sucker punch, thus setting up one of the classic lines of the series:

> You know what's wrong with karate, Jerry? It's based on the ridiculous assumption that both people will fight fair.

Rockford then reveals to Grimes (as well as the audience) that he had hidden a roll of nickels inside his fist before he punched him.

After reading and discussing the first draft with Cannell, Huggins suggested relocating the Rockford-Grimes confrontation to the men's room of a nightclub. "There's a man in there, and Rockford pretends to be an obnoxious drunk, to get the man out," according to Huggins' notes dated January 7, 1974. "The man leaves. Rockford unscrews the liquid soap container and douses half of the floor with it. Now Rockford can also use the roll of nickels, because he's really rigged it."

But Rockford still has to get Grimes to walk into the trap. This is where Cannell made the next contribution: "I have Rockford standing across the room saying, 'Well, I think there's a problem with big, overdeveloped guys like you.' And Bill Smith says, 'Meaning?' And Rockford says, 'You know—queer!' We'd already established that Smith was a martial arts guy, and so he plants his foot to make his kick. And of course, he goes down. Rockford steps over and whacks him with the roll of nickels—nothing but sucker punches. He'd never get into a fight with this guy, because *I* wouldn't get into a fight with this guy. And that was my whole idea with Rockford. I wrote him as if he were me."

NOTE. In crafting this particular element of the showdown between Rockford and Grimes, Cannell may have drawn inspiration from the sequence between James Garner and Bruce Lee in Marlowe *(1969), in which Marlowe (Garner) uses a similar derogatory remark to provoke an assailant (played by Lee) into taking a fatal leap off a balcony—thus saving Marlowe's life. While the basic setup between Rockford and Grimes is similar, Cannell's execution, of course, is completely different—and no less brilliant.*

Cannell and Huggins had determined that after Rockford stunned Grimes, he would strap Grimes' feet to the top of a bathroom stall, then slap the upside down Grimes with his own wallet. Huggins then suggested that while Rockford interrogates Grimes, he is interrupted by a bar patron who walks into the bathroom. Huggins originally had the man immediately turning around and walking out, only Cannell changed that. "Rockford and the man go into a kind of Alphonse and Gaston banter," Cannell continued, alluding to the characters from Beckett's *Waiting for Godot*. "The guy walks in and says, 'Oh, I didn't know the room was being used!' Then Rockford says, 'It's okay, we'll be through in a minute.' And the guy says, 'No, no, no. I can come back.' And then Rockford says, 'No, no, no. It's okay.'"

The bar patron is played by Jack Garner, James Garner's older brother. "That was a fun time," Jack recalled. "But I also remember that, the next time I did something on the show, the big joke around the set was 'Well, Jack, you finally got out of the bathroom!'"

       *   *   *

Near the end of the pilot episode, Rockford fires his pistol into the engine of a plane flying several thousand feet above him ... *and somehow manages to hit it.* But that wasn't how the scene was supposed to play. The script called for the plane to fly no higher than 15 feet above the ground, so that when it flew directly over Rockford, he would have a clear shot at the belly of the engine—and a good chance of causing some damage.

As the scene stands, however, it is the one moment of incredulity in an otherwise excellent film. (In fact, it was the subject of the one overwhelmingly negative finding in ASI's Program Test Report.) Huggins knew it, too. In fact, he became so concerned over that scene that he offered to put up his own money in order to reshoot it.

"I made a proposition to the Black Tower," he recalled. "[I said], 'Let me reshoot that, and if the pilot sells, you pay for it; but if it doesn't sell, I'll pay for it.' Because a scene like that could be the difference between the show selling and the show not selling. If we reshot it, and the pilot sold, it would have been worth the extra expense. And if I was wrong—if I reshot it, and the pilot still didn't sell—I was willing to pay for it myself."

Though the studio declined Huggins' offer (the scene stayed in), NBC purchased *The Rockford Files*, anyway. But that gives you an idea of how Huggins happened to approach his craft as a producer of television.

It is a given in television that if you have a popular show on the air, the majority of your audience (say, 80%) will tune in to watch it every week. Put another way, even if an episode one week is not up to par, you know that most viewers will still come back the next week. So, if you're a producer, there are two ways you can go about planning your series: you can aim for the mass core audience, or you can strive to reach the minority of viewers that might be a little more discriminating.

Roy Huggins went by the latter approach. "I had always tried to cater my shows to that 20% that might not come back the next week," he said. "If I thought there was something in the script or in the film that I knew would insult the intelligence of the upper tier of the audience, or be otherwise unacceptable to them, I would remove it. And I have always tried to follow that rule throughout my television career."

              *   *   *

Executive producer Meta Rosenberg was particularly involved with the casting of secondary characters and guest stars. Rosenberg had always wanted Noah Beery Jr. to play Joseph Rockford, but Beery was unable to film the pilot (he had been starring in a series with James Franciscus called *Doc Elliot*). By the time *The Rockford Files* was ordered as a series, *Doc Elliot* had been canceled—which meant that Beery was now available.

Photograph courtesy of TV History Archive
© 1979 Universal City Studios, Inc.

James Garner (left) and Stuart Margolin in a scene from "The Hawaiian Headache." Margolin's association with Garner began in 1971, when he played Mitch on *Nichols*.

"Noah Beery was a great choice," said Roy Huggins. "After all, he and Jim do kind of look like father and son." But Huggins thought that the casting of Beery brought another kind of verisimilitude to the series. "It's always bothered me that in the movies, the father is always bigger than the son," he said. "That's crazy. In the world we live in, the son is always bigger than the father. So I think the fact that Meta selected an actor who was shorter than Jim Garner added an element of realism to the series."

Rosenberg also made an excellent choice in casting Stuart Margolin as Angel Martin, Rockford's permanent cross to bear. Rosenberg had initially brought Margolin to Garner's attention in 1971 when she showed him clips of Margolin's work on *Love, American Style*. Margolin, a staff writer on *Style*, also appeared in many of the zany blackout vignettes that led into each episode of the series. Besides co-starring with Garner on *Nichols*, Margolin had played a character named Benny the Squealer in *Cops*, a pilot produced by Rosenberg in 1973.

It's difficult to picture anyone else in the role of Angel Martin. Margolin's expressive eyes say everything even when he isn't actually saying anything. It's not easy to take a character who has little, if any, redeeming qualities and portray it with conviction. Yet that's exactly Margolin managed to do with Angel.

"Jim Garner loves working with Stuart," said Juanita Bartlett. "From the moment they worked on *Nichols*, Jim said of Stuart, 'He gives you more than almost any other actor I can think of.' There's a wonderful thing that happens between Jim and Stuart. They just work so beautifully together."

Joe Santos has credited Stephen J. Cannell for casting him as Dennis Becker. Cannell had remembered Santos' work as a Mafia hit man in the first episode of *Toma*, as well as his co-starring role in the 1973 miniseries *The Blue Knight* with William Holden. Years later, Santos would work for Cannell again: he played Lieutenant Harper in Cannell's *Hardcastle and McCormick* series.

Rockford Facts

For syndication purposes, the 90-minute pilot was re-edited into a two-part episode called "Backlash of the Hunter," and is included in the rerun package that continues to air on cable networks and independent stations throughout the world. Interestingly enough, when *The Rockford Files* first went into reruns in September 1979, the pilot was inexplicably inserted among the fourth season episodes in the original syndication package released by MCA/Universal under the title *Jim Rockford, Private Investigator*. Most stations, however, air "Backlash of the Hunter" in its proper sequence at the beginning of the rotation of episodes.

*   *   *

In the pilot, Rockford tells Sara that he was wrongly convicted of armed robbery and served five years in San Quentin before he received a pardon from the Governor of California. In his original story, Roy Huggins provided some additional background explaining how Rockford was eventually cleared of the charges, as well as why he became a private investigator. "[Rockford] kept writing letters to people, and he finally found this old retired lawyer who became interested in his case [and] found the answer—literally found the guy who was guilty," Huggins wrote in October 1973. "When [Rockford] got out, he went to the old man and asked what he could do to repay him. The old man said Rockford could work with him. The old man died a couple of years ago, and Rockford stayed in the investigating business ... Rockford feels strongly about closed cases because he was the victim of one."

Huggins had considered dramatizing these aspects of Rockford's past in the first season (in an episode aptly called "Flashback"). Although that particular segment was never made, the series frequently referred to Rockford's prison background, either by introducing a character who served time with Rockford (such as Gandolf Fitch), or by having Jim tell a story about some lesson he learned while doing time (as he does in the pilot, as well as in "To Protect and Serve"). Interestingly enough, the fourth-year episode "The House on Willis Avenue" features the man who was Rockford's mentor—only the character was changed from a retired lawyer to a veteran P.I.

*   *   *

In addition to the audience tests conducted at the ASI facility on March 22 and March 27, 1974, the *Rockford* pilot was tested using both "specially recruited and self-selected samples." According to the NBC Program Test Report for the pilot,

> Both in San Francisco and in a national Trendex survey, 250 to 300 people who had, of their own volition, tuned in to watch *The Rockford Files* were interviewed and their opinions of the show were elicited. Concurrently, 250 homes in San Francisco and 250 homes in Boston, Massachusetts were recruited and asked to watch *The Rockford Files*. After the telecast, these homes were contacted and the attitudes of the participants were obtained.

The final report submitted to NBC reflected the data obtained from these surveys, as well as the reactions from the two test audiences that screened the pilot at ASI. Overall, viewers found the pilot to be "very entertaining" and the Rockford character "very appealing."

*   *   *

The pilot episode was later adapted by mystery writer Mike Jahn as *The Unfortunate Replacement*, a paperback novel published by Popular Library in 1975. Years later, Jahn would create a Rockfordesque character of his own: private eye Bill Donovan, whom Jahn first introduced in the 1982 novel *Night Rituals*.

The Unfortunate Replacement, Mike Jahn's novelization of the *Rockford Files* pilot, published by Popular Library in 1975.

*   *   *

According to the pilot script, Angel's given name is "Al Martin." However, the character was only identified as "Angel" throughout the pilot. Later, however (in the second-season episode "Chicken Little is a Little Chicken"), we are told that Angel's first name is "Evelyn." Though there is no mention in the original series of how Angel obtained his famous nickname, Rockford provides an explanation in the 1995 reunion movie *A Blessing in Disguise.*

*   *   *

Although Huggins had come up with the *Rockford Files* title when he first conceived the idea for the pilot, he also submitted several alternate titles (*Rockford, Rockford's Files, The Rockford Style*) for NBC's consideration shortly before production of the pilot got underway. The underlying assumption would be that the title would somehow incorporate the name "Rockford"—a point about which series star James Garner felt very strong.

Rockford Familiar Faces

William Smith appeared as one of the riverboat gamblers in the 1994 feature film version of *Maverick* starring James Garner.

Nita Talbot (Mildred Elias) was a fixture on television throughout the '60s and '70s. Among her many roles on the small screen, she played opposite James Garner in an episode of *Maverick* entitled "The Resurrection of Joe November."

Bill Quinn (Harvey Butler) played Mary Richards' dad on *The Mary Tyler Moore Show*, as well as the blind Mr. VanRenssalaer on *All in the Family* and *Archie Bunker's Place*. In real life, he was the father-in-law of comedian Bob Newhart. In addition to the pilot, Quinn appeared in three episodes of *The Rockford Files*: "Pastoria Prime Pick," "The Dog and Pony Show," and "White on White and Nearly Perfect."

Appendix A
Rockford's Phone Messages

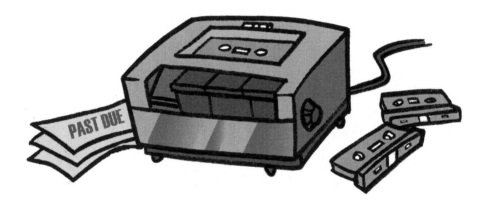

Original art © 2005 by Darin Bristow

This is Jim Rockford.
At the tone, leave your name and message.
I'll get back to you.

Stephen J. Cannell originated the idea for what has become one of *Rockford*'s signature elements: the decidedly offbeat telephone messages that we hear at the beginning of every episode. The messages were almost exclusively written independent of the script, and often do not pertain to the episode, although there are some exceptions, such as the tag in "Chicken Little is a Little Chicken," in which Beth asks Rockford to babysit her cat (which we actually see him doing later in that episode).

For the most part, writing those one-liners was a collaborative effort on the part of the writers and producers. "I've got to tell you," said Juanita Bartlett, "toward the end of our run, we were getting 'messaged out.' I'm not kidding. We had everybody doing them. I remember that Jackie Cooper and Lou Antonio [two of our directors] would often come up with ideas for the phone messages—which we would immediately pounce on! Sometimes it was a matter of 'If you have any ideas, come see us, please.'"

In some episodes (such as "Beamer's Last Case," "Rosendahl and Gilda Stern are Dead," and "Guilt"), Rockford plays back the messages on his phone machine as part of the story. Those shows posed an extra challenge, because they would require the writers to come up with two or three messages in addition to the eight-second tag at the beginning of the show.

The person who was responsible for making sure that each episode included the phone message tag was usually Charles Floyd Johnson. "And that wasn't always easy," he said. "The writers would be busy with writing and preparing the episodes, and I would be busy taking care of other things. The picture would be dubbed, and ready to go, but it would still need to have a phone message added before we could deliver it to the network. I would say, 'Hey, guys, we need to add a tag,' and they would sometimes groan or put a 'hex' on me. Sometimes out of self-defense, I would write out four or five and present them to Steve or Juanita or David [Chase] and say, 'Okay, choose the one you like, because we need one.' So it was very much a collaborative effort, and we all had fun writing them."

Though the pilot did not include a telephone message when it originally aired on NBC, the two-part syndicated version does open with the following message from Officer Billings (Luis Delgado):

> *Billings, L.A.P.D. You know, Thursday is Chapman's 20th year, and we're giving a little surprise party at the Captain's. I think you should come. By the way, we need five bucks for the present.*

Officer Billings does not appear in the pilot—the character was not introduced until *Rockford*'s third season. The phone message was actually lifted from "The Hawaiian Headache," an episode from the sixth season.

Luis Delgado, however, does appear in the pilot ... as himself! Delgado plays the groom whose back is to the camera during the wedding sequence near the end of the film. As the scene ends, the minister addresses him as "Luis Delgado."

NOTE: The phone messages for each episode are included in the episode guide. They appear between the guest cast listings and the plot synopsis for each show.

Appendix B
What If Jamie Farr Played Angel ...?

While Noah Beery, Stuart Margolin and Joe Santos were the preferred choices for their respective roles on *The Rockford Files*, Roy Huggins requested a list of additional actors to consider in the event one or more of the above actors were not available for the pilot. This, of course, is a standard practice in television. In the case of Noah Beery, he clearly wasn't available, which accounts for why Robert Donley wound up playing Joseph Rockford in the 90-minute pilot. While Donley did a serviceable job, the chemistry between he and James Garner was nowhere near as strong as that which was achieved once Beery began playing the character.

With that in mind, it might be fun to take a look at some of the alternatives that were initially considered when it came to casting the pilot. No doubt the dynamics between Rockford and his father would have considerably different, for example, had Broderick Crawford (*Highway Patrol, All The King's Men*) played the role. Crawford was among the additional actors originally suggested to play Rocky, as were James Gregory (*Barney Miller, The Manchurian Candidate*), Richard Basehart (*Voyage to the Bottom of the Sea*), Paul Stewart (*The Bad and the Beautiful*), Don Porter (Gidget's dad on television), Lloyd Nolan (*Julia*), character actor John Randolph (*Seconds, Serpico*), and noted acting teacher Jeff Corey.

Paul Sorvino and Charles Durning were among the original suggestions for Sergeant Dennis Becker, as were Vic Tayback (Mel on *Alice*), Victor French (Mr. Edwards on *Little House on the Prairie*), Ed Flanders (*St. Elsewhere*), M. Emmet Walsh (*Blood Simple*), Mills Watson (*The Misadventures of Sheriff Lobo*), Dana Elcar (*MacGyver*) and longtime Clint Eastwood company players John Larch and John Vernon. (Charles Durning, of course, would later co-star with Garner on *First Monday*, while Walsh, Watson and Elcar would each appear as guest stars on *The Rockford Files*.)

Jamie Farr (Corporal Klinger on *M*A*S*H*), Al Molinaro (Murray the Cop on *The Odd Couple*) and Len Lesser (Uncle Leo on *Seinfeld*) were among the options considered in case Stuart Margolin was unavailable to play Angel. So were Abe Vigoda (*Barney Miller*) and future Oscar nominee Michael Lerner

(*Barton Fink*). Lerner eventually won the role of Dr. Ruben Seelman in the pilot, while Vigoda had a memorable turn as a syndicate leader in the premiere episode, "The Kirkoff Case."

As for the female leads in the pilot ... Margot Kidder, who had co-starred with Garner in *Nichols*, was among the actresses suggested for the Sara Butler character. Donna Mills (*Knots Landing*), Valerie Perrine (*Lenny*), Kim Darby (*True Grit*) and Brenda Vaccaro (*Midnight Cowboy*) were also considered for the role that was eventually landed by Lindsay Wagner.

Meanwhile, Joan Van Ark (*Knots Landing*), Joanna Pettet (*The Group*), Stefanie Powers (*Hart to Hart*), Barbara Feldon (*Get Smart*), Valerie Harper (*Rhoda*), Susan Howard (*Dallas*) and Loretta Swit (*M*A*S*H*) were all considered for Mildred Elias, the character that was ultimately played by Nita Talbot. Van Ark, Powers and Howard would later guest-star on the series.

Finally, a young Nick Nolte was among the alternatives for the Jerry Grimes role that eventually went to William Smith. So were James Wainwright (*Jigsaw*), Richard Jaeckel (Lt. Marty Quirk on *Spenser: For Hire*), Bo Swenson (*Walking Tall*), Andrew Robinson (the Scorpio killer in the original *Dirty Harry*), and former movie Tarzans Mike Henry and Denny Miller. Swenson would eventually join the regular cast of *Rockford* in 1978, while Wainwright and Miller appeared as guest stars.

Part 2:
The Original Series

First Season: 1974–1975

Photograph courtesy of Movieland Productions
© 1974 Universal City Studios, Inc.

Because of the apparent effortlessness that he brings to his performances, it's often said that James Garner doesn't so much act as merely play himself. The fact that Garner really does work hard is often overlooked. "Jim is a very, very intelligent actor who hasn't gotten the credit that he deserves because he makes it look so easy," said writer/producer Juanita Bartlett. "When you see him on *Rockford Files*, he isn't playing himself—he is playing a character. But he makes it look so real that you think you're looking at Jim Garner."

It isn't easy to make yourself look natural and easy—nor is it easy for Garner to explain exactly why he excels at his craft. "I don't know what I bring to my roles—if I bring anything at all," the actor said in an interview for this book. "And I don't really 'create'—at least, as far as I know. I read the script, and if I understand the character, I do it. I don't try to 'do things' with it.

"In the case of *Rockford*, I understood the humor, and what the writers were trying to do, just by reading the script. I just went with what the writers wrote—in fact, you'd have to ask the writers [what I bring], because, to me, it's all in the writing. And if the words aren't on the paper, I ain't gonna make 'em any better."

According to Roy Huggins, the key to Garner's success with Rockford (and with Maverick before that) lies in the actor's absolute understanding of the character's thought process and motivations. "That was a very important part of Jim's great success with that Maverick/Rockford character," he said. "In the case of those two shows, the dialogue is never as important as understanding what the character has in mind. I know Jim would not have done those shows as well as he has if he didn't have great insight into how that character thinks and what motivates him."

During a 1986 interview on ABC-TV's *20/20*, Garner said that one of the most important skills an actor can learn is how to listen. "That was one of the first things I learned in this business," he said. "By listening, you put yourself in it. You know what's going on. You're reacting to it. I never learned dialogue—I learned thoughts."

That brings to mind something else that Garner brings to the package. He is one of the finest reactors the film industry has ever known, rightly compared with the likes of Cary Grant, Jack Benny, Jack Lemmon, and Bob Newhart. Oftentimes, you'll know exactly what his character is thinking simply from watching the look on Garner's face. *The Rockford Files* exploited Garner's skills as a reactor by constantly placing Rockford in situations with characters who were decidedly off the wall.

For example, Stephen J. Cannell's "White on White and Nearly Perfect" pairs Rockford with Lance White (Tom Selleck of *Magnum, p.i..*), an intrepid gumshoe who behaves as if he's a character in a pulp fiction story. Rockford and Lance investigate a kidnapping, but the trail soon runs cold. Lance, who lives a very providential life, suggests returning to his office, where he believes a clue will be waiting for them. Rockford can't believe what he's hearing: "There's not going to be a clue waiting for us in the office—it just doesn't work out that way!"

"Oh, yes, it does," Lance insists. "You go back to the office, and you sit down and you wait, and somebody will come in and tell you what you need."

Rockford and Lance proceed to Lance's office, where, sure enough, a statuesque beauty named Belle Labelle is not only waiting for them, she also brings them a vital clue that leads to a break in the case.

Watch Garner's reactions throughout that sequence, and you'll see a man who is thinking to himself, "I can't believe I'm in the same room with these people." Knowing what Rockford is thinking makes the few lines he has in the scene ("Would you mind if I run out and get some popcorn?") that much more funny.

"Rockford is an island in a world where people can be pretty bizarre," said Bartlett. "He is a very reasonable, very sane man who recognizes the insanity—and you can see that in his eyes, and in his face and his expression. Rockford recognizes the insanity, and he accepts it, although he certainly can do without it."

James Garner provides the impetus for *Rockford*'s sophisticated sense of humor. Situations or lines of dialogue that ordinarily may not be funny suddenly are funny because of Rockford's character and Garner's impeccable understanding of how to play it. "Jim can take a ordinary line and hand it back to you gift-wrapped, because he'll know how to deliver it," said Bartlett.

Yet, even after it had purchased *The Rockford Files*, NBC apparently didn't understand what made the series work. "The programming department had a big problem with the first script," recalled Frank Price. "They didn't like it because they weren't getting the humor."

Price met with NBC's West Coast programming executives to try to straighten out the problem. "They didn't see the script as funny," he said. "I kept telling them, 'It *is* funny,' and they kept saying, 'No, it's not.' I finally decided to read the script aloud to them, which helped them understand the humor—they'd laugh a little, or at least smile, at some of Rockford's lines. I'd then say, 'These lines will be funnier when Jim Garner is saying them!'"

Take, as an example, this sequence from that first episode, "The Kirkoff Case" (also written by Cannell), in which Rockford tries to clear a man accused of murdering his parents. Two thugs kidnap Rockford and transport him to an abandoned warehouse, where they proceed to pummel him severely. After Rockford is worked over, the ringleader (a creep named Muzzy Vinette) advises the private eye to drop out of the case.

VINETTE
You're a private detective, and I know you gotta work for a living. I understand that. But your client is guilty of murder. You know, *murder*. Yeah, and I know it to be a fact, the D.A. knows it, and the cops and every newspaper editor knows it. So how come you're trying to prove it otherwise?

ROCKFORD

Why, that was this morning. I just stopped working for him. I never really liked him very much.

VINETTE

It ain't that I really care that much about Larry Kirkoff. No. I think the kid's a creep for killing his mom and dad. But that's not the reason why I want you to quit fooling around with this.

ROCKFORD
(agreeing to anything)

You're right. I understand.

VINETTE

No, you don't understand.

ROCKFORD

No, I don't.

In the interests of fairness, NBC wasn't the only one that missed the humor in this particular sequence. Both *The San Francisco Chronicle* and *Weekly Variety* cited the above scene as a "violence-for-violence's sake beating that contributed nothing to the story." And it's true that a situation in which someone is being beaten is not ostensibly funny.

But if you found yourself in Rockford's position, there's a good chance you might also do whatever it takes, without hesitation—be it dropping your client, or contradicting yourself—simply to get Muzzy Vinette to leave you alone. Once Muzzy goes away, Rockford's free to resume his investigation, which is exactly what he does. That's what makes this scene funny. The humor in this situation works because it's humor based on a character: the kind of character that James Garner understands masterfully.

"That was one of the greatest readings I ever heard Jim do," added Huggins. "Only Jim Garner can say those lines ['*You're right, I understand.*' '*No, you don't understand.*' '*No, I don't.*'] in a way that makes the audience laugh like crazy. Nobody else can do that."

Still, in light of the network's problems with recognizing some of the humor in "The Kirkoff Case," it's worth noting the following comments from NBC's Standards and Practices upon its review of the script:

Please exercise extreme caution while filming these scenes wherein "Rockford is pummeled around good" by Muzzy and his two hood-lums. When they drag Rockford out in front of his headlights and prop him up, please avoid such grotesque makeup as described. (The script says "They have turned him into jelly.") Final acceptance of this scene must be determined at the rough cut viewing.

While Rockford certainly takes quite a beating on film—the sequence ends with Jim realizing that he has lost a tooth—the scene as shot is nowhere near as brutal as it was apparently first conceived.

That same memo from Standards and Practices also advised:

There should be a minimum of violence in this and future episodes. Rockford the principal character will reflect and inherit distaste for violence. Even though there will be times when the action must move beyond words, it should be apparent that any physical con-frontation is one that Rockford cannot avoid, and will conclude as quickly and as painlessly as possible. While Rockford does not like to hurt, neither does he like to be hurt. Thus, his wits and charm will help him avoid such violence as would befall a lesser man.

Given that Rockford began as a modern-day Bret Maverick, the character's aversion to physical violence was already well established. Though Rockford could usually handle himself in a fight if push came to shove, more often than not he would avoid such trouble as a matter of self-preservation. On this point, Roy Huggins was very consistent, as were as his successors Stephen J. Cannell, Juanita Bartlett, David Chase, and Charles Floyd Johnson.

NBC's comments about Rockford's wits and charms helping him stay clear of such trouble "as would befall a lesser man" are also worth noting in light of the concerns both the network and Universal would have over the character's

Promotional materials for *The Rockford Files,* circa 1974. At left is an ad that originally appeared in Universal's annual preview of its fall lineup of shows. At right is an ad syndicated to newspapers across the country for their weekly TV supplements.

apparent *lack* of intelligence in the early second-season episodes produced by Cannell in the summer of 1975.

         ✳   ✳   ✳

Perhaps Cleveland Amory said it best when he reviewed *The Rockford Files* for *TV Guide* in December 1974. Describing the appeal of James Garner, Amory wrote:

> A lot of what Mr. Garner does in this show is funny. It's not *fast* funny, mind you—everything Mr. Garner does, including think, is done slowly. But the fact remains that he is—in a kind of instant-replay, double-take way—slow funny. In other words, he grows on you.

Even *Variety,* despite its criticism of the first episode, recognized Garner's style ("sardonic, and sometimes a little whimsical") as one of the show's strengths. The trade paper also predicted that *Rockford* would benefit from "a good audience rollover" following its lead-ins on NBC's Friday schedule, *Sanford and Son* and *Chico and the Man*.

A look at the ratings figures for the season bear that out. *Rockford* finished in the Top 30 during each of its first five weeks of the season. As *Variety* noted, *Rockford* had a tremendous advantage heading into the season: its 8:00-9:00 p.m. lead-in was anchored by *Sanford and Son*, the No. 3 show on television in 1974 (and No. 1 on Friday nights), averaging nearly 50% of the total television-watching audience every week. *Rockford* held onto the majority of this enormous built-in audience, with an average share of 37.8%.

But, more importantly, *Rockford* won its own time slot on a consistent basis throughout its first season. The series cracked the Top 20 in its fourth week (the episode "Exit Prentiss Carr," which finished No. 14), then made its way into the Top Ten after Week 13 ("Caledonia, It's Worth a Fortune!," which ranked No. 10). *Rockford*'s audience grew over the course of the season—in fact, ABC changed its Friday 9:00-10:00 p.m. lineup three times that season, to no avail. Over the course of the final six weeks of the campaign, *Rockford* was averaging nearly 28% of all television households (and 43% of all televisions in use). *The Rockford Files* finished the year in the Top 20 (it ranked No. 12), with an overall average rating of 23.8.

The ratings figure refers to the estimated percentage of all U.S. "television households" (i.e., households that own at least one TV set) who watched *Rockford Files*. The share, or "HUT number," refers to the percentage of all "households using television," or households whose TV sets were actually in use at the time of the broadcast. In other words, of the total number of people watching television from 9:00-10:00 p.m. on Fridays during the 1974-1975 season, nearly 40% of that audience, on average, watched *Rockford Files*.

Rockford's average audience share in 1974-1975 becomes even more impressive once you consider that it was a Friday night show. The television industry traditionally considers Friday and Saturday to be low HUT nights because, as a rule, the majority of TV-viewing consumers aged 21-49 (i.e., the key demographic that most advertisers primarily try to target) are not at home. Not surprisingly, *Rockford*'s demographics consisted primarily of older viewers (ages 50 and up), an audience that likely recognized in *Rockford* the sophisticated character-driven humor they remembered from *Maverick*. (Interestingly enough, according to newspaper reports, NBC had originally considered scheduling *Rockford* for Sundays at 10:00 p.m.—a time period during which as many as 70% of the "TV-watching universe," particularly those in the all-important 21-49 demographic, are at home watching television.)

The Rockford Files succeeded not only because it had a star with proven audience appeal in James Garner—it also told stories featuring a character with proven audience appeal. The strength of the Maverick/Rockford character is that he is not only unorthodox, he is also ultimately smarter than anybody else. This is worth pointing out because it explains why *Rockford* stumbled in its second season: the series suffered a huge loss in audience during the period of time when the series featured stories that went against the character's strength.

        *   *   *

The success of a film or television series often depends on the lead actor—and not just in terms of performance. The principal sets the tone of the entire production by virtue of his or her demeanor. James Garner's contributions in this regard cannot be overstated. Not only was he the star of the show, he was the owner of the company that made it, which meant that he was ultimately responsible for the makeup of the crew.

"Jim Garner is perhaps the all-around best series lead that I've ever encountered," said supervising producer Jo Swerling. "He really was a leader on the set. He set a tone on the set. And this is terribly important to having an efficient operation, and also one that does good work. He protected the crew.

"Now, if he saw somebody that wasn't pulling their weight on the crew, he would speak up and we would make a change. That didn't happen very often, though. Because there was such an atmosphere of family on the set that he created, and that he was responsible for, changes didn't happen very often, because everybody did try very hard to live up to their responsibilities. The morale on the set was always high no matter how many hours they had to work. And that is all attributable to Jim."

In many respects, Garner is a practical person; this is particularly illustrated in his approach to hiring people. "I want people who want to go to work every day, and put in a full day's work, so that they can walk up to the pay window proudly and say, 'I got my check,'" he said in an interview for this book. "I like people who are proud of their work. And I have a crew that's wonderful. Every one of them is like that."

Garner knows that the key to maintaining a happy work environment requires both taking care of little things (such as providing the members of his crew with the best coffee and food available), as well as providing the people he hires with the room they need to do their best. As an executive, he remains aware of every aspect of the operation without being obtrusive. "I like to let people do whatever they do," he said. "I think you get better work that way. They know that they won't have somebody looking over their shoulder all the time. Now, I know what everybody's doing on the show, and they realize that, but they also don't feel as if I'm looking over their shoulder."

In particular, Garner always placed total confidence in the people who write for him—a quality that has never been lost on Juanita Bartlett. "I was on the set one day while they were filming an episode [of *Nichols*] I had written," she recalled. "I was standing over to the side when Jim came in to do a scene. Jim crossed over to me, and he said, 'Juanita, is it all right if I changed a line from so-and-so to so-and-so?' I said, 'No.' And he said, 'Oh, okay,' and he turned around and walked away. Jim took another look at the script, and they filmed the scene. He did it exactly as it was written.

"After the scene had been shot, I went over to him and I said, 'Jim, there was a reason I didn't want you to change that line.' Jim looked at me and said, 'I assumed there was.' He didn't care what the reason was. If it was okay to change it, fine—but if I said, 'No,' he figured, 'Well, she must have a reason.'

"I went back to the office, and I told [*Nichols* producer] Frank Pierson what had happened. Frank looked at me and he began to laugh uncontrollably. I didn't understand what he thought was so funny. And Frank said, 'You told not just the star, but *the owner of the series*, that he couldn't change one of your lines?'

"And I said, 'But, Frank, if he changed it, it would have changed the whole meaning of the scene.'

"Frank couldn't believe it—he just came unglued. But that's the way Jim is. He said to me once that he let people do what they did. And if we used a director that was a bad director, Jim would say, 'We may not use him again, but first, I'm going to give him a chance to do his thing. And if a writer can't write for me, we don't use that writer again. But let the writer write, let the director direct, and I'll do what I'm supposed to be doing.' And, believe me, that is refreshing, and rare, beyond belief.

"Jim Garner is such a joy to work for, because he truly is a rare one."

Many of the members of the *Rockford* crew have been with Garner so long, it's as if they really are a family. Luis Delgado, assistant director Cliff Coleman, stunt coordinator Roydon Clark, and chief electrician Gibby Germaine all knew or worked with Garner since before the days of *Maverick*. Meta Rosenberg was with Garner for almost 25 years, acting as his agent in 1958 before heading Cherokee Productions from 1964 until the spring of 1982. Lamar Boren was the cinematographer on *Nichols*; when Boren left *The Rockford Files* after two seasons, he was replaced by Andrew Jackson, whom Garner met on *The Castaway Cowboy*. And Bartlett had been Rosenberg's secretary for several years before she made her first break as a writer on *Nichols*.

"Jim is so loyal to his staff and crew," said Bartlett. "It really is his family, and he wants to keep it together. There are people working on these *Rockford* movies for CBS that I first met on *Nichols*, and who have been with him all that time. Whenever Jim works, if they're available, they're with him."

Photograph by Robert Howe   *Photograph by Robert Howe*

Director of photography Andrew Jackson   Stunt coordinator Roydon Clark

Photograph by Robert Howe

Sound man John Carter

Three members of the *Rockford Files* crew

"Jim had a lot to do with hiring the right kind of people," added Luis Delgado. "In fact, you'd be surprised at the number of people that are in line waiting to work with Jim on *Rockford Files*, or on anything he makes, because they know that he'll see to their needs, and that he treats his crew as if they were a family."

Familiar guest stars in *Rockford*'s first season include Joseph Cotten, James Woods, Jill Clayburgh, Julie Sommars, Roger Davis, Dick Gautier, Linden Chiles, Lara Parker, George DiCenzo, Thayer David, James McEachin, Sharon Gless, Suzanne Somers, Paul Michael Glaser, Linda Kelsey, Shelley Fabares, Ramon Bieri, Greg Mullavey, Bill Mumy, Diana Muldaur, Neva Patterson, Gordon Jump, Lindsay Wagner, and Tony Musante.

Appendix C
Writing *The Rockford Files*

Pre-production for a 22-episode season scheduled to premiere in September starts several months in advance, depending on exactly when the network orders the series. Back in the '70s, the networks usually announced their fall schedules sometime in April, giving producers at least two months to develop scripts for the season before filming began in June.

For Roy Huggins, script preparation often began with one of his patented "story trips," during which time he would embark on a three-or-four-thousand-mile drive and dictate stories for his shows into a tape recorder as he drove. As mentioned previously, the stories on these tapes were fully developed with notes on characterization, the nature of the relationships in the story, and actual dialogue. Upon his return, Huggins would have his stories transcribed, revised, and then dictated a second time for clarity. Before assigning a writer to write the story into script form, the producer would meet with the writer at his office at Universal and go over the story. This meeting would also be recorded and transcribed for the benefit of the writer. After the writer wrote the teleplay, he or she would then meet with Huggins once again for any input and/or revisions.

In theory, Huggins' approach was foolproof. Because his stories included detailed character descriptions as well as actual dialogue, all the writer had to do was transform them from prose to teleplay form. In practice, however, that wasn't always as easy as it sounds. In writing the script, the writer had to reflect an absolute grasp of the producer's original concept. If the script failed to do that, one of two things happened. Either the writer would have to revise the teleplay so that it conformed with Huggins' vision, or Huggins would reassign the story to another writer—but not before going over the story in detail with that new writer in a session that would also be recorded.

Huggins' meticulous approach to stories and scripts did not sit well with everyone who worked with him. By his own admission, he could be extremely uncompromising in the area of story and script development, and he could be brutal with his criticism. But others in the film and television industry, including Stephen J. Cannell and Juanita Bartlett, swear by Huggins' methods because they respected his expertise in the craft of storytelling, and because they recognized his desire to develop the talent he saw in them to its fullest possible extent.

"Roy was really a teacher at heart," said Jo Swerling. "In fact, at one point in his life, he wanted to be a professor of political theory, and actually left television for a time to work on his doctorate in that field until he was lured back to television by Universal to produce *The Virginian*.

"While Roy was very easy with his praise when you did something well, he was also not shy about being stern whenever you screwed up. Roy could be tough—but in a lot of ways that was good, because he would always back off and say, 'You know, if I thought you had no talent, I wouldn't bother. I only do this because I think you have something to offer, and that you'll learn from the experience.'"

Swerling adds that there was also a very practical reason behind the producer's use of criticism. "Roy used to tell me, 'If I say nothing, or if I only say "That's okay," then you're not going to learn anything—and at some point, your option at the studio will not get picked up.'

"So he was a stern mentor, but he was also a wonderful man to work with. He was marvelously creative … the way he could come up with stories bordered on the supernatural. While he would certainly borrow from himself on occasion, he would always change it around so that you couldn't recognize it. And if he ever borrowed a story from himself, [he usually made sure that] it wouldn't have been one that he had done recently.

"He was a lot of fun to work with. I learned everything from him—and I think Steve Cannell will tell you the same thing. We both look at Roy as our mentor."

Cannell in fact does echo the sentiment. "Roy was such a terrific mentor for me," he said. "I just loved working with him."

Cannell actually coaxed Huggins back into television in 1985 after a five-year retirement from the industry. Cannell called on his mentor to take over the reins of *Hunter*, a show Cannell had created for NBC about a "Dirty Harry"-esque cop played by former NFL standout Fred Dryer. Though *Hunter* struggled to find an audience throughout its first season (1984-1985), then-NBC president Brandon Tartikoff was said to have liked the show and decided to renew it. With Huggins aboard as executive producer for the second season, the series immediately found its footing. By the time the writer/producer left the show in 1988, *Hunter* was an established Top 20 hit.

∗   ∗   ∗

Huggins' influence can be seen in the approach *Rockford*'s other producers took to story preparation after he left the series in 1975. "We would hire outside writers, and we would work with the writer to put the story together," said Juanita Bartlett, who along with Cannell supervised the process beginning in the show's second season. "At some point, however, the script would have to go through our typewriters. This is not to say anything against these writers— they contributed some excellent stories. However, if you're [on staff] on a show, you 'know' that show. You know what the characters would say, how they would act, how they wouldn't act. So we would *Rockford*-ize the script."

Cannell and Juanita Bartlett were joined by David Chase and Charles Floyd Johnson beginning in 1976. Their style as producers may have been less methodical (at least, in comparison to Huggins), but they were no less committed to making sure that the scripts were conformed to reflect an absolute grasp of the *Rockford* concept.

Appendix D
Rockford, Marlowe and Abel Marsh

In its March 1974 review of the *Rockford Files* pilot, *Daily Variety* suggested that *Rockford* may have been inspired in part by a 1969 feature film in which James Garner starred as Raymond Chandler's legendary gumshoe Philip Marlowe:

> Garner's Rockford was reminiscent of the interpretation he brought to Stirling Silliphant's *Marlowe* movie of a few years back, with elements of dry wit, irony, unforced light romance and that peculiar sense of stubborn contrariness just below the surface that is an appealing part of Garner's professional image. Garner has a way of underplaying his way through required action and violence sequences, milking humor from the encounters and projecting an effortlessly laconic air to light romantic footage.

The daily trade paper further speculated on a *Rockford/Marlowe* connection in its write-up of the premiere episode "The Kirkoff Case":

> *Rockford* may have found its inspiration in a sort of sleeper feature Garner made, titled simply *Marlowe*, in which he played Chandler's detective in a style attractive to the trade.

Granted, there is a connection in the sense that while Jim Rockford was definitely "made for TV," the character does have ties to the great literary gumshoes of our time. *Rockford*'s co-creator Roy Huggins was not only a successful novelist in the Chandler vein prior to his career in television, he was also the creator of *The Outsider* (NBC, 1968-1969), a *noir*-ish private eye show with a Chandleresque protagonist in the downtrodden David Ross (Darren McGavin).

But given the fact that Huggins did not think much of the Silliphant adaptation of *Marlowe*—an assessment of the film shared by most newspaper critics at the time—it's hard to imagine he would have ever considered using it as a source. If he were to "borrow" from a film or story, Huggins was far more likely to adapt one of his own properties than anything else. Indeed, Huggins did that several times in developing the early episodes of *Rockford*.

Furthermore, the matter of *Rockford*'s origin, as discussed before, is also very clear. Once Huggins was apprised of Garner's desire to return to series television, he decided to update *Maverick* as a private eye series, knowing that Garner's success with the Maverick character could also carry over into the TV mystery genre. Thus, any corollary between *Marlowe* and *Rockford* on the part of Huggins would seem more coincidental than not.

That said, it's possible that co-creator Stephen J. Cannell may have been inspired (at least, subconsciously) by elements of the movie. As noted earlier, the basic setup of Cannell's scene from the *Rockford* pilot in which Rockford goads Jerry Grimes (William Smith) into lunging after him in the men's bathroom is reminiscent of the sequence in which Marlowe outwits Winslow Wong (Bruce Lee) in *Marlowe*. In addition, when Marlowe is accosted by thugs about halfway through the picture, he makes a wisecrack—"Does your mother know what you do for a living?"—that would later surface in the premiere episode of *The Rockford Files* ("The Kirkoff Case"), which Cannell also wrote. (Rockford makes the same remark as he is being transported to the warehouse where he is about to be beaten up by Muzzy Vinette's goons.) While these occurrences may also be coincidental, they are nonetheless interesting to note.

Beyond that, any further similarities between Jim Rockford and the character Garner played in *Marlowe* are mostly cosmetic. Both are L.A. private eyes with a high set of values. Both charge a hefty fee for their services (Marlowe charges $100 a day, plus expenses, while Rockford charges $200/day), and yet they're also interminably broke. Both like to eat Oreo cookies, although that probably had more to do with James Garner liking Oreo cookies than anything else. Neither is above resorting to using a phony name to wheedle information out of an unsuspecting source. In addition, several actors who co-starred with Garner in *Marlowe*—William Daniels, Rita Moreno, Christopher Cary, H.M. Wynant, Jason Wingreen, Kenneth Tobey, and Paul Stevens—would later appear on *Rockford*.

Another Garner movie that is occasionally likened to *Rockford* is *They Only Kill Their Masters* (1972). In this vehicle, Garner stars as Abel Marsh, a police chief in a small town in Northern California who investigates the bizarre murder of a beautiful young woman. Garner's performance in the film certainly brings to the mind the easygoing manner that he would eventually bring to his portrayal of Jim Rockford, while the script by Lane Slate surrounds Garner with no shortage of offbeat characters. In addition, the harmonica-and-guitar score by Perry Botkin Jr. is reminiscent of the "country rock" sound that Mike Post would bring to *The Rockford Files*. (Botkin, in fact, was among the composers initially considered to score the *Rockford* pilot in 1974.) While these similarities are again more stylistic than substantive, they are still worth mentioning.

On a historical note, *They Only Kill Their Masters* was the last movie ever made on the memorable MGM backlot, home of some of the great film classics of our time, including *The Wizard of Oz, Gone With the Wind, Mutiny on the Bounty, Grand Hotel, Ben-Hur, Singin' in the Rain, An American in Paris* and *The Bad and the Beautiful*. With MGM facing grave financial trouble in 1970, control of the studio was taken over by Las Vegas land mogul Kirk Kerkorian, who promptly hired onetime CBS-TV production head James Aubrey and installed him as president. "The new management," wrote Ephraim Katz in *The Film Encyclopedia*, "began an economy drive, ranging from a sharp reduction in personnel and production schedules to the sad end-of-an-era auction in 1970 in which hundreds of thousands of props and costumes from the studio's glorious past were put on the block." The studio's remaining assets were then channeled into the construction of yet another lavish resort in Las Vegas, The MGM Grand Hotel (now known as Bally's).

In the meantime, with Aubrey concentrating primarily on building the hotel, MGM's feature motion pictures noticeably declined in quality. As one critic rather harshly noted:

> *They Only Kill Their Masters* was typical of MGM's theatrical output during Aubrey's Reign of Terror. A cheapjack mystery no better (and in most ways worse) than the average TV movie-of-the-week, this abomination was especially horrific in unintended ways. For one, it was the last movie made on the memorable MGM backlot (soon to be bull-dozed and sold to realtors) ... Congratulations to Mr. Aubrey for cannibalizing the heritage of MGM, its wondrous backlot, and its rightful boasting that its contract players at one time constituted "more stars than there are in heaven."

While *Masters* is by no means a great film, it performed very well at the box office in 1972. It also holds up well on television and as a video rental today ... certainly more so than the above reviewer would perhaps give it credit for.

They Only Kill Their Masters is also of interest in the sense that it was one of two Garner films (*Skin Game* being the other) that were developed for television around the time that *Rockford Files* began production. Indeed, as mentioned earlier, Garner was considering an offer from MGM when he was presented the script for the *Rockford* pilot. Though no one can recall for sure, it's not inconceivable that the project he was mulling over from MGM was the pilot for the TV adaptation of *They Only Kill Their Masters*.

Production Credits
1974–1980

NOTE. The majority of names on this list were obtained from the screen credits that appear at the end of each episode of The Rockford Files. *Some names, however, were obtained from additional sources, including the MCA syndication kit and* The Internet Movie Database.

JAMES GARNER
in
THE ROCKFORD FILES

Also Starring
Noah Beery *as Joseph "Rocky" Rockford*
Joe Santos *as Dennis Becker*
Gretchen Corbett *as Beth Davenport (1974-1978)*
and
Stuart Margolin *as Angel Martin*

Co-Starring
Tom Atkins *as Lieutenant Diel (1974-1976, 1977-1978)*
Luis Delgado *in various roles (1974-1976)* and *as Officer Billings (1976-1980)*
James Luisi *as Lieutenant Chapman (1976-1980)*
Jack Garner *in various roles (1974-1979)* and *as Captain McEnroe (1979-1980)*

Executive Producer: Meta Rosenberg
Supervising Producers: Jo Swerling Jr. (1974-1975), Stephen J. Cannell (1975-1980), Juanita Bartlett (1979-1980)
Produced by: Stephen J. Cannell (1974-1975), Charles Floyd Johnson (1976-1980), David Chase (1976-1980)
Created by: Roy Huggins and Stephen J. Cannell

Associate Producers: Charles Floyd Johnson (1974-1976), William F. Phillips (1974), J. Rickley Dumm (1978-1979), John David (1978-1980)
Creative Consultant/Executive Story Editor: Juanita Bartlett (1974-1979)

Musical Score: Mike Post and Pete Carpenter
Additional Music: Dick DeBenedictis and Artie Kane (1974-1975), Velton Ray Bunch
Musical Supervision: Hal Mooney (1974-1975), Morrie McNaughton (1976-1980)
Directors of Photography: Lamar Boren (1974-1976), Andrew Jackson (1976-1980), Leonard J. South (1974), Steve Yaconelli
Art Directors: Robert Crawley Sr., Robert Luthardt (1974)
Set Decorators: Gary Moreno (1974-1975), Robert L. Zilliox (1975-1980), Ed Baer (1975)
Assistant Directors: Robert Jones (1974-1979), Cliff Coleman (1974-1977, 1979-1980), Dave Menteer (1976-1979), Leonard R. Garner (1978-1979), Jan Lloyd (1978-1979), Pat Duffy (1978-1979), Reuben Watt (1979-1980), David Beanes (1979-1980), Cal Naylor (1979-1980), Robert J. Doherty (1979-1980), Michael Kane (1979-1980)
Unit Production Managers: Les Berke (1974-1978), Rowe Wallerstein (1976-1977), Zane Radney (1978-1979), Sam Freedle (1979-1980), Bill Carroll (1979-1980)
Casting: Dodie McLean, Joe Scully (1974-1975)
Film Editors: George R. Rohrs, Buford F. Hayes (1974-1977), Diane Adler (1976-1980), Roderic Stephens (1977-1979), Edward A. Biery (1974-1975), Frederic Baratta (1974-1975), John J. Dumas (1974-1975), John Kaufman (1974-1975), Robert Leeds (1975-1976), I. Robert Levy (1975-1976), Robert L. Kimball (1976-1977), Lawrence J. Vallario (1976-1977), Jerry Dronsky (1977-1978), Gloryette Clark
Sound Mixers: John Carter, John Kean (1974-1975), Vic Carpenter (1974-1975), Albert D. Cuesta (1974-1975), Jack F. Lilly (1976-1977)
Sound Effects Editors: Walter Jenevein, Dave Schonleber (1976-1977)
Editorial Supervision: Richard Belding
Stunt Coordinator: Roydon Clark
Stunt Doubles: Roydon Clark, Dave Cass, Nick Dmitri, Dick Durock, Tony Epper, Chuck Hicks, Leslie Hoffman, Gene LeBell, Terry Leonard, Fred Lerner, Conrad E. Palmisano, Sherry Peterson, Jesse Wayne
Assistant to Mr. Garner: MaryAnn Rea
Costume Designer: Charles Waldo (1974-1978), Kent Warner (1978-1980)
Make-Up Artists: Dick Blair, Dave Grayson, Jack Wilson (1974-1975)
Hair Department Head: Allen Payne
Property Masters: William Fannon, Craig Binkley

Helicopter Pilot/Aerial Consultant: Ross Reynolds
Main Title Design: Jack Cole
Color by Technicolor
Titles and Optical Effects: Universal Title

A Public Arts/Roy Huggins Production
in Association with
Cherokee Productions
and
Universal—an MCA Company

Episode Guide for the First Season

All episodes for the first season and all subsequent seasons are listed in the order in which they were originally broadcast on NBC. All synopses of episodes have been written by the author of this book.

NOTE. Strictly speaking, Gretchen Corbett (Beth), Stuart Margolin (Angel), Tom Atkins (Diel) and James Luisi (Chapman) were always listed as guest stars whenever they appeared on Rockford in their respective recurring roles. That was also the case for Joe Santos (Becker) during the first season, as well as Luis Delgado and Jack Garner (both of whom played a variety of characters before eventually appearing on a regular basis as Billings and McEnroe, respectively).

However, for purposes of this book, Santos, Corbett, Margolin, Delgado, Garner, Atkins and Luisi are all considered regular cast members; therefore, with the exception of James Luisi in the second-year episode "Joey Blue Eyes," their names are not included in any of the guest casts listed for seasons one through six. (Because Luisi played the main villain in "Joey Blue Eyes," his name is listed among the guest stars for that show.)

1.   THE KIRKOFF CASE
(Originally Entitled: "The Kirkoff Killings")

Production Number: 41401
Original Air Date: September 13, 1974
Teleplay by: Stephen J. Cannell
Story by: John Thomas James
Directed by: Lou Antonio

Guest Cast: Julie Sommars (Tawnia Baker), Roger Davis (Travis Buckman), James Woods (Larry Kirkoff), Philip Keneally (Muzzy Vinette), Milt Kogan (Marsh), Abe Vigoda (Al Dancer), Sandy DeBruin (Hostess), Dino Seragusa (Maitre D'), Dennis McCarthy (Calvin Carras), Fred Lerner (Parking Attendant), Melissa Mahoney (Carhop)

Jim, it's Norma at the market. It bounced—you want us to tear it up, send it back or put it with the others?

Photograph courtesy of TV History Archive
© 1974 Universal City Studios, Inc.

James Garner as Jim Rockford in the opening sequence of "The Kirkoff Case"

Synopsis. *Larry Kirkoff was indicted for the double murder of his parents, but he was never convicted because the prosecution couldn't place him at the scene of the crime, and the police never found the murder weapon. Larry hires Rockford to find evidence that would clear him of both crimes. Although Jim believes Kirkoff is guilty, he can't quite resist the potential payoff: a $20,000 fee if he cracks the case. Rockford discovers that the Kirkoff murders may be linked to a real estate fraud, but he also finds that his investigation could have fatal ramifications after mobsters work him over and warn him to drop the case.*

A filmed story is told three times: first by the writer; then by the actors and the director, who interpret the writing; and finally, in the post-production process, which includes editing, the most crucial part of post-production. Film editing requires not just a mastery of technical skills [such as splicing footage and dubbing sound], it also requires an understanding of the craft of telling stories. In fact, many "cutters" (as they're known in the industry) who are particularly gifted storytellers often graduate to other fields of the film industry. Frequent *Rockford* director William Wiard and writer/producer Gordon Dawson, to name just two, began their film careers in the cutting room.

If an editor is not in sync with what the writer or producer has in mind, then the cut of the film may include (or exclude) footage that could alter the complexion of the entire story. For that reason, Roy Huggins, who originated the stories for nearly every series episode or TV-film he ever made, paid close attention to the editing of all his projects—and often served as an auxiliary editor. "Roy was incredible in the cutting room, in terms of what he could do with film," said Jo Swerling. "If he saw some footage that he thought might detract from the story, Roy would try to change it: he'd flip it around, blow it up, run it backwards, put wild lines on it, or do whatever it took to make the film work."

As an example, once while watching dailies [the footage of scenes filmed the previous day], Huggins decided that a scene depicting a holdup would be more effective if the actor playing the gunman fired a shot—which he hadn't done in the original footage. Rather than reshoot the entire sequence to include the gun shot, Huggins "manufactured" the gun shot just by working with the footage he had, first by instructing his editor to scratch the film at the point where the actor is seen holding the gun for approximately ten frames, then by asking the sound effects technician to dub a gunshot effect onto the film.

"Roy used to say that editing a film was like peeling the layers of an onion," said Swerling. "Each time you take a pass at the picture, you peel a layer off the onion, until you finally get it down to where the thing is lean and hard. Sometimes, after you're finished cutting, you end up short on footage; if that happens, you have to selectively build the film up back to where it's on footage. That was Roy's technique, and it's the technique that Steve Cannell and I still use today." *NOTE. "Footage" refers to both the material contained within the film, as well as its total running time. In series television, the final cut of an one-hour episode must run approximately 48 minutes. The network sells the remaining portion of the program's air time to sponsors.*

Huggins firmly believed that the quality of what went on the air was reflected by the amount of time spent in post-production—after all, it was always his philosophy to cater his shows to the "minority" (the 20% of the audience that might not otherwise tune in next week). Huggins' philosophy didn't always sit well with Universal, whose Business Department often complained that Huggins' shows cost one-third more than any other show produced at the studio. The extra expenditures were always tied to post-production. But it was hard to argue with the results. The quality of Huggins' shows were usually reflected by high audience figures and, in some cases, recognized by professional associations within the industry. *The Rockford Files*, for example, was recognized by the Motion Picture Sound Editors Association as the Best Sound Edited Television Series of 1974.

Rockford Facts

Huggins had originally designed "The Kirkoff Case" for *Toma* (as an episode entitled "How to Get Away with Murder"). Because that segment was never produced, Huggins took his story and reworked it as a *Rockford* episode.

Early in the episode, after Tawnia Baker (Julie Sommars) drugs Rockford in her apartment, Travis Buckman (Roger Davis) removes Rockford's pants while our hero is incapacitated. The scene originally called for Rockford to make a remark about his sitting around in his "Jockey shorts" once he came to. After reviewing the script, however, NBC's Standards and Practices had the line changed to simply "shorts" because "Jockey is a brand name." Of course, in this age of blatant product placement in films and television shows, the line would likely have remained "Jockey shorts" had this episode been filmed today.

Stephen J. Cannell named Sommars' character "Tawnia" after his eldest daughter.

"The Kirkoff Case," along with the 90-minute episode "This Case is Closed," were later adapted as *The Deadliest Game*, a paperback novel published by Popular Library in 1976. "The Kirkoff Case" is also available through MCA/Universal Home Video as part of its *Rockford Files* collection.

2. THE DARK AND BLOODY GROUND

Production Number: 41402
Original Air Date: September 20, 1974
Teleplay by: Juanita Bartlett
Story by: John Thomas James
Directed by: Michael Schultz

Guest Cast: Linden Chiles (Elliot Malcolm), Nancy Malone (Elizabeth Gorman), Patricia Smith (Ann Calhoun), Walter Brooke (Clyde Russell), Tom Bower (Officer Hensley), Mark Alaimo (Farber)

Hey, Jim, this is Louie down at the Fish Market—you gonna pick up these halibut or what?

Synopsis. *This episode introduces Gretchen Corbett as Rockford's attorney Beth Davenport, who (as Becker puts it) "collects lost causes like they were rare coins." Beth's client Ann Calhoun has been accused of the murder of her husband, poet Kevin Calhoun. Jim would rather pass on the case, since the evidence linking Ann to the crime seems insurmountable (not to mention the fact that Ann has no money), and he becomes less inclined to pursue the matter after two attempts are made on his life. But the case takes an interesting turn after Rockford uncovers a connection between the murder victim and the legal rights to the novel* The Dark and Bloody Ground.

Gretchen Corbett recalls having a hunch at the time she filmed this episode that the role of Beth Davenport might ultimately prove to be very important for her. "I had recently signed a television contract with Universal, and had appeared in several of their shows: *Kojak, Columbo, Marcus Welby*," she said. "And I believe it was during my first year as a contract player that I auditioned for a guest role on *The Rockford Files*. There was something about the character Beth that I knew—it 'spoke' to me, because I'm a reasonably intelligent woman, and they didn't write such roles at the time. That is, there weren't as many 'strong, smart' female characters on television as there are today; back then, women were usually limited to playing the wife, or the girlfriend.

"I was treated with such gentle hands by Monique James, the woman who ran the contract system at Universal, that I didn't have the feeling that there was ever any heavy-duty competition for the role. And I'm not sure that there ever was. It was a guest shot. And so, I think, Monique said to Meta Rosenberg,

Photograph courtesy of Movieland Productions
© 1974 Universal City Studios, Inc.

Gretchen Corbett as Beth Davenport

'I've got your gal,' and I came in and met with Meta and the folks, and I got the job.

"And it was in the shooting of that show that I had a gut feeling that it was a terribly important time for me, and I really needed to do it 'good.'"

That, she did. Beth became a recurring character which Corbett would play in a total of 32 episodes throughout the first four seasons of the series. "They liked the character, and I think they also liked the rapport I had with Jim," she said.

"Gretchen was perfect for that part," added Roy Huggins. "She was a very bright actress to begin with, and it wasn't difficult for me to imagine her playing a lawyer."

"The Dark and Bloody Ground" establishes that there was once a romantic relationship between Rockford and Beth. Given the age difference between Corbett and James Garner (she is 20 years younger), that made Beth a particularly challenging role for Corbett to play. "In that show, the producers pushed me to look and behave a little older than I appeared, because they didn't want to make Rockford look like he was disgusting," she said. "Jim was very sensitive about that kind of stuff. Every now and then, there would be a hint about their past—in fact, there was one show ['A Portrait of Elizabeth'] with a scene where it was the morning after, and Rockford was in my apartment. But there was never anything explicit between those two characters."

Because of the mature and intelligent manner in which Corbett played Beth, the notion of a past relationship between Rockford and her is believable, regardless of the age difference. "I think that's what the producers were going for," the actress continued. "They wanted to make sure that relationship came across 'okay.'"

Rockford Facts

Sometimes it takes a while to find the right vehicle for a story. Roy Huggins first wrote "The Victim Who Never Was" (the story on which "The Dark and Bloody Ground" is based) in July 1972. Over the course of the next two years, he developed the story on three separate occasions: first as a two-hour TV-movie, then as a one-hour series pilot, and later as an episode of *Toma*. Although each of these projects was scrapped for various reasons, Huggins never gave up on "The Victim Who Never Was," and eventually produced it as a segment of *The Rockford Files*.

Perhaps Huggins kept returning to the story because of its terrific plot twist: 17 U.S.C. § 24, the peculiar loophole in U.S. copyright law which stipulated that if a publisher purchased a book, but the author died before the copyright is renewed, all rights to the book reverted to the author's surviving spouse. *NOTE: This statute was later revised in 1978.*

Interestingly enough, *The Rockford Files* had its own in-house expert on copyright law: Charles Floyd Johnson, an attorney who served as an advisor in the U.S. Copyright Office in Washington D.C. from 1967-1970 before moving into television. Johnson worked as a production coordinator for many series at Universal, including *Toma*. Johnson was *Rockford*'s production coordinator on the pilot and early in the first year before eventually becoming the show's associate producer (and, later, one of its producers).

In 1967, during his stint at the U.S. Copyright Office, Johnson published a pamphlet entitled *Copyright and Developing Countries*. "I remember I was asked a lot of questions when they made that episode because of my experience in that area," he said.

3.　THE COUNTESS
(Originally Entitled: "Call Girl Countess")

Production Number: 41410
Original Air Date: September 27, 1974
Teleplay by: Stephen J. Cannell
Story by: John Thomas James
Directed by: Russ Mayberry

Guest Cast: Susan Strasberg (Deborah Ryder), Art Lund (Mike Ryder), Dick Gautier (Carl Brego), Harold J. Stone (Sorrell), Todd Martin (Policeman), James Cromwell (Terry), Florence Link (Old Woman), Jeanne LeBouvier (Woman), Mel Allen (Cab Driver)

Hey, Rockford! Very funny. I ain't laughing—you're gonna get yours.

Synopsis. *Socialite Deborah Ryder hires Rockford to stop an extortionist named Carl Brego, who knows that Deborah was once linked to a numbers racket in Chicago. As part of his surveillance, Rockford videotapes a meeting between Deborah and Carl. Then, while pretending to be another blackmailer who wants a piece of the action, he confronts Carl and threatens to turn the tape over to the police unless Carl cuts him in. But Rockford's ploy backfires. A mysterious assailant shoots Carl dead—and when an elderly couple who witnessed Rockford at the scene of the crime notifies the police, the P.I. becomes the prime suspect in the killing.*

One of the more endearing trademarks of *The Rockford Files* is its sly sense of humor. Besides clever dialogue, the show also had a penchant for working in the names of actual series personnel in the course of a given episode. About halfway through "The Countess," for example, during the sequence in which Rockford breaks into Carl Brego's house in order to search for evidence, Jimbo comes across a phone book near Brego's night stand and begins flipping through it. The film then cuts to an insert of a page with handwritten names and numbers. In addition to the name "Leah Richards"—the woman who was with Brego when he brawled with Rockford on the beach earlier in the episode—we see the following names: "C. Johnson," "Dorothy B.," "Helen A.," "Steve Rubinstein" and "D. Bailey."

"C. Johnson," of course, is a reference to associate producer Charles Floyd Johnson. "Dorothy B." and "D. Bailey" both refer to Dorothy Bailey, Roy Huggins' longtime assistant at Universal Television. "Helen A." alludes to Helen Alexander (Jo Swerling's assistant at the time of the series), while "Steve Rubinstein" was the name of an executive at Universal.

Rockford Facts

In this episode, Sergeant Becker makes a brief reference to his wife Nancy. However, either Becker remarried or his wife's name was changed, because when Pat Finley (*The Bob Newhart Show*) began playing Mrs. Dennis Becker (beginning with the second season episode, "The Farnsworth Stratagem"), the character's first name was Peggy.

According to this episode, Rockford's address is 2354 Pacific Coast Highway in Los Angeles. Later in the series, it will be changed to 29 Cove Road in Malibu.

Rockford Familiar Faces

Best known for his Oscar-nominated role in *Babe* (1995), James Cromwell's television roles include Stretch Cunningham on *All in the Family* and George Sibley on *Six Feet Under*. Cromwell, who appears briefly as the tennis instructor in this episode, also played opposite James Garner and Clint Eastwood in the box office sleeper *Space Cowboys* (2000).

Susan Strasberg (Deborah) was the daughter of Lee Strasberg, the legendary acting coach who taught at the famous Actors Theatre in New York City. Among her many roles in film and television, Strasberg starred as the wife of Tony Musante in *Toma*, the police drama inextricably linked to the creation of *The Rockford Files*.

Dick Gautier (Brego) played Hymie the Robot on *Get Smart*. He also starred as Robin Hood in *When Things Were Rotten*, a short-lived sendup of the legend of Sherwood Forest that Mel Brooks produced for ABC in 1975.

4.   EXIT PRENTISS CARR

Production Number: 41405
Original Air Date: October 4, 1974
Teleplay by: Juanita Bartlett
Story by: John Thomas James
Directed by: Alex Grasshoff

Guest Cast: Corinne Michaels (Janet Carr), Warren Kemmerling (Lieutenant Furlong), Mills Watson (Sergeant Larsen), Stephen McNally (Chief Bailey), William Jordan (Terry Warde), Wallace Rooney (Eric Saunders), Hank Rolike (Eddie), Thomas Rubin (Delivery Boy), Roberta Collins (Nancy Helmond), Heath Jobes (Jack Clark)

It's Morrie. Got a call from Davis at the IRS. You were right—they bounced your return. Call me.

Synopsis. *Rockford's old flame Janet Carr hires him to tail her philandering husband Prentiss. Rockford locates Prentiss at the Bay City Motel, but he finds the man dead—an apparent murder victim. Rockford reports the matter to the authorities, albeit without telling them that he's already investigated the scene of the crime (a fact could possibly implicate Jim and his client to Prentiss' death). When Lieutenant Furlong and Sergeant Larsen of the Bay City Police report that Prentiss apparently committed suicide, Rockford accuses them of tampering with the evidence. After the cops throw him out of town, Rockford surreptitiously continues to probe—and discovers a link between Prentiss' death and an embezzlement scheme at the insurance company where Prentiss worked.*

Although Roy Huggins wrote nearly all the stories for every television series he produced (and then assigned to another writer to compose the teleplay), his name rarely appeared among the writing credits for his shows because he usually gave the credit to whomever wrote the teleplay. However, beginning in the 1960s and continuing through the 1970s, Huggins' name did appear in the story credits—as "John Thomas James," a pseudonym named after three of Roy's sons.

Supervising producer Jo Swerling Jr. recalled that "John Thomas James" was once very much in demand by other studios. "We used to get calls from agents and from other producers who would ask, '*You know, that John Thomas James is pretty prolific. Who's his agent?*' Depending on what they wanted, we'd either make up a story or level with them. Universal even had the name on a separate parking space, which meant that Roy had two parking spaces on the lot. So a lot of people thought that 'John Thomas James' was an actual guy."

"John Thomas James" received individual writing contracts from the studio, as well as separate correspondence from the networks. In one instance, ABC wanted to include footage from a *Toma* episode written by "John Thomas James" in a montage of TV detectives it was preparing as a segment to be featured on the Emmy Awards telecast in 1974. The network needed the author to sign a release form, and in fact had the form addressed to "John Thomas James." Huggins signed the form on behalf of James.

Though clearly the most famous of Huggins' pen names, "John Thomas James" was not the only one the producer used over the years. In fact, at the time *Rockford* was produced, Huggins had at least six other pseudonyms on file with the Writers Guild of America: "Bret Huggins" (named after Roy's eldest son), "F.D. Averno," "James Patrick," "John Francis O'Mara," "Thomas Fitzroy," and "Roy O'Haogain" (the Irish name from which Huggins' surname has its origin).

Rockford Facts

This episode features character actors Warren Kemmerling and Mills Watson, both of whom were were among the early considerations for the role of Dennis Becker in the *Rockford Files* pilot.

Also, the fictitious town of "Bay City," where much of the action in "Exit Prentiss Carr" takes place, is presumably an homage to Raymond Chandler. Bay City was the town run by crooked cops in Chandler's classic Philip Marlowe novel *Farewell My Lovely* (1940). Bay City would also be the focus of another Rockford investigation in the second season (the episode "The Girl in the Bay City Boys Club").

5. TALL WOMAN IN RED WAGON

Production Number: 41415
Original Air Date: October 11, 1974
Teleplay by: Stephen J. Cannell
Story by: John Thomas James
Directed by: Jerry London

Guest Cast: Sian Barbara Allen (Sandra Turkel), George DiCenzo (Harry Stoner), John Crawford (Dr. Kennilworth), Susan Damante (Charlotte Duskey), Angus Duncan (Joe Baron Jr.), Ryan MacDonald (Motel Manager), Dave Morick (James Darrow), Rudy Diaz (Maddey), Robert Raymond Sutton (Morrie), James Murtaugh (Steve McWilliams), Jack Stamberger (Station Manager)

It's Lori at the Trailer Park. A space opened up … Do you want me to save it, or are the cops gonna let you stay where you are?

Synopsis. *The "tall woman in red wagon" is one Charlotte Duskey, a newspaper copy editor (and former gangland moll) who suddenly vanished—along with the $1.2 million she inherited from her late paramour, gangster Joe Baron. Sandra Turkel, a co-worker of Charlotte's who is unaware of her friend's checkered past, hires Rockford to investigate the disappearance.*

"Tall Woman in Red Wagon" features Sian Barbara Allen, a contract player at Universal who appeared in many of the studio's high-profile series and movies-of-the-week throughout the early 1970s, including episodes of *Ironside, Columbo, Adam-12, The Bold Ones: The Lawyers, Marcus Welby, M.D.,* and *Baretta*, as well as the acclaimed TV-movie *The Lindbergh Kidnapping Case* and the Roy Huggins-produced miniseries *The Captains and The Kings*. At the time she filmed this episode, Allen was dating actor Richard Thomas (*The Waltons*), whom she met on the set on the 1972 feature motion picture *You'll Like My Mother*.

Other guest stars include *Dark Shadows* alumnus George DiCenzo, who played Los Angeles County District Attorney Vincent Bugliosi in the original *Helter Skelter* (1976), and character actor John Crawford, who previously appeared with James Garner in *The Americanization of Emily* (1964).

Rockford Facts

"The secret of a good confidence game," Rockford explains to Sandra in this episode, "is the right props. You can waste a lot of time on people if you don't have the right props." In "Tall Woman in Red Wagon," we're introduced to one of Rockford's most valuable (and most memorable) "props"—the portable printing press that he keeps in the back seat of his car.

6.   THIS CASE IS CLOSED (90-minute episode)

Production Number: 41403
Original Air Date: October 18, 1974
Teleplay by: Stephen J. Cannell
Story by: John Thomas James
Directed by: Bernard L. Kowalski

Guest Cast: Joseph Cotten (Warner Jameson), Sharon Gless (Susan Jameson), James McEachin (David Shore), Fred Sadoff (Howard Kasanjian), Joseph Della Sorte (Torrance Beck), Norman Bartold (Hollis Cotton), Eddie Fontaine (Lieutenant Larry Pierson), Del Monroe (Vic), Jude Farese (Harry), Stu Nisbet (Bartender), Geoffrey Land (Mark Chalmers)

You really want Issue in the 7th? Come on, that nag couldn't go a mile in the back of a pick-up truck! Call me.

Synopsis. *Warner Jameson believes that Mark Chalmers, the jetsetting Ivy Leaguer engaged to his daughter Sue, is not all that he appears to be, so he hires Rockford to check into Mark's past. Rockford's investigation takes him to Newark, New Jersey, where he is hounded by local police and federal agents. The matter becomes worse for Rockford when he returns to L.A.: first, he's tailed by another private investigator, then he's kidnapped (and almost killed) by mobster Torrance Beck and his goons. Federal agents rescue Rockford from Beck, but then they interrogate him for reasons they won't make clear. Rockford becomes so fed up that he not only quits the case, he drops out of the P.I. business all together. Meanwhile, when Mark Chalmers discovers that Jameson is having him investigated, he abruptly calls off the engagement. A stunned Sue Jameson asks Rockford to investigate why Mark mysteriously changed his mind, but Jim can't help her (even if he wanted to) without compromising his professional relationship with her father. But Rockford becomes drawn back into the case anyway once he discovers Mark has been murdered.*

James Garner competed against himself on the night this episode was first broadcast (October 18, 1974). "This Case is Closed" went head-to-head with *They Only Kill Their Masters*, the 1972 Garner feature that aired on *The CBS Friday Night Movie*. *Rockford* bested *The CBS Friday Night Movie* in that night's Nielsen ratings.

As noted earlier, *They Only Kill Their Masters* was written by Lane Slate, who briefly served as producer of *The Rockford Files* during the 1975-1976 season. It was also developed an astonishing four times for television, with Andy Griffith taking over for Garner on each occasion. *They Only Kill Their Masters* was initially retooled as *Winter Kill*, a 1974 pilot that led to the short-lived series *Adams of Eagle Lake*, which ran on ABC for two weeks in the summer of 1975. Though Griffith's character was essentially the same as Abel Marsh (the small town police chief originally played by Garner in *Masters*), for some reason the character's name was changed both times for the ABC projects.

Two years later, Griffith tried again with *The Girl in the Empty Grave*, a two-hour movie produced and written by Slate that aired on NBC in September 1977. This time, Griffith played Abel Marsh, with James Cromwell cast as his slow-witted deputy Malcolm Rossiter. Though *Girl in the Empty Grave* did well enough to commission yet another pilot—*Deadly Game* (written and directed by Slate), which aired on NBC in December 1977—no Abel Marsh series would ever materialize.

Photograph courtesy of Photofest
© 1974 Universal City Studios, Inc.

James Garner and Joseph Cotten in a scene from "This Case is Closed"

Photograph courtesy of TV History Archive
© 1974 Universal City Studios, Inc.

James McEachin with Garner, also from "This Case is Closed"

Rockford Facts

This episode also features noted screen actor Joseph Cotten (*Citizen Kane*), who reprtedly agreed to do the guest shot on the basis of his longtime friendship with executive producer Meta Rosenberg.

"This Case is Closed," which airs as a two-parter in syndication, was one of two episodes novelized by mystery writer Mike Jahn as *The Deadliest Game*, a licensed paperback tie-in published by Popular Library in 1976. As previously noted, the other source for *The Deadliest Game* was the premiere episode "The Kirkoff Case."

Rockford Familiar Faces

James McEachin (Shore) was a mainstay on television detective shows for over 30 years. Under contract at Universal at the time this episode was filmed, McEachin had just finished starring in *Tenafly*, a short-lived but nonetheless memorable private eye series that was part of the *NBC Mystery Movie* franchise. In 2002, McEachin played Supreme Court Justice Jerome Morris in *First Monday*, a legal drama featuring James Garner as the Chief Justice of the United States. *First Monday* was also produced by *Rockford* alumnus Charles Floyd Johnson.

Like the original 90-minute pilot, this episode was re-edited into a two-parter when *Rockford* was released in syndication in 1979. Also like the pilot, "This Case is Closed" was apparently shown out of sequence for a time when the series first went into reruns. For some reason, both the pilot and "This Case is Closed" were originally inserted among the fourth season episodes, appearing between "Dwarf in a Helium Hat" and "The House on Willis Avenue" in the rotation of shows. At some point, however, the error was corrected. Both the pilot and "Case" continue to air in their original broadcast sequence, which is the order in which most stations air the episodes.

Rockford Fun

The character "Howard Kasanjian" was presumably named after the assistant director with the same name who worked on the *Rockford Files* pilot.

7.   THE BIG RIPOFF

Production Number: 41416
Original Air Date: October 25, 1974
Teleplay by: Robert Hamner and Jo Swerling Jr.
Story by: John Thomas James
Directed by: Vincent McEveety

Guest Cast: Jill Clayburgh (Marilyn Polanski), Normann Burton (Melvyn Moss), Fred Beir (Steve Nelson), Bruce Kirby (Carl LeMay), Nedra Dean (Nancy Frazier), Warren Vanders (Earl Pitt), Kelly Thordsen (Sheriff Neal), Suzanne Somers (Ginny Nelson), Christine Dixon (Stewardess), Jenny Maybrook (Ticket Clerk)

It's Audra. Remember last summer at Pat's? I've got a 12-hour layover before I go to Chicago. How 'bout it?

Synopsis. *Nancy Frazier hires Rockford to investigate the death of her lover Steve Nelson, who allegedly perished in a plane crash. Nancy believes that Steve's wife Ginny arranged for the accident, but Rockford suspects that Steve is alive—and that he and Ginny faked the accident as part of a scheme to bilk their insurance company out of $400,000. Jim also believes that Nancy may be part of the scam, because Nancy skipped town almost immediately after Rockford reported back to her. Rockford persuades the insurance company to hire him in order to find Steve Nelson and recover the money.*

"The Big Ripoff" features another *Maverick* touch. After the two operatives beat up Rockford and leave him to die along the side of a lonely road, model Marilyn Polanski (Oscar and Emmy nominee Jill Clayburgh) rescues Rockford after following him in his own car. Marilyn urges Jim to take it easy, but our hero is determined to press on with the case.

"Is there anything you won't do for money?" asks Marilyn.

"I won't kill for it, and I won't marry for it," replies Rockford. "Other than that, I'm open to just about anything."

Other guest stars include Suzanne Somers, who at the time of this episode was three years away from her breakthrough role opposite John Ritter and

Joyce DeWitt in *Three's Company* (ABC, 1977-1984). Ritter, of course, went on to star as Paul Hennessy in *8 Simple Rules for Dating My Teenage Daughter* (ABC, 2002-), the family comedy based on the popular column and book by W. Bruce Cameron. James Garner joined the cast of *8 Simple Rules* following the untimely death of Ritter in September 2003.

Rockford Facts

"The Big Ripoff" is a retooled version of "The $20,000 Carrot," a private eye story which Roy Huggins had originally developed as an episode of *The Outsider* in 1968.

This episode is available through MCA/Universal Home Video as part of its *Rockford Files* collection.

8.   FIND ME IF YOU CAN

Production Number: 41412
Original Air Date: November 1, 1974
Teleplay by: Juanita Bartlett
Story by: John Thomas James
Directed by: Lawrence Doheny

Guest Cast: Joan Van Ark (Barbara Kelbaker), Paul Michael Glaser (Ralph Correll), Richard Drout Miller (Sergeant Doane), Joseph Stern (Morgan Tallman), James Lydon (Wyatt), Adrian Ricard (Miss Connor)

This is the Blood Bank. If you don't have malaria, hepatitis or TB, we'd like to have a pint of your blood.

Synopsis. *Barbara Kelbaker approaches Rockford with an unusual request: she wants to hire him to find out if she can be "found." But Barbara refuses to explain why—in fact, she doesn't even give Rockford her real name—because she's frightened for her life. Barbara witnessed her boyfriend, Denver crime lord Ralph Correll, murder a man. Barbara believes that Correll is after her, and she figures that if Rockford can find her, so can Correll.*

The storyline of "Find Me If You Can" is very similar to that of "Girl on the Run," a Roy Huggins short story which Huggins later adapted in 1956 as the basis for the pilot of the TV series *77 Sunset Strip*. Although Huggins acknowledges the similarities between the two stories, he recalls that he'd been thinking along a different line when he first came up with "Find Me If You Can." "That story began simply with that idea: somebody comes up to Rockford and says, 'I want to know if I can be found. I won't tell you a thing about me, but I want to know whether I can be found.

"Although I now can see that the background story is very much like 'Girl on the Run,'" continued Huggins, "I don't recall deliberately using that story as a *Rockford*. But it may have been done subconsciously."

Rockford Funnies

Rockford sustains a nasty-looking gash near his left eye after he's been knocked around by one of Ralph Correll's goons. Although his father is understandably concerned about the mishap ("Look at that gash—two inches to the right, and you'd have been missing that eye!"), Jim remains remarkably optimistic. "Look at it this way," he tells Rocky. "Two inches to the left, and he would've missed me completely."

Also, the scene between Rockford and the officer at the Pacific Grove Pacific Department features another instance of inside humor. "Mr. Yaconelli" (the name of the bogus client Rockford uses to get information from the cop) is a reference to Steve Yaconelli, a cinematographer on both the original series as well as the CBS movies.

9.   IN PURSUIT OF CAROL THORNE

Production Number: 41406
Original Air Date: November 8, 1974
Teleplay by: Stephen J. Cannell
Story by: John Thomas James
Directed by: Charles S. Dubin

Guest Cast: Lynette Mettey (Carol Thorne), Robert Symonds (Miles Keeley), Jim Antonio (Cliff Hoad), Bill Fletcher (Nate Spinella), Irene Tedrow (Dixie), Sandy Ward (Detective Boris Sausman), Vince Howard (Patrolman), Laffit Pincay Jr. (Himself)

This is the Message Phone company. I see you're using our unit … now how 'bout paying for it?

Synopsis. *An elderly couple who claim to be the parents of Cliff Hoad hire Rockford to tail Carol Thorne, a recently paroled convict who is also Cliff's former girlfriend. Rockford doesn't realize that his client is really Miles Keeley, a master con artist named who, along with Cliff and two other men, robbed a Marine Corps payroll of $1.2 million three years earlier. Because of a snafu, Cliff alone ended up with all the money (although Miles and the others managed to escape). Miles wants Carol to lead him to Cliff—and to where Cliff stashed the money.*

Like all other aspects of production, planning the look of a show requires a total understanding of what the writer and producer want to accomplish. Because *Rockford* was primarily written "in house," the writers were usually available for consultation in the planning of the look of the show. This is particularly helpful if you encountered an element of the script that may pose a practical difficulty. "Say you have a two-page scene that was written to take place outside a gas station in Santa Monica," explained supervising producer Jo Swerling. "During the prep time, we might find a location in Santa Monica that's perfect for that scene. Only there's one problem—there's nothing else around that location that could be used for that script. That means that scene would require a major company move across town just to shoot two pages.

"Now, normally, you try to shoot anywhere from 8-10 pages a day. By going out of your way just to shoot that one scene, by the time you're finished loading the trucks, moving everything across town, unloading, setting everything up, shooting the scene, breaking for lunch, wrapping everything up, loading up the truck again, and then heading off to the next location (or back to the studio), you will have burned off at least one-third of your shooting time. In the meantime, you still to have to shoot eight pages in whatever is left of the day. And you really don't want to make two moves in one day, because you're not grinding out film when you're moving—you're spending your shooting time inside a truck.

"So we would say to whoever wrote the script, 'You know, there's a diner nearby the location where we're shooting several other scenes. Would you mind if we play this scene in a diner instead of a gas station, because that would save us an additional company move.' Now, of course, the gas station can't be critical to the scene—and in many cases, it isn't. The writer is simply picking a location that works for him or her, whereas another location might work equally as well."

Rockford Family

Jim Antonio (Cliff) is the brother of prolific television director Lou Antonio, whose many credits include such top-rated shows as *The West Wing*, *CSI: Crime Scene Investigation* and the Emmy-nominated made-for-TV movie *Something for Joey*. Like James Garner, the Antonio brothers are native Oklahomans. Jim and Lou were born in Oklahoma City, Oklahoma while Garner was born in Norman, Oklahoma.

Jim Antonio later appeared with Garner in the 1985 miniseries, *Space*. Lou Antonio helmed five segments of *The Rockford Files* ("Roundabout," "The Aaron Ironwood School of Success," "The No-Cut Contract," "Foul on the First Play," and the premiere episode "The Kirkoff Case"), as well as episodes of Garner's Supreme Court drama *First Monday*. Lou's wife Lane Bradbury also guest-starred on *Rockford*: she played Houston Preli in the second-season episode "Where's Houston?"

Rockford Fillies

This episode also features a cameo appearance by legendary jockey Laffit Pincay Jr., who became thoroughbred horse racing's all-time winningest jockey in December 1999 with his 8834th career win. A six-time Eclipse Award winner, Pincay won the Kentucky Derby in 1984, as well as the Belmont Stakes three years in a row (1982, 1983, 1984).

10. THE DEXTER CRISIS
(Originally Entitled: "Cherchéz la Femme," *or* "Find the Woman")

Production Number: 41408
Original Air Date: November 15, 1974
Written by: Gloryette Clark
Directed by: Alex Grasshoff

Guest Cast: Lee Purcell (Susan Parsons), Linda Kelsey (Louise Adams), Ron Soble (Kermit Higby), Tim O'Connor (Charles Dexter), Joyce Jameson (Marge White), Burke Byrnes (Deputy), Bing Russell (Lieutenant)

I staked out that guy, only it didn't work out like you said. Please call me—Room 234, County Hospital.

Synopsis. *Wealthy entrepreneur Charles Dexter hires Rockford to locate his mistress, Susan Parsons, but doesn't disclose his true motives until much later (Susan ran off with over $250,000 of Dexter's money). Rockford joins forces with Susan's roommate, law student Louise Adams, who thinks there's a connection between Susan's disappearance and the driver of a car which had been following Susan for several days. Rockford and Louise travel to Las Vegas, where they not only find Susan, they also come across the man who'd been tailing her: Kermit Higby, a private investigator with whom Rockford has clashed in the past.*

This episode was written by Gloryette Clark, who enjoyed a long association as a film editor, writer and director at Universal, particularly on projects produced by Roy Huggins. Clark was nominated for an Emmy in 1972 for Outstanding Achievement in Film Editing on *The Lawyers*, a series produced by Huggins as part of the NBC dramatic "wheel" *The Bold Ones*.

Prior to becoming a film editor, Clark was the resident stock footage librarian at Universal Pictures. "Gloryette was superb at finding good stock film," recalled supervising producer Jo Swerling Jr. "They had a pretty good film library at Universal, but they also had access to [stock footage at] other studios, as well as other independent film libraries. Gloryette would find all sorts of good stuff for us [whenever we would need it]."

In the case of "The Dexter Crisis," for example, even though part of the action takes place in Las Vegas, the episode was not filmed there. (According to studio production sheets, location filming for this segment actually took place in nearby Lancaster and Palmdale, California.) Given Clark's background, she may have had a hand in selecting the stock footage of Las Vegas used in this episode to establish Rockford's travels.

Rockford Facts

Because Jim Rockford is essentially Bret Maverick in modern dress, it seems only fitting that Rockford is as much an expert in games of chance as his TV Western ancestor. Like Maverick, Rockford knows that playing roulette, like playing poker, is a game you can only win if you're patient. "No roulette wheel is ever in perfect balance," he explains to Susan (Lee Purcell) in this episode. "All you have to do is figure out the bias, and keep playing until they catch onto what you're doing. That gives you a 6-7% advantage. If you can keep them from figuring your action, you can rip 'em good." Rockford then tells Susan that he once hit one of the Grand Hotels on the Vegas Strip for over $50,000.

Rockford Fun

"The Dexter Crisis" features some more inside humor. When Rockford enters the roulette room upon his arrival in Las Vegas, one of the patrons being paged in the background has the same name as associate producer Charles Floyd Johnson.

Photograph courtesy of TV History Archives
© 1974 Universal City Studios, Inc.

Jim Rockford (James Garner) uses his knowledge of roulette to win the confidence of Susan Parsons (Lee Purcell) in "The Dexter Crisis."

11.   CALEDONIA—IT'S WORTH A FORTUNE!
Originally Entitled: "No Stone Unturned")

Production Number: 41414
Original Air Date: December 6, 1974
Teleplay by: Juanita Bartlett
Story by: John Thomas James
Directed by: Stuart Margolin

Guest Cast: Shelley Fabares (Jolene Hyland), Ramon Bieri (Sheriff Prouty), Richard Schaal (Leonard Blair), William Traylor (Wilson), Sid Haig (B.J.), Rudy Challenger (Dr. Watkins), Don Eichner (Gerald Hyland), Robert Ginty (Gib Moore), Robert Ellenstein (Motel Manager)

It's Doc Jones. What'd you do to the hand, son? Three fractured knuckles ... You hit somebody?

Synopsis. *Gerald Hyland, who was convicted of embezzling over $4 million several years ago, is brutally beaten by two prison inmates. Shortly before slipping into a coma, Hyland leaves his wife Jolene a cryptic clue to where he had supposedly buried nearly $750,000 in rare stamps which Hyland had purchased with the stolen money shortly before his arrest. However, in order to recover the stamps, Jolene must team up with Jerry's former cellmate Leonard Blair—with whom, unbeknownst to her husband, she once had an affair. The conniving Len has the map leading to the stash, but the map is useless without Jolene's directions. Because she knows Len will doublecross her at the first opportunity, Jolene hires Rockford to protect her interest.*

One reason why *The Rockford Files* has endured for 30 years is its timelessness. With few exceptions, the series has very little in the way of topical humor or subject matter that would specifically date it to the time period in which it was made (the mid-to-late 1970s). Interestingly enough, some of the fashion trends seen on the series, such as miniskirts for women and long sideburns for men, have even come back "in vogue" in recent years.

However, there are some behaviors seen on the series that may have been acceptable 30 years ago, but which are now considered socially unacceptable (and, in some cases, illegal). For example, many characters, including Rockford, are depicted smoking cigarettes—something that would clearly be verboten if the series were done today. Also, as we see in several instances throughout "Caledonia," passengers in motor vehicles do not always wear their seat belts because the mandatory law had not yet gone into effect.

As it happens, NBC's Standards and Practices department, which monitored the content of every series episode and TV-movie for accuracy and/or questionable material, *did* object about the non-use of seat belts in "Caledonia," and stated its displeasure explicitly in a memo to Roy Huggins:

> There is no reason why [seat belts] should not have been in use. Please inform all concerned that this is a serious matter which will continue to be reviewed. We hope it will not become necessary to edit future scenes because they do not properly support our concern regarding the use of safety belts and harnesses.

While Huggins usually strove to eliminate anything that might offend the upper tier of his viewership, he apparently overlooked that detail. The producer did, however, make a big notation in red ink on his copy of the memo: "PLEASE NOTE."

Rockford Facts

"Caledonia—It's Worth a Fortune!" recycles a line that Huggins had first used in "Point Blank," the pilot episode of *Maverick* which he wrote in 1956.

At the end of "Point Blank," the sheriff orders Maverick "to get out of town in ten minutes," to which Maverick replies, "Sheriff, I've gotten out of towns this size in *five* minutes." Similarly, in the first act of "Caledonia," Sheriff Prouty, who has taken an immediate dislike to Rockford, asks how long it would take Jimbo to leave town.

"About fifteen minutes," says Rockford.

"Why don't you make it ten?" cracks Prouty.

Incidentally, Sheriff Prouty is played by character actor Ramon Bieri, who later co-starred with James Garner in *Bret Maverick*.

12./13. PROFIT AND LOSS (Two-Parter)
(Originally Entitled: "Fiscal Dynamics, Inc." and "Programmed to Destroy")

Production Numbers: 41417/41418
Original Air Dates: December 20 and 27, 1974
Teleplay by: Stephen J. Cannell
Story by: John Thomas James
Directed by: Lawrence Doheny

Guest Cast: Ned Beatty (Leon Fielder), Sharon Spelman (Doris Parker), Paul Jenkins (Stan Gorrick), Val Bisoglio (Carl Bovino), Albert Paulsen (Kurt), Michael Lerner (Arnold Love), Priscilla Pointer (Helen Morris), John Carter (Alec Morris), Ray Girardin (Ted), Don Billett (Don Shavelson), Joe E. Tata (Solly Marshall), J. Jay Saunders (Computer Programmer), Tracy Bogart (Teresa), Tom Rosqui (Norm Mitchell), Al Stevenson (L.J.), Barry Cahill (Sergeant)

Hey, Jimmy—this here's Teeter Skerritt. Remember me? From the Army. I'm stuck here in town. How 'bout I come over and bunk with you, buddy?

This is Mrs. Bosley at the library. We billed you for your overdue book, Karate Made Easy. We abuse our library if we don't get our cards renewed ...

Synopsis. *Computer programmer Alec Morris comes to Rockford for protection upon discovering that his employer, the powerful corporation Fiscal Dynamics, Inc., has been forging information on its annual report in order to carry off plans to purchase another corporate giant. Rockford witnesses two men abduct Morris, but after reporting the matter to the police, he not only finds Morris safe and sound, he also faces a false report charge when Morris denies that anything ever happened. In addition, CEO Leon Fielder threatens to sue Rockford for $10 million unless he stays out of FDI's affairs. Rockford is about to drop out of the matter when he is hired by Doris Parker, who has long suspected FDI of murdering her husband (who also worked as a computer programmer for the company). Upon reading that the man who printed FDI's annual report was found dead in his shop, Jim deduces that both Doris' husband and the printer were killed after* *they, like Morris, discovered the forgery scheme. With the help of Doris (and his father), Rockford sets out to prove it.*

Noted character actor Ned Beatty (*Deliverance, Network*) makes the first of his two appearances on *The Rockford Files*. Beatty, who also played a former Army commander of Rockford's in the third season episode "Return to the 38th Parallel," would later star with James Garner in *Streets of Laredo*, the 1995 mini-series based on the novel by Larry McMurtry.

Rockford Facts

According to "The House on Willis Avenue" (an episode that aired at the end of the fourth season), Rockford's efforts in cracking the FDI case were recognized in a front-page story that ran in the *Los Angeles Times*—an article that would help cement Rockford's reputation as one of the top private detectives in Los Angeles.

Val Bisoglio, who plays the ill-fated printer Carl Bovino in Part One of this episode, was among the early considerations for the role of Dennis Becker in the *Rockford* pilot. Bisoglio's best-known television role was Danny Tovo, the owner of the restaurant and bar that Jack Klugman frequented on *Quincy*.

Part Two of "Profit and Loss" marks the first of Al Stevenson's four appearances as Rocky's friend L.J. Al Stevenson would reprise the role in "Guilt," "New Life, Old Dragons," and the first episode of the two-parter "Gearjammers."

Rockford Flubs

Early in the first act of Part One, after he is beaten up by the two men who kidnap Alec Morris, Rockford calls the police and asks for "Lieutenant Becker." Either this was an oversight, or Becker must've gotten into big trouble with the department, because by the time we see Dennis again (in the episode "Sleight of Hand"), he has been bounced back to sergeant. Becker, of course, was promoted to lieutenant for good in the fifth season episode "Kill the Messenger."

14.　AURA LEE, FAREWELL

Production Number: 41413
Original Air Date: January 3, 1975
Teleplay by: Edward J. Lakso
Story by: John Thomas James
Directed by: Jackie Cooper

Guest Cast: Lindsay Wagner (Sara Butler), Robert Webber (Senator Evan Murdock), Greg Mullavey (Dirk Shaefer), Kelly Lange (Commentator), Bill Mumy (Trask), Melissa Greene (Aura Lee Benton), Henry Slate (Oscar), Tom Scott (Motel Clerk), Linda Dano (Ellen Murdock), Ed Crick (Campaigner)

Mr. Rockford, you don't know me, but I'd like to hire you. Could you call me at—My name is, uh—Never mind. Forget it.

Synopsis. *Once again, Rockford teams up with Sara Butler, the woman who hired him in the pilot episode to solve the murder of her father. This time, Sara wants Jim to prove that the apparent suicide of her girlfriend and employee Aura Lee Benton was really a homicide. Aura Lee died of a heroin overdose, but Sara suspects foul play because she knows that Aura Lee did not use drugs. After some probing, Rockford and Sara discover that a high-profile state senator, a drug pusher, a fatal hit-and-run accident, a blackmail scheme and over $2,600 in hush money are all linked to Aura Lee's death.*

Like Maverick, Rockford is capable of having a romantic relationship with a woman without ever losing sight of his own self-interest. At the end of this episode, Rockford asks Sara Butler how she plans to pay him. Sara tells Jim that she'd planned on paying him with the cash she found in Aura Lee's apartment, only to find that she can't because the police have confiscated the money. As an alternative, Sara offers to pay Rockford on the installment plan ("like we did before"), then leans forward and kisses him in order to seal the deal. As much as Jim enjoys the kiss, he doesn't lose sight of the bottom line. Once they finish smooching, Rockford smiles at Sara and says, "I want the pink slip to your car."

Emmy winner Lindsay Wagner (*The Bionic Woman*) returns as Sara, the role she had originated in the *Rockford Files* pilot.

Bill Mumy (*Lost in Space*), who had played Sara's brother in the pilot, also appears in "Aura Lee, Farewell," albeit in a completely different role. Mumy plays an

Photograph courtesy of Movieland Productions
© 1974 Universal City Studios, Inc.

James Garner and Lindsay Wagner in a publicity shot for "Aura Lee, Farewell"

artist named Trask, who sells his paintings on the streets of Venice in the funniest scene of this episode. Rockford asks if Trask needs a permit to sell his paintings. "I told you, I paint what I feel," Trask replies.

Upon glancing at one of the paintings, Rockford cracks, "You must not feel well."

15.   SLEIGHT OF HAND
(Originally Entitled: "Nightmare")

Production Number: 41423
Original Air Date: January 17, 1975
Teleplay by: Stephen J. Cannell and Jo Swerling
Based on the Novel *Thin Air* by Howard Browne
Directed by: William Wiard

Guest Cast: Lara Parker (Diana Lewis), Pat Delany (Karen Mills), Allan Miller (Michael Cordeen), John Steadman (Morrie Blauner), Gerald McRaney (Irv), Howard Curtis (Vince Minette), Wayne Wynne (Detective Olson)

Rockford, this is Mr. Dow. If you think I'm gonna pay to have your car repainted, you're nuts—you can take your expense bill and stuff it!

Synopsis. *Rockford makes an exception to his own rule of never interfering with an open police case when he investigates the disappearance of his girlfriend Karen Mills, who mysteriously vanished in front of her home moments after returning from a trip to San Francisco with Jim and her daughter Julie. While the police link Karen's disappearance with the brutal murder of her next door neighbor, Rockford's probe eventually uncovers a connection between his girlfriend, a mysterious woman named Diana Lewis, and a fugitive underworld kingpin.*

In January 1973, Roy Huggins and Jo Swerling Jr. took over the reins of *Jigsaw*, a low-rated police drama starring James Wainwright as an investigator for the California State Bureau of Missing Persons. In an effort to save the series, Huggins and Swerling reworked the premise of the show and made Wainwright's character a private eye. To generate attention for "the new, improved *Jigsaw*," Universal Studios put out an aggressive publicity campaign that resulted in the series getting a second review in all the major newspapers and trade journals, including *Variety*. Although Huggins' first episode of *Jigsaw* (an adaptation of the Howard Browne mystery novel *Thin Air*) was critically acclaimed, the ratings for the series did not improve. *Jigsaw* was canceled in the spring of 1973.

Huggins had always liked *Thin Air*, and so he decided to adapt it once again—this time, as a story for *The Rockford Files*. "It's tough to come up with good stories, week after week after week," he confessed. "I liked *Thin Air*. It was a story that I'd always thought had a great opening, and it happened to be written by an old and dear friend of mine, Howard Browne.

"I knew that I had done a *Thin Air* story only a couple of years before [on *Jigsaw*]. But I also remembered that *Jigsaw* never had high audience numbers. And so, I figured, 'Here's a story that was on a show that nobody watched, so I'm going to adapt it again. I'll make changes in it—with Jim Garner, it will look completely different.' That was pretty much what was going on in my mind at the time."

However, Huggins did catch some flak from *Variety*, whose reviewer accused the producer of "cribbing from himself" after recognizing "Sleight of Hand" as a remake of the *Jigsaw* episode of 1973. "Well, that shows you that *Variety* had a very good reviewer," the producer smiled. "He was showing that he was on his toes. And I'll tell you, two years is a little soon to bring something back. If you're going to do that, you ought to wait at least seven." (Or, in the case of *Maverick* as *The Rockford Files*, maybe as long as twenty.)

Ironically, while *Variety* may have been astute in recognizing the recycled plotline of "Sleight of Hand," the trade journal neglected to mention that the episode itself is excellent. The hour is also unusual in that it presents Rockford as more hardboiled and less "tongue in cheek" than we are ordinarily accustomed to seeing. There is an intensity to the character, particularly in the scenes in which he roughs up the desk clerk at Diana Lewis' apartment building (then later, Michael Cordeen) that, while jolting, is very effective.

All told, Jo Swerling and Stephen J. Cannell create a faithful adaptation of Browne's classic whodunit, while James Garner delivers one of his finest performances in the entire series.

Rockford Funnies

Helen Alexander, who was Jo Swerling's assistant at the time, volunteered her beige handbag as one of the props for the *Jigsaw* adaptation of *Thin Air*. When Alexander learned that Huggins was going to remake that episode on *The Rockford Files*, she wrote a witty memo (which she signed "Helen Alexander's handbag") asking Huggins if she could "reprise" the role.

> I am Helen Alexander's handbag. I have recently been informed that the *Jigsaw* episode in which I starred—well, had a featured lead—well, I did have a big zoom closeup—and for which I was personally selected by Roy Huggins, is being remade as an episode of *Rockford Files*. Naturally, I'd like to play the part again.

In case you may be worried that I have aged in the meantime, I'd like you to know that I have since had my face lifted. In addition, although my figure is still the same, I have a varied wardrobe, so that I am available in black, tan, and navy, in addition to the beige outfit in which I previously played the role. Please keep me in mind when you start casting. Somehow or other, I missed being nominated for an Emmy, but I'm sure that if you gave me another chance, that honor will be in the bag.

P.S. Although I do not belong to SAG, I do belong to BAG.

Although Alexander's white handbag was used in the episode (it has a zoom closeup midway through the first act), it was somehow once again overlooked in the Emmy Awards nominations for 1974-1975.

16.   COUNTER GAMBIT

Production Number: 41420
Original Air Date: January 24, 1975
Written by: Howard Berk and Juanita Bartlett
Directed by: Jackie Cooper

Guest Cast: Mary Frann (Valerie Thomas), Eddie Fontaine (Moss Williams), Burr deBenning (Harry Crown), Ford Rainey (Manny Tolan), M. Emmet Walsh (Edgar Burch), Garry Walberg (Arnold Cutter), Eric Server (Daniel Kramer), Barbara Collentine (Miss Bolting)

Jim, it's Jack—I'm at the airport. I'm going to Tokyo and I want to pay you the $500 I owe you. Catch you next year when I get back ...

Synopsis. *Insurance agent Edgar Burch hires Rockford to recover a $250,000 pearl necklace that was apparently stolen by Moss Williams three years ago—shortly after Williams asked Jim to locate the woman who supposedly stashed the pearls. Rockford decides to play both sides of the fence, but instead gets burned. The "stolen" necklace was never stolen. Williams hired Burch to get Rockford to find the pearls so that he can steal them and frame Jim for the theft. With the help of Valerie Thomas (the owner of the pearls), jewel appraiser Manny Tolan, and his old stir mate Angel Martin, Rockford sets out to clear himself.*

Like Maverick, Rockford's not above committing a little larceny so long as no one gets hurt. In this episode, Rockford takes advantage of Valerie's affections for him in order to get the combination of her apartment safe.

Jim asks Valerie to store a box, which allegedly contains valuable papers for another client, inside her safe while they're out on the town. Valerie doesn't realize that the box contains a sound-activated tape recorder, which began to play once Rockford spoke to Valerie and continued to record as Valerie locked the safe. After retrieving the box the following day, Jim rewinds the tape, plays it back, and determines the combination by counting the clicks. (Rockford knows that most safes are insulated from the outside, but not from the inside. Once you figure how to get a tape recorder inside a safe, you can record the combination.)

Rockford Facts

"Counter Gambit" marks Stuart Margolin's first appearance as Angel since the pilot movie. Margolin went on to play the character in a total of 32 episodes, winning two Emmy Awards for Best Supporting Actor along the way.

Rockford pays Angel a backhanded compliment in this episode when he tells Angel that he makes a great informer. "It's a gift," says Angel.

In an interesting coincidence, Moss Williams, whom Angel helps Rockford outwit in this episode, is played by Eddie Fontaine—who was briefly considered for the role of Angel that eventually went to Margolin. Fontaine, a regular on the Warner Bros. World War II drama *The Gallant Men* (ABC, 1962-1963), appeared in several episodes of *Rockford*, including "This Case is Closed," "Joey Blue Eyes," and "White on White and Nearly Perfect."

Rockford Familiar Faces

Other guest stars include character actor M. Emmet Walsh (*Blood Simple*), who would later appear with James Garner in the motion pictures *Sunset* (1988) and *Twilight* (1998). Prior to *Rockford Files*, Walsh had acted with Garner in three episodes of *Nichols*.

This episode also features Mary Frann (*Newhart*), who would later guest star in the fifth season show "A Fast Count," and longtime film and TV character actor Ford Rainey, who was briefly considered for the role of Joseph Rockford in the *Rockford* pilot.

Rockford Funnies

Early in this episode, we see Rockford on the phone with his dentist, "Dr. Boren" (named after Lamar Boren, the show's director of photography).

17.   CLAIRE
(Originally Entitled: "Lady on the Run")

Production Number: 41422
Original Air Date: January 31, 1975
Written by: Edward J. Lakso and Stephen J. Cannell
Directed by: William Wiard

Guest Cast: Linda Evans (Claire Prescott), W.L. LeGault (Stone), Jackie Cooper (Captain Highland), Lane Smith (Willett), M.P. Murphy (Carl), Douglas V. Fowley (Ted)

Mr. Rockford, this is the Thomas Crown School of Dance and Contemporary Etiquette. We aren't going to call again. Do you want these free lessons, or what?

Synopsis. *Rockford's former fiance Claire Prescott asks him to find Charlie Manning, an undercover police detective who used Claire as an informant as part of an important narcotics investigation. When Manning is found dead, Claire becomes the prime suspect. When Claire becomes the target of the real killers, Jim tries to smuggle her out of town. But the killers kidnap Rocky and threaten to kill him unless Rockford delivers Claire.*

This episode features Jackie Cooper, the onetime child film star who starred in the *Little Rascals* comedies of the early 1930s. Cooper is the youngest male performer ever to be nominated for an Academy Award: he was only nine years old when he was nominated for Best Actor in the 1931 comedy *Skippy*. Cooper, who also co-starred with Wallace Beery (Noah Beery's uncle) in the 1931 film classic *The Champ*, remains one of the few child stars who would also enjoy a successful acting career as an adult. Besides headlining two popular television comedy series in the 1950s (*Hennesey, The People's Choice*), he played Perry White in the *Superman* movies of the '70s and '80s. Cooper was also an accomplished director in television. He helmed multiple episodes of many popular series throughout the '70s and '80s (including *Magnum, p.i., The Mary Tyler*

Photograph courtesy of TV History Archive
© 1974 Universal City Studios, Inc.

James Garner and Noah Beery Jr. in a scene from "Claire"

Moore Show and *The Rockford Files*), and won directing Emmys for his work on *M*A*S*H* and *The White Shadow*.

Rockford Writeoffs

When we first see Rockford in this episode, he's helping his father do his taxes. Rocky is trying to claim a check for $260, which he said he loaned Jim to help him pay for his car. "That check bounced," Rockford reminds his dad. "You can't claim a check as a deduction if the check bounced. No wonder you have tax problems."

Truth be told, Rocky should have declared his truck as a tax writeoff. After all, his son often borrows it whenever he's on a case, as we see in this episode.

18.   SAY GOODBYE TO JENNIFER
(Originally Entitled: "The Witness Vanishes")

Production Number: 41407
Original Air Date: February 7, 1975
Teleplay by: Juanita Bartlett and Rudolph Borchert
Story by: John Thomas James
Directed by: Jackie Cooper

Guest Cast: Hector Elizondo (John Micelli), Pamela Hensley (Jennifer Ryburn), Ken Swofford (Floyd Ross), Kate Woodville (Marilyn Rae), Thayer David (Carl Birrell), Regis J. Cordic (Dr. Evan Stuart), Len Lesser (Colby), Clint Young (Harrison), Beverly Gill (Mary Ann), Vince Cannon (Ricky Pont)

This is Mrs. Landis. Three times this month I come to clean and it always looks like people've been fighting in there: furniture broken, things tipped over. I'm sorry, but I quit!

Synopsis. *Supermodel Jennifer Ryburn allegedly died in a fiery car accident that occurred shortly after the fatal shooting of her boyfriend Ricky Pont, a murder that the police (and the mob) believe she actually committed. But Jennifer's photographer and former lover John Micelli thinks she's alive and hiding in Seattle, and he wants Jim to find her and to prove her innocence. Rockford is reluctant to take on the case: not only does he believe Mitch is too distraught over Jennifer's death to think clearly, he also knows that his involvement could implicate Mitch, who was very jealous of Pont, in Pont's murder. Mitch and Rockford's lives becomes endangered when mobster Carl Birrell, who raised Pont like a son, learns about their investigation. Birrell wants Jennifer found and killed.*

Keep an eye out for two Hollywood landmarks and another sly bit of humor during the scene in Act I in which Mitch meets Rockford downtown after returning from Seattle. Rockford and Mitch take a walk along Hollywood Boulevard, pass by the venerable Roosevelt Hotel (where the first Academy Awards were presented in 1929), and make their way up the famous Hollywood Walk of Fame. That particular scene begins with a closeup of the star of actor Robert Young, who in 1975 was one of the biggest names in television. Young was the star of the top-rated *Marcus Welby, M.D.*, which, like *The Rockford Files*, was produced at Universal. (Coincidentally, Pamela Hensley, who plays Jennifer in this episode, joined the cast of *Marcus Welby, M.D.* in the fall of 1975.)

In real life, James Garner and Stephen J. Cannell each have a star along the Hollywood Walk of Fame. Garner's star is in front of the world-famous Mann's Chinese Theater (across the street from the Roosevelt Hotel), while Cannell's star is actually located in front of the Roosevelt. Also, the West Coast head-quarters of the Cannell Studios are located in the Lareina Building on Hollywood Boulevard, one block away from the hotel.

Rockford Fashion

This episode features a rarely seen aspect of Rockford's sartorial personality. For the first and only time in the series, he wears a lot of turtleneck sweaters (his choice of fashion while in Seattle).

19.   CHARLIE HARRIS AT LARGE
(Originally Entitled: "Crime Without Witness")

Production Number: 41409
Original Air Date: February 14, 1975
Teleplay by: Zekial Marko
Story by: John Thomas James
Directed by: Russ Mayberry

Guest Cast: Tony Musante (Charlie Harris), David Spielberg (Sergeant Tom Garvey), Warner Anderson (Alfred Bannister), Diana Muldaur (Linda Bannister), Eddie Firestone (Haines), Mel Stewart (Police Lieutenant), Zekial Marko (Dr. Gabriel)

Hey, Jim, it's me—Suzie Lewis, from the laundromat. You said you were going to call, and it's been two weeks. What's wrong—you lose my number?

Synopsis. *Charlie Harris, a "high society hustler" who was Rockford's cellmate for two years at San Quentin, is the leading suspect in the murder of a socialite whom he recently married. Charlie is innocent, and he even has an alibi (a woman he knows only as "Cassandra"). But when Cassandra disappears, Charlie needs Rockford to help him find her and clear his name. Rockford soon discovers that Charlie's mystery woman is married to Alfred Bannister, a powerful business magnate who wants to suppress any knowledge of his wife's involvement with Charlie. Bannister threatens to have Rockford killed unless he drops the case.*

This episode features Tony Musante, who played the title role in *Toma*, the series produced by Roy Huggins and Stephen J. Cannell, and the vehicle for which the Jim Rockford character was originally created. "Tony is a very focused actor with a great sense of his craft," recalled Huggins. "We once did a story on *Toma* about someone who was deaf. I ran into Tony one day while we were shooting that episode, and I noticed he was carrying some books. He showed them to me—they were books about the deaf. That shows you the kind of conscientious, serious actor that Tony is."

Other guest stars include Diana Muldaur (Rosalind Shays on *L.A. Law*) and Warner Anderson, the onetime star of the '50s detective drama *The Lineup* who was also among the early considerations for the role of Rockford's dad in the *Rockford Files* pilot.

Rockford Fun

Listen carefully to the baseball game that Rocky is watching on television during Act IV and you'll catch the names of *Rockford*'s executive producer ("Last time up, Rosenberg really shelled him"), associate producer ("Here comes Johnson, with the hook"), co-creator ("Now Cannell's coming in") and executive story consultant ("Here comes Bartlett from the bullpen"). In addition, Zekial Marko, who wrote the teleplay for this episode, has a small role as police doctor Gabriel.

20.   THE FOUR POUND BRICK

Production Number: 41421
Original Air Date: February 21, 1975
Teleplay by: Leigh Brackett and Juanita Bartlett
Story by: Leigh Brackett
Directed by: Lawrence Doheny

Guest Cast: Edith Atwater (Kate Banning), William Watson (Ross), Jess Walton (Laura Smith), Paul Carr (Sergeant Andrew Wilson), John Quade (Tennen), Jack Knight (Officer Drexel), Bruce Tuthill (Waiter), Frank Campanella (Morrie), John Furlong (Minister)

This is Shirley, from the bank. The answers are No, No, and Yes. No, we won't loan you money. No, we won't accept any co-signors. And yes, your account's overdrawn. I get off at 4:30 ...

Synopsis. *Rocky's friend Kate Banning always knew that her son David, a rookie police officer, took better care of his car than he did himself. She therefore becomes suspicious when Dave is killed in a matter the L.A.P.D. has officially classified as a traffic accident. (According to Kate, there was nothing wrong with the brakes of Dave's car because Dave had just brought the vehicle in for a tuneup.) Jim agrees to look into the matter, but he soon faces a dilemma. While Rockford does find signs that point to foul play, he also uncovers evidence that could implicate Dave in a crooked narcotics operation. Thus, by probing further, Rockford could impugn Dave's good name even as he resolves the nature of his death.*

"Noah Beery had a great career, and he came from a really talented family of actors," said makeup artist Jack Wilson. "His dad was one of the great movie villains of the silent screen era, and his uncle, Wallace Beery, won an Oscar in 1932 for *The Champ*. I worked with him quite a bit on *Rockford*, and he was truly wonderful to be around. It's kind of funny ... back then, I hadn't really thought about what he had done, but lately, I've come to realize what a marvelous performer he was. On any given day, you could turn on the TV and catch him in some really great films: *Inherit the Wind, Sergeant York, Of Mice and Men, Inherit the Wind, Red River*. He was in all kinds of great pictures. He was a fine actor whose career spanned a long time."

Although the character he played on *Rockford* was always addressed on camera by his nickname ("Rocky"), Beery's speeches in the *Rockford Files* scripts were actually headed "Joseph," because series co-creator Stephen J. Cannell named the character after his father Joseph Cannell. Indeed, when Cannell was originally interviewed for this book in 1995, every time he mentioned Rockford's father, he always referred to the character by his given name, "Joseph."

In addition, on every call sheet and production schedule pertaining to episodes that featured Rocky, Beery's character was always listed under "Joseph."

Rockford Facts

This episode originated from Leigh Brackett, the distinguished writer of science fiction and fantasy who was also active in the field of detective fiction. A novelist in the Chandler tradition, Brackett wrote the screenplay for *The Big Sleep*, the 1945 film classic (based on the 1939 Chandler novel that introduced Philip Marlowe) that is widely considered to be one of the finest movies of its kind ever made. A mentor of Ray Bradbury, Brackett also published many novels and short stories in the sci-fi genre. At the time of her death in 1978, she had just completely the first draft for the screenplay of the first *Star Wars* sequel, *The Empire Strikes Back* (1980).

21.   JUST BY ACCIDENT

Original Air Date: February 28, 1975
Production Number: 41427
Written by: Charles Sailor and Eric Kalder
Directed by: Jerry London

Guest Cast: Neva Patterson (Louise Hartman), Steven Keats (Duane Bailey), David Spielberg (Sergeant Tom Garvey), Fred Sadoff (Matt Springfield), E.J. Peaker (Jeannie Szymczyk), Joey Aresco (Billy Jo Hartman), Oliver Clark (K. Julian Krubm), Alan Bergmann (The Doctor), Millie Slavin (Assistant Bank Manager), Beatrice Colen (Woman Bettor), Michael Fox (The Announcer), Gordon Jump (Freddie), Fritzi Burr (County Clerk), Sal Acquisto (Gas Station Attendant), Susan Keller (Vivian)

This is Thelma Sue Binkley. It's about the research I called you about—the family tree? Did you talk to your daddy? We may be kin!

Synopsis. *Demolition derby driver Billy Jo Hartman's plans to retire from the field and move into dirt racing are cut short when his car is pushed off a cliff by a man named Duane Bailey. Although the police classify the death as accidental, Billy Jo's mother Louise hires her longtime friend Rockford to investigate. The matter becomes more intriguing when Louise discovers that her son had named her as the beneficiary on a $200,000 life insurance policy he'd taken out on himself. Although Billy Jo was a champion driver, he didn't make enough money to afford such an expensive policy. Louise doesn't realize that Billy Jo was involved in an elaborate life insurance scam orchestrated by Bailey and crooked salesman Matt Springfield, and that her son was killed because he wanted out. When Rockford discovers that Springfield and Bailey were behind Billy Jo's death, his own life becomes endangered.*

David Spielberg reprises his role of Tom Garvey, whom we first saw in "Charlie Harris at Large." As originally conceived, Garvey was much more hard-nosed: in fact, Roy Huggins' original story for "Charlie Harris" likened Garvey to Sergeant Joe Friday, describing him as having "an inhuman coldness, a distance quality about him, and a deadly politeness that is impolite as hell."

Apparently a decision was made to soften the character, because Garvey's demeanor toward Rockford in "Just by Accident" is considerably more friendly.

Also appearing in this episode: Neva Patterson, who had previously co-starred with James Garner and Stuart Margolin on *Nichols,* and Gordon Jump, a few years away from becoming Mr. Carlson on *WKRP in Cincinnati.*

Rockford Facts

"Just by Accident" was the last episode filmed for the first season, which in turn makes it the last episode of *The Rockford Files* produced by Roy Huggins. The matter of Huggins' departure from the series is discussed in our review of the second season.

22.   ROUNDABOUT

Production Number: 41424
Original Air Date: March 7, 1975
Teleplay by: Mitchell Lindemann and Edward J. Lakso
Story by: Mitchell Lindemann
Directed by: Lou Antonio

Guest Cast: Jesse Welles (Nancy Wade), Ron Rifkin (Tom Robertson), Mills Watson (Edward Moss), Frank Michael Liu (Kenneth Mamato), Virginia Gregg (Eleanor Wainwright), Joe E. Tata (Agent Hanzer), George Wyner (Strock), Robert Ward (The Hotel Clerk), Fred Lerner (Freeman), Chuck Hicks (Klaus)

This is Marilyn Reed. I want to talk to you—Is this a machine? I don't talk to machines! [Caller hangs up. Phone goes dead.]

Synopsis. *An insurance company hires Jim to deliver a $10,000 check to Nancy Wade, the sole beneficiary on her late mother's policy. Rockford travels to Las Vegas, where Nancy works as a lounge singer, and eventually discovers that she has been exploited by her manager Tom Robertson, who has been using her money to fund business ventures owned and operated by the syndicate. After he is attacked and robbed of the check by some of Robertson's men, Rockford schemes to turn the tables on the slick operator. Aiding him in the cause is Japanese electronics executive Kenneth Mamato, another victim of Robertson's maneuvers.*

Filmed partly on location in Las Vegas, "Roundabout" features one of the slowest chases in the history of prime time television (and quite possibly, in all of film). In Act IV, Rockford is wired for sound when he meets Robertson outside Hoover Dam. As soon as Rockford says the code word ("Geronimo!"), FBI Agent Hanzer and the rest of the police are supposed to converge on the scene. But Robertson panics and dashes inside, forcing Rockford to chase him on foot throughout the entire Hoover Dam building and grounds. Because Rockford, unlike most private eyes, is a little out of shape, it doesn't take long for him to become winded. However, Robertson is not in great condition, either—in fact, both men are gasping and chugging by the time Rockford finally catches up to Robertson and tags him ("I got you!"). As the two men both sit down and catch their breath, the camera pulls away, enabling the viewer to see that Rockford chased Robertson all the way to the bottom of the dam.

Interestingly enough, the foot chase was not in the original script. For that matter, neither was the Hoover Dam location. According to the final shooting script (dated January 28, 1975), after Rockford says "Geronimo" for the third time, the gunman Klaus takes a shot at Rockford, who then dives behind the rocks for protection. At that point, the script called for a car chase to ensue between Rockford and Robertson, to be staged as follows:

> SERIES OF SHOTS. Rockford runs back to his rental car, takes off after Robertson, the federal agents and police officers close in, shots are exchanged, Robertson's car tries evasive action, broadsides off the road, slams into sand and jerks to a bone-jarring halt.

The script also called for this particular sequence "to be staged to accommodate location yet to be selected." Indeed, while the episode was set for three days of location shooting in Las Vegas on February 5, 6, and 7 of 1975, the production report for those three dates makes no mention of any scheduled filming at Hoover Dam. The report only mentions scheduled "exterior footage at a highway dirt road, and then a country road."

Though no one could recall for sure, Roy Huggins believed it was Steve Cannell who came up with the idea of staging the climactic action sequence at Hoover Dam and changing it from a car chase to a foot chase. Regardless of how it came about, the end result is clearly one of the more memorable moments of the entire series.

Rockford Facts

"Roundabout" also includes a sequence in which Rockford visits Nancy Wade at the Las Vegas lounge where she performs. As it was originally written, however, the scene called for Rockford to walk past a bevy of showgirls (one of whom offers him "an appreciative look") as he makes his way toward Nancy. After reviewing the script, NBC's Standards and Practices cautioned: "Let's keep television propriety in mind concerning the costuming of the 'scantily-clad chorus girls,' avoiding such anatomical exposure as might make the scene unacceptable." For whatever reason, the scene was changed. Rockford is instead filmed walking past a bunch of casino patrons on his way to the lounge.

Earlier in the season, Standards and Practices had also made similar comments regarding the "propriety" of the brief bikini worn by Mildred Elias (Nita Talbot) in the *Rockford Files* pilot, as well as the bikini worn by Tawnia

Baker (Julie Sommars) in the opening scene of "The Kirkoff Case." On both occasions, S&P urged the producers to "please stay within the expected standards of propriety concerning [the] costume of [these characters]."

While these remarks may seem prudish today, bear in mind they were made in 1974, at a time when such standards as "propriety" in television were considerably more stringent than they tend to be today. No doubt if the original sequence featuring Rockford and the showgirls were to be staged today—or even a few years after this episode was originally filmed, when the likes of *Three's Company* and *Charlie's Angels* ushered in the era of "jiggle" television— it would not only include gratuitous footage of cleavage and bare midrifts, the showgirls themselves would probably be filmed in slow motion. (Of course, if the episode were filmed for HBO, the showgirls in all likelihood would be shown with no tops at all, a la the Bada Bing dancers on *The Sopranos*.)

Still, these comments are interesting precisely because they provide us with a window into what was considered acceptable at the time and what wasn't. For instance, Standards and Practices frequently objected to the number of times the words "damned" and "hell" appeared in the *Rockford Files* scripts (whereas today, a script containing those two expletives, and none other, would be considered fairly tame). In fact, Roy Huggins recalled that S&P once asked him to remove the word "danged" from a script because "they [S&P] thought the audience might hear it as 'damned.'"

"Long, Long Time," the song that Nancy Wade is performing when Rockford catches her act, was originally recorded by Linda Ronstadt for Capital Records. The song appears on the album *Silk Purse*, released by Capital in October 1970.

Rockford Familiar Faces

Jesse Welles (Nancy) and Ron Rifkin (Robertson) would later play husband and wife in the short-lived comedy series *Husbands, Wives & Lovers*, which aired briefly on CBS in the spring of 1978. Created by comedienne Joan Rivers, the series was unusual in that it was one of the few hour-long sitcoms in the history of television.

Photograph by Robert Howe

This was the banner affixed to Rockford's trailer whenever it was transported from Universal Studios to Paradise Cove for location shooting

Second Season: 1975–1976

The circumstances under which executive producer Roy Huggins departed from *The Rockford Files* remains one of the cloudier episodes in the show's history—at least, based on the accounts that were published at the time. In 1974, for example, *TV Guide* reported that Huggins had been banned from the *Rockford* set because he and Garner couldn't get along. Another item in 1979 claims that Huggins left the show after a few episodes because he and Garner disagreed "over how the show should be done."

A closer look at these allegations, however, shows that there's more to them than meets the eye. For one, Huggins rarely set foot on the set of any of his shows, unless he was directing an episode, or if an emergency came up that required his immediate attention. Huggins primarily concerned himself with only two areas of production: the development of stories and scripts, and the editing of the film. All other aspects of the show were left in the hands of Jo Swerling, Stephen J. Cannell, and others like them. Huggins also tended to work "swing shift" hours, often arriving at the studio around five or six in the evening (when most shows were wrapping up production for the day) and working well into the early hours of the morning. As a result, an actor working on a show produced by Huggins wasn't likely to see him on an everyday basis.

The matter of Garner and Huggins disagreeing over how *Rockford* should be made is also easy to disprove. It was not at the time (nor has it ever been) Garner's style to tell his producers, directors and writers how to do their jobs. He respected their capabilities and let them be.

However, relations between the actor and the producer have not always been smooth—and they became particularly strained as the result of an article published two weeks before *Rockford*'s premiere in September 1974.

Shortly before embarking on a five-week vacation in Europe, Huggins was contacted by a reporter from *Daily Variety* to comment on a situation that was widely known throughout Hollywood at the time: the never-ending search for new talent, and the challenge television producers often face when it came to replacing talented individuals who are suddenly lured away from a show by a bigger and better offer. With production in the industry at a peak level, and the number of exceptional professionals at a premium, it had become increasingly difficult for producers such as Huggins to fill those vacancies whenever they occurred with equally experienced talent.

For example, say you have a talented film editor on your staff who is offered the opportunity to direct on another series. Finding a replacement for that editor is not as easy as it sounds. After all, none of the other "top level" editors would be available, because they would have already been hired by other studios and production companies. Therefore, as a matter of necessity you may find yourself filling that vacancy with an editor who has a great deal of upside, but nowhere near as much experience as the one you just lost.

While this condition certainly affected a number of television series, Huggins told the reporter that it had no impact whatsoever on *The Rockford Files* because the entire makeup of the crew was excellent. Huggins also noted that the series was fortunate enough to have top-quality directors, many of whom did not ordinarily do hour-long episodic television, but who agreed to do *Rockford* because of the unique qualities of the show, and because of their relationship with James Garner.

The following morning, however, *Variety* published the article under the banner headline *TV SERIES TALENT SHORTAGE*. The tone of the article gave readers the impression that Huggins believed that *Rockford* was plagued by a lack of talent, "not only in above-the-line [personnel], to actors, writers, and directors, but below-the-line, where [*the article quotes Huggins, totally out of context, as saying*] 'we are using people who have had no experience whatever in film.'" By the time the paper came out, Huggins had already left for Europe, so he had no idea had badly he had been misquoted until after his return. The item caused a stir throughout the film industry—and particularly incensed Garner and Meta Rosenberg, both of whom were personally responsible for selecting many of the personnel who worked on the show.

Supervising producer Jo Swerling Jr. interceded on Huggins' behalf by stating in a memo to Rosenberg that Huggins had indeed been misquoted. Rosenberg, however, did not believe that, insisting that the reporter who interviewed Huggins had a reputation for accuracy. In response, Swerling countered with a memo to Rosenberg stating that while the journalist in question may have been "accurate relative to other trade reporters," he was still prone to errors even after he'd been supplied with accurate information. To illustrate his point, Swerling recalled a recent instance in which the Publicity Department at Universal supplied the same reporter who had interviewed Huggins with a promotional flyer regarding the production of *The Story of Pretty Boy Floyd,* an ABC *Movie of the Week* produced by Swerling earlier in 1974. While the press materials provided by Universal clearly stated that the TV-movie was "written and directed by Clyde Ware for producer Jo Swerling Jr.," the reporter wrote in

Variety that the film was "written by Clyde Ware and directed by producer Jo Swerling Jr."

"Let me emphasize that this serious error was made even though the accurate information was clearly furnished in writing," Swerling wrote Rosenberg. "If [this reporter] can make that kind of error, he is certainly capable of making more serious errors when his article is based on a telephone conversation."

Swerling's memo also noted that Huggins' assistant Dorothy Bailey was present in his office at the time of the interview. Bailey heard Huggins' comments during the conversation and also believed that the producer had been misquoted, based on the following facts:

(1) The interview was not solicited by Huggins but rather resulted from a casual call to Huggins by the reporter.

(2) Important information stated by Huggins yet omitted in the article included the fact that the entire crew on *The Rockford Files* was "excellent," which [Huggins pointed out] "was extremely difficult to come by because of the shortage of competent manpower in the industry due to high production activity."

(3) Another statement by Huggins that was omitted in the article addressed the fact the while most of the top directors will not ordinarily do episodic television, "we have been fortunate to get some because of the unique qualities of the show and especially because of Jim Garner."

(4) Huggins, said Bailey, stated to the reporter that "*The Rockford Files* is a difficult show to do." However, that statement appeared in the article as "I have a difficult show to do."

Swerling concluded his memo to Rosenberg by submitting that had the reporter accurately quoted Huggins, the article would have emerged, as Huggins had intended, "as nothing more than an interesting commentary on conditions in the industry which we all know exist." Swerling further noted:

Clearly, the tone of the article is [the reporter's], and not Roy Huggins's, and flawed as it is, it nowhere states that the directors we have used or the key people in our crew are incompetent or inept.

I must state categorically, as the one who has known Roy the best and the longest in a continous day-to-day relationship for the past twelve years, that he has neither the lack of taste nor the lack of intelligence with which he has been credited as a result of this trade paper article. And, more importantly, I have never heard him express anything but respect for you and fondness and deep admiration for Jim Garner.

I have never known a talented person in a high executive position who doesn't acquire some enemies along the way or who doesn't have a fair share of ego. Roy is very rough on the people who do not deliver what they are paid for, but he is considerate and loyal to those who do. I think Steve Cannell can vouch for that, if you have any doubts about my credibility in this area.

Roy is also extremely productive and talented. I have been told that Jim Garner has somehow come to the conclusion that Roy doesn't do anything on the show and cares less. The facts are that he has a deep personal commitment and puts in more hours than anyone else with the possible exception of Garner. The development of stories, particularly in the detail with which Roy develops them, is an extremely difficult and indispensable creative effort for which Jim has apparently not given him credit, and his efforts in post-production are time consuming and vital to the ultimate quality of the episodes. He is also fully informed as to the day-to-day operation and makes many important contributions. To conclude that he does nothing is absurd, unfair, and unacceptable. I can't imagine how Jim could be so misinformed.

When he returned from vacation, Huggins clarified his comments in a rebuttal published in *Variety*. "The fact is that the *Rockford* crew is one of the best I have ever had the good fortune to have in the 20 years I have been in TV," he wrote. "That is largely because of Jim Garner, who has a way of attracting good people and keeping them. That is the basic crew, but that isn't what I was talking about.

What I was talking about is the difficulty you run into when you suddenly need additional personnel. You have one helluva time finding people who are experienced.

People say there are a lot of talented people. That's true, but the problem is how do you find them. Meta Rosenberg, executive producer of our series, had a secretary, Juanita Bartlett, and she was given an opportunity to write on *Nichols* by Meta and Jim. She turned out to have extraordinary talent and when *Nichols* was canceled both Meta and Jim called me about Juanita, and asked me to try her. I did, because I am constantly looking for talent.

I am not retracting my previous statement. There is a problem both in the shortage of talent and in finding them. Production is at such a high level that all the good people we know are already working. We have been lucky on *Rockford* in getting some actors and directors who work for us because of Jim, who attracts people. There is a shortage, but there is talent out there, and their problem is to be discovered.

Despite the efforts of Swerling and Huggins to smooth things over, the relationship between Huggins, Garner and Rosenberg remained prickly throughout *Rockford*'s first season. A rift developed over the course of the year between the Huggins camp and the Garner/Rosenberg camp, which often led to the kind of published remarks against Huggins that appeared in the likes of *TV Guide*. Huggins never retaliated, with the exception of one remark that encapsulates the peculiar nature of his relationship with Garner. "Jim and I have a love/hate relationship," Huggins said on *60 Minutes* in 1980. "I love him, and he hates me." (The "feud" between the actor and the producer was never entirely resolved until several years after *The Rockford Files* left the air.)

Although Garner and Huggins were alike in many ways (both are introverted, both are personable, both are extraordinarily gifted in their respected crafts), they were also two fundamentally different people. For Garner, it is very important to create a sense of family in the working environment. Ask anyone who has ever worked with Garner, and they will inevitably use the word "family" when describing their experience with him. Garner thrives on surrounding himself with people that he trusts and cares for.

Huggins, however, never became a part of that family circle—although, by his own admission, that was a matter of choice. Huggins, keep in mind, was preeminently a writer, which means that he was often reclusive by choice: as mentioned previously, he would often isolate himself for days at a time in order to concentrate on developing stories. "When I was producing television, I lived in a world of story development: telling the stories, reading them, rewriting them, and editing them," he explained. "That was predominantly my world ... until the time I'd come home, when that would become my world."

Also factoring in the equation was Garner's film career, which stumbled after a promising start. Though Garner had starred in some successful and acclaimed motion pictures in the 1960s (*The Wheeler Dealers, The Americanization of Emily,*

Photograph courtesy of TV History Archive
© 1974 Universal City Studios, Inc.

James Garner

The Great Escape, Grand Prix, Support Your Local Sheriff), he never quite became a "big movie star." While that in part may have been attributed to bad choices, the fact that Garner had been so closely identified with *Maverick* didn't help him, either. Garner had created such a lasting impression with his portrayal of the silver-tongued grafter that for years he was perceived (by filmmakers and moviegoers alike) as an actor who could only play "tongue in cheek" characters. Only within the past two decades has Garner been able to shake that perception completely through his efforts in such films as *Heartsounds, Promise, Decoration Day, My Name is Bill W., Barbarians at the Gate, Twilight, The Notebook*, and his Oscar-nominated performance in *Murphy's Romance*.

While he and Garner were never close friends, Roy Huggins knew Garner for so long and so well that he believed he understood Garner like few other people. Huggins agreed that Garner was determined to shake the "tongue in cheek" label. But he also believes there was a little more to it than that.

"This is only my opinion—and I could be wrong," Huggins cautioned. "But I believe that when Jim first returned to television, it was very important to him that his new show should succeed. Now, as you know, *Nichols* failed, and that was a trauma, so much so that he gave a series of interviews over several years saying things like: '*This show was a great show; it was a show that was so good no one understood it, because it was ahead of its time.*' And that allowed him to live with the suggestion that he couldn't do it alone—that if he wanted a success, he had to work with a strong producer. And in that first season, Jim had to face it: he had succeeded with *Maverick*, failed with *Nichols*, and now he was succeeding with *Rockford*—which may be why he was so eager to get me off the show. My colleagues, however, are of the opinion that the close relationship of Garner and Rosenberg was at the heart of the move to have me taken off the show."

Be that as it may, this much is clear. Garner did come to Huggins at a pivotal point in his career: after the failure of *Nichols*, and at a point when his once-promising motion picture career was on the decline. The tremendous success of *The Rockford Files*, particularly during its first season, resuscitated Garner's career. Although *Rockford* struggled in its second season, this much is also clear: the show continued for four successful years after Huggins left, during which time Garner won the Emmy Award for Best Dramatic Actor, and the series itself won the Emmy for Best Dramatic Series. That was important to Garner because it proved that he could succeed on his own.

As a rule, Huggins left all his series after one or two seasons because that was the point at which he felt he had exhausted all storytelling possibilities for a given series. In the case of *The Rockford Files*, he had decided to move on by the time Garner spoke up. The producer's decision to leave the series was also based in part on the fact that his plate was full. By the end of the 1974-1975 season, Huggins had launched another series, *Baretta*, and had begun developing another private detective series (*City of Angels*). However, since *The Rockford Files* was a big hit, Huggins wanted to ensure that the series would remain that way—his contract provided that once he lauched a show, he would be paid his production fee (which increased from season to season), regardless of whether he continued to be involved in the show or not. This particular provision had already been applied to several other shows that Huggins had either created or produced for Universal.

But Huggins knew that *Rockford* had someone who was perfectly capable of running the show in his place. "I had Steve Cannell, and I knew that he could do it," said Huggins. "And I honestly believed that was the only way the studio could avoid losing him. Steve was far too great a talent to be restricted to just writing and acting as a secondary producer."

Just as Huggins was about to break the news to Frank Price, Garner met with Price and asked to have the producer removed from the show.

Price was reluctant to make any change. "One of the reasons that I wanted so strongly to keep Roy on *Rockford Files* is that I didn't know anybody who was better with a certain kind of sophisticated humor in that dramatic form than he was," he said. "*Maverick*'s been a good example of that, and certainly *Rockford*. In the case of both shows, there's a danger of getting carried away with the fact that the show was funny, and starting to turn it into a farce. And if it goes that way, it destroys the show—it's amusing for a while, but the credibility of the show just goes away. Roy was always good at making sure the show measured up in that regard."

Since Huggins had planned to step down anyway, the matter of his departure was a *fait accompli*. However, Huggins did convince Price to turn over the critical area of story and script supervision to Cannell. While Meta Rosenberg retained the title "executive producer," it was Cannell who ultimately ran the show after Huggins left *Rockford* at the end of the first season.

*   *   *

Meanwhile, after taking a beating by NBC's Friday night lineup all year long the previous season, CBS went for the jugular by moving *M*A*S*H* and *Hawaii Five-O* (both Top Ten shows in 1974-1975) to Friday nights beginning in September 1975. The Eye Network scheduled *Hawaii Five-O* opposite *The Rockford Files* in the critical 9:00-10:00 p.m. time slot. The head-to-head competition between *Rockford* and *Five-O* was one of the most heavily anticipated events of the Fall.

Legend has it that NBC and Universal became so concerned over *Hawaii Five-O* that they exerted tremendous pressure on Cannell and Meta Rosenberg to "remove the humor" from *The Rockford Files* in order to make *Rockford* more like *Hawaii Five-O*. However, like most legends, that story doesn't really hold up once you examine the facts.

In the first place, *Rockford* had everything going for it heading into its second year. For one, it was a huge hit, having won its time slot throughout the previous year; and its huge audience continued to grow, particularly during the summer, when the reruns attracted many new viewers to the show. No network in its right mind would want to tamper with something that's already working.

Secondly, as discussed previously, network executives usually think in terms of "What makes this show different?" *Rockford*, by virtue of its irreverent attitude toward the private eye genre, already *was* different. It would not have made sense for NBC to insist on having the show conform to *Hawaii Five-O* by removing the humor in its entirety.

Finally, Universal Studios (and, in particular, its head of television Frank Price) loved the humor of *The Rockford Files*. It was Price who had to act out the scripts before the network programming executives who were befuddled by the show's sophisticated brand of humor.

However, late in the summer of 1975, Price became concerned over the direction that *Rockford* seemed to be taking early in the second season, particularly with respect to its approach to humor. A pattern seemed to be developing. Whereas in the first season, much of the humor of the series was derived from Rockford's character, in the early going of the second season, much of the humor came at Rockford's expense. Seven of the first nine scripts produced for the second season ("Chicken Little is a Little Chicken," "The Aaron Ironwood School of Success," "The Great Blue Lake Land and Development Company," "The Italian Bird Fiasco," "Pastoria Prime Pick," "The No-Cut Contract," and "A Bad Deal in the Valley") all revolved around the following theme: Rockford is either duped/swindled (in some cases, by his own friends) or otherwise thrust into a set of circumstances in which he is the last to know what's going on.

There is nothing wrong with taking the conventions of a genre and turning them inside out. After all, that's what Roy Huggins had done with *Maverick*. Unlike most TV heroes, Maverick didn't always come up on top. By the end of any given episode, he was likely to find himself broke, or swindled, or even tied up in the middle of nowhere.

But Huggins also knew that the key to playing with conventions was to do so with restraint. The audience would grow tired of watching if Maverick ended up with egg on his face every week.

That, ultimately, is why NBC and Universal were equally concerned that the broad approach to humor in the second season would ultimately hurt *The Rockford Files*. After watching a few of these stories, the audience might wonder just how smart Rockford is if he continues to fall for such cons time and again, particularly at the hands of his own friends.

This was the exact problem NBC had encountered with Garner four years before with regard to *Nichols*. The Program Test Report for *Nichols* indicated that the character Garner played on that show "lacked a very important quality for the protagonist of a series—intelligence. [The Nichols character] did not project an impression of intelligence to the viewers and came across as a well-liked but dumb hero." In comparing the pilot test results for *Rockford* with those of *Nichols*, the Program Test Report from NBC's Program Research Division noted:

> Fortunately, as Jim Rockford, Garner projects the image of an intelligent man who outsmarts his enemy, rather than fight him head on.
>
> As we have continually seen over the past two pilot seasons, and through *Probe* [an unsuccessful detective series produced for NBC in 1972], the viewing audience is growing weary of the detective/investigator format. Consequently, in order to achieve success, a detective program must strive to have some distinguishing characteristic that will separate it from other detective programs. *The Rockford Files* appears to have such a characteristic in James Garner and the character he portrays. *However, in our judgment, special care should be taken to insure that a series based on this pilot not lose or diminish these attributes of the Rockford character that set him apart from other detectives.* (Emphasis added.)

The Program Test Report for the *Rockford* pilot concluded by making the following three recommendations:

1. The juxtaposition and balance of action and humor should be maintained, with judicious and increased use of humor.

2. Great care should be taken to highlight Rockford's cleverness and to insure that the character's casualness is never mistaken for lack of intelligence.

3. Stunts that appear too impossible or phony [a reference to the sequence in which Rockford shoots down a light plane with a hand gun] should be avoided.

Clearly, from the point of view of NBC and Universal, the problem with *Rockford* early in the second season was not over humor *per se*, but rather the approach to humor that the show was beginning to take and its potentially damaging impact on the Rockford character and the series in general.

Word of the network and studio's concerns over *Rockford* eventually made its way to James Garner. However, either Garner apparently misunderstood the problem, or someone had miscommunicated it to him. Garner was under the impression that NBC and Universal wanted *all* the humor taken out of the show. For that reason, the actor requested a meeting with Frank Price, which took place at the Riviera Country Club in West Los Angeles, where the series was on location filming the episode "Joey Blue Eyes."

"We had a meeting in Jim's motor home," Price said. "I told him that I thought that the shows were headed in the direction of broad farce, which is what I had seen on *Nichols*—and that I thought that was wrong for *Rockford Files*. You can't play Rockford for a chump every week. Rockford has got to be a sophisticated guy. He is *smarter* than everybody else, not dumber.

"Jim became very angry over the position I was taking—and he was particularly offended that I cited *Nichols* as an example of what I didn't want done, because he thought *Nichols* was the best thing he'd ever done. I said, 'Jim, I don't know what to say, because I saw *Nichols*, and I don't agree with you about that.' All I know is that last year, we did the kinds of shows we wanted to do on *Rockford*. Now we're moving into silly stuff this year, and if we don't do anything about it, it will kill the series.'"

Although Garner usually maintains a laidback, easygoing personality, he does have a temper which occasionally gets the best of him. Garner himself has acknowledged this on many occasions, including an appearance on *The Tonight Show with Johnny Carson* in 1986:

> CARSON: You're pretty much reserved and quiet, until someone either puts you in a corner, or pushes a little too hard ... and then, it's "Lights out, Harry." True?
>
> GARNER: Pretty much ... [*Carson, Garner and the audience laugh.*] Yeah, I think that about says it.
>
> CARSON: What is it about that quirk in your personality?
>
> GARNER: I don't know what that quirk is—but it's there ... where something snaps, and I'm not too sane.

As soon as Price mentioned *Nichols*, Garner lost control. "I was sitting in the driver's seat of the motor home, and Jim was standing between me and the door," Price continued. "Once I brought up *Nichols*, he became violently angry, and he took the coffee table that was in the motor home and started smashing it against the rest of the furniture ... At that point, the argument had really ended, and so, I began to say things to Jim, to calm him down, and I eventually eased by him and made my way out the door."

To understand this incident requires examining it from the point of view of both parties. One of the most respected men in the motion picture industry, Frank Price is a rarity: an executive who came from a creative background, as opposed to a legal- or business-oriented one. Price had spent many years as a writer-producer on such top-rated shows as *The Virginian*, *It Takes a Thief*, and *Ironside*, so that certainly qualified him as a good judge in the area of storytelling. It was Price's responsibility as head of television production at Universal to sell series and to keep them on the air as long as possible, so when he expressed his concerns to Garner about the impact the direction of the early second-year episodes might ultimately have on the series, he was simply providing his expertise and doing his job.

On the other hand, *Nichols* was still very much a sore spot with Garner, so the mere mention of the show was likely to set him off—and Garner did overreact in this instance. However, his outburst can be tempered in light of his numerous other exceptional instincts. As discussed earlier, Garner has absolute trust in the abilities of his writers. Because he would never tell them how to do their jobs, he may have felt compelled to protect them from what he perceived to be outside interference.

"That's why NBC didn't want the combination of Meta and Jim, because they'd been through all that," said Price. "It was only when Roy came to me and said 'I think I can work with them' that I overcame my reservations and tried to sell the network on the idea."

Price and Garner have remained amicable in the years since the incident at the Riviera Country Club. However, from that point on Price never again met with Garner alone.

Fortunately, as far as Price and the network were concerned, Garner was not the key decision-maker in the area of story and script—that was left in the hands of Stephen J. Cannell. "The key was talking to Steve," said Price. "From a creative standpoint, you had to get to Steve, to try to make sure he agreed with and understood what needed to be done."

Photograph courtesy of TV History Archive
© 1974 Universal City Studios, Inc.

James Garner

What NBC wanted were more shows that reflected the sophisticated humor of the first season and less of the pattern they had seen in the early second-year episodes—to the extent that it was possible. By the time the matter was addressed, not only were five episodes already filmed, most of the scripts for the remaining 16 shows were completed and being readied for production. It would have been practically impossible (not to mention very expensive) to order new scripts.

Cannell had to work with what he had—and to his credit, he corrected the problem. For the most part, the rest of the episodes produced in 1975-1976 were "on target," so far as the network was concerned: they portrayed Rockford more as a problem solver than as a patsy, and featured less evidence of the broad humor that the network and the studio found off-target.

NBC, which ultimately determined the broadcast schedule, decided to refrain from airing the problem shows until later in the year. That meant that many of the episodes that were produced later in the summer were often broadcast almost immediately upon completion. For instance, "The Farnsworth Stratagem" and the two-parter "Gearjammers," which were both filmed in August, each aired in September, while "A Bad Deal in the Valley," another early-made show in which Rockford is duped, was held back until the very last week of the season.

However, by the time NBC voiced its concerns over the direction of the second season, the date of the first September broadcast was only a few weeks away. That left the network with little choice but to open the year with one of the five problematic shows that were already "in the can" (that is to say, ready to air) and hope that any damage they might cause to the show's audience numbers would be minimal. Ironically, the show NBC selected as the season premiere—"The Aaron Ironwood School of Success," in which Rockford is hung out to dry by his own foster brother—was an episode that epitomized the problem. Of the four other episodes from which it had to choose ("Chicken Little is a Little Chicken," "The Great Blue Lake Land and Development Company," "The Italian Bird Fiasco" and "Pastoria Prime Pick"), the network would have been better off had it gone with either "Great Blue Lake," "Fiasco" or "Pastoria." While Rockford is duped in these three episodes as well, in each case he is taken in by characters that we are clearly not supposed to like.

In any event, that set the stage for the much ballyhooed competition between *The Rockford Files* and *Hawaii Five-O*. The first round went to *Rockford*, with *Five-O* finishing a distant 3rd (behind *The ABC Friday Night Movie*). *Rockford* not only took the time slot that night with a 35 share and a 24.4 rating, it also ranked No. 5 among all shows telecast that week.

Again, *Rockford* had a huge advantage over *Five-O* heading into the season because it had been averaging a 40 share in its time period throughout its first year. However, while *Rockford* continued to beat *Five-O* during the next five weeks, *Five-O* steadily began to close the gap. By the end of October, *Five-O*'s total audience had increased by 10% from the first week of the season—which meant that *Rockford* had lost 10% of its audience during the same period of time.

The numbers get worse. After two months, *Rockford* dropped from 12th to 23rd in the overall rankings, and its average rating for that time (19.7) was almost 20% lower than its overall average for the first season (23.8). In terms of total audience, that's a loss of approximately 11,392,000 television households from the previous year. Although *Rockford* did come out on top in its head-to-head battle with *Hawaii Five-O* (CBS moved the show to Thursday nights in November), it was a pyrrhic victory at best. While the overall numbers did improve slightly (the series finished with a seasonal average of 19.9), *Rockford* never recovered the sizeable chunk of its total audience it had lost during the first seven weeks of the season. By the end of the year, *Rockford* was finishing third in the time slot it had once owned. For the 1975-1976 season, the series finished in 32nd place (out of 97 shows).

Yet the news on the second year is not all bad. Cannell may have made some mistakes in the early going, but he also demonstrated much of the promise and ability that made him the one of most sought-after talents in the industry at the time—and ultimately, one of the most successful producers in television history. In the years since *The Rockford Files*, Cannell created and/or produced such critical and commercial successes as *Baretta* (co-created with Roy Huggins), *City of Angels* (co-created with Huggins), *Baa Baa Black Sheep*, *The Greatest American Hero*, *Tenspeed and Brownshoe*, *The A-Team*, *Hunter*, *Wiseguy*, *21 Jump Street*, *The Commish*, and *Profit*. It was under Cannell's guidance that *Rockford* won the Emmy for Best Dramatic Series of 1977-1978. In addition, the producer has been honored by the Writers Guild of America, the Mystery Writers of America, the International Film and Television Association, the People's Choice Awards, Media Access, and the Academy of Family Films and Family Television.

In many respects, Cannell put his stamp on *Rockford* by virtue of the many singular characterizations he created for the show. For example, early in the episode "Foul on the First Play" (which Cannell wrote), we are introduced to a gangster who happens to have asthma. Later in the story, Rockford finds himself in a car chase with this same gangster. The chase takes them into L.A.'s Griffith Park, where Rockford pulls up in front of a museum and gets out of his car—forcing the gangster to continue the chase on foot. The asthmatic, of course, doesn't get very far, because he has to stop and administer his medication. Thus, Rockford is able to escape. What seemed at first to be a gimmicky detail (the gangster with asthma) ultimately contributed something very special to the story. "Steve can't write a scene that doesn't have character in it," said Roy Huggins. "He will not write a scene that is meaningless or that has someone who is characterless. The characters in his stories all have some bent or quirk that makes them terribly interesting."

Cannell also carried over the attitudes of *Maverick* to a new generation of viewers. In "The Great Blue Lake Land and Development Company," for example, Rockford stores $10,000 overnight in a safe in a small town, only to discover the next day that the money is gone. He soon discovers that a corrupt real estate company has been bilking senior citizens out of their life savings through a phony land development project. The premise of this episode is straight out of *Maverick* (it's a variation of the classic "Shady Deal at Sunny Acres"). So is Rockford's reluctance to become involved in the matter (much to his father's chagrin) once he manages to get his money back. Rockford may really want to help the victims of the fraud, but he also realizes there's only so much he can do by himself. He's not out to be a hero, although he is pressed into becoming one by the end of the story. That is the *Maverick* attitude—the reluctant hero—which Cannell understood almost as thoroughly as Roy Huggins himself.

Even "Chicken Little is a Little Chicken," which Cannell also wrote, is admittedly fun to watch. The problem with the premise notwithstanding, the episode provides Rockford with yet another opportunity to display some of his *Maverick* qualities by hatching a scheme designed to cheat the cheater.

The second season also boasts two of *Rockford*'s most memorable hours: "The Girl in the Bay City Boys Club," the only episode directed by series star James Garner; and "The Hammer of C Block," the first of three shows featuring Isaac Hayes as Rockford's onetime prison mate Gandolf Fitch. Garner does a yeoman's job at the helm of "Bay City," while Hayes' performance and a poignant final twist are among the highlights of "C Block."

Prominent guest stars this season include Louis Gossett Jr., Linda Evans, Stefanie Powers, Joan Van Ark, Joe E. Tata, Robert Hays, Michael Conrad, Sherry Jackson, Ray Danton, James Hampton, Mitchell Ryan, David Huddleston, Charles Siebert, Blair Brown, Rob Reiner, Dick Butkus, John Saxon, Michael Ansara, Joseph Campanella, Robert Mandan, Veronica Hamel, and Susan Strasberg.

Appendix E
The Theme to *The Rockford Files*

The role of the music composer in film or television is to create music that reflects the particular goals and attitudes of the writer and/or producer of the film or series. Series co-creator Stephen J. Cannell wanted music that captured *Rockford*'s sophisticated yet sassy brand of humor, but he also wanted the show to have a fresh sound. He turned to his friend Mike Post, who (along with his collaborator Pete Carpenter) had revolutionized the art of film and television scoring a few years earlier by infusing it with contemporary music.

Most film composers through the early 1970s were either classically-based or big-band jazz-based. Post brought a rock and folk background to television (he was music director on *The Andy Williams Show* from 1969-1971), while Carpenter had worked with Earle Hagen in scoring such series as *The Danny Thomas Show*, *That Girl* and *I Spy*. "Nobody had done rock 'n' roll music on dramatic television prior to the time when Pete and I began [in 1972]," said Post, who won a Grammy Award in 1968 for his arrangement of the Mason Williams instrumental "Classical Gas." "Nobody before us knew how, because nobody had a background in rock 'n' roll who could also fit music precisely to film."

Post and Carpenter broke ground in film scoring by taking the approach originated by the great Henry Mancini and applying it to contemporary music. "Before Mancini," Post explained, "everyone scored film and television in a style that had been derived from the silent movies, taking music that was classically based and trying to fit it to film. Then, as the art of film scoring became more perfected, and the art of fitting music to picture became more precise, a lot of composers became (as we say in the music industry), very 'queuey.' In other words, practically every time the camera moved, or every time someone said a line of dialogue, the music changed.

"Mancini saw that it wasn't necessary to change the music so many times within a given score. All you needed to do was come up with a tune for a scene, and play the tune from Point A to Point B. Unless there was a big shift in the locale, or the feeling, or the timbre of the scene, there was no need to change the music. And so, in a two-or-three-minute queue, Mancini may have made only two or three changes. Whereas before him, you might have heard as many as 25 changes in the mood of the music for that one scene. Pete and I took Mancini's template and applied it to what was [at the time] more contemporary music."

While Carpenter came from a more traditional music background, he also had a feel for contemporary music. "We had kind of a strange orchestra, in that it was half-legit, half-rock 'n' roll," said Post. "We were the first to use volume pedals [for spooky scenes], the first to use breakup guitar [for action scenes], and the first to use the harmonica as a blues instrument. Prior to us, the harmonica had only been used in Westerns."

Post and Carpenter were also the first duo to use the Dobro guitar, which had previously been considered strictly a bluegrass instrument, on an action-adventure series. "That's why the music on *Rockford* sounds, if not country, then country rock," said Post. "It could also sound Midwestern, which is exactly what James Garner is (he's from Oklahoma)."

Post credits Cannell with providing the musicians with the necessary impetus to translate *Rockford* into music. "I can't say enough about how much it means to sit down and talk to a guy like Cannell," said Post. "He's the real guide. He's really good at telling me what I need to know in order to get inspired."

Cannell provided Post with a vivid description of *Rockford*'s attitudes. "We talked about the kind of guy Rockford was, how he was more interested in collecting his $200-a-day plus expenses than in catching bad guys," Post said. "And that he was kind of quirky—how, because he'd been to the joint, he had a 'Kiss my ass' attitude toward the police (despite his friendship with Becker); how he was friends with Angel, even though he knew Angel would steal him blind if he could; and how he also had a wryness and sweetness about him, which you could see in his relationship with Rocky."

Duly inspired, Post and Carpenter went to work. "We tried to write music that has humor," said Post. "We wanted to create music that was 'tongue in cheek,' but at the same time, with your fist on your hip—as if you're saying 'Hey, kiss my ass!'"

"It's catchy," said James Garner in a 1974 press interview. "I think viewers will like the theme music by Mike Post. It's a driving beat with a harmonica backed up by a big band."

In fact, if there's one instrument in the entire composition that truly captures the flavor of *The Rockford Files* onto music, it's the harmonica. "I always thought the harmonica sounded kind of sassy," said Post.

During the spring of 1975, Post added a bridge to the series theme, re-recorded the theme, and released the music as a single ("I'd always thought it would make a good record," he said). "The Theme of *The Rockford Files*" ranked as high as Number 10 on the Billboard charts, and would earn Post and

Carpenter a Grammy Award for Best Instrumental Arrangement of 1975. The lengthened version of the theme was so popular that it was ultimately included into the opening sequence of the series, beginning with the second season.

In the years since *The Rockford Files,* Post has in effect become the John Williams of dramatic television. He has scored the music for nearly every major dramatic TV series in the past 20 years, including many of the shows produced in that period by Stephen J. Cannell and Steven Bochco. Along with Pete Carpenter, Post created the themes for *Hill Street Blues, Magnum, p.i., The A-Team, Hunter, Wiseguy,* and *L.A. Law.* After Carpenter's death in 1987, Post composed the music for *NYPD Blue, Murder One, The ABC Mystery Movie, Law and Order, ER, Silk Stalkings, Dragnet* and other television series.

Post won an Emmy in 1995 for his work on *Murder One,* as well as numerous other Grammy Awards and BMI TV Music Awards for various television series.

Episode Guide for the Second Season

23. THE AARON IRONWOOD SCHOOL OF SUCCESS

Production Number: 42607
Original Air Date: September 12, 1975
Written by: Stephen J. Cannell
Directed by: Lou Antonio

Guest Cast: James Hampton (Aaron Ironwood), Ken Swofford (Federal Agent Patrick), Jonathan Lippe (Nino), Jerome Guardino (Vito Ginoso), Robert Broyles (Hauss), John Petlock (Dave), Gammy Burdette (Cabbie), Don Furneaux (Russo)

Hi, Jim. We couldn't reach you, so we went ahead with the job, and I know you're really gonna dig it—but if you don't, I suppose we could always tear it out ...

Synopsis. *Aaron Ironwood, an orphan who once lived with the Rockfords for many years, is now a self-made multi-millionaire who travels around the country giving motivational seminars that promote "Dare to Win," a $5,000 program that purports to teach people the secrets of his success. But Aaron is also a fraud artist, and Jim becomes his latest victim. After agreeing to take over control of Aaron's company on a temporary basis, Rockford discovers that Ironwood is wanted by both federal agents and the mob.*

The second season gets off to a fast start right off the bat. Three hoods try to abduct Rockford, but the plan stalls, literally, because the engine of their limousine won't start (a problem that recurs throughout the episode). When an elderly couple volunteers to help with the car, Rockford takes advantage of the delay and makes his escape by commandeering a VW Bug, although he soon finds the limousine hot on his trail. Because the car Rockford "borrowed" has a giant pizza plastered on top (it's the delivery vehicle for Pizza Dan's Restaurant), the chase sequence has an added element of fun.

Luis Delgado, who appears as the limousine driver, did his own stunt driving for this and other episodes of *The Rockford Files*. Delgado learned from one of the best in the business: formula race car driver Bob Bonderant, who had tutored James Garner years before for the motion picture *Grand Prix*. "Roy Clark, our stunt coordinator, had also taken lessons from Bob," said Delgado. "I thought that I could make a few extra bucks by doing some driving on the show, so I called Bob, and I spent about a week-and-an-half at his driving school at Sears Point [in Northern California]. Bob was an excellent teacher, and he showed me everything I wanted to learn: how to do a 90° slide, a 180° slide, a reverse 180°, and to do chases. He easily could have taught me more, but I wasn't interested in getting into it that deep. I didn't want to learn how to flip a car over, or how to jump a car from one spot to another. Those things, I did not care to do at all."

Although Delgado handled a car very well, he did have to prove himself before he earned the respect of some of the other stunt drivers. "I remember one show where I had to perform the same stunt four times because no one could believe it was me driving," he said. "I was driving a police car with a passenger, and I had to cut across a park in order to prevent the heavies from going into the park. I had to do a 90° slide between a tree and a fence, which left me about a foot-and-a-half in the front and a foot-and-a-half in the back.

"The stuntpeople didn't think I could do it, because they had never seen me drive a car or anything else before. But I brought the car in and, boom, dropped it right where they wanted it. They were amazed—they thought it was a fluke—and so they said, 'Well, let's see you do it again.' And I did it again—boom, right in the same spot. They still couldn't believe it. They made me do that slide four times—and all four times, I put the car right in the same spot. So I guess that convinced them that I knew what I was doing."

Rockford Facts

According to this episode, Becker is fifth on the list for lieutenant ("If I do well, I can make lieutenant in two or three months"). Although it took him a little longer than anticipated, Becker finally earned his promotion in the fifth season episode "Kill the Messenger."

Rockford Familiar Faces

Aaron Ironwood is played by Jim Hampton, the burly, affable character actor perhaps best known as "Caretaker" in *The Longest Yard* (1974). A native Oklahoman like series star James Garner, Hampton appeared frequently on television throughout the '60s and '70s. He played Trooper Dobbs on *F Troop*, and was among the ensemble actors (along with Stuart Margolin) who appeared in the various blackout skits that opened and closed each episode of *Love, American Style*.

Photograph courtesy of TV History Archive
© 1974 Universal City Studios, Inc.

Joe Santos as Dennis Becker

24.   THE FARNSWORTH STRATAGEM

Production Number: 42616
Original Air Date: September 19, 1975
Written by: Juanita Bartlett
Directed by: Lawrence Doheny

Guest Cast: Linda Evans (Audrey Wyatt), H.M. Wynant (Danzil), Paul Jenkins (Simon Lloyd), Pat Finley (Peggy Becker), John Crawford (Christian), Eric Server (William MacKenzie), Gerald McRaney (Manager), Al Hansen (Gardell), Steven Parr (Stewart Zilliox)

Rockford, this is Tony. Now, your car's ready—I couldn't reach you, so I went ahead and put in the new pistons. The tab's $527.54—and this time, we're talking cash!

Synopsis. *Dennis and Peggy Becker apparently purchase 2-1/2% ownership of a posh hotel resort in a deal brokered by Simon Lloyd, a flim-flam artist who does-n't tell the Beckers that the "hotel" actually houses condominiums, all of which are fully owned. To their embarrassment, the Beckers discover that they not only spent $7,500 (on a lobby!!), they're also indentured into paying a $700,000 trust deed. Dennis hires Jim to win back their money. Drawing on his own vast grifting skills, Rockford concocts an elaborate scheme designed to beat Lloyd at his own game.*

Although we've seen Rockford the grifter in operation before (as Becker reminds us in this episode, he pulled off a masterful scam in "Counter Gambit"), as a rule he won't resort to such tactics unless either he himself or one of his friends have been cheated. This is another characteristic taken straight out of *Maverick*.

Not only does Rockford run a "big store" con game in "The Farnsworth Stratagem," he also lays out the entire process (including the lingo) for the benefit of the viewers:

> In a con, there's always more than one grifter involved. Simon Lloyd was the operator, but somebody put up the marks [found the victim], and somebody roped 'em. A "roper" steers the marks to the inside man. They tell him the tale, show him the game, take off the touch, and blow him off.

Rockford will hold other "seminars" in the art of grifting in the episodes "There's One in Every Port" and "Never Send a Boy King to Do a Man's Job."

Rockford Facts

In this episode, we learn that Becker's rank is Investigator, 2nd Grade. Over the course of the series, Becker will be promoted to Investigator, 3rd Level (in the third-year episode "Piece Work") and finally to Lieutenant (in the fifth season's "Kill the Messenger").

Rockford Funnies

The name of the hotel assistant manager is "Zilliox," named after Robert Zilliox, the show's set decorator.

25./26. GEARJAMMERS (Two-Parter)

Production Numbers: 42626/42627
Original Air Dates: September 26 and October 3, 1975
Teleplay by: Don Carlos Dunaway
Story by: Stephen J. Cannell
Driected by: William Wiard

Guest Cast: Ted Gehring (Johnny LoSalvo), Scott Brady (Hammel), Rosemary DeCamp (Mary Ramsey), Jack Kruschen (John Koenig), Bobby Hoy (Scheib), Al Stevenson (L.J.), Peter Brocco (Hodges), Charles Cooper (Jack), Robert Raymond Sutton (Paco), Joe E. Tata (Willie Thompson), Bucklind Beery (Officer Mazursky), Terry Leonard (John Smith), Reb Brown (Lifeguard), John Dullaghan (Sergeant Sullivan)

Hey, Jimmy, it's Angel. Don't pay no attention to my other message. You're out of it. You're clean. No trouble at all. Just ignore the first message ...

Okay, pal, it's Harry. I just checked my car. You kept the battery charged, all right. You also put 3500 miles on it!

Synopsis. *Rocky's life becomes endangered after he inadvertently witnesses an illegal business transaction between his trucker friend Johnny LoSalvo and LoSalvo's ruthless boss Hammel, who has plotted to hijack six of his own trucks as part of a master plan to steal an incoming cargo of valuable sable furs. Although Rocky has absolutely no idea what's going on, Hammel wants the old man eliminated simply because Rocky can identify him. LoSalvo tries to save Rocky, but Hammel has him killed. Rockford protects his father from danger—while Rocky helps his son solve the case.*

The second act of Part One ends with an extensive chase in which Rockford is tailed by two of Hammel's goons. After Rockford pulls into a garage, he whips out his gun (he came prepared for trouble), gets the drop on them, then

Photograph courtesy of TV History Archive
© 1974 Universal City Studios, Inc.

Noah Beery Jr. and James Garner

pays the two men a compliment. "It's sort of an honor to be tailed by two people who drive so well," he says.

Rockford ought to know good driving when he sees it. After all, the man who played him was one of the best in the business. James Garner not only did his own stunt driving on *The Rockford Files* and in many other motion pictures (including *Grand Prix* and *The Getaway*), he even raced professionally for a time during the late 1960s/early 1970s. "I've been asked the question more than once: *If I hadn't been an actor, what would I have done?*" Garner told *Autoweek* in 1999. "There are two things I would like to have done. One would have been to be a race driver, one a professional golfer. But I don't think I'd have made much money at either one of those.

"I always admired the drivers [in the '60s] because it took a great deal of talent," the actor continued. "You had to be pretty brave to get into a race car. I found they were all very warm. They were open to me. They accepted me. Of course, I was in awe of them. And to be on the same tracks as them, not necessarily racing, but driving with them—there wasn't competition there. Well, there was a little ..."

Drivers not only "accepted" Garner, they respected his considerable abilities behind the wheel. "Jim handles a car very well," said Luis Delgado. "He handles a car better than 99% of the stunt drivers in the business."

Rockford Facts

According to "The House on Willis Avenue" (an episode from the fourth season), the trucking operation that Rockford thwarts in this episode was one of two major cases that established his reputation as one of the top private eyes in Los Angeles. The other case was the fraud scheme he stopped in "Profit and Loss."

Rockford Familiar Faces

This episode features veteran character actors Ted Gehring and Scott Brady, who were both among the actors originally under consideration for the role of Dennis Becker in the *Rockford Files* pilot. Gehring, who eventually won the role of Norm Mitchell in the pilot, later appeared with James Garner in *Murphy's Romance* (1985). Other guest stars include Joe E. Tata (best known as Nat, the owner of the Peach Pit, on *Beverly Hills 90210*) and Bucklind Beery (the real-life son of series star Noah Beery Jr.).

27.   THE DEEP BLUE SLEEP

Production Number: 42620
Original Air Date: October 10, 1975
Teleplay by: Juanita Bartlett
Story by: Charles Floyd Johnson
Directed by: William Wiard

Guest Cast: Robert Webber (Bob Coleman), Michael Conrad (George Macklan), Janet MacLachlan (Adrienne Clarke), Ric Mancini (Ray Porter), Melendy Britt (Millie), Doria Cook (Margaux Adams), Robert B. Hays (Darren Weeks), John Furlong (Medical Examiner), Ed Crick (Gas Station Attendant)

Hi, Jim—thanks for the dinner invitation. I'd love to, but does it have to be the taco stand?

Synopsis. *When the body of premier fashion model Margaux Adams is found at the scene of an apparent car crash, the police classify her death as either accidental or suicidal. But Beth, who was one of Margaux's best friends, suspects foul play— particularly since she received a frantic phone call from Margaux shortly before she died. Although clearly an open case, Jim agrees to look into the matter after Beth agrees to provide free legal services in the event the police hassle him. Rockford's investigation uncovers a romantic triangle between Margaux, fashion designer Adrienne Clarke, and accountant Bob Coleman—and the likelihood that Margaux was killed upon discovering Coleman's link to organized crime.*

Two-time Emmy nominee Diahann Carroll was the original choice to play the female lead in "The Deep Blue Sleep." "When I first wrote the original story for this episode, I did have her in mind—and Diahann wanted to do the show, too," said Charles Floyd Johnson. "But her schedule didn't work out. We just couldn't work out the dates."

The role of fashion designer Adrienne Clarke eventually went to Janet MacLachlan, whom Johnson says was "excellent."

28.   THE GREAT BLUE LAKE LAND AND DEVELOPMENT COMPANY

Production Number: 42603
Original Air Date: October 17, 1975
Produced by: Lane Slate
Written by: Juanita Bartlett
Directed by: Lawrence Doheny

Guest Cast: Richard B. Shull ("Fast Harry" Danova), Dennis Patrick (Walter Hart), Dana Elcar (Sheriff Mitchell), Mary Ann Chinn (Billie Carlton), Bob Hastings (Paul Tanner), Noble Willingham (B.J.), Ray Girardin (Murray Johnson), Bartine Zane (Mildred Jensen)

[Caller speaks in a robotic tone:] Hello, Jim Rockford's machine. This is Larry Doheny's machine. Will you please have your master call my master at his convenience? Thank you. Thank you. Thank you ...

Synopsis. *En route to Los Angeles to deliver a client's $10,000 bail money, Rockford becomes stranded in the small desert town of Great Blue Lake after his car breaks down. Needing a place to store the money overnight, he deposits the cash with Murray Johnson, a salesman at the Great Blue Lake Land and Development Company (the only building in town with a safe). But when Jim arrives to pick up the money in the morning, he finds that the money is gone— and that nobody named Johnson works for the company. A determined Rockford plots a sting (and recruits Rocky and con artist Harry Danova for key roles) in order to recover his money, but he drops his plans when company president Walter Hart suddenly returns the $10,000. However, when the phantom Murray Johnson is found murdered, Rockford becomes the prime suspect. Rockford believes that Hart murdered Johnson, but he has to break himself out of jail in order to prove it.*

Juanita Bartlett found the basis for this episode in a segment she'd once seen on *60 Minutes.* "They had done a show on land fraud," she said. "One of the things that really got to me about that show was seeing how these people were selling land out in the middle of nowhere in Arizona. And I mean *literally*—there was a ribbon of a road, and desert on either side of the road. And it wasn't a matter where the investors were being taken in through the mail. They would actually go out there and look at it and say, 'No, that's too close to the road, or that's too close to the country club. I want my house to be over there.' In addition, the report showed that most of the people who were bilked were retired: people who were living on a fixed income, and who therefore had the most to lose.

"I found it so appalling, and infuriating, to see that people could be gullible. So I did 'The Great Blue Lake,' which had to do with the land fraud scheme. And my thinking was, 'If I can bring what has been happening to the attention of some of these people, maybe they won't bite if something like that comes their way.'"

Bartlett's script marks the first instance in which the series uses the Rockford character to address certain social inequities. This is a characteristic for which *Rockford* would become particularly known beginning in the third season.

"The Great Blue Lake Land and Development Company" was produced by Lane Slate, who wrote the screenplay for *They Only Kill Their Masters* (1972), which starred James Garner and Katharine Ross. Slate won an Edgar Award from the Mystery Writers of America for the TV-movie *Isn't It Shocking?* (1973), as well as an Emmy Award for writing the teleplay for *Tail Gunner Joe* (1977).

Rockford Familiar Faces

Dana Elcar (Sheriff Mitchell) is best known for playing Peter Thornton on *MacGyver* (ABC, 1985-1992). When Elcar began losing his sight to glaucoma in 1991, the Thornton character was also given the same affliction on the series. Elcar continues to act, appearing in such series as *ER* and *Law and Order* while relying on special computer equipment in order to read printed text in scripts. Prior to *MacGyver*, Elcar had starred in a number of series produced by Stephen J. Cannell, including *Baretta*, *Baa Baa Black Sheep* and *The Duke*.

Noble Willingham (B.J.) co-starred with James Garner in *Fire in the Sky* (1993). Shortly after completing that film, he began a six-year run as C.D. Parker on *Walker, Texas Ranger*.

Bob Hastings (Tanner) has been a voiceover artist in television for over 40 years. He has supplied the voice of Commissioner Gordon on the *Batman* animated series and related videos produced by Fox since 1992. Back in the '60s, Hastings played Lt. Elroy Carpenter on *McHale's Navy*, the popular comedy produced at Universal for ABC.

29.   THE REAL EASY RED DOG

Production Number: 42628
Original Air Date: October 31, 1975
Written by: Stephen J. Cannell
Directed by: Ivan Dixon

Guest Cast: Stefanie Powers (Christina Dusseau), Bruce Kirby (Aaron Friedler), Sherry Jackson (Jennifer Sandstrom), Wayne Grace (Deek), Larry Cook (Dave), George Wyner (Tom Brice), Nick Ferris (Pete Finch), Connie Bryant Milton (Policewoman)

Jim, it's Shirley at the cleaners. You know that brown jacket—the one that looks so great on you—your favorite? We lost it.

Synopsis. *A woman who identifies herself as Jennifer Sandstrom hires Rockford to delve into the apparent suicide of her sister Alice. Jim doesn't realize that his client is a private investigator, Christina Dusseau, who actually has paid him to play decoy. (An insurance company hired Tina to deliver a ransom payment to thieves who had stolen a $3 million jewelry collection—and to keep the authorities out of the matter. When Tina found herself followed by two police officers, she needed to create a diversion to throw the cops off her trail. Enter Rockford.) But Tina's charade turns up an unexpected dividend. Although Tina pulled the Sandstrom suicide from a newspaper article, Jim stumbles onto evidence suggesting that Alice really was murdered. When Rockford and Tina link Alice's death to a black market baby racket, their lives become endangered.*

For a short time during the 1974-1975 season, Tom Atkins had recurring roles on two different series: in addition to playing the snarling Lieutenant Diel on *The Rockford Files*, he also played the delightfully dimwitted Sergeant Frank Cole on *Harry O*. Atkins played Diel in a total of six episodes throughout the first, second and fourth seasons. He also reprised the role in three of the *Rockford* reunion movies, including what turned out to be the final film in the series, *If It Bleeds ... It Leads.*

In 1997, shortly after completing production of *If It Bleeds*, Atkins looked back fondly on his experience on *Rockford* in an interview published in *Images.*

"I had a wonderful time," he said. "Jimmy Garner is a very gracious guy, as he was then and he is still today. We've all aged some, but I just did, this past summer, another *Rockford Files* movie with the whole gang out there: Joe Santos and everybody else. I think it's called *If It Bleeds ... It Leads* and hopefully it won't be the last one—though I think Jim thinks it might be. He's feeling a little old, and also feeling as if CBS didn't pay enough attention to the movie-of-the-weeks as we were doing them these past couple of years. But I certainly hope it's not the last, 'cause we all had a great time over many, many years of doing these things. And he's a wonderful core, center, for all of us to gather around and do good work around. I'll miss them if they're finished."

Although Atkins' character was known as "Alex Diel" throughout the first season, the lieutenant apparently underwent a name change. According to this episode (as well as a later show, "The Battle of Canoga Park"), Diel's first name is "Thomas."

30.   RESURRECTION IN BLACK AND WHITE

Production Number: 42629
Original Air Date: November 7, 1975
Written by: Juanita Bartlett and Stephen J. Cannell
Directed by: Russ Mayberry

Guest Cast: Joan Van Ark (Susan Alexander), William Prince (Arnold Newcomb), Sandra Smith (Shirley Atwater), Milton Selzer (Patrick Elber), John Lawlor (Dave Krueger), John Danheim (Roy Pierce), Elvin Howard (Police Officer)

Hey, Jimmy, it's Cousin Lou! Gonna be in town a coupla days. Know you won't mind puttin' us up. It's just me, and Aunt Cissy, and B.J., and the kids, and little Freddie, and …

Synopsis. *Investigative reporter Susan Alexander believes that Dave Krueger was wrongfully convicted six years ago of the brutal murder of his girlfriend Cheryl Wilson, and she wants Rockford to help her prove him innocent. First, Jim is skeptical. He suspects Krueger of playing Susan for a sucker, then doubts he could proceed far in a case whose principals are either long dead or long retired. Rockford is also reluctant to stay involved when he learns that someone has been trying to kill Susan. (Remarkably enough, Susan is unfazed by the attempts on her life. The way she sees it, the death threats only serve to convince her that she's on the right track.) But Rockford ultimately becomes curious when the police later identify a murder victim as Cheryl Wilson—the woman Dave Krueger allegedly killed!*

"Resurrection in Black and White" features some of the most memorable lines of the entire series, including Rockford's classic retort upon learning Susan was nearly killed while investigating the Krueger case—a detail the crafty journalist neglected to mention when she originally hired our hero for help. "Why didn't you tell me [about the man who nearly drove your car off the road]?" he asks his client.

"Physical violence has a tendency to put some people off," explains Susan.

"Yeah," cracks Rockford. "I'm one of them!"

Moments later, it's Susan's turn to be flabbergasted when she realizes Rockford, whom she believes will protect her from future harm, is traveling unarmed. "But *you're a private investigator*," she says in amazement. "Why don't you carry a gun?"

"Because I don't want to shoot anybody," Rockford replies.

In Act IV, however, Jim decides to pack his gun before he and Susan head out to the dock to confront Elber and Pierce. "I thought you didn't like to shoot people," Susan reminds him.

"I don't shoot it," clarifies Rockford. "I just point it."

This episode also recycles elements from the first season's "Tall Woman in Red Wagon," including a further explanation of the portable printing press Rockford keeps in his car. Jim tells Susan he got the machine from a client who once had been a printer.

31. CHICKEN LITTLE IS A LITTLE CHICKEN

Production Number: 42602
Original Air Date: November 14, 1975
Produced by: Lane Slate
Written by: Stephen J. Cannell
Directed by: Lawrence Doheny

Guest Cast: Ray Danton (Chester Sierra), Frank Campanella (Marty Frishette), Angelo Gnazzo (John Little), Sandy Ward (The Sheriff), Nicholas Worth (Kessler), Dave Cass (Sid), Kenneth Strange (Don), Charlie Horvath (Jose), Tom Williams (Minister)

Jim, it's Beth. You have the vet's number, the flea collar, and extra litter. One thing I forgot: keep him away from other cats. He's not very discriminating.

Synopsis. *Angel finds himself in trouble with both the police and two rival crime lords after he unwittingly agrees to launder money for a former cellmate named John Little. Angel doesn't realize that Little, a convicted forger, swindled $30,000 from the newspaper where Angel works, then framed Angel by planting the counterfeiting evidence inside Angel's desk. Meanwhile, Angel's association with Little runs him afoul of underworld kingpins Chester Sierra and Marty Frishette, whom Little both doublecrossed. Rockford finds himself stuck in the middle after Angel hides the $30,000 inside his car. In order to bail themselves out of trouble, Rockford fakes Angel's death, then plans a variation of the old "shell game" designed to play Sierra and Frishette against each other at the "funeral."*

Despite the problems both NBC and Universal had with the initial premise of this episode, "Chicken Little is a Little Chicken" does have its share of clever moments. Like "The Farnsworth Stratagem" before it, Rockford provides the audience with a detailed explanation of the scam he intends to pull to try to get Angel and him off the hook. In this case, Rockford tells us that Angel's "death" is part of a shell game designed to nail Frishette and Sierra:

We'll have three people, and two briefcases. Now, Frishette will have the money from the swindle in his, and I'll have the evidence that we found in your desk in mine. Frishette is gonna try to lay the evidence off on Sierra by making him think he's giving him the money back. In order to doublecross Chester Sierra, Frishette is going to have bring along an extra, identical briefcase, which will be empty. So, now we'll have three attache cases, and, like the three shells in a carnival, we've set the stage for the old shell game: *which shell has the pea?*

Now, when all this is over, I'm going to end up with the money, instead of Frishette. Frishette is going to end up with the one with the evidence in it—only the cops are gonna nab him on the way out of the chapel. Sierra is gonna come up dry, which is gonna make him very angry at Frishette. And Frishette is gonna be angry at Sierra for laying the evidence on him! We'll end up out of the middle, with the 30 grand.

Rockford claims to have worked this con successfully on at least ten different occasions. "The whole idea is to 'keep your eye on the pea,' as they say—or in this case, keep your eye on the right briefcase—and to set it up so that you have an accomplice who will make the switch at the right moment."

Jim tells Angel that Rocky will act as his accomplice. While Angel is pleased to hear that Rocky will be attending his "funeral," he does admit to finding Rockford's scheme a tad bit confusing.

"Angel," assures Rockford, "when this con is in the hands of a master, it's a joy to watch. All I have to do is get these jokers to play." Rockford does indeed execute the shell game in a masterful way reminiscent of his spiritual ancestor Bret Maverick.

The entire funeral sequence is well done. In fact, if you pay too much attention to all the shuffling suitcases, you can easily miss the "eulogy" of Angel that drones on in the background. The eulogy is particularly funny in light of what we learn about Angel in this episode. Far from serving "with great distinction" in Korea, Angel was actually court-martialed for desertion under fire and served time at the federal penitentiary at Railworth.

Rockford Facts

"Chicken Little" also reminds us that Angel and Rockford did time together at San Quentin. "I guess you could say we owned a piece of the rock," cracks Angel—a reference to "Get a piece of the rock," which at the time of the show was a popular advertising jingle for Prudential Life Insurance.

Finally, this episode establishes that Angel's real name is "Evelyn." However, the matter of how Angel acquired his famous nickname would remain a mystery until 1995, when Rockford gives us the back story in the reunion movie *A Blessing in Disguise*.

Rockford Friends

At first, Rockford is perfectly willing to walk away and let Angel sink in his own mess. "You were meant for this frame," he tells him in this episode. "It was built for a dummy, and it looks good on you!" However, Jim feels compelled to help Angel because, like Maverick before him, he has a conscience—or at the very least, an ethical code. Rockford can't walk away once Angel appeals to him on a basic level: the man, after all, is his friend.

"That relationship has always puzzled me," James Garner told CBS in 1994. "I've never understood why Rockford likes this guy so much, even though he's just rotten to the core. I guess there is something lovable about Angel. I just don't know what it is."

Rockford Familiar Faces

Frank Campanella, who would also guest-star along with his brother Joseph Campanella later in the second season (in the episode "In Hazard"), was one of the actors originally considered to play Rockford's father in the *Rockford Files* pilot.

Rockford stunt man Dave Cass plays one of Chester Sierra's thugs.

32.   2 INTO 5.56 WON'T GO

Production Number: 42630
Original Air Date: November 21, 1975
Written by: Stephen J. Cannell
Directed by: Jeannot Szwarc

Guest Cast: Jesse Welles (Shana Bowie), Charles Napier (Billy Webster), Mitchell Ryan (Colonel Hopkins), Frank Maxwell (Colonel Daniel Hart Bowie), William Boyett (Sergeant Harvey Slate), Harvey Gold (Quentin Davis), Carol Vogel (Terri), John Kerry (Lieutenant Doug Fenton), Kenneth Washington (Guard), Eddie Firestone (Dwight Davis)

Jim, it's Maria over at the laundromat. There's a yellow dress in with your things—is that a mistake, or a special handling, or what?

Synopsis. *Moments after leaving an urgent message on Rockford's phone machine, Colonel Daniel Bowie is abducted by his aide, Sergeant Harvey Slate, and a former soldier named Quentin Davis. Bowie is later found dead, the victim of an apparent car accident. When the military discover that Bowie had contacted Rockford prior to his death, they question Rockford (who had also served under Bowie during the Korean War) for possible involvement. Meanwhile, Bowie's daughter Shana, who believes her father was murdered, hires Jim to investigate. When Rockford determines that Davis, a mortician, has been teaming with Slate to steal military weapons (by smuggling them inside funeral caskets), he suspects that Bowie was killed after he stumbled onto the operation.*

Rockford apparently had a colorful career in the Army. According to his military file, after he was wounded in action (an injury also mentioned in the episode "The Hawaiian Headache"), he received a Silver Star and was promoted to sergeant. However, six months later, he was bumped down to PFC (private first class) after he was busted for trading 400 cases of C-rations for a North Korean tank. (What the file doesn't mention, though, is Rockford was merely following orders. Colonel Bowie had told Rockford to commandeer a tank *fast* because the troop needed to blow their way out of a pocket—and he wasn't specific about whether it had to be a U.S. tank.) For his fast thinking,

Rockford received a battle field promotion to sergeant, although he was demoted to private once again after he was caught setting up a string of pool halls in Puo Sang and stealing a major general's staff car right in front of the Seoul Korean Hilton.

In real life, James Garner was wounded on two occasions during the Korean War, and was awarded two Purple Hearts. He was also something of a "dog robber" (Army lingo for someone who operates just barely within the law). During an interview with *Playboy* in 1981, he recounted some of the exploits he pulled off while stationed at a base postal office in Japan. "Guys in the Army like their mail and they become very unhappy if they don't get it," he said. "I decided to spruce up our unit, and if they didn't give me what we needed, they didn't get their mail. The base post office was stationed in a bombed-out shoe factory, and I turned it into a showplace. In exchange for their mail, other units got us the materials to build a bar and then kept it stocked with whiskey. Nobody over there had ice except us, courtesy of the Graves Registration Unit. I built us a theater in the biggest room in the shoe factory, got a baseball diamond laid out, got us hot water and showers. My crowning achievement was a swimming pool … The smallest room in the shoe factory was the basement. We cleansed it all out, whitewashed it, cemented the floor, put a ladder up the side and filled that sucker up with water."

Garner played a "dog robber" in *The Americanization of Emily* (1964), which remains the actor's favorite film.

Rockford Familiar Faces

Mitchell Ryan (Colonel Hopkins) starred in *Chase*, a police drama that Stephen J. Cannell created for Jack Webb in 1973. More than two decades later, he would return to series television as Dharma's uppercrust father-in-law Edward Montgomery in the popular sitcom *Dharma and Greg* (ABC, 1997-2002).

33. PASTORIA PRIME PICK

Production Number: 42609
Original Air Date: November 29, 1975
Written by: Gordon Dawson
Directed by: Lawrence Doheny

Guest Cast: Warren Kemmerling (Vern Soper), Richard Herd (Sheriff Gladish), William Lucking (Officer Pete Kolodny), Kathie Browne (Mayor Karen Sanders), Smith Evans (Rita Sanders), William Zuckert (Emmett Byrd), Don Billett (Gilbert Univaso), Bill Quinn (Judge Russell Cline), Robert Ward (Honcho), Bruce Tuthill (First Hood), Barbara Collentine (Waitress)

Hey, Jimbo—Dennis. Really appreciate the help on the income tax. Do you want to help on the audit now?

Synopsis. *Rockford becomes the latest victim of a horrifying blackmail scheme orchestrated by the mayor and sheriff of a small community called New Pastoria. Lured into town to find a man who allegedly abandoned his family, Rockford finds himself stung by a hornet's nest of manufactured charges ranging from grand theft auto to possession of narcotics and statutory rape. The county prosecutor, who is also in on the scheme, then offers to drop the charges if Jim pays an outlandish fine of $15,000—money which is intended to "build a better New Pastoria." Rockford, however, finds an ally in retired sheriff Emmett Byrd, who helps the P.I. uncover evidence that could bring down the operation.*

Early in this episode, Rockford calls himself collect in order to retrieve his messages. Although he asks the operator to dial 555-9000, according to the closeup of his phone that appears at the beginning of each episode, Rockford's phone number is 555-2368.

34.   THE REINCARNATION OF ANGIE

Production Number: 42631
Original Air Date: December 5, 1975
Written by: Stephen J. Cannell
Directed by: Jerry London

Guest Cast: Elayne Heilveil (Angie Perris), Wayne Tippet (FBI Agent Dan Shore), David Huddleston (Sherm Whitlaw), Sharon Spelman (Susan), Eugene Peterson (Tom Perris), Charles Siebert (Bettingen), George Skaff (Bundy), Jenny O'Hara (Operator), Jeanne Bates (Lady in Bank), Louise Fitch (Maid)

Hi, Jim. It's Jamie at the Police Impound. They picked up your car again—lately, they've been driving it more than you have ...

Synopsis. *Angie Perris receives a late night phone call from her brother Tom, who asks her to remove an envelope from his safe, but Tom is abducted before he can give her the combination. Angie hires Rockford. After disarming both the man who had seized Tom, as well as another man who had been following Angie, Jim retrieves the envelope—which contains $500,000 in cash. Rockford later learns that Tom, a stockbroker, had been working with a federal agent named Bettingen to determine who had been selling forged stock certificates to Tom's firm. Bettingen provided Tom with $500,000 to make the purchases; when Bettingen is found dead, and both Tom and the money disappear shortly thereafter, the feds become suspicious. Meanwhile, the kidnapers notify Rockford that they'll release Tom in exchange for the money. Jim arrives at the appointed place, only to find himself set up—federal agents converge on the scene and discover Tom's dead body stuffed inside the trunk of Rockford's car.*

When Rockford meets Angie at a bar, he confronts the man who had been following her. The man claims to be a federal agent, but Rockford quickly determines that the man is lying after noticing that the picture on the man's I.D. card was taken against a blue field—as it would appear on a driver's license. "Feds have their pictures taken against a yellow field," Rockford later explains to Angie. "What that guy did was cut his picture out of his driver's license, paste it into a federal I.D. and encase it in plastic."

Angie is impressed. How on earth did Rockford know about that trick? "Because that's what I did," Rockford tells her, having tried it once before himself.

Rockford Facts

Strictly speaking, this episode marks the first of Wayne Tippet's three second-season appearances as Federal Agent Shore, the character previously played by James McEachin in "This Case is Closed." Technically, however, it's actually his second. Tippet also appears in "The No-Cut Contract," an episode that was filmed prior to "The Reincarnation of Angie," but held for broadcast until later in the season.

Tippet, whose last name is occasionally misspelled as "Tippit" (as we see in the credits for this episode), had regular roles on the daytime serials *Guiding Light* and *Search for Tomorrow*, as well as such prime time dramas as *L.A. Law* and *Melrose Place*. Besides "The Reincarnation of Angie" and "The No-Cut Contract," Tippet also played Shore in "A Portrait of Elizabeth."

Rockford Fun

According to this episode, Agent Shore's first name is "Dan," but in "This Case is Closed," the character's first name was "Dave." Perhaps the change in monikers was an attempt to obfuscate the fact that a character that had previously been played by a black actor (McEachin) was now being played by a white actor (Tippet).

35.   THE GIRL IN THE BAY CITY BOYS CLUB

Production Number: 42632
Original Air Date: December 19, 1975
Written by: Juanita Bartlett
Directed by: James Garner

Guest Cast: Blair Brown (Kate Doyle), Joel Fabiani (Tompkins), Stewart Moss (Burton Kimball), Paul Stevens (George Welles), William Phipps (Sergeant), William Bryant (Paul Flanders), Sharon Ullrick (Clerk), Julio Medina (Gardener), Stacy Keach Sr. (Cy Mosher), Todd Hoffman (Young Man), Byron Morrow (Ted Thatcher), Norman Bartold (Thatcher)

Hi, Sonny. It's Rocky. I got the bill—I've been trying to figure out what everybody owes on L.J.'s birthday party. Tell me, did you have the Pink Lady?

Synopsis. *A man named Phelps hires Rockford to determine if the weekly Thursday night poker game held at the Bay City Boys Club is fixed. Rockford doesn't realize that his client is really Burton Kimball, a prominent deputy district attorney heavily in debt to racketeer George Welles, who founded the club as a front to his operation. Kimball, who has been blackmailed by Welles into fixing cases, needs evidence against Welles in order to escape his grasp. When Kimball is later found dead, Jim deduces that the D.A. was close to obtaining the proof he needed. With the help of fellow investigator Kate Doyle, Rockford tries to put Welles and the Bay City Boys Club out of business by determining how the game was rigged.*

This episode is the first and only film directed by James Garner. According to the actor, the circumstances that resulted in his debut behind the camera were brought on by accident. "We lost a director," he explained. "The person who was scheduled to direct that show, for some reason, couldn't do it, and had to pull out. It was a last-minute situation, so I went ahead and did it myself."

It is a challenging task for an actor to direct a film in which he or she is also appearing. That task becomes even more difficult when the actor/director has to appear in 90% of the scenes—which was the case with Garner and *The Rockford Files*. "That show asked a great deal of him," said Juanita Bartlett. "As the director, he had to get everything going in each scene, and then he'd have to pop into it and play Rockford, while still directing the other actors in the scene. It was an extremely hard thing for him to do, and he came through."

That, he did. Garner kept the story moving at a brisk pace, particularly during the climactic chase sequence inside the gym, and elicited a sparkling effort from guest lead Blair Brown (*The Days and Nights of Molly Dodd*, in one of her early roles). And while the added burden of directing can sometimes impair an actor's own performance, that wasn't the case with this episode. Garner as Rockford was definitely "on."

Although "The Girl in the Bay City Boys Club" was Garner's only "official" effort behind the camera, he is often looked upon as an auxiliary director on the set, particulary in regard to the production of *The Rockford Files*. His input and suggestions, coming from over 40 years in the business, are welcomed. But Garner never imposes himself on the director. That's never been his style.

"I talk a lot with the directors, so I know what they're doing," he said. "Sometimes, I'd make suggestions. But I'd never, ever say, 'You've got to do it this way.' When I hire people, I let them do whatever they do, because I think you get better work that way."

Though Garner proved that he can act and direct in the same picture, he also knows that doing so is an extra burden that he could do without. "After that show, Jim said, 'I am never going to do this [star and direct] again,'" said Bartlett. "However, he did say that he might direct again ... so long as he wouldn't have to appear in the picture."

Ten years after "The Girl in the Bay City Boys Club," Garner and Brown starred together in *Space*, the 1985 mini-series based on the novel by James A. Michener. Brown, whose husband Joseph Sargent directed *Space*, would also hook up with Garner in a brief but funny sequence in the 2000 film *Space Cowboys*.

Rockford Facts

In this episode, we see that Rockford has a portable set of lock picks, which he usually keeps handy inside the breast pocket of his jacket.

36.   THE HAMMER OF C BLOCK

Production Number: 42622
Original Air Date: January 9, 1976
Written by: Gordon Dawson
Directed by: Jerry London

Song "Gandy's Theme"
Music and Lyrics by: Isaac Hayes
Sung by: Isaac Hayes

Guest Cast: Isaac Hayes (Gandolf Fitch), James A. Watson Jr. (Arthur Bingham), Annazette Chase (Debbie Bingham), Jack Somack (Oliver Prey), Lynn Hamilton (Eunice Charles Bingham), Allan Rich (Charles "Pebbles" Runkin), Bill Walker (Rosie), Sandy DeBruin (Receptionist), Hank Stohl (Wino), Helen Schustack (Betty)

It's Jack. The check is in the mail. Sorry it's two years late. Sorry I mis-figured my checking account and I'm overdrawn. Sorry I stopped payment on it. So when it comes, tear it up. Sorry!

Synopsis. *Gandolf Fitch received the death penalty after he was convicted of the brutal murder of his girlfriend Lila McGee, but the sentence was reduced to life imprisonment after one year. Released after serving 20 years, Fitch calls on former prison mate Rockford to collect on a five-year-old debt (Jim lost $1,500 to Gandy in a crap game one night). But Gandy, who claims he was framed, offers Rockford*

Photograph courtesy of Photofest
© 1975 Universal City Studios, Inc.

Gandolf Fitch (Isaac Hayes) turns to Jim Rockford (James Garner) for help in "The Hammer of C Block"

a deal: he'll waive the debt if "Rockfish" (as he calls Jim) can help him find the real killer. Although their trail starts cold, Rockford and Gandy eventually locate a former prostitute named Eunice Charles who may have proof of Gandy's innocence. But Eunice also holds a secret that, if revealed, could absolutely devastate Gandy.

Grammy and Academy Award-winning vocalist/composer Isaac Hayes had just started his acting career around the time "The Hammer of C Block" was being cast. "Isaac's agency contacted us, and they recommended that we let him read for the role of Gandy Fitch," said Charles Floyd Johnson. "He was in Memphis at the time, and he wanted to do it—his agent told us that he was going to fly himself in. So we said, 'Sure.' It was near the beginning of his acting career; in fact, I remember that I kept saying, 'Isaac Hayes, *the singer?*' But when we heard him read, we all knew he was perfect for the part. Isaac helped create a very, very interesting character, and we brought him back to do two more shows."

Hayes appears to have composed the haunting "Gandy's Theme" exclusively for *The Rockford Files*. The song is not listed on any of the artist's charted albums (i.e, albums that made the official Billboard charts).

Rockford Familiar Faces

Lynn Hamilton (Eunice) had a recurring role as Judge Fulton on *The Practice*, as well as regular roles in the daytime serials *Rituals*, *The Young and the Restless*, and *Port Charles*. In real life, she is the wife of Bernie Hamilton, the actor best known for playing Captain Dobey on *Starsky & Hutch*.

Character actor James A. Watson Jr., who along with Stuart Margolin appeared regularly in the blackout vignettes on *Love, American Style*, also had a memorable turn as First Officer Dunn in *Airplane II: The Sequel* (1982). Watson appeared in three of the *Rockford* reunion movies, *I Still Love L.A.* (1994), *If the Frame Fits ...* (1996) and *If It Bleeds ... It Leads* (1999).

37.   THE NO-CUT CONTRACT

Production Number: 42615
Original Air Date: January 16, 1976
Produced by: Lane Slate
Written by: Stephen J. Cannell
Directed by: Lou Antonio

Guest Cast: Rob Reiner (Larry "King" Sturtevant), Dick Butkus (Himself), Wayne Tippet (Agent Dan Shore), Milt Kogan (Norman), Sharon Cintron (Sharon), Gene Tyburn (Bill), Barbara Flicker (TV Coordinator), J. Jay Saunders (Agent Prizer), Mary Angela (Lisa), Kathy Silva (Judy)

Horas fantasticos. La unique opportunidad en su vida la frescia rosaria llantas realiades. Call toll free—cinco-cinco-cinco, tres-uno-dos-uno.

Synopsis. *Larry "King" Sturtevant, starting quarterback for the Southern Illinois Warriors (a second-rate team in a third-rate pro football league), knows that team owner Dale Fontaine has ties with the Chicago underworld, so he had Fontaine's conference room bugged in order to gain leverage in case he ever needed any. Sturtevant recorded a conversation in which Fontaine sold mob information to federal agents; when he learns that Fontaine planned to replace him with another quarterback, Sturtevant threatens to turn over the tapes unless Fontaine cancels the deal. However, when word of the tapes leaks out, Sturtevant finds himself on the run from both sides of the law. The weaselly Sturtevant, who claims he'd stashed the tapes with a private detective, supplies the mob and the FBI with a name he'd randomly plucked from the Yellow Pages: Jim Rockford.*

Like the character he played on *The Rockford Files*, James Garner enjoys watching NFL football—in fact, he has been a fan of the Oakland Raiders for over three decades. Back in the 1970s, Garner not only used to fly up to Oakland for Raiders home games, he was often seen standing on the sidelines, watching the game from the field alongside the Raiders players. "I got into that years and years ago," Garner said in 1996. "I used to go up there, and every time I went up, they won. And when I wasn't there, they lost. And I got to be the good luck charm. And pretty soon, if I didn't show up … they'd blame me!"

Garner's orthopedic surgeon, Dr. Robert Rosenfield (now deceased), was also the Raiders team doctor for many years. According to Garner's assistant MaryAnn Rea, Garner used to accompany Dr. Rosenfeld to and from Oakland on the Raiders team plane. Rosenfeld was also instrumental in helping Garner get season tickets at the Los Angeles Memorial Coliseum, where the team played its home games between the years 1982 and 1994 (when the franchise was known as the Los Angeles Raiders).

Rockford Facts

"The No-Cut Contract" is available through MCA/Universal Home Video as part of its *Rockford Files* collection.

Photograph courtesy of Photofest
© 1975 Universal City Studios, Inc.

Jim Rockford (James Garner) and King Sturtevant (Rob Reiner) take cover behind Rockford's Firebird in this scene from "The No-Cut Contract"

38.   A PORTRAIT OF ELIZABETH

Production Number: 42633
Original Air Date: January 23, 1976
Written by: Stephen J. Cannell
Directed by: Meta Rosenberg

Guest Cast: John Saxon (Dave Delaroux), Wayne Tippet (Agent Dan Shore), Cynthia Sikes (Susan Valero), Kate Woodville (Karen Silver), Robert Riesel (Mickey Silver), Ned Wilson (Arnold Adams), Joe E. Tata (Solly Marshall), James Murtaugh (Tom Hanson), Angus Duncan (Morey Dayton), Michael Thoma (Maitre D'), Victor Izay (Garvey), Chuck Winters (Fred Marley), Peg Stewart (Maid)

Jim, it's Harry. We've been waiting on you two hours. The forks—where's the forks?!? Lasagna ain't no finger food.

Synopsis. *Beth's client (and new boyfriend) Dave Delaroux, the controller for the local branch of a national corporation, wants Rockford to determine whether someone in his office has been stealing cashier's checks. Although Rockford is suspicious (and a little jealous) of Dave, he agrees to look into the matter and finds nothing amiss. Meanwhile, Dave, who along with two men swindled a San Diego bank out of $2 million (using cashier's checks from his company), not only frames Rockford for that crime, he also uses Rockford's gun to kill his two partners. But the real kicker is that Rockford has an alibi he can't use: Beth, who cannot reveal anything that could incriminate Dave without violating attorney/client confidentiality.*

Gretchen Corbett comes from an extensive theater background. In the seven years prior to signing with Universal in 1974, she appeared in numerous stage productions (on and off-Broadway), including *Arms and the Man*, *After the Rain*, *Forty Carats*, *The Effects of Gamma Rays on Man-in-the-Moon Marigolds*, and *The Master Builder*. She has also performed in such classics as *Othello* (as Desdemona), *Romeo and Juliet* (as Juliet), and *Saint Joan* (as Joan of Arc).

Although Corbett had done some films and television shows prior to *The Rockford Files*, "I was still relatively new to the world of camera when I first started the series," she recalled. "There are a lot of technical things that you need to be aware of when you're being filmed, and having come from stage, I didn't know all the technical stuff. Jim Garner was particularly helpful to me in that regard—he was like a mentor. He taught me where shadows were, and when I was in a light or not in a light, and when I was being lit well or when I wasn't being lit well.

"And Jim also taught me how to walk and talk at the same time. That may sound funny, but it's hard to do at first, particularly when you've got 150 technicians walking with you as you're being filmed."

Corbett also recalls the atmosphere of family that emanated from Garner. "Jim is an angel," she said. "He's a really wonderful man. His crew loved him. Whenever you're working on a film set, or a television set, the feeling on that set always comes from the top. And the feeling on *Rockford* was one of family, of looking out for each other, of caring for each other in a personal way. And that all came from Jim."

Rockford Funnies

Watch closely and listen carefully during the scene in which Rockford visits the Biometrics office early in this episode, and you'll catch the names of several key behind-the-scenes people. As Rockford examines the ledger, the camera cuts to a closeup of Rockford comparing the check numbers in the ledger to his own list of allegedly missing checks. From this closeup, you'll notice that some of the names in the ledger include "George Rohrs" (*Rockford*'s film editor) and "Charles F. Johnson" (the associate producer). Also, Rockford claims that he was sent by "Mr. Swerling of the Central Office," a reference to supervising producer Jo Swerling Jr.

Rockford Familiar Faces

Cynthia Sikes (*St. Elsewhere*) has a small role in this episode as Dave's former girlfriend.

39.   JOEY BLUE EYES

Production Number: 42613
Original Air Date: January 30, 1976
Written by: Walter Dallenbach
Directed by: Lawrence Doheny

Guest Cast: Michael Ansara (Joseph DiMina), Suzanne Charny (Paulette DiMina), Robert Yuro (Gannon), James Luisi (Bert Striker), Eddie Fontaine (Sweet Tooth London), James Lydon (Barrow), Sandy Kenyon (Mitchell), Michael Lane (Fred), Norman Bartold (Evans), Ril Raden (Fulton)

Sorry, Jim—this is for Rocky. Hey, Rock—Stan. I got that redhead and her sister. Ten-thirty, Stacy's Grill. [Chuckles.]

Synopsis. *Joseph "Joey Blue Eyes" DiMina, a reformed hood who has become a successful restaurateur, finds himself the victim of a conspiracy between his business partner Bert Striker and his attorney Larry Mitchell to force him out of his own business. To make matters worse: Joey borrowed money from loan shark Sweet Tooth London, who has Joey's daughter Paulette beaten up as a warning in case Joey fails to make payment. An enraged Joey assaults Sweet Tooth and ends up in jail. Although Rockford initially clashes with Joey, Beth (a friend of Paulette's) implores him to help. When Rockford learns that Striker also has financial problems, he sets up an elaborate con aimed at forcing Striker to pay Joey's loan with his own money.*

"Joey Blue Eyes" features Michael Ansara, who starred as the Apache chief Cochise in *Broken Arrow* (ABC, 1956-1958), the small screen version of the classic 1950 Western starring James Stewart and Jeff Chandler. Once married for 16 years to actress Barbara Eden, Ansara's brooding looks and rich baritone voice made him a fixture in films and television for over 50 years. Among his many roles, he played the Klingon warrior Kang in the original *Star Trek*, as well as in *Star Trek: Deep Space Nine* and *Star Trek: Voyager*. Prior to his appearance in this episode, Ansara had co-starred with James Garner in the lighthearted adventure *The Pink Jungle* (1968).

Other guest stars include James Luisi, who would join the cast of *The Rockford Files* as Lieutenant Chapman starting in the third season.

Rockford Funnies

The doctor who is being paged at the hospital where Rockford visits Paulette ("Dr. Rea, Dr. MaryAnn Rea, please pick up the phone") was named after MaryAnn Rea, James Garner's longtime assistant.

40. IN HAZARD

Production Number: 42634
Original Air Date: February 6, 1976
Written by: Juanita Bartlett
Directed by: Jackie Cooper

Guest Cast: Joseph Campanella (Arnold Bailey), Ben Frank (Howard Nystrom), Richard Venture (Fred Metcalf), Joe E. Tata (Solly Marshall), Frank Campanella (Marty Jordan), Melendy Britt (Connie), Skip Ward (Walt Raynor), Anne Weldon (Police Matron), Linda Dano (Marie), Bruce Tuthill (Murray Gaines)

Mr. Rockford, Miss Miller of the Bartlett Book Club. **Great Detectives of America** *is not in stock, so we sent you* **Cooking Made Easy.** *Hope you enjoy it.*

Synopsis. *Shortly after representing Arnold Bailey, a stockbroker accused of tax fraud, Beth is arrested on contempt-of-court charges. She learns that her office was burglarized, and then nearly dies after drinking cyanide-laced coffee. Rockford finds that the attempt on Beth's life is tied to the partnership between Bailey and another of Beth's clients in a scheme to skim money from the pension fund of a textile workers union controlled by syndicate leader Marty Jordan.*

This episode was the subject of "A Freudian Analysis of the Private Detective Tale," an insightful essay by Jeffrey H. Mahan that used the character of Jim Rockford to illustrate the classic psychoanalytic model of the *id, ego,* and *superego* originated by Sigmund Freud. "In applying these ideas to a television detective story," writes Mahan, "we can begin by identifying our central character with the ego.

> Thus, in looking at *The Rockford Files,* we can see Jim Rockford as an ego attempting to balance the pressures the narrative brings to bear upon him. Jim begins [a typical episode of the series] in a rational, ego control of his life. Each case creates a state of anxiety in which one or more of the pressures upon him attempts to gain ascendancy.

The tale ends when the pressures upon Jim's ego are relieved and he regains a healthy ego control over the forces that have come to bear upon him.

Rather than psychoanalyze Rockford, Mahan uses the character as a tool to explicate the basic concepts of the Freudian system, as well as Freud's theory that society is the product and enforcer of rationality. The essay concludes by using "In Hazard" as a specific application of Freud's social theory in action.

"A Freudian Analysis of the Private Detective Tale" was published as a chapter of *American Television Genres* (Nesson-Hall, 1985), which Mahan co-authored with Stuart Kaminsky, a onetime film professor at Northwestern University who has since become one of our country's leading mystery writers. Kaminsky has written over 50 novels, including two original *Rockford Files* mysteries: *The Green Bottle* (St. Martin's, 1996) and *Devil on My Doorstep* (St. Martin's, 1998).

Rockford Familiar Faces

Joseph Campanella (Arnold Bailey) has been a mainstay in television, as well as a familiar voice in radio commercials, for over 40 years. Among Campanella's many roles on the small screen, he starred as attorney Brian Darnell in *The Bold Ones: The Lawyers*, which Roy Huggins created and produced for Universal in the early 1970s. Campanella also played Mickey Ryder in *I Still Love L.A.*, the first of the eight *Rockford Files* movies produced for CBS.

Rockford Funnies

"In Hazard" features another inside joke. In Act II, when Rockford bumps into Bailey at the hospital, you can hear a page for "Dr. Robert Crawley" over the loudspeaker. Robert Crawley was the art director on *The Rockford Files*.

41. THE ITALIAN BIRD FIASCO

Production Number: 42605
Original Air Date: February 13, 1976
Written by: Edward J. Lakso
Directed by: Jackie Cooper

Guest Cast: William Daniels (Thomas Caine), Camilla Sparv (Evelyn Stoneman), William Jordan (Jeffers), Peter Palmer (Stack), Ron Silver (Ted Haller), Ivon Barry (Cryder), Dean Santorro (Collins), Eric Server (Whitlock), Karl Lukas (Officer), Gerald S. Peters (Edward Barrows), Peter Ashton (Clerk), D'Mitch Davis (Guard)

Jim—Sally. Hey, I just found out you're an Aries. Listen, if you have Virgo rising, give me a call.

Synopsis. *Thomas Caine, a shady dealer in* objects d'art, *hires Rockford to purchase a valuable cormorant modeled after one of three priceless originals by Italian sculptor Giacopo Lambrighni. Rockford doesn't realize that Caine's true interest lies in recovering a fortune in stolen jewelry that he had smuggled inside a series of imitation Lambrighni birds. Jim makes the purchase, but the cormorant is destroyed after two men attack him outside the gallery. (Neither Caine nor Rockford realize that the cormorant was in fact a genuine Lambrighni.) A determined Caine blackmails Rockford into purchasing another allegedly imitation Lambrighni. Meanwhile, the woman who helped Caine plan the theft starts her own search for the phony Italian birds.*

This episode features Emmy and Tony Award-winning actor William Daniels (*1776, St. Elsewhere, Boy Meets World*), who previously co-starred with James Garner in *Marlowe* (1969), and who would later play the unscrupulous federal prosecutor who violates Rockford's civil rights in the third season episode "So Help Me God."

Other guest stars include Ron Silver, who was nominated for an Academy Award for his brilliant portrayal of Harvard law professor Alan Dershowitz in *Reversal of Fortune* (1990).

Rockford Facts

The answering machine message that opens this episode tells us that Rockford is an Aries. (Later on in the series, in the episode "Beamer's Last Case," we'll learn that Rockford's birthday is April 14.) Like the character he plays on *Rockford*, James Garner is also an Aries. His birthday is April 7.

42.   WHERE'S HOUSTON?

Production Number: 42625
Original Air Date: February 20, 1976
Written by: Don Carlos Dunaway
Directed by: Lawrence Doheny

Guest Cast: Lane Bradbury (Houston Preli), Robert Mandan (Charles Blackhorn), Del Munroe (Charlie), Dabbs Greer (Peter Preli), Raymond O'Keefe (Hal), Murray MacLeod (Jerry Specht), Thomas Bellin (Clerk), Rodolfo Hoyos (Carlos Santoro)

Jim—Madame Arcana at the Zodiac Restaurant. You don't pay that dinner tab, we're gonna repo your birthday …

Synopsis. *Peter Preli, a longtime friend of Rocky's, hires Rockford after he believes his granddaughter Houston has been kidnapped. Early in his investigation, Rockford is beaten badly by three men who warn him to drop the case. When Jim reports back to Preli, he finds the old man dead, and the front door broken. However, when the police investigate the scene, they find no signs of forced entry, so they arrest Rockford for Preli's murder. Meanwhile, Houston returns unharmed—she'd been in Mexico on a geological expedition. Rockford soon realizes that the kidnapping hoax and Preli's murder are connected to a real estate conglomerate that plans to build a multi-milliondollar entertainment complex on the old man's property.*

This episode was written by Don Carlos Dunaway, who was one of the writers Roy Huggins cited as an example of the double-edged sword television producers often face when it comes to finding new talent. Dunaway was in Rome on a film working as an assistant director when Huggins came across a screenplay Dunaway had written but which had never been produced. "I read it, [told Don] he was talented, and brought him here [to Universal] from Rome," Huggins told *Daily Variety* in 1975. "I was only able to hold on to him for six months, because he was snatched up and is now doing screenplays for Paramount and 20th Century-Fox. He is getting $75,000 from 20th; how can he work for me? There is an irony, in that when you do find talent, you frequently lose it."

Dunaway, who wrote the screenplay for the film adaptation of Stephen King's classic horror novel *Cujo*, also produced the detective series *Stone* (ABC, 1980) for Stephen J. Cannell and Universal Television.

Guest stars include character Robert Mandan (*Soap*) and veteran character actor Dabbs Greer, whose many film and TV roles include appearances with James Garner in *Cash McCall* (1960) and the "Sleight of Hand" episode of *Nichols*.

Rockford Fun

"Where's Houston?" contains more examples of the inside humor that frequently permeated throughout *The Rockford Files*. Among the tenants who live in the Sunset Marquis Hotel, which Rockford investigates in this episode, are "R. Zilliox" (named after set decorator Robert Zilliox) and "R. Crawley" (art director Robert Crawley).

43.   FOUL ON THE FIRST PLAY

Production Number: 42635
Original Air Date: March 12, 1976
Teleplay by: Stephen J. Cannell
Story by: Charles Floyd Johnson and Dorothy J. Bailey
Directed by: Lou Antonio

Guest Cast: Louis Gossett Jr. (Marcus Hayes), Dick Davalos (Manny Stickells), David White (Martin Eastman), Pepper Martin (Greg Smith), James Ingersoll (Steve Sorenson), Al Ruscio (Tom Corell), John Mahon (Todd Morris), Chuck Bowman (Commissioner Bob Tremayne), Vincent Cobb (Ray Fairchild), Pamela Serpe (Receptionist), Ji-Tu Cumbaka (Sherm Addison), Al Checco (Leasing Agent), Janet Winter (Secretary), Jayne Kennedy (Janice)

Jim? It's Eddie. You were right about Sweet Talk in the 7th—he breezed in, paid $7,250. But I didn't get your bet down ...

Synopsis. *Rockford learns that his conniving parole officer Marcus Hayes has become a private investigator (after he was fired by the Parole Board). Marcus was hired by NBA Commissioner Bob Tremayne to find out which of the three prospective bidders of the Santa Monica expansion franchise has been using pressure tactics to influence the Commissioner's decision on who will get the new team. To get a lead on the case, Marcus tricks Rockford into acting as a decoy, but when Jim catches on, he forces Hayes to surrender half of his $10,000 fee. When Tremayne is found dead on the night before the announcement of the final decision—and one of the bidders implicates Marcus—Rockford must clear Hayes of the charges.*

The cagey Marcus Hayes was tailored specifically for Emmy and Oscar winner Louis Gossett Jr. (*Roots, An Officer and a Gentleman*), who had previously co-starred with James Garner in the 1971 Western satire *Skin Game*. "I was looking for any excuse to get Lou and Jim together again, because they had played so well off each other in that picture," explained producer Charles Floyd Johnson, who penned the original story for this episode along with Dorothy Bailey. "I think that when Dorothy and I wrote that story together, we did have Lou in mind—we pretty much designed Marcus as a character who was very similar to what Lou had played in *Skin Game*. And, fortunately, Lou was available to play it."

Other familiar faces in this episode include David White (Larry Tate on *Bewitched*), Ji-Tu Cumbaka (Jason on *Room 222*) and model/actress Jayne Kennedy.

Rockford Facts

Dorothy Bailey began her career in television as the longtime assistant to Roy Huggins. Bailey, who occasionally wrote under the pseudonym "Chris Wesley," was associate producer on a number of projects for Universal in the late 1970s, including the Emmy Award-winning mini-series *Captains and the Kings*. Bailey was also post-production supervisor on several high end made-for-TV movies, including the Emmy-nominated *Blind Faith* (1990).

Chuck Bowman, who plays NBA Commissioner Tremayne in this episode, produced and directed many of Stephen J. Cannell's other series for Universal, including *Baa Baa Black Sheep*, *Tenspeed and Brownshoe*, and *The Greatest American Hero*.

Finally, James Luisi, who would join the cast of *The Rockford Files* beginning in the third season, once played in the NBA before he became an actor. A former guard, Luisi appeared in 31 games for the old Baltimore Bullets (now known as the Washington Wizards) back in the 1953-1954 season.

Rockford Funnies

David Menteer, the name of the third (and unseen) bidder in this episode, was also the name of one of *Rockford*'s assistant directors.

44.   A BAD DEAL IN THE VALLEY

Production Number: 42618
Original Air Date: March 19, 1976
Written by: Donald L. Gold and Lester William Berke
Directed by: Jerry London

Guest Cast: Susan Strasberg (Karen Stiles), Jack Colvin (The Preacher), Veronica Hamel (Sandy Lederer), David Sabin (Murray Slauson), Rod Cameron (Jack Chilson), John Lupton (Tony Lederer), Gordon Jump (Appleby), Fritzi Burr (Maid), Russ McGinn (Fred Sutherland), Reg Parton (Jerry Sutherland), Dudley Knight (Agent), Laurence Haddon (Robert L. Braverman)

*Uncle Jim? It's Ralph! I got your letter—but I moved out here anyway.
I really want those detective lessons …*

Synopsis. *Rockford dates Karen Stiles, whose father Sam Stiles served time with him at San Quentin. Karen, a real estate agent, asks Rockford to deliver a suitcase containing escrow papers for a major property transaction—but doesn't tell him that the suitcase actually contains $100,000 in phony money. Later, after Rockford's release from jail, Karen is apparently abducted. But when Jim learns that Karen's father was a premier plate artist, he deduces that Karen staged her abduction so that the authorities would not suspect her of the counterfeit money fiasco. After linking Karen's real estate deal to a $500,000 jewel theft, Rockford tries to trip up Karen by recovering the jewels himself and collecting the finder's fee.*

This episode was written by *Rockford* unit production manager Les Berke, who also teamed with Donald L. Gold to write the episodes "Feeding Frenzy" and "Deadlock in Parma." Berke, who also contributed several teleplays for *Quincy* in the 1970s, would later return to *Rockford* as the second assistant director for the reunion movies produced for CBS in the mid-1990s.

Third Season: 1976–1977

James Garner likes to say that he never set out to become No. 1 in movies or on television because "once you've reached the top, you have nowhere to go but down. I'd much rather settle in at around No. 7 or 8, and just hang in there."

By the start of the 1976-1977 season, *The Rockford Files* had become a "middle-of-the-pack" show. In each of the next three years, the series would consistently finish somewhere between 40th and 50th overall [out of 100 shows] in the weekly Nielsen series rankings. During that period of time, *Rockford* would average about an 18-19% weekly audience rating. Translated into raw numbers, that means that despite sustaining a huge loss in audience during its second season, the series continued to draw approximately 13 million television households every week.

Granted, by television industry standards, those figures aren't spectacularly large, particularly when compared to the numbers *Rockford* had been pulling when the series was at the peak of its popularity in early 1975. Yet *Rockford*'s audience numbers during its third, fourth and fifth seasons remained remarkably steady—and that's what makes them intriguing. Although *Rockford* sustained a huge loss in audience (nearly 20%) over the course of the 1975-1976 season, the series would not suffer any other significant decreases in audience throughout the remainder of its network run. Put another way, while the show never regained the viewers it had lost, it held onto the viewers that it still had. In Garner's parlance, *The Rockford Files* "hung in there."

Those viewers who stayed with the show through the end did so to watch James Garner, who was ably supported by solid writing that remained tailored to his strengths. "Because television is such a character-driven medium, a lot of what you do with a character depends upon the actor you're working with," said Charles Floyd Johnson, who (along with newcomer David Chase) became co-producer of *Rockford* during the third season. "When you have an actor like James Garner, who has such a distinctive personality—which we've seen in *Maverick* and in the many other things that he's done—a lot of what you write is based on what you know he can bring or will bring to the material.

"In television, especially in developing episodic series, you draw on the character and the actor, in the sense that a lot of Jim Rockford may be a lot of Jim Garner. What happens, inevitably, in a series is that the actor and the writers expand upon each other. The writers see what the actor can do, and write that into the material. Then the actor takes the material and brings it to a new level; and with each subsequent week, you try to continue to build from that level.

"I used to watch *All in the Family* all the time. A lot of what was Archie Bunker was really Carroll O'Connor. The writers would write Archie Bunker as Carroll O'Connor, and you could just see that character grow and develop each week. I think the same holds true for Angela Lansbury in *Murder, She Wrote*, and Peter Falk in *Columbo*. In series where you have major personalities that dominate the screen, you get a lot of 'building' onto the main actor with each week."

In the case of *The Rockford Files*, a kind of synergy developed between a performer with particular strengths (Garner's ability to deliver wry, character-driven humor) and writers (Huggins, Cannell, Bartlett and Chase) who knew how to bring out that strength. But, as Johnson points out, the "building" of actor traits onto the character did not stop with Garner and Rockford. "You try to 'build blocks' with your other actors and the characters they play," he continued. "For example, the relationship between Rockford and his dad was just gold to begin with [on paper]. But after watching Jim and Noah Beery play those roles, you see that they would each bring nuances to the characters, and you start thinking, 'Wouldn't it be great to do a scene where you'd have Jim and Rocky bickering, because Jim and Noah play off each other so well.'"

The sheer nature of episodic television is not only volume-driven (you have to produce 22 one-hour films a year), but also speed-oriented (you have only six days to make each film). It's an industry where you never seem to have enough time, but you can never use that as an excuse: you simply try to make the best shows possible within the parameters.

Under these circumstances, the presence of a James Garner as your series lead is invaluable, both before the camera and behind the scenes. Garner's leadership on the set, as we have seen, inspires the members of his staff and crew to work hard because they know that he will support them. Similarly, Garner's uncanny knack for turning otherwise ordinary-sounding lines into "Christmas presents" provided the writers with an added incentive to deliver the best scripts possible. "When you have James Garner as your lead (or others who are as good as he is), you know that there'll always be something wonderful to watch—even if the episode or the writing isn't quite the way you want it—because Jim would make it work," added Johnson.

The Academy of Television Arts and Sciences recognized Garner's efforts by honoring him with the Emmy Award for Best Dramatic Actor of 1976-1977. Since that time, Garner has won several other major awards, including a People's Choice Award in 1979, a second Emmy in 1987, two Golden Globe Awards (one in 1991, the other in 1994), a Western Heritage Award in 1996, a Golden Boot Award in 1999, and induction in the Television Academy Hall of

Original art © 2005 by Darin Bristow

James Garner

Fame in 1990. *TV Guide* named Garner television's All Time Best Dramatic Actor in 1993. In addition, on February 5, 2005, the Screen Actors Guild honored Garner with its prestigious Life Achievement Award for career achievement and humanitarian accomplishment. The tribute from SAG is not only one of the highest honors an actor can ever receive, it is doubly significant because it comes from his peers.

Truly, Garner has received the recognition he deserves for his enormous talent. "I think Jim feels that he's established in the business, and people today realize what he can do," added Luis Delgado. "Jim is an excellent actor. I would put him up against any actor or any actress in the business, and he would outshine them."

Juanita Bartlett echoed that sentiment. "I think that over the past few years, people have become more aware of how talented Jim really is," she said. "In the past [20] years, done films like *Heartsounds*, where you can see his depth and appreciate some of the other things he can do."

Garner has modestly downplayed the importance of the individual awards. Although Garner realizes he is good at his craft, he never fails to remind himself of the important role his writers have played in his success. Johnson recalls discussing this very same matter with Garner during the planning stages of the 1994 *Rockford Files* episodes (of which Johnson and Garner are co-executive producers, along with Juanita Bartlett). "We were discussing how there are some actors who lose focus of what their jobs really are, so that they suddenly become very difficult to deal with," said Johnson. "Jim said to me, 'Well, it's a job you do. I don't write those words. I don't create that character. I embellish on it, and I know that the writers use a lot of me, but the words in the characters are from the writer. Without the writer, I don't have anything. So I never forget what the writers do—that they create Jim Rockford. Although I certainly have a big part in [the creation of Rockford's character], I don't let it become a focus of where I suddenly feel that I'm more important than the whole process.'"

Garner is one of the most esteemed performers in the business precisely because of this attitude. He recognizes and respects the contributions of his colleagues and workers, and that in turn brings him their respect. "I think that is what has kept Jim's feet on the ground over the years," Johnson continued. "He doesn't let himself get caught up in the hype. It's a job, and he enjoys it."

*   *   *

The Rockford Files also turned an important corner at the start of the third season. At a point when most television shows begin to repeat themselves—after all, there are only so many ways a particular kind of story can be told in the course of a given series—the addition of David Chase to the production staff completely reinvigorated *Rockford*. Besides sharing producer responsibilities with Charles Floyd Johnson, Chase joined Stephen J. Cannell and Juanita Bartlett as one of the three primary writers on the show, bringing along fresh ideas and an entirely new approach to Jim Rockford that would change the course of the series.

Chase's style was as versatile as it was cerebral. Though certainly known for exploring the depths of Rockford's soul (particularly in the poignant stories featuring Kathryn Harrold as Megan Dougherty), an episode by Chase was also capable of taking the show in any number of interesting directions. Chase wrote 17 episodes in all, tackling everything from film, music, politics, celebrity, old Hollywood, new age cults, and the peculiar world of the New Jersey mob. Like Cannell, Chase had also a knack for creating offbeat, idiosyncratic and unforgettable characters, including the blind psychologist Megan Dougherty, the insufferable L.A. party boy Jay Rockfelt, and the dangerously neurotic mob hit man "Anthony Boy" Gagglio—a character that, according to Chase, was in many ways the forerunner to Tony Soprano.

Just as Chase took *Rockford* in new directions, so increasingly did Cannell and Bartlett. Though the series would continue to honor its spiritual ancestry in shows such as "There's One in Every Port" (Cannell's reworking of the classic *Maverick* caper "Shady Deal at Sunny Acres"), as well as the episodes featuring "Jimmy Joe Meeker" (the smooth-talking Oklahoma oilman alias that Jimbo started assuming in the fourth season), it also began to use the Rockford character as a vehicle for addressing topical issues and social inequities that often were "straight from the headlines"—a device Dick Wolf would perfect 15 years later when he developed *Law and Order*. In the process, Jim Rockford became less a modern-day Bret Maverick and more an Everyman in a world of absurdities, the lone voice in the wilderness willing to stand up and wonder just what in hell is going on.

"We were free to write about anything," said Chase in an interview published in 2004. "[Writing for *The Rockford Files*] taught me the value of story."

Perhaps the best example of the reincarnation of Rockford—the character, as well as the show—is the brilliant third-season episode "So Help Me God" (written by Bartlett), a searing indictment of the grand jury system in which Rockford is jailed unjustly at the hands of an unethical federal prosecutor played by William Daniels. Lauded by law groups across the country, the episode is not only among James Garner's personal favorites, it was also the show that won him the Emmy Award for Best Dramatic Actor in 1977.

The bar having been raised, *Rockford* would see some of its finest episodes over the next three years: Bartlett's "The Paper Palace," introducing Rita Moreno as Rita Capkovic, a former prostitute who's so lonely for genuine friendship, she wheels an empty shopping cart up and down the supermarket just to be around people; Cannell's "White on White and Nearly Perfect," the first of two episodes featuring Tom Selleck (*Magnum, p.i.*) as the hilariously intrepid gumshoe Lance White; and Chase's "Quickie Nirvana," the show that won *Rockford* the Emmy for Best Dramatic Series in 1978.

Noah Beery Jr. received an Emmy nomination for Best Supporting Actor in a Dramatic Series in the 1976-1977 season.

Familiar guest stars this season include William Daniels, Ned Beatty, Robert Walden, Burt Young, Kim Richards, Susan Howard, Robert Loggia, Vincent Baggetta, John Anderson, James Wainwright, Avery Schreiber, Michael Lerner, Howard Duff, Steve Landesberg, Jack Riley, John Dehner, Strother Martin, Alex Rocco, Jack Carter, Jon Cypher, Leslie Charleson, Kathleen Nolan, Conchata Farrell, Roger E. Mosley, Martin Kove, Simon Oakland, Cleavon Little, and Jack Kelly.

*   *   *

Prior to the 1976-1977 season, James Garner amended his contract with Universal Studios. That in itself was not unusual; oftentimes, a lead actor in a successful series will use his clout as the star of the show in order to negotiate a substantial raise in salary and/or more creative control of the show. Peter Falk, for one, waged several such battles with Universal during the years he made *Columbo* (NBC, 1971-1978).

Garner's case, however, *was* a bit unusual because he wasn't asking for more money—at least, more money up front. Under the terms of Garner's original contract with Universal Studios, Cherokee Productions was entitled to 37.5% of the net profits of *The Rockford Files*, while Garner received a base salary of $30,000 per episode (a figure that would increase by five percent in each subsequent season the series was in production). The contract also stipulated an arrangement made between Cherokee and an unnamed third party whereby 20% of Cherokee's percentage [or 7.5% of the total net profits] would be set aside for that third party—which meant, in essence, that Cherokee would actually only be receiving 30% of the total net profits of the series.

In February 1976, Garner renegotiated his contract, reducing his salary in exchange for a percentage of Cherokee's actual percentage of the profits. Under the new agreement, Cherokee's 30% share of the series profits would be divided between Garner and the production company thusly:

> Such applicable percentage shall be divided between me and Cherokee in the same ratio as the number of photoplays produced hereunder bears to the number of Series photoplays produced prior to the term

hereof and in which I appear (including the *Rockford Files* pilot). Thus, for example, if (i) the total applicable percentage of net profits otherwise payable to me and Cherokee hereunder is 30% of 100% after reduction by the aforementioned participations to third parties; (ii) 44 Series photoplays (including the pilot) have been produced prior to the term hereof; and (iii) 66 photoplays in which I appear are produced hereunder, then I shall be entitled to 60% of 30% of 100%, i.e., 18% of 100% of the applicable net profits, and Cherokee would be entitled to the 40% balance of 30% of 100%, i.e., 12% of 100% under your agreement with Cherokee.

Garner had apparently estimated that *Rockford* would run a total of five 22-episode seasons, which was also the length of the contract between NBC and Universal with regard to the series.

Under the terms of the 1976 amendment, Garner's salary in 1976-1977 was $27,045 per episode, or roughly 18% lower than what Garner would have been entitled to that season under the terms of his original contract. (The amendment also stipulated that Garner's salary would be increased by 5% in each subsequent season the series was in production.) In essence, this meant that Garner took an 18% cut in salary in exchange for 18% of the total net profits from the series. In theory, he made a better deal for himself: although he was giving up about $1 million in salary over the final three years of the series (assuming that *Rockford* ran five seasons), he would more than make up that amount by receiving a personal share of the profits generated from the series once *Rockford* went into reruns.

The underlying assumption of this transaction, of course, was that *The Rockford Files* would indeed finish "in the black." This issue would come into play several years later, when the studio's claim that the series had lost over $9 million ultimately prompted Garner to take the matter to court.

Appendix F
The World's Most Famous Firebird

Photograph courtesy of Cinema Vehicle Services

The Pontiac Firebird Espirit, 1978 model

If *Family Feud* ever included a "Name a distinct characteristic of *The Rockford Files* other than James Garner" question in its national survey, no doubt one of the most popular answers would have to be the Pontiac Firebird Espirit. After all, only Garner appeared in more episodes of the series than the Firebird. In fact, *TV Guide* once thought the car should get a special Emmy Award for "most consecutive performances without a speeding ticket."

Ever wonder why the Espirit was chosen in particular? How'd it manage to run so fast? Was the Firebird on the CBS movies the same as the one on the NBC show?

Car expert and *Rockford* aficionado Steve Reich knows practically every-thing about the world's most famous Firebird. For many years, Reich worked for Ray Claridge, owner of Cinema Vehicle Services, the No. 1 provider of pro-duction vehicles in the film and television industry. From supplying the cars and trucks we see on-camera, to arranging and transporting the lights, props and other vehicles to and from location every day, Claridge's company has serviced the needs of just about every TV show and motion picture over the past 25 years, including the original *Rockford Files* and the eight reunion movies produced for CBS. Cinema Vehicle Services has over 500 vehicles in its fleet, as well as a complete facility that provides everything from mechanical work to body, paint, fabrication, glass, and upholstery.

The original Espirit was a 1974 model, equipped with a 400-cubic engine V8, dual exhaust, factory Pontiac wheels, a console, and automatic transmission—all of which, according to Reich, were standard features of every Firebird, regardless of the model. While the car used in the pilot episode had white-lettered tires, it had whitewall tires by the time *Rockford* went to series. Every model year, Pontiac supplied Garner's company Cherokee Productions with three cars for the sea-son: that way, there were always two extra vehicles on hand in case one broke down. Rockford had a brand new car each year (a 1974 model for the first sea-son, a '75 for the second, and so on) except for the last two seasons, when Garner elected to continue using the '78 model for the balance of the show.

Many car-savvy *Rockford* philes have wondered why Garner, an accom-plished performance car driver in the 60s and 70s, chose a base model like the Espirit over the more sexy TransAm. "Jim didn't think a guy like Rockford, who was always struggling to make ends meet, could afford a flashy car like that," explained Reich. "So he went with the Espirit. Pontiac had a Firebird for every taste. If you were Joe Lunchbucket, who wanted to go to the disco scene and pick up women every night, and make everybody think you were hot stuff, you got the TransAm, with the screaming bird on the hood, and all the fancy options. But if you were a guy on a budget, like Rockford, who wanted a nice-looking two-door, and didn't care about going fast or anything like that, then the Espirit was the car for you."

Still, the TransAm was the among top performance cars at the time—pre-cisely the kind of vehicle you'd want, ideally, for an action show like *Rockford*. So how did Garner manage to perform the stunts he did each week while driving an economy car? "Actually," explains Reich, "the cars on the original show were, underneath the hood, basically TransAms. They each had the body of an Espirit, but they also had the high-performance motor and suspension you'd ordinarily find inside a TransAm. That's why they were able to do all the things Jim needed them to do. He lost a lot of guys who were chasing him every week."

Original art © 2005 by Darin Bristow

Interestingly enough, Garner had apparently considered going with a TransAm convertible when *The Rockford Files* resumed production in 1994, but changed his mind after taking into account the tremendous following he had with the original car. Many, many viewers bought Firebirds in the 1970s just to emulate Jim Rockford.

Reich never missed an episode of the original *Rockford* while growing up in Northern California, so it was a real thrill to be part of the new series. "Everyone really went the extra mile on this one," he adds. "When we got the call that *Rockford* was coming back, and they needed cars, it was really special. I never knew how many *Rockford* fans we had in the shop. Everybody here knew the show, and so when we started throwing it around ('What kind of Firebird was it again?'), I said, 'This is exactly what it is,' and we went with it from there."

Some cars, though, are harder to match than others. This was the case with Rockford's Firebird. "The Espirit was not a car people kept," explains Reich. "Collectors aren't really into those kinds of base Firebirds—they're all into the TransAms. If Jim had chosen a TransAm [for the original show], we could've found those all day long.

"We also ran into trouble because the cars we bought for the new show didn't have the tan interiors like the originals had. They all had various other-colored interiors. We ended up having the upholstery specially made from a company in Kentucky." Reich adds that the Firebirds for the CBS movies had one feature that wasn't available on any of the original models: power windows.

One of the Cinema Vehicles Services Firebirds was showcased at the Peterson Automotive Museum in Los Angeles. Once again, Claridge's company took extra steps to get the car ready for display. "The original cars all had little chrome moldings up by the wheel wells," said Reich. "Today, however, you can only get them for the left front wells—you can't order them for the left rear. So we called the people we deal with at Pontiac Motor Division in Detroit. They happened to have a Firebird from that era on display at the plant. They took it off the display board and air-freighted it out to us. That gives you an idea of how involved this stuff gets sometimes."

One Firebird you'll probably never see on display is the one featured in the first reunion movie, *I Still Love L.A.* That vehicle, as you may recall, spent more time on the shelf than on the streets. "We used a fourth car for that show only," says Reich. "It was a car we'd bought for parts, and had stripped. When we saw the script for that movie, and what they had in mind for Rockford's car, we took the shell of that extra car, painted it to look like the Firebird, and used it on the show."

*   *   *

The original Firebirds were supplied by Vista Group, a company run by Eric Dahlquist, formerly of *Motor Trend* magazine. Dahlquist got to know James Garner quite well back in the days when the actor raced professionally. Vista Group handled the studio car fleet for Pontiac and GMC Truck and Coach. When Garner began production of *The Rockford Files* in 1974, he went to Dahlquist.

Pontiac has remained a prominent member of the Garner family ever since. When *Rockford* resumed production in 1994, for instance, Pontiac presented Garner with a custom-made black jacket with the company logo in appreciation being loyal to Pontiac for so many years. Garner proudly wore the special jacket (one of only two ever made) during an appearance on *The Tonight Show with Jay Leno* that November.

Reich recalls a time in 1995 in which Garner again went the extra mile for Pontiac: "We learned that the woman who was the secretary to John Middlebrook [former head of Pontiac, and current vice president and general manager of vehicle brand marketing and corporate advertising for General Motors] was seriously ill. We knew she was a huge fan of Jim, so we got a copy of *This is Jim Rockford* and asked Jim to autograph it for her. Jim not only signed the book, he made sure everyone on the entire cast and crew of *Rockford* signed the book before he sent it off to her. He went 90 miles more than he had to, and it really lifted her spirits. She made a full recovery."

✳   ✳   ✳

In order to completely recreate the Firebird for the CBS movies, Cinema Vehicle Services studied footage from the original show to determine the exact color of the original car. "We ended up watching the episode with Lauren Bacall ['Lions, Tigers, Monkeys, and Dogs'], where she and Jim drive up to the trailer at the end of the show," said Reich. "We freeze-framed that shot, and that's how we matched the color." *(NOTE. The precise color of Rockford's Firebird is "Medium Camel Tan.")*

✳   ✳   ✳

As every fan of the series knows, Rockford's license plate number was 853 OKG. However, on two occasions from the first season (the episodes "Find Me If You Can" and "Claire") the Firebirds used in those particular shows have a different license plate number: *835* OKG. Clearly, the numbers on the plates of the cars used on two shows were erroneously transposed.

Ironically, years after the series concluded, James Garner put in a request for "853 OKG" as a vanity license plate for his new Mini Cooper 2002 ... only the California Department of Motor Vehicles would not issue it. According to Garner's assistant MaryAnn Rea, the DMV's rule is pretty straightforward: had the car Garner purchased been a vintage model from the era when three-letter/three-numeral license plates were standard, the Department would have no problem issuing "853 OKG" as a vanity plate. But since Garner's car was a brand new model, the Department couldn't allow it.

Still, considering the significance of that particular license plate number (not to mention, the person who was making the request in the first place), you'd think the DMV could have somehow made an exception for the man who played Jim Rockford.

Episode Guide for Third Season

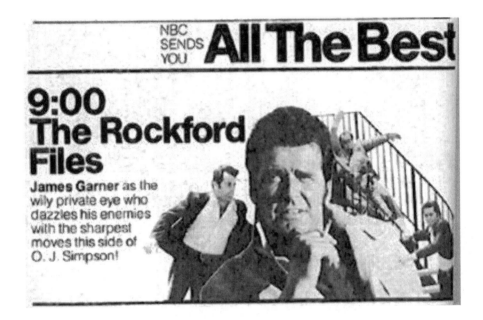

This ad promoting the start of *Rockford*'s third season appeared in newspapers across the country, as well as in the 1976 Fall Preview edition of *TV Guide*. Needless to say, the copywriters would have to rethink the last three lines if this ad were to run today

45. THE FOURTH MAN

Production Number: 45004
Original Air Date: September 24, 1976
Written by: Juanita Bartlett
Directed by: William Wiard

Guest Cast: John McMartin (Timpson Farrell), Sharon Gless (Lori Jenevein), Michael Bell (Stegler), Dianne Harper (Susan), Candace Howerton (Airline Clerk), Barbara Collentine (Maid)

Hi. Just want to put your mind at rest … found your address book in the theater last week. It's in the mail. By the way, Carol's okay—but Linda?

Synopsis. *Rockford's neighbor Lori Jenevein, an airline reservations clerk, becomes the target of a hit man named Timpson Farrell whom she recognizes as a regular passenger on the commuter flight. Farrell fears that Lori will link him to the recent deaths of three witnesses who were scheduled to testify before a Senate committee on organized crime (murders which all took place within the past month in cities serviced by the commuter flight). Jim is also threatened by Farrell, but he has no evidence linking Farrell to either the contract killings or the attempts on Lori's and his own life. Meanwhile, Farrell, who leads a double life as a respectable coin collector, sues Rockford for defamation of character.*

Early in this episode, Rockford temporarily rents a house (with Angel's help) as part of a plan to trap Timpson Farrell on trespassing charges. Rockford waits inside the house, hoping that Farrell will try to break inside, only to find Angel bungle the operation and nearly get them both killed. This sequence sets up one of the most often-remembered lines of the entire series.

ROCKFORD
Angel? What are you doing here?

ANGEL
You wouldn't shoot me for a lousy hundred dollars, would you?

ROCKFORD
I ought to shoot you on general principle!

Rockford Facts

The character "Lori Jenevein" (played by Sharon Gless of *Cagney and Lacey*) was named after sound effects editor Walter Jenevein.

46.   THE ORACLE WORE A CASHMERE SUIT

Production Number: 45006
Original Air Date: October 1, 1976
Written by: David Chase
Directed by: Russ Mayberry

Guest Cast: Robert Webber (Roman Clementi), Robert Walden (Barry Silverstein), Pepe Serna (Ray Ochoa), Terrence O'Connor (Eileen), Diane Sommerfield (Secretary), John Furlong (Detective Casselli), James Hong (Forensic Expert), Bonnie Bartlett (Casey Patterson)

Teddy's Treehouse—you've won our free landscaping services for one full year! We'll mow your lawn, top your trees, moat, seed, fertilize, and feed! Isn't that wonderful?

Synopsis. *Self-appointed "police psychic" Roman Clementi publicly accuses Rockford of withholding evidence that would link the investigator to the disappearance of a record company executive who, along with his girlfriend, vanished two days after Rockford was hired to surveil him. In fact, the grandstanding Clementi planted the rumor in order to make himself look good—and generate publicity for his upcoming book,* Crime and the Third Eye. *But the accusation causes Rockford no end of trouble. When he discovers that the record executive stashed away over $80,000 in cocaine, Rockford becomes the target of a drug-crazed drummer. When the executive is found murdered, Rockford becomes the prime suspect.*

William Daniels was originally cast as Clementi in "The Oracle Wore a Cashmere Suit," but he had to be replaced after injuring himself during the first day of filming. Filling in for Daniels was longtime TV villain Robert Webber, who narrowly avoids the dubious distinction of being the only guest star on *The Rockford Files* to be killed off in the third act in every episode he appeared in. Midway through the episode, Clementi takes what appears to be a fatal plunge down the hill ... only to emerge unscathed moments later.

William Daniels, of course, would return to *The Rockford Files* later this season as the ruthless federal prosecutor in "So Help Me God." In the meantime, his wife Bonnie Bartlett appears in this episode as desk sergeant Casey Patterson. Daniels and Bartlett would make history in 1986 by becoming the first real-life husband-and-wife to win Emmy Awards on the same night. (Daniels and Bartlett won for their roles on *St. Elsewhere*. Their characters on that show were also married to each other.)

Rockford Facts

This episode, the first written by David Chase, was nominated by the Mystery Writers of America for Best Television Episode of the 1976-1977 season. The award, however, went to James J. Sweeney and his script "Requiem for Murder" for *The Streets of San Francisco*.

47.   THE FAMILY HOUR

Production Number: 45002
Original Air Date: October 8, 1976
Written by: Gordon Dawson
Directed by: William Wiard

Guest Cast: Burt Young (Stu Gaily), Ken Swofford (Al Jollett), Kim Richards (Marin Rose Gaily), Paul Koslo (Pittson), Janice Carroll (Duty Clerk), Marge Wakely (Cecil Goss), Adrian Ricard (Receptionist)

Hey, Jim, it's Frank. Me and Ellie's down here for our convention. Can't wait to see you. [Hiccups] We should be over at your place around 1:00 a.m. Bonzai, buddy!

Synopsis. *Jim and Rocky's fishing trip to Baja is interrupted when they discover nine-year-old Marin Rose Gaily sitting outside Jim's trailer. While Rocky takes care of Marin, Jim searches for her father Stu, a convicted drug smuggler on the run from Al Jollett, a crooked DEA agent. Although Jollett claims that Stu stole $100,000 in government front money, Rockford discovers Jollett had been using Stu and another convict named Marty Goss to plant evidence for a series of drug busts that Jollett had rigged in order to pad his arrest record. Goss tried to use a log he'd kept of Jollett's phony operations to negotiate a reduced prison sentence. Instead, Jollett had him killed. Rockford must protect Stu, who has the book, from Jollett and his maniacal agents—one of whom wields a deadly electric cattle prod.*

Listen carefully to the game show and newscast that little Marin Rose watches during the second act of this episode. The game show contestant ("Okay, Mrs. MaryAnn Rea of Sherman Oaks, let's see what you've won ..."), emcee ("So until then, folks, Les Berke saying Good-bye and God Bless") and newscaster ("Ladies and gentlemen, good morning, this is Robert Crawley with the morning news ...") all are named after *Rockford Files* personnel. MaryAnn Rea is James Garner's longtime assistant, Les Berke was the unit production manager (and an occasional writer) on the original series, while Robert Crawley was the show's art director.

48.   FEEDING FRENZY

Production Number: 45007
Original Air Date: October 15, 1976
Teleplay by: Stephen J. Cannell
Story by: Lester William Berke and Donald Gold
Directed by: Russ Mayberry

Guest Cast: Susan Howard (Sandy Blaylock), Eddie Firestone (Charlie Blaylock), Luke Askew (Al), Pepper Martin (Mickey Wanamaker), Richard LePore (Lieutenant Dan Hall), Bill Phipps (Johnny Livingston), George Wyner (Max Steinberg), Roger Aaron Brown (Officer), Carmine Argenziano (Orin Wilson), Jon Cedar (Agent Raval), Joseph Della Sorte (Lucy Carbone), John Dennis Johnston (Grady Northcourt)

Hi, this is the Happy Pet Clinic. Your father gave us this number when he left town. The calico stray had six kittens. Please come get them— today?!?

Synopsis. *Charlie Blaylock, a former oil executive who now runs a bait stand on the pier, embezzled $500,000 from his company three years ago. Charlie has never spent the money, yet his conscience has gnawed at him ever since. Although the statute of limitations on the robbery is about to expire (which means that the police could not arrest him even if he confessed), Charlie hires Rockford to return the money to the company. But when mobsters kidnap Charlie's daughter Sandy, Rockford uses the money to pay the ransom. However, two factors complicate the matter further: (1) Rockford is arrested after learning that the statute of limitations is still valid, and (2) Sandy is kidnapped again, this time by the police lieutenant who worked with the insurance agent who originally investigated the heist.*

The corrupt police lieutenant who kidnaps Sandy Blaylock is played by Richard LePore, a dependable character actor who was a fixture in television for over three decades. LePore appeared in many top-rated network series— and particularly, shows produced by Universal, including *The Virginian*, *The Name of the Game*, *It Takes a Thief*, *Switch* and *B.L. Stryker*. "Richard was never under contract with the studio, *per se*, but because they liked him, and because he was good, he came to be one of those actors that producers at Universal liked to call on," said writer Frankie Montiforte, LePore's godson. "Richard was one of those reliable types who, if you needed an actor to come in for two or three days, he was your guy. He was always good for about three scenes. If you watch the shows he did, you'll notice that he usually played the kind of character who had about three really good scenes. *Rockford* is a perfect example of that.

"One of the things that I always loved about the character Richard played in 'Feeding Frenzy' is that it was so unlike him. Richard was not a screamer. I think I heard him raise his voice, seriously, maybe three or four times in my entire life. So to watch him just go into the kind of rage that he has for Rockford is just absolutely fascinating. Even Richard was surprised at the intensity of it—meaning, that the director [Russ Mayberry] would let him go at it like that. Because usually, whenever someone like Diel or Chapman said 'I'm gonna pull your chain, Rockford,' there was a reason for it: either Rockford was being a smart aleck, or whatever. But with Dan Hall [LePore's character in 'Feeding Frenzy'], there was a genuine hatred for Rockford the likes of which we'd never seen. It was a very powerful, very convincing performance.

"I think he told me that they shot the scene between him and Garner maybe once or twice—which was unusual. A lot of times in television, you'll do take after take after take until the director says you got it right. Not on *Rockford*. They put the camera on Jim, ran through the scene, then put the camera on Richard, ran through the scene, and that was it. Richard was always good for one or two takes. That's why television producers liked him. He would come right in and, boom, give it to you just like that."

Montiforte adds that of all the television episodes LePore did in his career, "Feeding Frenzy" was his favorite. "Richard just loved that character," he said. "He loved the way Hall spun around and went the other way. He enjoyed the scene with Jim, of course, and he also liked working with Joe Santos—because he had that scene in the end where he says to Becker, '*Sergeant, what are you doing, you can't do this to me ...*'"

Other guest stars include Susan Howard, who at the time of this episode had just completed a two-year stint playing Barry Newman's wife in *Petrocelli* (NBC, 1974-1976), an unorthodox legal drama produced by Leonard Katzman. Nearly three years later, in early 1979, Katzman cast Howard as Donna Culver, a character the actress would eventually play for nine seasons on *Dallas* (CBS, 1978-1991).

Rockford Facts

LePore was not only surprised (pleasantly, of course) at the freedom he was given in his interpretation of Hall, he was also surprised that NBC's Standards and Practices did not insist on changing the line in which Hall calls Rockford a "scumbag." "When he did that scene, he thought for sure they would take that out—which makes sense, considering what the word *scumbag* actually means," said Montiforte. "Remember, this was 1976, back in the day when they still clamped down on certain graphic language and obscenities on television. About the only show on TV at the time where you could really get away with politically incorrect slang like that was *All in the Family*. So when Richard watched the broadcast of 'Feeding Frenzy' on NBC, he was as surprised as anyone that they left it in there."

"Feeding Frenzy" features a clever twist of irony at the end of the story. Although the statute of limitations on the robbery has passed, Charlie learns that he must pay as much as $250,000 in back income taxes for the three years in which the $500,000 was in his possession. The episode ends with slow motion footage of Charlie walking along the beach as a cacophony of voices pounds inside his head. The final shot is a freeze frame of Charlie screaming in anguish once he realizes that by clearing his conscience, he has also ruined his life.

49.   DROUGHT AT INDIANHEAD RIVER

Production Number: 45021
Original Air Date: November 5, 1976
Written by: Stephen J. Cannell
Directed by: Lawrence Doheny

Guest Cast: Robert Loggia (Dominic Marcon), Vincent Baggetta (David Marcon), Anthony Carbone (Brad Charlotte), Ronda Copeland (Delores), Nick Georgiad (Danny), Jerome Guardino (Carl Dorado), Laurence Haddon (Dr. Sager), Buddy Foster (Terry), Judith Searle (Norma), George Fisher (Lo-Ball Pete), Nick Dimitri (Sammy)

Jim, thanks for taking little Billy fishing. He had a great time. Turns out he wasn't even really seasick ... Have you ever had chicken pox?

Synopsis. *Angel suddenly becomes the major player in a multi-million dollar real estate deal that serves as the front for a major tax fraud scheme. Angel doesn't realize that his business partners, a trio of tax felons led by Dominic Marcon, plan to kill him, then use the money from the life insurance policy to pay the taxes on the property. Rockford learns about the plot against Angel from Marcon's nephew David—who then retracts what he said. When Rockford continues to investigate, Marcon implicates him in the murder of a prostitute. In order to negotiate a way out of trouble, Rockford and Beth freeze Angel's assets (by having him temporarily committed to a mental institution) so that Jim can make a deal with Marcon.*

Juanita Bartlett recalled the first time she came to appreciate what a gifted performer Stuart Margolin is. "It was an episode of *Nichols* in which Mitchell [the rascally, Angel-like character that Margolin played on that series] asked Nichols to take care of his dog while he was out of town for a few days. The dog was a pit bull named Slump, and it was the ugliest mutt I've ever seen. Reluctantly, Nichols agrees to take care of the dog. When Mitchell returns, he sees that Slump has just fallen in love with Nichols. It's a story of alienation and affection—but it's with the dog! And as a result, Mitchell becomes jealous and angry. It's not as if Nichols set out to [steal the dog's affections from Mitchell]. It was just one of those things that happens.

"That turned out to be a wonderful, wonderful show, and it would take someone special like Stuart to play someone [who is as shifty as Mitchell or Angel] and yet still play it with great conviction."

Somewhere along the line, Bartlett must have also told the story about Nichols and the dog to Stephen J. Cannell and David Chase, because they would later use it themselves in an episode of *Rockford*. As part of the "B" story of "Dwarf in a Helium Hat" (a fourth-season show on which Cannell and Chase collaborated), Rockford saves the life of Romanoff, the dog that belongs to Jay Rockfelt (the insufferable playboy played by John Pleshette). After nursing him back to health, Rockford returns the dog to Jay at the end of the episode. Only Romanoff wants to be with Rockford—a fact that he makes clear to Jay by biting him on the hand!

Rockford Facts

Rockford demonstrates some of his golf prowess in this episode. In real life, James Garner and his brother Jack are both avid golfers. Jack Garner, in fact, has been a member of the Professional Golfers Association for many years.

50.   COULTER CITY WILDCAT

Production Number: 45009
Original Air Date: November 12, 1976
Written by: Don Carlos Dunaway
Directed by: Russ Mayberry

Guest Cast: John Anderson (Gerald O'Malley), Dennis Burkley (Howard), Patricia Stich (Phyllis), Noble Willingham (Claude Orzeck), Jerry Hardin (Walter Link), Sharon Compton (Beehive), Hal Bokar (Second Bidder), John Calvin (First Bidder), Gordon Hurst (Willie), Richard Kennedy (Third Bidder), Ed Deemer (Detective), Norman Blankenship (Russ), Terry Leonard (Driver), Don Nagel (Driver)

Photograph courtesy of TV History Archive
© 1976 Universal City Studios, Inc.

James Garner, Gretchen Corbett and Noah Beery Jr. in "Coulter City Wildcat"

It's Shirley at the Plant and Pot. There's just no easy way to tell you this, Jim—we did everything we could. Your fern died.

Synopsis. *Rocky wins a parcel of land in Kern County in a public auction sponsored by the federal government. Two men pistol-whip Rocky into signing away all oil and mineral rights to the property, even though he'd apparently sold back the land for $2,000 two weeks before. A curious Rockford intervenes, and together with his father, he discovers that Rocky's parcel is worth a fortune in oil, and that the auction was part of a plan to cheat the government out of a valuable oil lease. Rockford determines that Claude Orzeck, who sold Rocky the parcel, organized the scam along with a silent partner. When Orzeck is murdered (presumably by his associate), and the Rockfords are held in suspicion, Jim auctions off Rocky's parcel in order to flush out the identity of the silent partner.*

Usually in series television, an episode begins by displaying the titles and credits for that particular show ("Guest Stars," "Written by," "Directed by," etc.). However, this isn't always the case with *The Rockford Files*. Many episodes (including "Coulter City Wildcat") cut right to the chase, immersing the viewer into the storyline for a good 5-7 minutes before eventually pausing to flash the opening credits. "The way the stories were written, there was often a lot of important exposition at the beginning of the show, and we felt that it might distract the audience if they had to contend with the credits flashing while there was important dialogue or action going on," explained producer Charles Floyd Johnson. "In those instances, we would wait until there was a break in the action, or some kind of transition sequence, where we could put in the credits without taking away from the story."

You can see the influence of a Roy Huggins in this approach. Huggins always advised his writers not to bother with writing "breaks" (i.e., "End of Act I," "End of Act II," etc.) into their teleplays because he believed that if the story was strong, it could be broken anywhere and still carry suspense. Similarly, it isn't necessarily important whether you show the opening credits at the top of the show or several minutes into it. What matters is that the story is good and that the picture works. If flashing the credits at the outset of the episode takes the audience away from the story, then wait until the first available opportunity.

The "delayed credits" became a signature element of *The Rockford Files*, particularly with regard to the episodes that aired after the first season. "It did become a kind of stylistic choice, because we did do that quite a few times, to the point where the audience noticed it," said Johnson. "But it was always our thinking, whenever we'd hold back the opening credits, that if we ran them earlier, we would be taking the audience away from exposition that we felt they didn't need to be distracted from. And I think that, once we'd done it a couple of times, we'd do the same in other shows whenever we felt it worked."

51. SO HELP ME GOD

Production Number: 45020
Original Air Date: November 19, 1976
Written by: Juanita Bartlett
Directed by: Jeannot Szwarc

Guest Cast: William Daniels (Gary Bevins), Sandy Ward (Henshaw), Ted Gehring (Warden Furtell), Jason Wingreen (Clarence Rohrs), Vernon Weddell (Mike Prescott), Robert Raymond Sutton (Carl), John Lupton (Henry Franks), Lieux Dressler (Margaret Raucher), Cliff Carnell (Gordy), John B. Gowans (Doctor), Angelo Gnazzo (Pervis)

Dr. Soter's office. This is the third time you've canceled. Now, you have to have that root canal—a sore foot has nothing to do with your mouth!

Synopsis. *Rockford sees the judicial system at its worst when he is subpoenaed to testify before a federal grand jury investigating the alleged kidnapping of union official Frank Sorvino. Although Rockford doesn't seem to know Sorvino, federal prosecutor Gary Bevins produces evidence of an apparent phone conversation between the two men that occurred on the day of the kidnapping. Rockford invokes the Fifth Amendment when Bevins brings up his prison record, but instead of protection, he finds himself victimized by an abuse of judicial power and ultimately jailed for civil contempt. Jim receives a temporary reprieve when Beth has him freed on a technicality (the subpoena was addressed incorrectly), but he could face continued harassment indefinitely unless he can refute Bevins' evidence. While awaiting a second summons, Rockford investigates the phantom phone call, and deduces that Sorvino not only staged his own kidnapping, but actually hired Jim (while using an alias) to make sure that his accomplices had left town. Meanwhile, when he's called again to testify, Jim's caustic behavior lands him in the federal penitentiary—where Sorvino, whose embezzlement of union funds will become public if the phony kidnapping is exposed, attempts to have Rockford killed.*

Oftentimes there will be two or three stories going on over the course of a one-hour episode. The main story of the episode is known as the "A" story, while the subplot is called the "B" story. Juanita Bartlett had been looking for material around which she could build a "B" story for an episode she'd been developing when David Chase presented her with an item in the April 1976 issue of *The New Yorker* that pertained to the grand jury system. The article, "Annals of Law: Taking the Fifth," discussed a federal law passed under the Nixon Administration that provided for "use immunity," whereby persons who were compelled to testify before the grand jury could later be prosecuted themselves, provided that the government did not base its case on the persons' own testimony. Although the law was widely criticized by legal scholars who recognized its potential for abuse, it was still on the books at the time this episode originally aired in November 1976.

Although Chase suggested that the *New Yorker* article might provide the basis for a possible "B" story, Bartlett had other ideas. "This is more than just a possible subplot," she thought. "This is a story on its own." After drafting "So Help Me God," she asked the local chapters of the American Civil Liberties Union and the American Bar Association to review the script for accuracy. Except for one change (Bartlett had overlooked one step of the procedure), both groups lauded the script for its incisive treatment of the controversial issue.

Nearly thirty years later, "So Help Me God" remains a stellar example of how dramatic television can inform as well as entertain. "We were very proud of that show," said James Garner on *The Ronn Owens Program* in 1996. "It brought to light the inequities of the grand jury system, and they have changed those laws since then. And as I understand, our show had something to do with that."

"So Help Me God" also holds a special place in Garner's heart on two counts. Not only is the show one of his personal favorites, it was also the episode for which he won the Emmy for Best Dramatic Actor for the 1976-1977 season.

Rockford Facts

The foreman Clarence Rohrs (named after film editor George Rohrs) is played by Jason Wingreen, who had previously appeared with Garner and William Daniels in *Marlowe* (1969).

52.   RATTLERS' CLASS OF '63

Production Number: 45018
Original Air Date: November 26, 1976
Written by: David Chase
Directed by: Meta Rosenberg

Guest Cast: James Wainwright (Gene Chechik), Elayne Heilveil (Regine Boyajian), Avery Schreiber (Azie Boyajian), John Durren (Leo Kale), Rudy Ramos (Bobby Boyajian), Sandra Kerns (Robin Seidlitz), Stacy Keach Sr. (Reverend), Stanley Brock (Elliot Deutch), Ed Vasgersian (Hank Boyajian), Gerald Hackney (Jerryl)

Gene's 24-Hour Emergency Plumbing. Your water heater's blown? We'll have somebody out there Tuesday ... Thursday at the latest.

Synopsis. *Angel marries his way into an Armenian family he had fleeced in a variation of the "red barn" con. Angel and another flim-flam artist pretended to purchase an old dumping grounds from the Boyajian brothers, pulled out of the sale, then conned the family into "bribing" them. The scam hits a snag when Angel learns his partner has been killed. Angel thinks the Boyajians are responsible, so he hastily pulls out of the marriage. Meanwhile, when Bobby Boyajian, who had disapproved of the marriage, also turns up dead, the family blames Angel—and, by association, Rockford (the best man at the wedding). In order to get them both out from under, Rockford must determine who killed Bobby Boyajian. He soon finds a connection between both murders and the bodies of two motorcycle gang members who were buried on the dumping grounds in 1963.*

Reportedly Stuart Margolin's favorite episode, "Rattlers' Class of '63" presents Angel in a rare light. For a brief moment at the end of the episode (when he admits to Regine that "he's always scared"), Angel shows us that there may actually a human being tucked inside his exasperating persona. "I like you," he tells Regine. "There's nothing phony there, you understand?"

53.   RETURN TO THE 38th PARALLEL

Production Number: 45003
Original Air Date: December 10, 1976
Written by: Walter Dallenbach
Directed by: Bruce Kessler

Guest Cast: Ned Beatty (Al Brennan), Veronica Hamel (Marcy Brownell), Paul Stevens (John Stabile), Normann Burton (Markel), Robert Karnes (Captain Hulette), James Congdon (Alvin Thomas), Jeff David (Funeral Director), Michael Ebert (Lee Nejman), John Mahon (Lieutenant Hayes), Bart Burns (Fire Department Chief), Chuck Winters (Kevin Lindsay), Tom Stewart (Aarons), Michael Alldridge (Cab Driver), Sam Vlahos (Deck Hand), Ted Noos (Agent)

Tompkins of Guaranty Insurance. About your burglary claim … major loss, all right. Funny, you remembered to file, but you didn't pay your premium!

Synopsis. *Rockford's former Army commander Al Brennan, whose work as an insurance investigator has run aground, wants to become Jim's partner. Meanwhile, a woman wants to hire Rockford to find her missing sister; before Rockford can decline, Brennan accepts the case. Jim soon discovers that his "client" actually works for Brennan, who wants Rockford to lead him to a $3 million Chiang Yin vase that was stolen from a New York museum two years before. Rockford and Brennan compete with each other to recover the vase—and claim the 10% finder's fee.*

Rockford thinks the Chiang Yin vase may be on a train that's already left the station, so he asks Becker to order the train stopped. Becker can't believe Jim is serious. "Oh, come on," he says. "Stop a train with 300 people on it?"

"You're a cop, Dennis," reminds Rockford. "You can stop the whole Ventura Freeway at rush hour if you want to. I've seen it happen."

Becker concedes that point, but he still has a very practical reason for not wanting to stop the train. "[You do that] right here at the station," he tells Rockford, "and you have a great big credibility problem."

Photograph courtesy of TV History Archive
© 1976 Universal City Studios, Inc.

Joe Santos as Dennis Becker

Rockford Facts

Apparently Rockford served under three commanding officers during the Korean War: Al Brennan (according to this episode), Daniel Hart Bowie ("2 into 5. 56 Won't Go"), and "Howling Mad" Smith ("The Hawaiian Headache").

54.   PIECE WORK

Production Number: 45022
Original Air Date: December 17, 1976
Written by: Juanita Bartlett
Directed by: Lawrence Doheny

Guest Cast: Michael Lerner (Murray Rosner), Ned Wilson (Robert Spiker), Simon Scott (Gregory McGill), Ben Frank (Fred Molin), Frank Maxwell (Ciro Lucas), Jack Bannon (Herbert Deane), Michael Mancini (Angie Pictaggi), Deborah Landes (Lily Rosner), Harvey Vernon (Jerry Leedy), Ricky Powell (Junior Rosner)

It's Dr. Soter's office again, regarding that root canal? The doctor's in his office—waiting. He's beginning to dislike you ...

Synopsis. *Hired by an insurance company to investigate a suspicious accident at the Brent Air Health Club, Rockford stumbles onto a gun-running operation masterminded by club owner Ciro Lucas. Although arrested by federal agents (and, later, hassled by Lieutenant Chapman), Rockford finds his biggest threat is Murray Rosner, an incredibly paranoid informant who has been working with the FBI on the Lucas operation for over eight months. Rosner thinks Jim is an undercover agent whom the feds hired in order to circumvent paying Rosner for information. With a major gun shipment imminent (as well as a big score for himself), Rosner perceives Rockford as competition and decides to eliminate him permanently.*

The title "Piece Work" refers to the terms under which informants such as Murray Rosner work for the federal government. Rosner is paid per gun (or per "piece"), meaning that his fee based on the total number of guns the FBI confiscates as a result of his surveillance. The more guns the government collects, the more money Rosner collects—which explains why Rosner chides Rockford at the end of the episode for accepting a mere $5,000 for helping the feds bring down Lucas' operation. Considering how much the feds allocated to pay informants at that time ($10 million a year, according to Rosner), $5,000 is a drop in the bucket.

Rockford Facts

According to this episode, the first name of Officer Billings (Luis Delgado's character) is Jack. However, in the fourth season's "Quickie Nirvana," Becker refers to Billings as "Officer Todd Billings."

Rockford Funnies

Over the hospital intercom, you can hear the page "Dr. Adler, Outside Call Please." This is a reference to Diane Adler, one of the film editors for *The Rockford Files*.

55.   THE TROUBLE WITH WARREN

Production Number: 45008
Original Air Date: December 24, 1976
Written by: Juanita Bartlett
Directed by: Christian I. Nyby II

Guest Cast: Ron Rifkin (Warren Weeks), Paul Jenkins (Garrett Hudson), Joe Maross (Perry Lefcourt), John Dullaghan (Federal Agent Alpine), Tom Bower (Congressman), Ann Randall Stewart (Catherine Lefcourt), M.P. Murphy (Janitor), Jan Stratton (Hilda), Tom Williams (Wedding Guest), Ed Crick (Parking Attendant), Vince Howard (Kleinschmidt), Shirley Anthony (Secretary)

Jimmy, it's Phil in Puerto Rico. This is real important—[Inaudible due to bad phone connection.] He'll pay $20,000. Call me at— [Inaudible due to bad phone connection.]

Synopsis. *Beth implores Rockford to help her intellectually brilliant but socially inept cousin Warren, the prime suspect in the murder of his boss. The case lands Rockford in trouble with the police on a lengthy string of charges. Meanwhile, Jim's personal dislike for his client intensifies. First, he learns that Warren has been withholding information (he'd been fired from his job, plus he was fooling around with an executive's wife). Then, when the executive is also found dead, Rockford finds himself accused of acting as an accessory to that murder. But Rockford sees a way out when he discovers a possible link between the two murders and a Senate committee investigating Warren's company on charges of corporate bribery.*

This episode features Ron Rifkin, who was last seen catching his breath after his character had been chased by Rockford all the way to the foot of the Hoover Dam building in the closing moments of "Roundabout." Best known today as Arvin Sloane on *Alias*, Rifkin won a Tony Award for Best Supporting Actor in the 1998 Broadway revival of *Cabaret*.

Other guest stars include Shirley Anthony, a longtime friend of Juanita Bartlett. Besides this episode, Anthony had roles in two other *Rockford*s written by Bartlett ("Never Send a Boy King to Do a Man's Job" and "Lions, Tigers, Monkeys and Dogs"), as well as all three reunion movies written by Bartlett (*I Still Love L.A., If the Frame Fits ...,* and *Murder and Misdemeanors*). Anthony also had a recurring role in *Scarecrow and Mrs. King*, which Bartlett executive produced for CBS in the early 1980s.

56. THERE'S ONE IN EVERY PORT

Production Number: 45026
Original Air Date: January 7, 1977
Written by: Stephen J. Cannell
Directed by: Meta Rosenberg

Guest Cast: Joan Van Ark (Christina Marks), Howard Duff (Eddie Marks), John Dehner (Judge Lyman), Steve Landesberg (Kenny Hollywood), John Mahon (Victor Sherman), Jack Riley (Adrian Lyman), George Memmoli (Blast Gillette), Michael Delano (Sharkey), Byron Morrow (Ray Fahasateur), Kenneth Tobey (Captain), Stanley Brock (Morris), Christopher Winfield (Waiter), David Pansaris (Ski Mask)

Bum-mer! I called up with some good vibes and some positive energies, and I talk to a robot? Forget you, man!

Synopsis. *Another con artist acquaintance plays Rockford for a chump. Jim is told that Eddie Marks could die of a kidney disorder unless he's treated with a $50,000 dialysis machine. But Eddie has only $10,000, and he doesn't qualify for welfare because of his prison record. Eddie's daughter Christina begs Rockford to raise the money by playing in a highstakes poker game, using her father's money as a stake. Rockford gets into a game run by racketeer Blast Gillette. When three gunmen interrupt the game (and steal the $200,000 kitty), Blast suspects Rockford of orchestrating the robbery and threatens to kill him. When Jim realizes that Eddie and Christina set up the heist, he counters with an elaborate scheme designed to recover the money—and sting Eddie.*

Stephen J. Cannell liked to borrow elements that he remembered from watching *Maverick* (his favorite TV show as a kid) and implement them into *The Rockford Files*. As noted earlier, "The Great Blue Lake Land and Development Company" lifted a central plot device from the classic *Maverick* episode "Shady Deal at Sunny Acres," although the actual story for "Great Blue Lake" was completely different. "There's One in Every Port," however, is very much a modern rendition of "Shady Deal," in that Rockford recruits several con artist acquaintances in order to engineer a sting aimed at the man who had cheated him (just as Maverick had done in the original story). In fact, the episode actually weds elements from two classic *Mavericks*. The setup of this episode calls to mind a *Maverick* story entitled "The Seventh Hand," in which Maverick is staked $10,000 to play poker, then becomes accused of staging a robbery that interrupts the game.

"There's One in Every Port" is a thoroughly entertaining hour featuring typically colorful Cannell characterizations, including Kenny Hollywood (a con artist who is obsessed with washing his hands) and the Lyman brothers (who incessantly bicker with each other). There's also an inspired bit of casting: character actor John Dehner, who played Maverick's foil in "Shady Deal at Sunny Acres," appears as one of Rockford's cronies in this episode. Dehner also appeared with James Garner in the 1971 Western comedy *Support Your Local Gunfighter*.

57.   STICKS AND STONES MAY BREAK YOUR BONES, BUT WATERBURY WILL BURY YOU

Production Number: 45025
Original Air Date: January 14, 1977
Written by: David Chase
Directed by: Jerry London

Guest Cast: Simon Oakland (Vern St. Cloud), Cleavon Little (Billy Merrihew), Val Bisoglio (Marv Potempkin), Anthony Costello (Ted Clair), Robert Riesel (Wass), James Karen (John LaPointe), Jim Storm (Officer), Katherine Charles (Susan Hanrahan), George Pentecost (Carl Colavito), Linda Dano (Gwen Molinaro), Fritzi Burr (Receptionist), Hal Stohl (Guard), Brian Levy (Garth McCreary), Henry Gayle Sanders (Hard Hat)

This is the Department of the Army. Our records show that you are the "Rockford, James" who failed to turn in his service automatic in May 1953. Contact us at once.

Synopsis. *Waterbury Security Systems, one of the largest detective agencies in the world, has been systematically disenfranchising independent private investigators as part of its plan to reduce the market share of small agencies by 20 percent. Two victims, gumshoes Billy Merrihew and Vern St. Cloud, hire Rockford to investigate the matter. (Jim would have been victimized himself had he not been away on vacation.) Rockford realizes that Waterbury means business when he discovers a third private investigator has been murdered.*

David Chase not only helped pave the way for the many awards *The Rockford Files* won after he joined the show in the third season, he also helped established the formula for which the series is arguably best remembered. "*Rockford* is one of the few shows in television that never jumped the shark," said San Francisco radio talk show host Ronn Owens, an avid fan of the series. "There comes a point where most shows fall into a very familiar pattern: the writing is the same, the timing is the same, the show becomes very predictable.

"That was never the case with with *Rockford*. One week, the episode might be fast-paced, and very plot-oriented. The next week, the pace might be slower, and more of a character story. I think that was part of the charm and allure of the show. You didn't always know what to expect … other than the fact that you knew it would be good."

For James Garner, the freshness and unpredictability for which *Rockford* became known is a testament to the writing. "Each writer—Steve, Juanita, and David (who wrote the majority of the shows), they're all a little different," the actor said in 1996 when he appeared on Owens' top-rated talk show on KGO Radio. "David Chase is more literate. Steve Cannell is tricky. And Juanita is just wonderful, and fun, and always good on plot. I think that has a lot to do with it."

Indeed, as Stephen J. Cannell himself explained in 2003 during an interview with C.M. MacDonald, the different approaches each writer took to *Rockford* in many ways reflects their respective styles of writing:

> Juanita wrote very short. If you looked at a Juanita Bartlett script, her lines of dialogue were very short: one or two sentences. And she had this amazing ability in a very few number of words to say so much and be so funny.
>
> David [on the other hand] wrote soliloquies. Some of his speeches went on for half a page.
>
> I was somewhere in the middle of the two of them. My speeches were longer than Juanita's but not as long as David's. And we all wrote kind of differently. David is a very cerebral writer. I'm a very visceral writer. I think Juanita is a visceral writer. But all of us were able to write that show and make it slightly different. All of our minds were slightly different.
>
> I used to read David's stuff and go, *"God, I'm never going to be as good as this guy."* And he told me he used to read my stuff and felt the same way. I just talked to him [recently], and he said, 'I'd think, I've done it, this show has got nowhere to go. Then I'd read one of your scripts and think, *"Oh, there's still some stuff we haven't done. There's still stuff to do on this show."* We had that kind of great respect for one another.

Rockford Familiar Faces

"Sticks and Stones May Break Your Bones, But Waterbury Will Bury You" features James Karen, who later co-starred with James Garner in *First Monday*, the Supreme Court drama that aired for 13 weeks on CBS in the spring of 2002. Karen also appeared in the fifth season *Rockford* episode "The Deuce."

Other guest stars include Simon Oakland (*Toma, Kolchak: The Night Stalker, Baa Baa Black Sheep*), Cleavon Little (*Blazing Saddles*), and daytime soap opera star Anthony Costello (*Ryan's Hope*).

58./59. THE TREES, THE BEES AND T.T. FLOWERS
(Two-Parter)

Production Numbers: 45012/45013
Original Air Dates: January 21 and 28, 1977
Written by: Gordon Dawson
Directed by: Jerry London

Guest Cast: Strother Martin (Thomas Tyler "T.T." Flowers), Alex Rocco (Sherman Royle), Karen Machon (Cathy Royle), Scott Brady (Jack Meullard), Richard Venture (Dr. Ben Crist), Roy Jenson (Winchell), Paul Sylvan (Steve Fisher), Fred Stuthman (Homer Hobson), Jack Stauffer (Brubaker), Bob Hastings (Hank Gidley), Linda Ryan (Maid), Allen Williams (Dr. Norm Fellows), June Whitley Taylor (Nurse), Robert DoQui (SWAT Commander Willis), Tom Rosqui (Tom Brockmeyer), Dave Shelley (Division Commander), Ric Parrott (Attendant), Michael Lawrence (Newscaster), Fred Lerner (Lou), Dave Cass (Morris)

Jimmy, ol' buddy-buddy—it's Angel. You know how they allow you one phone call? Well, this is it.

Hello? He-hello? Hello …? Hello?!?

Synopsis. *Rocky's friend T.T. Flowers, a slightly eccentric beekeeper, is spirited away to a convalescent hospital. Rockford intervenes and discovers a link between the abduction and Sherman Royle, T.T.'s son-in-law. Sherm borrowed heavily from several sources (including land developer Jack Meullard) to cover up a bungled investment scheme which he'd financed with embezzled funds. The ruthless Meullard, who has long coveted T.T.'s property (located next to an apartment complex Meullard owns), fronted Sherm $100,000 in exchange for the land. Sherm convinced his wife Cathy to have T.T. committed. But Cathy doesn't realize that her father is in the hands of diabolical physicians, bankrolled by Meullard, who are feeding T.T. hallucinatory drugs as part of Meullard's scheme to have T.T. declared legally incompetent. Jim breaks T.T. out of the hospital, then scores another victory when a judge strikes down the incompetency ruling. But Rockford knows that Meullard will stop at nothing—not even murder—to win T.T.'s property.*

Photograph courtesy of TV History Archive
© 1976 Universal City Studios, Inc.

Left to right: Alex Rocco, Scott Brady, James Garner, Robert DoQui and Gretchen Corbett in a scene from "The Trees, The Bees and T.T. Flowers"

A few years prior to his guest appearance on *The Rockford Files*, Strother Martin had co-starred with James Garner in "Zachariah," an episode of *Nichols* written by Juanita Bartlett. A mishap occurred during the filming of that show (Garner nearly had his foot broken), but you'd never know it from watching the episode. "That's because Jim is a consummate pro," said Bartlett. "There was a scene in which Jim and Strother are in a hotel room. Strother is supposed to come up to Jim and try to throttle him from behind, but instead Jim flips him over his head and onto the bed. Strother asked Jim, 'What can I do to help?' Jim said, 'Don't help. Let me do everything, and that way, nobody gets hurt. You just relax, and I will see that you go over my head and onto the bed.' Strother said, 'Fine.'

"The cameras started rolling, and the scene began. Jim reached back, grabbed Strother, bent over, flipped him over his head onto the bed—and the bed collapsed! Strother's weight had caused the frame of the bed to break—and it landed on Jim's foot. But you wouldn't have known it, because Jim continued to play out the scene as if nothing had happened. Finally, the director yelled 'Cut!' and Jim said, 'Will somebody get this damned bed off my foot?'

"The piece of the frame that fell on him was sharp. If Jim hadn't been wearing boots, he would be missing the front part of his foot—because there was this huge dent in the toe of his boot! And his foot hurt like hell."

Bartlett, who was on the set to watch the filming of that scene, couldn't believe that Garner didn't say anything about the accident until after the scene had ended. "I went up to Jim," she continued, "and I said, 'My God, you didn't scream, you didn't tell the director to stop. Why didn't you tell him to stop?' And Jim said, 'Because I didn't want to have to do that scene again.'

"And I thought, 'My God, that is complete control. They got it in the one take, and Jim went limping off.'"

Rockford Facts

Joe Santos and Alex Rocco previously appeared together in the 1973 feature film *The Friends of Eddie Coyle*.

Rockford Funnies

Rockford cons his way into examining the admittance sheet at the Horizons Crest residence so that he can find T.T.'s room. Among the names he finds on the list is "William Fannon," which is also the name of the property master on *Rockford*.

This episode also includes references to "Bartlett Oil" (as in writer/producer Juanita Bartlett) and a patient named "Jackson" (cinematographer Andrew Jackson).

60.   THE BECKER CONNECTION

Production Number: 45028
Original Air Date: February 11, 1977
Teleplay by: Juanita Bartlett
Story by: Charles Floyd Johnson and Ted Harris
Directed by: Reza S. Badiyi

Guest Cast: Jack Kelly (Alex Kasajian), Jack Carter (Marty Golden), William Jordan (Officer Andy Dolan), Pat Finley (Peggy Becker), James B. Sikking (John Hickland), Lal Baum (Joey Holbrook), Rita George (Officer Hasty), Helen Schustack (Meter Maid), Warren Munson (Hotel Clerk), Bucklind Beery (Officer Al Mazurski)

Hi. I'm confused—is this Dial-a-Prayer? Well, should I come back when the Reverend is in the office, or what?

Synopsis. *Shortly after receiving a temporary transfer into the narcotics division, Becker finds himself suspended after someone stole heroin from the police property room and planted it in the spare tire of his car. A desperate Becker hires Rockford to find out who framed him. Rockford and Angel hit the streets and locate a dealer named Willie Hatton who may have information concerning "the Becker connection." But the matter becomes worse when Rockford finds Hatton dead and discovers evidence linking Becker to the murder.*

"The Becker Connection" is the first of two episodes featuring Jack Kelly, James Garner's co-star for three seasons on *Maverick*. In fact, Kelly "addresses" Garner in Act IV during their only scene together. When Kasajian (Kelly's character) has Rockford cornered, Kasajian says to Rockford, "We're gonna put you on hold, Slick." For many years, "Slick" has been Garner's nickname.

Jack Kelly also appeared in "Beamer's Last Case," the episode that opened *Rockford's* fourth season.

Rockford Facts

In order to stay active during his suspension, Becker takes a part-time job as a cab driver. In real life, Joe Santos drove a taxi for three years before he became an actor.

61.   JUST ANOTHER POLISH WEDDING

Production Number: 45030
Original Air Date: February 18, 1977
Written by: Stephen J. Cannell
Directed by: William Wiard

Guest Cast: Louis Gossett Jr. (Marcus Hayes), Isaac Hayes (Gandolf Fitch), Pepper Martin (Mel), Walter Brooke (Germanian), Dennis Burkley (Bartender), Anthony Charnota (Dancer), Barney McFadden (Fred Koska), Jack Collins (Finn O'Herlihy), George Skaff (Maitre' D), Melendy Britt (Musicians Union Secretary), Sidney Clute (Funeral Administrator), Raymond Singer (Johnny Goodbye), Alfred Dennis (Mr. Koska), Boni Enton (Hildy Mitchell), Holly Irving (Mrs. Martin), Jeanne LeBouvier (Mrs. Mitchell), Bruce Tuthill (Yacht Club Attendant)

George DeBolt, Malibu Space Watch. Had three sightings last week. You see anything unusual? Your television reception interrupted? Call 555-1313.

Synopsis. *Gandolf Fitch finds that he needs a new line of work, so he decides to become a private investigator and offers his services to Rockford. Jim declines Gandy's offer, proposing instead that Gandy form an alliance with parole officer-turned-private investigator Marcus Hayes. While Marcus and Gandy work out the details of their unlikely partnership, Rockford travels to San Diego, where he tries to locate a missing heir on behalf of the Probate Department. When Gandy mentions the case to Marcus, the opportunistic Hayes also decides to find the heir—so that he can ace Rockford out of the finder's fee.*

Normally, it took six working days to film a one-hour episode of *The Rockford Files.* But there were a few exceptions. In order to accommodate a request from the show's longtime director William Wiard, "Just Another Polish Wedding" was filmed in less than five days. "Bill's daughter was going to be married about the time he was scheduled to direct this show," remembered Juanita Bartlett. "There was going to be a conflict, and so he went to Meta and asked her if she would release him from his commitment to do that show. Meta said, 'Well, we'll certainly look for another director, but it's going to be very difficult to find someone who's available to step in.' Which was true, because you always have to schedule your directors several weeks in advance of when you actually need them.

"Bill said, 'I'll tell you what. If you'll let me do the show in five days, then I can do it.' Meta asked, 'Can you do it in five days?' Bill said, 'Yes, I can.' And he did. He actually did that show in four-and-a-half days."

Considering the complex nature of "Just Another Polish Wedding," that was no mean feat. "That was a very complicated show, because it had so many different things happening," said Bartlett. "You had three stories going on: Rockford's search, Gandy and Marcus' partnership, and the wedding party. But Bill did a wonderful job on that show, because of the way he planned. He was very efficient, yet creative at the same time. He was just wonderful."

Wiard had already directed several episodes of *Rockford* up to that point, so he was very familiar with the exceptionally proficient crew at Cherokee Productions. In addition, Wiard had previously filmed an episode of the show ("Sleight of Hand") in five days, so there was a precedent. Though the task at hand was not easy, the crew came through. "We were the fastest crew at Universal," said Luis Delgado. "We used to have the efficiency experts from the studio come down to our set and try to figure out what made us so efficient, why we did everything so fast, and got into less overtime, than any other show at Universal. And we did that show ['Just Another Polish Wedding'] in five days to show Universal how efficient we were and how fast we were—although we really had to crank that one out."

Needless to say, the studio was impressed by the crew's accomplishment on this episode—so much so, it apparently wanted to put the show on a permanent five-day shooting schedule. But James Garner wouldn't allow it. "Jim said, 'No way. We just did this to show you how efficient we are, and what can be done,'" Delgado continued. "We were all extremely tired after that show. And we stayed with our regular six-day schedule."

Rockford Facts

This episode served as the pilot for *Gabby & Gandy*, a proposed spinoff series featuring Marcus Hayes (Louis Gossett Jr.) and Gandy Fitch (Isaac Hayes). (Gandy calls Marcus "Gabby" throughout the episode because the fast-talking Hayes speaks at a rate of about 75 mph.) Although the chemistry between Gossett and Hayes was promising, NBC passed on the series. Hayes, however, returned to *The Rockford Files* for one more guest appearance in the fourth season ("Second Chance").

62.   NEW LIFE, OLD DRAGONS

Original Air Date: February 25, 1977
Production Number: 45019
Teleplay by: David C. Taylor
Story by: Bernard Rollins and Leroy Robinson
Directed by: Jeannot Szwarc

Guest Cast: Kathleen Nolan (Cathy Hartman), Irene Yah-Ling Sun (Pham Vam Mai), Charles Napier (Mitch Donner), Charles Siebert (Gary Stillman), Luke Askew (Benson Kelly), James Callahan (Lew Hartman), Clyde Kusatsu (Nguyen), Al Stevenson (L.J.), Bruce Tuthill (Officer), Jim Ishida (Pham Vam Vinh), Herb Kayde (Guard), Jay Gerber (Deputy Chief), Robert Phalen (Will Dunning)

It's Pete. Hope you enjoyed using the cabin last week. Only next time, leave the trout in the refrigerator, huh? Not in the cupboard!

Synopsis. *Pham Vam Mai, a Vietnamese refugee, wants Rockford to find her brother Vinh, whom she believes was abducted by a trio of former American soldiers. Although Mai speaks English fluently, she addresses Rockford in pidginese because she doesn't want him to discover the real reason why she hired him—she has smuggled over $500,000 in American government payroll money that her brother and a Vietnamese colonel obtained through the black market during the Vietnam War. In addition to rescuing Vinh from the abductors, Rockford must protect his client from her American sponsor, a treacherous former Army CID agent who also has his sights on the money.*

From the collection of Robert Howe

Rockford's ad in the Yellow Pages, as it appears in the pilot episode

Rockford's ad in the Yellow Pages has changed since we first saw it in the pilot. The ad now features an actual photograph of Rockford, as opposed to the pen-and-ink drawing that appeared in the old version.

According to the new ad, Rockford's state investigator's license number is 9749; he speaks Spanish; and his phone number is 555-2867. (Previous episodes have listed 555-2368 and 555-9000 as his phone number.)

Rockford Familiar Faces

Guest stars include Kathleen Nolan (*The Real McCoys*), who at the time of this episode was the president of the Screen Actors Guild. Nolan was elected president of SAG in 1975, the first woman ever named to that post.

Like Nolan, James Garner was also actively involved in the Screen Actors Guild. During his three terms as a member of the SAG board, he served on the union's television negotiating committee and was twice elected 2nd vice-president.

63/64. TO PROTECT AND SERVE
(Two-Parter)

Production Number: 45027/45029
Original Air Dates: March 11 and 18, 1977
Written by: David Chase
Directed by: William Wiard

Guest Cast: Joyce Van Patten (Lianne Sweeney), Leslie Charleson (Patsy Fossler), Jon Cypher (Michael Kelly), George Loros ("Anthony Boy" Gagglio), Pat Finley (Peggy Becker), Luke Andreas (Syl), James Coleman (Officer Haydu), Charles Parks (Officer Drumm), Jason Ledger (Sergeant Salcedo), Bob Peterson (Bartender), Lou Frizzell (Wes Wesley), Angus Duncan (John Fossler), Bucklind Beery (Officer Mazurski), Douglas Ryan (Deputy), Charles Bateman (First Detective), John Lucarelli (Bowling Alley Customer), Nick Dimitri (Dorsey)

This is Dusty, your father's friend. So you helped me move—that's it? You couldn't call, see if maybe I liked the new place? See if maybe there's some painting to be done?

This is incredible. Do you know last night I had one of my dreams? I dreamed that if I called you, you wouldn't be home—and you're not!

Synopsis. *New York attorney Michael Kelly hires Rockford to locate his fiance Patsy Fossler, who apparently fled to Los Angeles after she abruptly canceled their wedding a few days earlier. After two thugs from the East Coast who are also look- ing for Patsy break into Rockford's trailer and beat him up, Jim tries to quit the case, but Kelly won't let him—in fact, he threatens to kill Rockford if he can't find Patsy within 24 hours. The matter becomes clearer to Rockford once he tracks down Patsy. Kelly represents New York crime lord Joseph Minette, who was recently acquitted of jury tampering charges. Because Kelly told Patsy about many of the Minette family dealings, Minette wants her silenced for his own protection. Rockford must therefore protect Patsy from both his own client and Minette's goons. Complicating the situation: Lianne Sweeney, a meddlesome "police buff" whose efforts to assist the investigation nearly get Rockford and Patsy killed.*

Joyce Van Patten, who plays Lianne Sweeney (the police buff who also runs a shoe concession stand in this episode), is the sister of Dick Van Patten (*Eight is Enough*). For a time in the late 1970s, she was married to Dennis Dugan, the actor who starred in the *Rockford* spinoff, *Richie Brockelman, Private Eye*. Van Patten is also the mother of actress Talia Balsam (*Rocky*), as well as the half-sister of award-winning director Tim Van Patten—one of the primary directors on David Chase's *The Sopranos*. Joyce Van Patten previously acted with James Garner in "Paper Badge," an episode of *Nichols*.

This episode also marks George Loros' first appearance as East Coast mobster "Anthony Boy" Gagglio, the character that David Chase has since said was a prototype for New Jersey mobster Tony Sopranos in *The Sopranos* (HBO, 1999-). Loros, who has a recurring role as Raymond Curto on *The Sopranos*, reprised Anthony Boy in the fifth-season episode "The Man Who Saw the Alligators." Loros also played another tightly-wound bad guy in "The Dog and Pony Show," as well as a good guy in "Only Rock 'n' Roll Will Never Die."

Other guest stars in "To Protect and Serve" include James Coleman (Officer McCabe on *S.W.A.T.*), Jon Cypher (*Hill Street Blues, Major Dad*) and daytime soap icon Leslie Charleson (*General Hospital*).

Rockford Funnies

Early in Part One, Jim and Rocky are watching a football game on television when the announcer remarks, "We haven't seen much action from Price this season." This was probably a reference to Frank Price, then-president of Universal Television.

65. CRACK BACK

Production Number: 45031
Original Air Date: March 25, 1977
Written by: Juanita Bartlett
Directed by: Reza S. Badiyi

Guest Cast: Joseph Mascolo (Gibby), Howard McGillin (Davey Woodhull), John Calvin (Coach Preston Garnett), Sondra Blake (Doreen Carpenter), Conchata Farrell (Ella Mae White), Nick Ferris (Cab Driver), Bo Kaprall (Willie Gunter), Robert Miller Driscoll (Defense Attorney Rosecrans), Norman Bartold (Judge Carroll), Glenn Robards (Doorman), Robert Ward (Reporter No. 1), Bill Woodard (Football Player), Gloria Dixon (Reporter No. 2), Bill Baldwin (Jury Foreman)

This is Dr. Soter. Now, my nurse tells me you've blown four root canal appointments. Well, you're finished in this office!

Synopsis. *Beth hires Jim to find a woman who allegedly could clear her client, pro football player Davey Woodhull, of first degree murder charges. Meanwhile, just as Woodhull's trial begins, Beth is harassed by crank phone calls, stalkings, and a series of sexually explicit gifts sent to her through the mail. When Woodhull's mystery woman is murdered shortly after Rockford locates her, Jim suspects Woodhull of masterminding an insidious scheme that would cover all bets in case he's convicted—by showing that Beth was distracted, Woodhull could appeal on the basis that she could not render an effective defense. Rockford then tries to prove that Woodhull orchestrated the harassment.*

Rockford frequently resorts to phony names and cheap disguises in order to wheedle information out of some of the people he investigates, often using the portable printing press in his car to print up business cards for such ruses. In this episode, we learn that Rockford will sometimes put his father's phone number on the business card he'll leave with his "mark." This makes perfect sense: he can't leave his own phone number, of course, because if he's not at home, his cover would be blown as soon as his answering machine kicks in. (Then again, Rockford could solve that problem by changing his outgoing message every time he uses a phony name. However, as often as he goes through names in the course of an investigation, it wouldn't take long before he finally wore out the machine.)

Rockford Familiar Faces

Guest stars include daytime serial star Joseph Mascolo (*Days of Our Lives*), Sondra Blake (who at the time of this episode was the wife of *Baretta* star Robert Blake), and character actress Conchata Ferrell, who later appeared along with James Garner and Jack Lemmon in the 1996 comedy *My Fellow Americans*.

66.   DIRTY MONEY, BLACK LIGHT

Production Number: 45005
Original Air Date: April 1, 1977
Written by: David C. Taylor
Directed by: Stuart Margolin

Guest Cast: John P. Ryan (Dearborn), Wesley Addy (Agent Steiner), Roger E. Mosley (Electric Larry), Joshua Bryant (Agent Wolf), John Chappell (Blake), Martin Kove (Harry Smick), Victor Argo (Jud Brown), Michael Lane (Tony), Mary Carver (Receptionist), Dick McGarvin (Bank Teller), Craig Wasson (Steve), Edward Knight (Fed), Naomi Grumette (Second Receptionist), Charles Hutchins (Trainer), Dani Heath (Switchboard Operator)

This is Tony. I forgot what I was calling for. Your recording is so boring.
Spike it with some humor, some personality—something!

Synopsis. *Rocky wins an all-expenses-paid trip to Hawaii as part of a contest sponsored by a public relations company that serves as the front for an elaborate money racket. The company uses the addresses of the unsuspecting participants to funnel dirty money back and forth while the prize winners are out of town. Jim, who'd been collecting his father's mail while he was away, stumbles onto the scam when he opens four envelopes addressed to Rocky containing over $44,000 in stolen $100 bills. The complications increase when Angel steals two of the bills in order to repay a debt to loan shark Electric Larry—and promptly gets arrested once he tries to break them.*

Photograph courtesy of TV History Archive
© 1976 Universal City Studios, Inc.

Foreground from left to right: James Garner, Stuart Margolin and Gretchen Corbett

The second of two episodes directed by Stuart Margolin, "Dirty Money, Black Light" features some very effective P.O.V. shots. For example, the sequence where Angel is being questioned by the two federal agents is shot from Angel's perspective: the agents are filmed with the camera tilted slightly upward, as if the viewers are looking at the agents from where Angel is seated. Also, because Angel speaks quickly and acts very nervously throughout this scene, the camera frequently cuts back and forth from one agent to the other.

Guest stars include Roger E. Mosley (*Magnum, p.i..*), Martin Kove (*Cagney and Lacey*), and jazz drummer and longtime L.A. radio personality Dick McGarvin.

Rockford Facts

According to several television reference books, Angel resides at the Hotel Edison. However, the scene in this episode in which Jim and Beth visit Angel's apartment begins with an establishing shot of an apartment building. In the foreground, you can see a sign that clearly reads "Hotel Madison."

Rockford owns an ultra-violet detecting mechanism that enables him to determine whether or not currency is marked.

Fourth Season: 1977–1978

Judging from the numbers, *Rockford*'s fourth season would seem no different than its third. While the series did slip five notches in the overall rankings (from 41st at the end of 1976-1977 to 46th at the end of 1977-1978), its overall average rating (18.3) was not appreciably different from its seasonal average of the third season (18.8). However, as we saw in the case of *Rockford*'s showdown with *Hawaii Five-O*, the raw numbers do not always reflect the entire story. In the case of the fourth season, *Rockford* started on par (averaging a 34 audience share and an 18.8 rating after three weeks), stumbled during the middle (sustaining a 10% loss in viewers from October through December), then finished strong (its audience numbers increasing by 10% in the last two months of the season). *Rockford* also enjoyed its strongest season in three years with regard to the writing, which rivaled that of the outstanding first season in terms of overall quality. At the end of the season, the series reaped an Emmy Award, the Television Academy recognizing *Rockford* as Best Dramatic Series of the year.

Still, it does seem ironic that *Rockford* should win the Emmy in a year when its overall audience numbers were comparatively low—particularly when you consider that in 1974-1975, when the show's popularity (in terms of Nielsen ratings) was at its peak, the series wasn't even nominated. In truth, many factors come into play when it comes to the Emmy Awards. Much depends on which shows are nominated, which particular episodes are sent to the awards panel for consideration, and the makeup of the panel itself. There's also a great deal of lobbying that takes place in order to bring certain shows to the Academy's attention.

"I think it took a while for the Academy to recognize *Rockford* for what it was," said producer Charles Floyd Johnson. "By the time we were nominated, we'd been on four years, and the show had become a staple on Friday nights, and I think it was a matter of where people recognized how clever the show was. I think it kind of got to where [1977-1978] was its year."

Series co-creator Roy Huggins agrees that, while the quality of the fourth season definitely factored into the equation, the series was ultimately recognized for the characteristics it had developed over four years—including the many idiosyncratic characters that reflect the brilliant mind of Stephen J. Cannell. "It was more than just one year was better than the other," said Huggins. "It was a

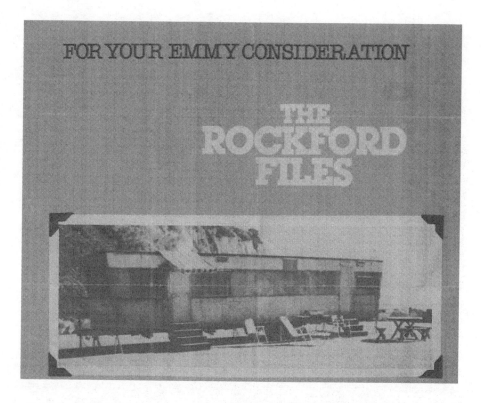

From the collection of Robert Howe

This ad appeared in trade papers prior to the announcement of Emmy nominations

recollection of characters on the Academy's part, and not just the character of Rockford, but all the characters surrounding him: those that Steve created and those that Steve embellished. That's what kept the show going, and I think that's why it ultimately won the Emmy Award."

Another factor to consider was James Garner, who had won the Best Dramatic Actor Emmy for *The Rockford Files* for 1976-1977. While Garner's award in the previous season may not have had any actual bearing on the final selections for 1977-1978, it certainly couldn't have hurt *Rockford*'s chances. "Jim is one of a kind," said supervising producer Jo Swerling. "There's never been anybody like him, and there'll *never be* anybody like him, who has that unique personality that he has, and who has Jim's ability to read wry, ironic, humorous lines. He can do that like nobody else can. You can have another actor do the same role, and the same script, word for word, and it'll be the difference between it being ordinary, or being so good it sparkles."

By all accounts, "Quickie Nirvana" (written by David Chase) was the episode submitted that year to the Academy's Blue Ribbon Panel. A mixture of humor, drama and social satire, the story pairs Rockford with an off-the-wall woman (Valerie Curtin) on a perpetual search for self-enlightenment. In many respects, the episode epitomizes everything about *The Rockford Files*, particularly in the years after Chase joined the show. The humor comes out of Rockford's reactions to Sky's behavior, but never at Sky's expense. Yet the story ends on a somber note, because Sky is still very much a lost soul at the end of the episode.

Rockford's win was something of an upset. Insiders had predicted that the Best Dramatic Series award would go to *Lou Grant*, the *Mary Tyler Moore Show* spinoff starring Edward Asner as the editor of a major Los Angeles newspaper. In fact, Charles Floyd Johnson recalls being as surprised as anyone that *Rockford* won. "Earlier that evening, we (Meta, David, Steve, Juanita and me) were all at Steve's house, getting ready for the awards ceremony," Johnson said. "Steve asked me, 'Do you think we'll win?' And I said, 'Give me a break! It's our fourth year on the air, we've never been nominated before … we're just lucky to be nominated!' And I really believed that. I didn't think at that stage of the game we'd get a win.

"We went to the auditorium that night. And I don't know whether it was a matter of wish fulfillment (in the sense that if I believed it wasn't going to happen, then it wouldn't happen), or that I just didn't want to be disappointed, but I honestly didn't believe we'd win. So when they opened the envelope later that night, and they announced 'The Rockford Files,' I was the most nonplussed person in the world!"

Stephen J. Cannell, Meta Rosenberg, David Chase, and Charles Floyd Johnson all received Emmys on behalf of the show. Only Johnson nearly didn't made it to the podium. The producer was so dumbfounded by the announcement, he could barely move from his seat. "Juanita sat next to me that night," Johnson continued, "and she started punching my arm: 'Charles! Charles, they said your name!' I looked up and I saw that David, Steve and Meta were all standing up on the stage, and I was still sitting in my chair! Juanita kept nudging me, and I finally got out of my chair. From that point on, I was sort of on automatic pilot, because I couldn't believe we had won. It was the strangest feeling. I remember, as I went down the aisle, that Lou Gossett reached out and grabbed my hand, and that I saw Rita Moreno, then Jim Garner. But it was as though I were in this dream. It was a wonderful feeling.

"And I remember that when I had the Emmy in my hand, I thought to myself, 'I know they want to take this back and have it engraved, but I'm never letting it go!'"

The fourth season is also marked by two cosmetic changes, plus another subtle difference in the approach to Rockford's character. The opening title sequence was altered slightly. Inserted among the montage of Garner/Rockford in action are stills of Rockford interacting with Angel (Stuart Margolin), Beth (Gretchen Corbett) and Rocky (Noah Beery); then toward the end of the sequence, two stills of Rockford with Dennis Becker (Joe Santos) are also inserted. The closing title sequence was also changed. During the first three years of the show, a head shot of Jim and Rocky was used as the background against which the closing credits were flashed. However, beginning with the fourth season, and continuing through the end of the series, the closing credits of each episode are flashed against still frames selected from that particular episode.

In addition, for the second consecutive year a new wrinkle is introduced that further distinguishes the Jim Rockford of the "David Chase era" (i.e., the episodes produced after Chase joined the series in 1976) from the character as originally conceived by Roy Huggins. While Rockford never failed to remind his clients that he charged "$200 a day plus expenses," in truth he was more likely to be stiffed than be paid. Beginning in the fourth season, however, Rockford not only gets paid more often than not, in one episode ("The Mayor's Committee from Deer Lick Falls") he even gets paid by a client who technically hadn't even hired him.

Not only that, in one episode ("The House on Willis Avenue") we learn that Rockford has become a "living legend among the private eyes in the L.A. area" on the basis of front-page stories in *The Los Angeles Times* that recognized him for his work in two of his earlier cases: the Fiscal Dynamics fraud scheme ("Profit and Loss") and the trucking operation that he broke with the help of his father ("Gearjammers"). (Rockford's reputation would eventually spread beyond the boundaries of Southern California. A character in the sixth-season episode "Lions, Tigers, Monkeys, and Dogs" refers to him as a "world famous private investigator.") And while the likes of Lieutenant Chapman may still sneer at Rockford, our hero continues to merit the respect of his friends and peers, to the point where some people (like Richie Brockelman and Freddie Beamer) even want to emulate him.

These two nuances further the appeal of Jim Rockford. "You're always looking for ways in which you can enhance your characters, and the series," added Charles Floyd Johnson.

Noteworthy guest stars in *Rockford*'s fourth season include Larry Hagman, Anthony Zerbe, Dionne Warwick, James Whitmore Jr., Gerald McRaney, Carlene Watkins, Ed Nelson, Malachi Throne, Ed Lauter, Gary Crosby, Chuck McCann, Jason Evers, Valerie Curtin, Barbara Babcock, Edward Binns, Charles

Aidman, Richard Sanders, Priscilla Barnes, Jerry Hardin, Larry Linville, Arlene Golonka, Rick Springfield, Stephen Elliott, John Fiedler, Howard Hesseman, Pernell Roberts, and Rita Moreno.

Episode Guide for the Fourth Season

67. BEAMER'S LAST CASE

Production Number: 47509
Original Air Date: September 16, 1977
Teleplay by: Stephen J. Cannell
Story by: Booker Bradshaw and Calvin Kelly
Produced and Directed by: Stephen J. Cannell

Guest Cast: James Whitmore Jr. (Freddie Beamer), Jack Kelly (Ralph Steel), Bibi Besch (Monica Steel), Robert Loggia (Manny Arturez), Cal Bellini (Pedro E. Ramirez), Howard George (Phil "Golf Bag" Moreno), Phil Hoover (Dallas Walker), John Davey (Delivery Man), Paula Victor (Receptionist), Arthur Eisner (Floyd Arturo), Raymond O'Keefe (Tony), Carlene Watkins (Girl on Bus)

Jimmy, this is Angel. Listen, I got this new pad, right over by the Hollywood Freeway, and some friends are coming. Can I borrow your record player?

Photograph courtesy of Photofest
© 1977 Universal City Studios, Inc.

Jim Rockford (James Garner) is not happy about the mess Freddie Beamer (James Whitmore Jr.) made of his life while Rockford was out of town in this scene from "Beamer's Last Case," the episode that launched *Rockford*'s fourth season on NBC

Synopsis. *Rockford returns from an aborted fishing vacation in the Carribean to find that someone has wrecked his car, disturbed his home, used his credit card to purchase several expensive detection devices, and even impersonated him. The culprit: Freddie Beamer, a mechanic at Tony's Body Shop who is also a private detective wannabe. Rockford not only has to clean up the mess Freddie made of his own life, he must also save Beamer's neck after discovering that Beamer stumbled onto a taxicab company owner's plot to sabotage his own business.*

In this episode, writer/director Stephen J. Cannell borrows a concept from the classic *Maverick* episode "The Saga of Waco Williams" by pairing Rockford with a character with a penchant for landing in the middle of situations that Rockford would normally avoid. For example, when the rambunctious Beamer tries to take on the tempestuous Ralph Steel (*Maverick* star Jack Kelly), Rockford acts quickly to break up the fight.

> BEAMER
> I had the situation totally under control. I don't know what you came here for. I don't know what you pulled me that guy off me for—-I could've handled the guy.

> ROCKFORD
> Freddie, let me tell you something. A guy like that can go get a gun and shoot you, me, or both of us!

> BEAMER
> Well, sometimes a private detective's gotta take risks!

> ROCKFORD
> Well, not me—-I make a habit of *avoiding* risks. That's why I've still got a full set of teeth.

This ad promoting the launch of *Rockford*'s fourth season ran in newspapers
nationwide, as well as in the 1977 Fall Preview issue of *TV Guide*

When Beamer insists that he's "not the kind of guy you blow away with a
threat," Rockford simply replies, "Well, I am."

Cannell would return to "Waco Williams" in the fifth season and carry it
one step further by updating the entire episode in the form of "White on White
and Nearly Perfect."

Rockford Felines

Rockford "sort of" has a cat: Valentino, a stray who wanders in and out of
the homes of the trailer park.

68.   TROUBLE IN CHAPTER 17

Production Number: 47508
Original Air Date: September 23, 1977
Written by: Juanita Bartlett
Directed by: William Wiard

Guest Cast: Claudette Nevins (Ann Louise Clement), Ed Nelson (Edgar R. "Bud" Clement), Arthur Roberts (Jack Avery), Donna Bacalla (Jan Avery), Tasha Martell (Marty Bach), Al Checco (Sam), Michael Laurence (Second Reporter), Bob Novarro (Third Reporter), Toni Berrell (Woman), Candace Howerton (Gloria), Mario Machado (First Reporter), Scott Ellsworth (Zinberg), Mike Steele (Lyle Van Houghton), Molly Dodd (Daisy)

[NOTE: The caller is calling from a pet center. You can hear dogs barking in the background.]

Jim, this is Donna. Boy, we've really been swamped today—No, sit!—We should be closing in about—Sit!—I'll meet you at—Oh, get down!

Synopsis. *Author Ann Louise Clement, whose bestseller* Forever Feminine *advocates that "total happiness" for women lies in traditional feminine values, hires Rockford to investigate a series of threats that she believes have been carried out by militant women's liberation groups who resent the widespread acceptance of her book. Rockford soon realizes that he's been sucked into a publicity campaign: Ann Louise and her agent Marty Bach staged the "attacks" in order to generate publicity for the book. He also suspects the author of using him to help her win back her husband Bud, who has been fooling around with his secretary Jan Avery. But the matter turns into a real-life murder mystery when Marty is shot to death in Ann Louise's study.*

The Ann Louise Clement character was based on Marabel Morgan, a Miami housewife and author who attracted a tremendous amount of attention in the mid-1970s by encouraging women to behave in a manner that was decidedly against the feminist movement. Morgan's two books (*Total Woman* and *Total Joy*) suggested that housewives could only find happiness through total submission to their husbands. Among other things, she thought women should try to "put sizzle back into their marriages" by wearing erotic costumes when they welcomed their husbands home from work. Although Morgan herself thought that "a frilly new nightie and heels will probably do the trick," some readers followed her recommendations to the extreme. One woman greeted her husband wearing nothing but Saran Wrap and red ribbon.

Though both books were huge bestsellers, Morgan was soundly panned by critics who found her methods demeaning to women because they ultimately suggested that happiness for women could only be found through deception and manipulation. Others found Morgan's ideology näive and ridiculous.

Juanita Bartlett chose to address the issue constructively by patterning a character after Morgan and placing her in a situation with the always discriminating Rockford. "Rockford was, and is, a no BS guy," explained Bartlett. "So if you put him with someone who is all BS, you're going to have fun. Something will happen (they may connect, or they may clash) that will be interesting and fun to watch. So I wrote 'Trouble in Chapter 17,' because I knew that Rockford would find a character like Marabel Morgan absolutely repulsive. He'd hate everything she stood for, because it was so manipulative. There's no honesty in that kind of a relationship. So, given that backdrop, that episode was particularly fun for me to write."

69.   THE BATTLE OF CANOGA PARK

Production Number: 47505
Original Air Date: September 30, 1977
Written by: Juanita Bartlett
Directed by: Ivan Dixon

Guest Cast: Nora Marlowe (Viola Wenke), Adrienne Marden (Lee Ronstadt), John Dennis Johnston (Hank Schlaeger), Elliott Street (Leonard Wenke), Ted Gehring (Walter Chalco), John Perak (Pete Semple), Brion James (Clamshell), Charles Hallahan (Brian), James Parkes (Records Clerk), Art Koustik (Second Officer), Bruce Tuthill (Bomb Squad Officer)

It's Betty from up the street. I'm phoning all the neighbors because Spotty is loose. If you see him, call me. Oh, don't wear Musk cologne. Leopards have a thing about that ...

Synopsis. *Jim's gun is stolen and used to murder Robert Reidy, a gas station owner and a member of a local paramilitary group. Without an alibi, nor any explanation for what happened to his gun, Rockford becomes the primary suspect in the killing. Although he and Reidy served in the same Korean War outfit, Jim never knew the man, and knows of nothing else that could link him with the murder victim. In fact, there is no link—the gun was stolen by Hank Schlaeger, another member of the paramilitary group, who had no idea that the weapon belonged to Rockford. When Lee Ronstadt, the group's leader, discovers Schlaeger's mistake, she orders the P.I. killed before he uncovers the connection between Reidy and the organization's radical activities.*

"The Battle of Canoga Park" was one of eight episodes directed by Ivan Dixon, whose association with James Garner began with *Nichols* and continued after *Rockford* with *Bret Maverick*. Prior to becoming a director in 1970, Dixon had been a mainstay in films and television as an actor throughout the '60s, including five years as a regular on *Hogan's Heroes*.

Rockford Facts

According to this episode, Rockford belonged to the 5th Regimental Combat Team, 24th Division of the U.S. Army—the same unit to which James Garner was assigned during the Korean War.

70.   SECOND CHANCE

Production Number: 47503
Original Air Date: October 14, 1977
Written by: Gordon Dawson
Directed by: Reza S. Badiyi

Guest Cast: Isaac Hayes (Gandolf Fitch), Dionne Warwick (Theda Best), Malachi Throne (Shapiro), Tony Burton (Joe Moran), Sean Garrison (Lanark), Frank Christi (Brill), Richard Seff (Arnold Rose), Vivi Janiss (Pawn Shop Proprietor), Milton Oberman (Farnum), Janet Day (Secretary), Rudy Diaz (Raoul), Michael J. London (Grizelli)

This is Globe Publications. Our records show you did not return your free volume of The Encyclopedia of Weather, *so we'll be sending you the remaining 29 volumes. You'll be billed accordingly.*

Synopsis. *Gandolf Fitch now works as a bouncer at a dive bar in San Pedro—and he's in love with Theda Best, a onetime singer in Las Vegas who's now on the verge of getting another recording contract. Gandy and Theda's happiness is threatened when she is kidnapped by her ex-husband (and former singing partner) Joe Moran, who was convicted of murder five years earlier. Moran, who also was once involved in a counterfeit poker chip operation, received his parole through "Second Chance," a rehabilitation program that serves as a front for one of its sponsors, a shady industrialist named Shapiro, who arranges for the release of convicts so that he can use them to carry out his criminal operation. Shapiro has Moran kidnap Theda because she knows the whereabouts of the stereo system where Moran has hidden the counterfeiting equipment. Gandy and Rockford try to rescue Theda.*

Photograph courtesy of Photofest
© 1977 Universal City Studios, Inc.

Music legends Isaac Hayes and Dionne Warwick in "Second Chance"

Rockford wants to back out of the case once he and Gandy locate where Shapiro has hidden Theda because he's perfectly willing to let the police handle the matter from that point on. But Gandy begs Rockford to see it through to the end, and even offers Rockford 25% of the percentage he stands to make from Theda's contract with Pacific Records. Although Jim still wants out ("It's too dangerous"), he changes his mind once Gandy addresses him by his real name ("I really need your help, Rockford"). This is the only time in the series that Gandy calls Rockford by his given name.

Rockford Facts

"Second Chance" features Grammy Award-winning vocalist Dionne Warwick in a rare acting appearance. Warwick's hit singles include "Walk on By," "I'll Say a Little Prayer," "I'll Never Love This Way Again," "Do You Know the Way to San Jose?" and "That's What Friends are For."

Other guest stars include veteran character actor and voiceover artist Malachi Throne, whose many TV roles include that of Robert Wagner's boss in *It Takes a Thief* (ABC, 1967-1970), one of several series executive produced by Frank Price for Universal before he became president of the studio's television division.

71.   THE DOG AND PONY SHOW

Production Number: 47502
Original Air Date: October 21, 1977
Written by: David Chase
Directed by: Reza S. Badiyi

Guest Cast: Joanne Nail (Mary Jo Flynn), Ed Lauter (Joseph Bloomberg), Walter Brooke (NIA Agent Simonds), George Loros (Tommy Lorentz), Michael Bell (NIA Agent Krasny), Gary Crosby (Beau), Al Ruscio (Vic Cassell), Howard Honig (Dr. Alan J. Adler), Bill Quinn (Judge Raymond Ordonez), Robert Lussier (Leo), Louisa Moritz (Helen), Dan Barton (Hal), Ken Sidwell (Attendant), Harriet Matthey (Girl)

Jimmy—Lou. You owe me five bucks. Matarozo's average in the '68 Series was .310, not .315. Oh, and—uh, Fran and I are getting divorced.

Synopsis. *Rockford meets his latest client, Mary Jo Flynn, in a group therapy session after a judge convicts him of petty theft and sentences him to undergo psychiatric counseling. (Not surprisingly, it was all Angel's fault: he stole $200 worth of silverware, then tried to haul the stash away in Jim's car.) While she was recently institutionalized for paranoid schizophrenia, Mary Jo met another patient named Joseph Bloomberg, who claimed to be an intelligence agent victimized by the U.S. government. But "Joey B" is really a renowned mob informer who was committed by his own family in order to prevent rival crime factions from killing him. Rockford must protect Mary Jo from Bloomberg's family, who perceive her as a threat because she could leak Joey's location.*

The premise of this episode is that Rockford is hired by a paranoid schizophrenic woman who believes someone is trying to kill her. Ironically, Rockford's client turns out to be the sanest person he meets in the entire story. In the course of the hour Jimbo finds that both the NIA agents and the mobsters (particularly, the hit man Tommy Lorentz) all display more signs of paranoid schizophrenia than his client does.

Guest stars include Gary Crosby (son of legendary crooner Bing Crosby), character actor Ed Lauter (*The Longest Yard, Stephen King's The Golden Years*), and George Loros, who would reprise his signature *Rockford* role of "Anthony Boy" Gagglio in the fifth season episode "The Man Who Saw the Alligators."

72.   REQUIEM FOR A FUNNY BOX

Production Number: 47511
Original Air Date: November 4, 1977
Teleplay by: James S. Crocker
Story by: Burt Prelutsky
Directed by: William Wiard

Guest Cast: Chuck McCann (Kenny Bell), Robert Quarry (Lee Russo), Jason Evers (Paul Sylvan), Judian Rousseau (Maxine), Meredith MacRae (Lori Thompson), Gilbert Green (August Sylvan), Thomas A. Geas (Waiter), Del Hinkley (Poco), Hank Stohl (Officer), Joel Lawrence (Newscaster)

Mr. Rockford? Sue Ellen. Our class is having that great scavenger hunt I told you about—if you're wondering what happened to your trailer door, it's gonna win me first prize!

Synopsis. *Moments before comedian Lee Russo is about to deliver a brand new monologue on national television, his former partner Kenny Bell scoops him by performing the routine first and taking all the credit. Kenny placed a bugging device in Lee's home in order to steal material for his own "funny box" (a catalog of jokes and funny material). But Kenny also stumbled onto a well-kept secret: Lee is a closet homosexual who has been involved with his personal manager Paul Sylvan, whose father is a major crime lord. Later, Kenny's funny box is stolen and held for a $10,000 ransom. Kenny suspects that Russo and Sylvan were behind the theft, so he hires Rockford to make the drop. After discovering Russo dead at the place of exchange, Jim finds himself arrested on suspicion of murder. Rockford explains that he was hired to retrieve Kenny's funny box, but when the police question Kenny, the comedian denies the entire story.*

At the beginning of the episode, Rocky is extremely excited to be part of the audience at a live television show. In real life, of course, the man who played him was quite at home in front of a camera. Noah Beery Jr. came from a family of actors—in fact, many of his early roles were in action serials that were filmed at Universal Studios, where *The Rockford Files* was produced. Beery once said, "I feel as though I'd been born [at Universal]."

Beery also once told *TV Guide* that of all the films he made in his career, *Red River* was his favorite because of his love for the Old West. "Working on that picture was like living in the West, like really being on that cattle drive," he explained. "I could have stayed on that picture forever."

Rockford Facts

"Requiem for a Funny Box" was based on a story by Burt Prelutsky, the award-winning humor columnist for the *Los Angeles Times* who also penned episodes of *M*A*S*H*, *The Mary Tyler Moore Show*, and other series in the '70s and '80s. A few months before this episode aired, Prelutsky's profile of *Rockford* star Joe Santos was published in the August 27, 1977 edition of *TV Guide*.

73.   QUICKIE NIRVANA

Production Number: 47513
Original Air Date: November 11, 1977
Written by: David Chase
Directed by: Meta Rosenberg

Guest Cast: Valerie Curtin (Sky Aquarian), Kenneth Gilman (Alan Bayliss), Quinn Redecker (Gordon Borchers), Dick Anthony Williams (Maceo Prentiss), Larry Cook (Dijon), Patricia Pearce (Girl at Ashram), Carl Crudup (Eddie McBrare), Elta Lake (Ann), Aesop Aquarian (Cook), Michael Grandcolas (Panhandler), Dan Magiera (Conga Drummer)

Hey, I saw your ad in the classified—three African goats for sale. I keep calling. All I get is a machine. Is that a typo in the paper, or what?

Synopsis. *Rockford becomes embroiled in the perils and anxieties of Sky Aquarian (real name: Jane Patton), a 40-year-old waif on a perpetual search for personal fulfillment. Sky's failure to deliver an envelope for her boss, attorney Alan Bayliss, may prove fatal. The envelope contained $30,000 in hush money intended for a witness who can link Bayliss' client, recording star Maceo Prentiss, to the murder of musician Joe Vivyan. Rockford returns the envelope to Bayliss—without realizing that someone had stolen the money. When he learns that Sky had told her "consciousness guru" Gordon Borchers about the $30,000, Jim suspects that Borchers took the money and ran. Meanwhile, an impulsive Maceo decides that without the money, his only option is killing the witness—as well as Rockford and Sky.*

Part of the fun of "Quickie Nirvana" lies in watching Rockford's (and James Garner's) reactions whenever Sky begins to speak in tongues—that is to say, sing the praises of whatever new age ideology she happens to be into at the moment. "I'm not into structured living or accumulated things," she tells Rockford. "I'm into my consciousness."

"Consciousness!?" retorts Rockford. "You're practically unconscious 24 hours a day."

Sky is played by Valerie Curtin, the cousin of *Saturday Night Live* alumnus Jane Curtin, and the wife of Academy Award-winning director Barry Levinson (*Rain Man, Wag the Dog*). In 1979, Curtin and Levinson co-wrote the courtroom satire ... *And Justice For All* and received an Oscar nomination for Best Original Screenplay.

Rockford Facts

Becker's police handle is "1Y9."

74.   IRVING THE EXPLAINER

Production Number: 47507
Original Air Date: November 18, 1977
Written by: David Chase
Directed by: James Coburn

Guest Cast: Barbara Babcock (Katarina Korper), Paul Stewart (Buddy Richards), Maurice Marsac (Chief Inspector Jeneau), Irene Tsu (Daphne Ishawahara), Robert Etienne (Inspector Mage), Peter Von Zernick (Ruprecht), Byron Morrow (Irving), Lester Fletcher (Gertler), Brooke Palance (Gilda), Alex Rodine (Willie Schindler), Shep Sanders (Desk Clerk)

So you put your machine on at night, huh? Just because I call you at 3:00 a.m.? You know how bad my insomnia is! Thanks a lot, Jim.

Synopsis. *A woman who is apparently writing a biography of controversial film director Alvah Korper hires Rockford to help her research the book. Rockford doesn't realize that his client is really Korper's daughter Katarina, who hopes that the private investigator will lead her to a priceless painting by 17th-century artist Antoine Watteau that Alvah Korper allegedly purchased and hid during the 1940s. Rockford soon finds himself thrust into a convoluted mess involving French police officers and German spies (both of whom also want to find the painting) and the long unsolved murder of Korper's wife, which may hold the key to the entire puzzle.*

Though originally conceived as a modern-day Bret Maverick, Jim Rockford is also steeped in the tradition of literary gumshoes originated by Dashiell Hammett and Raymond Chandler. Series co-creator Roy Huggins was certainly well versed in the genre, having penned three mystery novels in the Chandler tradition before moving into film and television. Huggins' first novel, *The Double Take* (1946), introduced Stu Bailey, the Los Angeles private eye that the writer/producer would later bring to television in *77 Sunset Strip* (ABC, 1958-1964), the popular private eye series created by Huggins for Warner Bros. Television.

Given the character's literary roots, some fans of the genre consider Jim Rockford to be the quintessential L.A. private eye. That being the case, one could argue that "Irving the Explainer" is the quintessential L.A. private eye story. "Out of all the episodes in *The Rockford Files*, 'Irving the Explainer' comes the closest to capturing not only the Chandler style, but also the flavor of old L.A.," said writer and *Rockford* fan Frankie Montiforte. "You're dealing with Hollywood in the '40s, you're dealing with corruption, you're even dealing with Nazis—I mean, once you throw Nazis into the mix, it doesn't get much bigger than that.

"Granted, 'Irving the Explainer' is a very talky script. There's not a lot of detective work going on—it's mostly people telling stories, with Rockford going from one person to another, to another, and so on. But once you get into the unsolved murder of Alvah Korper's wife, and the Watteau, and how everyone says that Korper was this crazy director, you can't help but think of the old Black Dahlia case from the 1940s." *NOTE: The Black Dahlia case refers to the death of Elizabeth Short, a 22-year-old aspiring actress whose mutilated body was found in a vacant lot near Hollywood in January 1947. One of the great unsolved mysteries of the 20th century, the Black Dahlia case has inspired several books (including the novel* The Black Dahlia *by James Ellroy), as well as four films—including an episode of* Hunter *produced by Roy Huggins in 1988 to commemorate the 41st anniversary of the murder.*

Stylistically, "Irving the Explainer" also has an unmistakable "old Hollywood" vibe to it. For one, the episode brims with elements of *film noir*, the dark, gritty genre of film that was very popular in the '40s, and which also had a permeating effect on television detective series in the '50s and '60s.

"Even though it was shot in color (which is not a trademark of *film noir*), [director James] Coburn and [writer/producer David] Chase wisely used night shots to darken the tone and heighten the tensions whenever possible to convey a mysterious old L.A. atmosphere—that is to say, the *noir* perspective, which is indicative of the genre," Montiforte adds. "We see this, among other places, (1) in the scene where the Nazis first menace Rockford in a vacant and under-lit weight room, (2) in the darkened bowels of the old L.A. police station, where Rockford and Becker dig into the long forgotten murder of Julio Sanchez amid evidence boxes of the city's unsolved crimes of yore, (3) the scene in which Rockford finds Buddy Richards shot and dying in his lonely valley office late at night, the man's thoughts adrift of a bygone era minutes before 'the big sleep'—which, of course, was also the title of Chandler's first novel, which introduced Philip Marlowe, (4) the sequence in which the Nazis kidnap Rockford at gunpoint in a dead-of-night fog-induced haze, and (5) the subsequence sequence at the cemetery.

"Then you have the inspired casting of Paul Stewart as Buddy Richards, Alvah Korper's longtime assistant director. Paul Stewart was in *Citizen Kane*, he was part of the old Orson Welles Mercury Theater of players, plus he appeared in many classic *noir* films of the era. Paul Stewart also played Kirk Douglas' best friend in *The Bad and the Beautiful* (1952), which many consider to be one of the finest movies ever made about movies and filmmaking. So to watch Paul Stewart, 25 years later, playing the friend of this crazy director in 'Irving the Explainer,' you know there's a connection there. You also have a reference to Benedict Canyon Drive, which is the scene of yet another famous unsolved Hollywood mystery [the death of actor George Reeves]. They even shot it at one of those old-style mansions up in the Hollywood hills. Put it all together, and you have the quintessential L.A. private eye story. I think that's why the episode resonates so much with me."

In addition to being memorable, "Irving the Explainer" also spawned one of the more interesting urban legends pertaining to *The Rockford Files*. One television reference book claims that NBC refused to broadcast the episode in 1977 because the storyline concerned Nazis. However, a look at the newspaper listings from November 18, 1977 clearly indicates that "Irving the Explainer" aired that night as scheduled. Producers Charles Floyd Johnson and Juanita Bartlett further dispelled this claim. All 118 episodes produced for the original series were broadcast on NBC without incident.

Rockford Facts

"Irving the Explainer" was the first and only directorial effort by distinguished actor James Coburn, who won the Oscar for Best Supporting Actor as Nick Nolte's alcoholic father in *Affliction* (1997). A versatile performer throughout his career, Coburn starred with James Garner in three films: *The Great Escape* (1963), *The Americanization of Emily* (1964), and the motion picture version of *Maverick* (1994).

Paul Stewart was also among the actors originally considered to play Joseph Rockford in the *Rockford Files* pilot. Other guest stars include Irene Tsu (*Flower Drum Song*) and Barbara Babcock, the future *Dallas* and *Hill Street Blues* star who would also appear with James Garner in *Space Cowboys* (2000).

75. THE MAYOR'S COMMITTEE FROM DEER LICK FALLS

Production Number: 47506
Original Air Date: November 25, 1977
Written by: William R. Stratton
Directed by: Ivan Dixon

Guest Cast: Edward Binns (Everett Benson), Richard O'Brien (Art Kelso), Charles Aidman (Noah Deitweiler), Priscilla Barnes (Lauren Ingeborg), Jerry Hardin (Knute Jacobs), Clark Howat (Mr. Rankin), Richard Sanders (Samuel Rooney), Fritzi Burr (Miss Hornick), Ian Sander (Christian), David Rupprecht (David)

Jim, this is Manny down at Ralph's Bar. Some guy named Angel Martin just ran up a 50-buck bar tab, then he wants to charge it to you. You gonna pay it?

Synopsis. *Four eccentric businessmen from Deer Lick Falls, Michigan hire Rockford to help them purchase a used fire engine on behalf of their town's mayor. Rockford soon discovers his clients have a much more horrifying proposal in mind: they offer him $20,000 to arrange for the murder of actress Lauren Ingeborg (the niece of one of them), who has threatened to report them to the IRS after she uncovered their scheme to pocket over $750,000 in falsified tax deductions. The businessmen retaliate viciously after Rockford reports them to the police: they not only deny the charges, they also arrange to have Jim's private investigator's license suspended. In order to clear his name, Rockford must find Lauren and get her in touch with the local branch of the IRS before the mayor's committee has her killed.*

The fictitious locale of "Deer Lick Falls" made its way into at least one other Stephen J. Cannell series. The character played by Connie Sellecca in *The Greatest American Hero* (ABC, 1981-1983) also had a father who was the mayor of Deer Lick Falls ... only that town was located in Minnesota.

76.   HOTEL OF FEAR

Production Number: 47514
Original Air Date: December 2, 1977
Written by: Juanita Bartlett
Directed by: Russ Mayberry

Guest Cast: Gerald McRaney (D.A. John Pleasance), Frank DiKova (Nova), Vincent Baggetta (Murray Riddle), Madison Arnold (Del Kane), Eugene Peterson (Louie Gaedel), Barry Atwater (Roach), Barbra Rae (Teddy), Fred Carney (Howe), Stephen Coit (Thompson Welles), James Whitworth (Krauss), Rene Djon (Waiter), Peter Forster (Judge Bertram Hovis), Sal Acquisto (Bailiff)

Hey, am I too late for those African goats? Haven't got the whole $300 in cash, but, like, I got a lot of homemade cheese. Maybe we can work something out ...

Synopsis. *Del Kane, a syndicate hit man from New Jersey, was hired to kill a bookie named Gaedel, but the contract was canceled at the last minute. However, Kane, a decidedly loose cannon, decided he had to kill someone in order to save face, so he shot a prostitute named Muriel Nafac. Angel witnessed the murder, and later agrees to testify against Kane at a preliminary hearing in exchange for non-stop police protection. But when the D.A. fails to present a prima facie case against Kane, the killer is set free—and immediately goes after Angel.*

This episode features Gerald McRaney, a frequent guest star in television throughout the '70s before becoming a star in his own right in the '80s, first in the offbeat detective series *Simon & Simon* (CBS, 1981-1988), then in the family comedy *Major Dad* (CBS, 1989-1993). Often cast as a villain early in his career, McRaney holds the distinction of being the last guest star to have a face-to-face shootout with Marshal Matt Dillon (James Arness) in the long-running Western *Gunsmoke* (CBS, 1955-1975).

Rockford Facts

According to this episode, Angel's address is 21150 Sierra Bonita, Apartment 202, in Los Angeles. Also according to this episode, fear makes Angel hungry, which accounts for why he is constantly eating throughout this story.

77.   FORCED RETIREMENT

Production Number: 47512
Original Air Date: December 9, 1977
Written by: William R. Stratton
Directed by: Alexander Singer

Guest Cast: Larry Hagman (Richard Lessing), Margaret Impert (Susan Kenniston), Denny Miller (Chris Jenks), Ron Masak (Virgil Cheski), William Joyce (Harcourt), Conrad Bachmann (Rundstedt), Derek Murcott (Maitre' D), John Davey (Sergeant Jacobson), Doug Hale (Restaurant Manager), Bill Hart (Benish)

Hi, there. If you're interested in selling your product via computerized telephone sales, stay on the line, and one of our representatives will speak with you.

Synopsis. *Beth asks Jim to investigate the Minerva project, a highly speculative off-shore drilling venture whose investors include Beth's boss. Beth's concerns stem from her relationship with the project's engineer (longtime college rival Susan Kenniston), but they intensify considerably, first after her apartment is broken into, then after an attempt is made on her life. Meanwhile, Rockford becomes curious after discovering that Richard Lessing, the primary investor, has a shaky credit history—and a string of businesses that all folded after the CEO died under accidental circumstances. After Chris Jenks, the president of Minerva, dies in a plane crash, Jim deduces that Lessing manufactured the accident in order to collect the insurance money. When Rockford learns that Lessing also took out a life insurance policy on Susan, he tries to prevent another fatal accident from happening.*

"Forced Retirement" marks the first appearance of Jimmy Joe Meeker, the Oklahoma oilman who's "smoother than oil on a blister." Rockford adopts this alter-ego on several occasions over the course of the remainder of the series. In many ways, "Jimmy Joe" resembles the Maverick character. Not only does Rockford as Meeker dress in Western duds and wear a Stetson pushed back (very much like the way in which Maverick wore his hat), he also speaks in folksy aphorisms, such as "When you're looking at a man right in the eye, it's hard to get your hand in his wallet."

As a running gag in this episode, Richard Lessing (guest star Larry Hagman) keeps addressing Rockford/Meeker as "Joe Jimmy" instead of as "Jimmy Joe." Rockford, in turn, counters by sardonically calling Lessing "Dick."

Photograph courtesy of TV History Archive
© 1977 Universal City Studios, Inc.

Rockford as Jimmy Joe Meeker

One month after "Forced Retirement" aired, Larry Hagman traveled to Dallas, Texas to commence filming on the five-part pilot that would eventually launch the long run of *Dallas* (CBS, 1978-1991). The character he plays in this episode, Richard Lessing, was one in a series of less than scrupulous roles

Hagman played in films and on television in the four years leading up to *Dallas* that helped shape his portrayal of J.R. Ewing. "I couldn't have been more ready to step into J.R.'s boots," Hagman wrote in his autobiography *Hello Darlin'* (Simon & Schuster, 2001). "I'd been working on his character for years, particularly in *Stardust* [a 1974 feature in which he played a J.R.-like business manager named Porter Lee Austin]."

Hagman, by the way, once shared a role with James Garner. In 1973, Warner Bros. decided to develop a TV pilot based on *Skin Game* (1971), a satire of the Old West in which Garner and Lou Gossett played con artists who exploit slave traders in the years before the Civil War. Gossett agreed to reprise his role for television, but Garner was unavailable because of his commitment to another pilot: *The Rockford Files*. Producer/director Burt Kennedy hired Hagman to take over for Garner for the 90-minute pilot, which aired on CBS in March 1974 under the title *Sidekicks*. Though Hagman's efforts were well received by critics, *Sidekicks* was not picked up as a series.

Four years later, of course, Hagman began his 13-year run on CBS as J.R. on *Dallas*.

Rockford Facts

In this episode, Beth decides to quit her job at Harcourt & Lowe and start her own practice. Because she can't raid the client list at her old law firm, Beth is concerned whether she can develop enough of a client base to survive as a sole practitioner.

Rockford tries to encourage her. "Well, you've always got me as a client."

"Thanks, Jim," replies Beth, "but I mean *paying* clients."

Apparently, Beth became quite busy after this episode. Aside from a brief appearance in "The Queen of Peru," it would be almost 20 years before we ever saw her again. By the time she came back into Rockford's life (in the 1996 reunion movie *If the Frame Fits …*), she was not only a success as a lawyer, she had also written *The Brief*, a hugely successful legal thriller that was at the top of the *New York Times* best seller list for over 19 months.

78. THE QUEEN OF PERU

Production Number: 47519
Original Air Date: December 16, 1977
Written by: David Chase
Directed by: Meta Rosenberg

Guest Cast: George Wyner (Stephen Kalifer), Ken Swofford (Karl Wronko), Christopher Cary (Ginger Townsend), Joe E. Tata (Mike Trevino), Luke Andreas (Lou Trevino), Hunter Von Leer (Skip), Jennifer Markes (Shareen Wronko), Michael Morgan (Sean Wronko), Susan Davis (Dot Wronko), Paul Cavonia (Donnie B. Waugh), Tara Buckman (Girl)

Photograph courtesy of TV History Archive
© 1977 Universal City Studios, Inc.

Left to right: Noah Beery, Gretchen Corbett and James Garner in a scene from "The Queen of Peru," the episode that marked Corbett's final appearance as Beth Davenport in the original series

Jim, it's Grace at the bank. I checked your Christmas Club Account.
You don't have $500. You have $50. Sorry ... computer foulup.

Synopsis. *An insurance company hires Rockford to assist in the recovery of a stolen diamond worth over $1 million. Rockford and insurance agent Stephen Kalifer deliver the ransom money to Donnie Waugh and Mike Trevino (two of the thieves), but learn that Waugh hid the diamond inside the ashes of Rockford's barbecue grill. Jim returns home, only there's no grill: it was inadvertently stolen by the Wronkos, a family from Indiana who had spent the night on the beach near his trailer. When Waugh clubs Kalifer and runs off with the money, Rockford must recover both the diamond and the ransom. Complicating the matter: Ginger Townsend, the mastermind of the theft, who wants the diamond back (he was doublecrossed by Waugh and Trevino); and the Wronkos themselves, who kept the grill, but lost the diamond (without realizing it) after they emptied the ashes at a roadside dumping grounds.*

Christopher Cary, who along with Ken Swofford would also appear in the sixth season episode "The Hawaiian Headache,"previously appeared with James Garner in *Marlowe* (1969).

This episode also features character actor George Wyner, who co-starred with Garner in the short-lived series *Man of the People* (NBC, 1991).

Rockford Facts

Gretchen Corbett appears briefly as Beth Davenport, the character's final appearance in the original series. The circumstances surrounding Corbett's departure from *Rockford* are discussed in detail in our examination of the fifth season.

79.   A DEADLY MAZE

Production Number: 47521
Original Air Date: December 23, 1977
Written by: Juanita Bartlett
Directed by: William Wiard

Guest Cast: Larry Linville (Dr. Eric Von Albach), Corinne Michaels (Tracy Marquette), J. Pat O'Malley (Billy Baines), Lance LeGault (Phil D'Agosto), Johnny Seven (George), Cliff Carnell (Max Savatgy), Jack Collins (Victor Kreski), John McKinney (Nick Commandini), Ken Anderson (Tod Posner), Gail Landry (Student Receptionist)

Hey, Jimmy, I tried to catch you before you left. Hey, buddy, I was wrong—you know that rally in Mexico? That was yesterday.

Synopsis. *Facing a serious cash flow stoppage, Rockford agrees to find a man's missing wife—a case he'd decline under normal circumstances. Jim doesn't realize that his client, Eric Von Albach, is a behavioral scientist who is using him as a guinea pig in a government-funded study to determine how monetary reinforcement influences certain people's ability to complete their work under stress. The "missing wife" case was part of the charade Von Albach concocted in order to measure Rockford's reactions. The experiment hits a snag, however, when the woman Von Albach hired to play his wife is later found murdered.*

Larry Linville was an inspired choice to play the cold, calculating, eccentric and ever scientific Professor Von Albach. At the time of this episode, Linville had just completed his five-year stint as Major Frank Burns on *M*A*S*H*.

Rockford Facts

Juanita Bartlett's "A Deadly Maze" was one of three scripts nominated by the Mystery Writers of America for the Edgar Allan Poe Award for Best Television Episode of the 1977-1978 season. The Edgar, however, went to "The Thighbone is Connected to the Knee Bone," an episode of *Quincy* written by Tony Lawrence and Lou Shaw.

80.   THE ATTRACTIVE NUISANCE

Production Number: 47520
Original Air Date: January 6, 1978
Written by: Stephen J. Cannell
Directed by: Dana Elcar

Guest Cast: Victor Jory (Eddie LaSalle), Ken Lynch (Vince Whitehead), Dick Balduzzi (Don Silver), Hunter Von Leer (Skip Speece), Rudy Bond (Bennie), John Morgan Evans (Vinnie), Jess Nadelman (Bruce Weinstock), Jeanne Fitzsimmons (Joy Silver), Joey Tornatore (Sid), Paul Sorenson (Inspector Claybourn), Jerome Guardino (Hank), Joseph Della Sorte (Dave Young), Will Gill Jr. (FBI Agent), Anne Gee Byrd (Woman on the Beach), Richard Doyle (Paramedic)

Jimmy Scott? This is Aunt Bea from Tulsa. Cousin Randy just gradu-ated high school and wants to be a movie producer. Now, you live out in Hollywood—you just do something!

Synopsis. *Rocky opens a truckstop diner with a man named Vince Whitehead. Neither Jim nor Rocky realize that Whitehead, a onetime major mob figure, is using the garage located behind the restaurant to market stolen auto parts. Jim soon discovers that he and Rocky have been under the surveillance of Eddie LaSalle, a retired FBI agent who has long been obsessed with apprehending Whitehead—the man who murdered his partner over 40 years ago. Meanwhile, Rockford finds himself sued by a man hired by LaSalle hired to bug his home. The man fell off the roof of Jim's trailer after planting an electronic bugging device.*

"The Attractive Nuisance" is the second of two episodes this season in which Rockford demonstrates his prowess handling his father's CB (citizens band) radio, the popular fixture among truckers and radio buffs in the late '70s. Though Jim seemed very familiar with CB lingo in "The Queen of Peru" (the episode filmed immediately before this one), clearly there were some CB terms even he hadn't heard of. "Steak on the grill," for example, is trucker talk for "I just ran into a cow," while "I've got the hammer down" means "I don't have time to talk."

Rockford Facts

According to this episode, Rockford's middle name is Scott, which means that the character's full name (James Scott Rockford) is similar to the given name of the man who plays him (James Scott Bumgarner).

81.   THE GANG AT DON'S DRIVE-IN

Production Number: 47516
Original Air Date: January 13, 1978
Written by: James S. Crocker
Directed by: Harry Falk

Guest Cast: Anthony Zerbe (Jackson Skowron), Arlene Golonka (Jeanne Rosenthal), Lawrence Casey (Bob Atcheson), Mills Watson (Stan Collier), Dick Bakalyan (Porter), Elaine Princi (JoAnn), Connie Sawyer (Mrs. Fornechefski), Jordan Rhodes (Dr. Kozoll), Paul Pepper (Don Brakeman Jr.), Al Rossi (Fred Stassi), Fredd Wayne (Curtis Meyer), Chuck Hicks (Walton Hettie), Lynn Hurst (Reporter)

Jim, I have finally finished 12 long years of psychotherapy and I am now able to tell you just what I think of you—would you please call me?

Synopsis. *Author Jackson Skowron, whose career has run aground in the 20 years since his only success (the bestselling novel* Free Fall to Ecstasy*), hires his old friend Rockford to help him research his new book on the John C. Fremont High School graduating class of 1962. Rockford doesn't realize that Jack has discovered that onetime classmate Bob Atcheson, whose powerful family owns the* Los Angeles Tribune *newspaper, accidentally killed young Nancy Fornechefski, then covered up the homicide with the help of two other classmates. If Jack can prove that Fornechefski was murdered, he'll have the makings of a guaranteed best seller. But Jack may never live to write that book because Atcheson will resort to anything, including murder, to protect his secret.*

The running gag of this episode: while everyone has heard of *Free Fall to Ecstacy* (a 1,040-page stream-of-consciousness narrative whose protagonist jumps off a roof in the first chapter, while the rest of the novel depicts the character's random thoughts as he continues his descent), nobody's ever managed to finish it. Although most readers gave up on the novel after approximately four chapters, Rockford tells Jack that he had only finished reading the first 15 pages when someone stole his copy.

Jack Skowron is played by accomplished stage and screen actor Anthony Zerbe (*Behind the Broken Words, The Young Riders*). Though Zerbe won an Emmy in 1976 for playing a good guy (Lieutenant Trench on *Harry O*), he is best known for his colorful portrayals of villains in films and television shows, including the gunslinger who killed James Garner's character in "All in the Family," the famous final episode of *Nichols*. Zerbe found roles like Trench and Skowron a refreshing change of pace. "Not that heavies aren't fun," he added. "I did say once, '*All heavies had a mother somewhere ...*'"

Other guest stars include film and TV mainstay Dick Bakalyan, whose many screen credits include *Chinatown* (1974), the Oscar-winning homage to Chandler and 1930s Los Angeles starring Jack Nicholson as private eye Jake Gittes. Bakalyan played the cop who winds up gunning down Evelyn Cross (Faye Dunaway) at the end of the movie. *Chinatown* was also developed for television as *City of Angels*, a short-lived but nonetheless memorable period piece produced by Roy Huggins for NBC in 1976.

Rockford Facts

According to this episode, Skowron and Rockford previously worked together as carpet layers for two years. In real life, James Garner had once worked with his father (a carpet layer) prior to becoming an actor.

82.   THE PAPER PALACE

Production Number: 47522
Original Air Date: January 20, 1978
Written by: Juanita Bartlett
Directed by: Richard Crenna

Guest Cast: Rita Moreno (Rita Capkovic), Bruce Kirby (Sid Loft), Pat Finley (Peggy Becker), David Lewis (Burton Woodrup), Trish Donahue (Eleanor Loft), Rena Assa (Jeannot Turner), Shirley O'Hara (Maggie Gilson), James Jeter (Officer McRainey), Norwood Smith (Henry Helpern), Gene Scherer (Rudy Ganse)

This is Mrs. Owens with the Association for a Better Malibu. Thanks for your contributions. We've made great strides, but it would help, dear, if you could move your trailer!

Synopsis. *Rita Capkovic is a career prostitute who aches for genuine friendship: she's so lonely that she often wheels an empty cart around a supermarket just to socialize with other people. After meeting Rockford at a disastrous dinner party with Dennis and Peggy Becker, Rita finds herself needing his help after two French-speaking men nearly kill her inside her own apartment. Rita then stays at the home of her friend Maggie Gilson—only to find the woman murdered the following night by the same two men. Rita assists Rockford as he tries to find a connection between the two attacks.*

There's a built-in advantage in writing for a television series, regardless of whether the writer is a freelancer or a member of the show's staff: you know who the regular characters are and the actors who play them, and that often proves helpful in writing the story. However, the freelancer and the staff writer both face the same obstacle when it comes to writing guest characters. "You usually don't know who your guest stars are going to be when you're writing your story," said Juanita Bartlett. "Those decisions aren't made until long after the script is finished. You have to write the character that you feel is correct for the story, and then you cast it. That's the way you always do it."

Sometimes, though, it helps to have a particular actor in mind as you create a character. "When I wrote the Rita Capkovic character, I did have Rita Moreno in mind—but that didn't mean we were going to get Rita Moreno," said Bartlett. "In that case, as it turned out, we did. But for the most part, you write the character, and then after that character is down on paper, and fully realized as a character, you start saying, 'Who could play this? Well, so-and-so would be excellent, or do you think we could get this person, or that person?' So, usually, it's a matter of writing the character out of your head, and casting it."

Rita Moreno won an Emmy for her performance in this episode, making her one of just three actresses (Barbra Streisand and Helen Hayes being the other two) to be honored with all four major awards in the entertainment industry: the Oscar, the Emmy, the Grammy and the Tony. Moreno won the Oscar for Best Supporting Actress in *West Side Story* (1962), the Tony for *The Ritz* (1975), and the Grammy for her performance on *The Electric Company Album* (1972). Moreno's Emmy for "The Paper Palace" was actually her second such statuette; she had previously won an Emmy in 1976 for a guest appearance on *The Muppet Show*.

Moreno's friendship with James Garner dates back to the early '50s. "I did Jim's first screen test years and years ago," she said on *The Ronn Owens Program* in early 2005. "This was before he was Maverick, this was before he was the James Garner that everybody knew about. He was this gorgeous, gorgeous hunk, and we did a screen test together [for 20th Century Fox]. And as Jim is the first to tell you … he was awful! In those days the studios were still doing screen tests for people, and if they thought you were promising, they would sign you up. So they didn't sign him to a contract. But, ha ha, I guess he showed them, because he became Maverick a few years later [for Warner Bros.]."

Moreno added that in many respects, Jim Rockford, the character, is very much like James Garner, the person. "What you see is practically what he is," she said. "Jim is obviously more complicated than what you see on the screen, but that character is so very like him."

83.   DWARF IN A HELIUM HAT

Production Number: 47524
Original Air Date: January 27, 1978
Written by: Stephen J. Cannell and David Chase
Directed by: Reza S. Badiyi

Guest Cast: John Pleshette (Jay Rockfelt), Rebecca Balding (Carol Lansing), Gianni Russo (Gianni Tedesco), Milton Selzer (Irving Rockfelt), Rick Springfield (Keith Stuart), Ted Markland (Mel), Scott Ellsworth (Norman Appet), Robina Suwol (Amy Rockfelt), Bea Silvern (Edith Rockfelt), Mary Nancy Burnett (Susan), Marie Reynolds (Janaique), Robert Mayo (Santo)

Here's the tally, Jimbo. You had Atlanta on even money—tough break—and you got bombed on the new Wake Forest fiasco, and you split the Cornell at Hollypark, so you're in the book $450. Any time before Friday, huh, buddy?

Synopsis. *After receiving a strange phone call from a man who tells him "your dog is dead" and that "you and that Lansing girl are next," Rockford determines that the message was meant for Jay Rockfelt, whose name appears directly above Jim's in the phone book. After rescuing Rockfelt's dog (Romanoff) and girlfriend (Carol Lansing), Jim learns that the problem stems from a lavish birthday bash Rockfelt threw for Gianni Tedesco, an aspiring actor who also has connections with the mob. Gianni suffered the embarrassment of having to pay the $30,000 tab for his own party—an incident which has made him a laughingstock in Hollywood. Gianni blames Rockfelt, who left the party early to fly to Puerta Vallarta. The irresponsible Jay, however, blames his parents, who have refused him to loan him any money after cutting off his inheritance. Although Rockford doesn't like Jay, he feels compelled to help him after learning that Gianni has kidnapped Rockfelt's sister.*

"Rockford's attitudes toward the police, the FBI, the CIA, the Mafia, or any other American authority figures present a consistently anti-authoritarian viewpoint," observed Tom Stempel in *Storytellers to the Nation* (Continuum, 1992). "This was usually present in traditional private eye shows, but *Rockford* takes it a step further. It also goes further than Roy Huggins did in *Maverick*. In the Western, the authority figures were those of the past, while on *Rockford* they are contemporary. In other series, representatives of the Federal Government and the Mafia are both treated seriously. In *Rockford*, they are not."

Rockford certainly knows his way around the legal system, so he doesn't easily succumb to whatever pressure tactics police officers or FBI agents may try to exert. In one particular instance ("The Girl in the Bay City Boys Club"), when the cocky deputy district attorney who had originally hired Jim tries to intimidate him by threatening to suspend his private investigator's license, Rockford not only doesn't flinch, he dares the D.A. to make the call: "Go ahead and do it—I'll appeal, of course, and there'll be a hearing, and our relationship will have to come out in the open. Unless you're completely clean [which Rockford and the D.A. know is not the case], everything you've got at stake will have to come out, too."

Rockford's writers may have thumbed their noses at the system from time to time, but they never went so far as completely ridicule it. "We always tried to give Rockford worthy opponents, because his triumph wouldn't mean much if it wasn't against a formidable foe," said Juanita Bartlett. "There's no triumph in outwitting a stupid person."

The one exception would appear to be Lieutenant Chapman (James Luisi), who was much more thickheaded than Rockford's previous police foil, Lieutenant Diel (Tom Atkins). Chapman has a penchant for either sticking his foot in his mouth, or simply setting himself up for some of Rockford's ridicule, as is the case in this episode ("Come on, Chapman, does this keep coming, or are you really just a giant bag of gas in a three-piece suit?").

But Bartlett says that the Chapman character is hardly stupid at all. "He didn't like Rockford, but a lot of police don't particularly like private investigators," she explained. "Chapman wanted to run things his own way, because he was on his own turf. He also knows that whenever Rockford's on a case, he's making one hell of a lot more money than he is, and he's putting in less hours, and he can quit whenever he wants to, and he doesn't have any of the restrictions that a cop has. Rockford doesn't have to go by the book—he just has to stay out of trouble. But Chapman wasn't stupid, by any means. Of course, he could be impossible to deal with ..."

Rockford Familiar Faces

The insufferably spoiled Jay Rockfelt is played by character actor John Pleshette (*Knots Landing, Murder One*), whose famous cousin Suzanne Pleshette (Emily on *The Bob Newhart Show*) co-starred with James Garner in the 1966 feature film *Mister Buddwing*—and, years later, in *8 Simple Rules* (ABC, 2002-) as part of the story arc that introduced Garner's character "Grandpa Jim" to the series following the death of John Ritter in the fall of 2003.

The Mick Jagger-like "Keith Stuart" is played by singer/actor Rick Springfield, whose single "Speak to the Sky" was a Top 20 hit in April 1972. Later in 1978, Springfield would have another hit in "Bruce," an autobiographical song written by Springfield which talks about how he was often mistaken for the much more popular Bruce Springstreen because their names happened to be similar. Springfield, who also starred in the daytime soap *General Hospital*, would enjoy a musical comeback in 1981 after the release of *Working Class Dog*, a Top Ten album that included the No. 1 single "Jessie's Girl."

84.   SOUTH BY SOUTHEAST

Production Number: 47523
Original Air Date: February 3, 1978
Written by: Juanita Bartlett
Directed by: William Wiard

Guest Cast: Dorrie Kavanaugh (Christine Van Deerlin), Don Chastain (John Van Deerlin), Carlos Romero (Agent Sam Goroll), Don Diamond (Coelho), Jim B. Smith (Agent Whitaker), Isaac Ruiz Jr. (Jorge), Bert Rosario (Second), Mark Roberts (Agent Kleinhoff), George Clifton (Agent Mallardi), Jim Scott (Agent Ben Bast), Eric Mason (Emilio Rivera), Don Dubbins (Agent Frazee), David Panceri (Bodyguard), Robert Clockworthy (Tommy), Yolanda Marquez (Hotel Operator), Gloria Dixon (Party Guest)

Bill Skelly with ICO. I'd like to interest you in some new private detection equipment, including the 440A Telephonic Bug. We'll demonstrate it in a friend's home for one full week, at no charge.

Synopsis. *Government agents who have mistaken Rockford for an operative named Terence Halsey fly the private investigator to Mexico to prevent heiress Christine Van Deerlin from selling 50,000 shares of her father's aircraft company to Arab countries—a move which could adversely impact both the economic structure and strategic defense of the United States. Without any choice, Rockford meets Christine and discovers that she's being blackmailed by her fortune-hunting husband John, who threatens to expose the unsavory truth behind her father's legend unless she carries out the sale. Although Rockford has a chance to walk away once the matter of his identity is straightened out, he decides to stay—even at the risk of his own life—when he learns that Christine's safety is endangered.*

"South by Southeast" is ostensibly an espionage thriller in the tradition of Alfred Hitchcock's *North by Northwest*, but it's also a very poignant love story that brings out a tenderness in Rockford that we rarely see him display.

Although Rockford has shown that he's capable of falling in love without losing sight of how to make a profit, in this episode he is willing to risk his life for someone he genuinely cares about—without any consideration of his own personal gain.

85. THE COMPETITIVE EDGE

Production Number: 47504
Original Air Date: February 10, 1978
Written by: Gordon Dawson
Directed by: Harry Falk

Guest Cast: Stephen Elliott (Dr. Herb Brinkman), Jim McMullan (Perry Brauder), Robert Hogan (Lester Shaw), John Fiedler (James Bond), Neile McQueen (Joyce Brauder), George Murdock (Doc Holliday), Pepper Martin (Gustav), Logan Ramsey (Dr. Carl Brinkman), John Lupton (Marty Sloan), Harold Sakata (John Doe), Anthony Charnota (Robert W. Zachary), Dennis Fimple (Rhino), William Boyett (Morris), Charles Howerton (Councilman Moore), Dick Gjonola (Security Guard), Barbara Leigh (Sylvia), Sandie Newton (Gail)

Okay, Jimbo—Dennis. I know you're in there. And I know you know it's ticket season again ... Policeman's Ball, and all that. So come to the door when I knock this time. I know you're in there!

Synopsis. *Joyce Brauder hires Jim to find her husband Perry, an accused embezzler who has jumped bail. After infiltrating an affluent men's health club directed by Dr. Herb Brinkman, Rockford discovers that Brinkman has been running a drug-and-extortion racket—he laces the "vitamin treatments" of his clients with amphetamines financed by exorbitant monthly membership fees. When Rockford suspects that Perry's disappearance may be linked to his membership in the health club, Brinkman intervenes by drugging the P.I. and imprisoning him in a mental institution run by Brinkman's equally heinous brother.*

While he is incarcerated in the insane asylum, Rockford encounters a Stetson-wearing inmate (played by veteran character actor George Murdock) who thinks he's Doc Holliday—and that Rockford is Wyatt Earp. In real life, James Garner actually played Wyatt Earp in two films: *Hour of the Gun* (1967) and *Sunset* (1988).

Rockford Familiar Faces

This episode features also John Fiedler (Mr. Peterson on *The Bob Newhart Show*), Hawaiian actor Harold Sakata (best known as the villainous Oddjob in *Goldfinger*), daytime soap star Robert Hogan (who later in 1978 would co-star with Dennis Dugan in the short-lived *Rockford* spinoff *Richie Brockelman*), and Neile McQueen, whose onetime husband Steve McQueen co-starred with James Garner in the classic prison camp drama *The Great Escape* (1963).

86. THE PRISONER OF ROSEMONT HALL

Production Number: 47510
Original Air Date: February 17, 1978
Teleplay by: Stephen J. Cannell and David Chase
Story by: Charles Floyd Johnson and MaryAnn Rea
Directed by: Ivan Dixon

Guest Cast: Frances Lee McCain (Leslie Callahan), Kenneth Tobey (Max Kilmore), Joyce Easton (Valerie Douglas), Danny Ades (Machmoud), Maurice Sherbanee (Kadahfi), Barney McFadden (Bert Hannon), Bill Thornberry (Paul Lowe Douglas), Paul Coufos (Thomas Tate), Ric Carrott (Pledge Miller Claussen), Buck Young (Jake Sand), Michael Swan (Cal Morris), Kathy Richards (Judy), Julia Ann Benjamin (Melinda), Douglas Ryan (Herb)

That No. 4 you just picked up from Angelo's Pizza? Some scouring powder fell in there. Don't eat it! Hey, I hope you try your phone machine before dinner ...

Synopsis. *Rockford's friend Paul Lowe Douglas, a promising journalism student at Rosemont University, is abducted outside of Jim's trailer by members of a popular college fraternity. With the help of Leslie Callahan (Paul's teacher—and lover), Rockford discovers that Paul had gathered evidence of a plot to kidnap student Mustahfa Ben Ali, the son of a prominent Arab ruler. Max Kilmore, the head of campus security, had hoped to exhort $2 million from the boy's father, but the plan backfired when Ali died of a heart attack. While the paranoid Kilmore tries to fend off the Arab agents who are investigating the matter, he also tries to eliminate Rockford and Leslie.*

In the "B" story of this episode, Rocky asks Jim to help him prepare his income taxes. Rockford, however, reminds his father that he'll only "help" him by allowing him to use his adding machine. Perhaps it wasn't a pleasant experience for Jim when he last helped his father with his taxes (back in the first-season episode "Claire").

Rockford Facts

MaryAnn Rea, who collaborated with series producer Charles Floyd Johnson to write the story on which this episode was based, has been James Garner's assistant for over three decades.

87.   THE HOUSE ON WILLIS AVENUE (Two-hour episode)

Production Numbers: 47597/47598
Original Air Date: February 24, 1978
Written by: Stephen J. Cannell
Directed by: Hy Averback

Guest Cast: Dennis Dugan (Richie Brockelman), Jackie Cooper (Garth McGregor), Simon Oakland (Vern St. Cloud), Howard Hesseman (Albert Steever), Philip Sterling (Supervisor Thomas Nardoni), Pernell Roberts (B.J. Anderson), Paul Fix (Joe Tooley), Irene Tedrow (Mrs. Tooley), Lou Krugman (Sam Detonis), Brett Hadley (Computer Operator), Vince Howard (Billy Mayhew), Vince Milana (Tim), Brian Culhane (Second Deputy), Jay Fenichel (Morgue Attendant), Nancy Conrad (Receptionist), John Van Dreelan (Hans Gunderson), Robert Hogan (Sergeant Ted Coopersmith), Russell Thorson (Arthur Kenner), Hank Brandt (Mr. Davis), Ben Wright (Derek Halsted), Tom Stovall (Baker), Larry McCormick (Newscaster)

Good morning. This is the telephone company. Due to repairs, we're giving you advance notice that your service will be cut off indefinitely at 10 o'clock—that's two minutes from now.

Sonny, this is Dad. Never mind giving that talk about your occupation to the Gray Power Club. Hap Dudley's son is a doctor, and everybody sort of—would rather hear from him. But, thanks ...

Synopsis. *Rockford and greenhorn investigator Richie Brockelman probe the suspicious circumstances surrounding the accidental death of their mentor, veteran P.I. Joe Tooley, who died in the middle of a case involving a series of properties housing an extensive computer system. After questioning Tooley's last client, political activist Albert Steever, Rockford and Richie determine that Tooley had run afoul of Garth McGregor, an electronics expert who plans to install a national computer network capable of providing access to personal information on over 250 million Americans—for his own means. Rockford and Richie try to pull the plug on McGregor's operation.*

Photograph courtesy of Photofest
© 1979 Universal City Studios, Inc.

Richie Brockelman (Dennis Dugan) makes a point to Jim Rockford (James Garner) in "The House on Willis Avenue," the episode that led directly to the short-lived *Rockford Files* spin-off series *Richie Brockelman, Private Eye*.

Richie Brockelman is amazed to see how much information Rockford can elicit from people through sheer blarney. But Richie himself has a little bit of "Rockford" in him, in that he's capable of changing his mind in a second if it gets him out of trouble:

> RICHIE
> This guy actually lives in a trailer.

> ROCKFORD
> What does that mean?

> RICHIE
> Oh, I don't know. It just seems to me like living in a trailer is kind of the bottom.

> ROCKFORD
> I live in a trailer.

> RICHIE
> Well, no, not exactly the bottom—more like the middle. And, of course, depending on the trailer, it could be more like the upper middle.

Although Richie clearly looks up to Rockford, it's also apparent as the story unfolds that Jim respects Richie on his own terms. This is particularly important to Richie, who is extremely aware of the fact that, because of his age (he's 23) and his appearance (he looks like he belongs in high school), he isn't always taken seriously as a private eye. In fact, Richie is a little too sensitive about the impression people have of him—at one point, he jumps all over Rockford for saying "Good boy, Richie" when Jim was actually *complimenting* him on a particularly brilliant piece of deductive reasoning.

However, Richie also admits that sometimes he uses that perception as an advantage. "I count on people underestimating me," he tells Rockford.

Rockford Facts

"The House on Willis Avenue" was actually the second pilot for the *Richie Brockelman, Private Eye* series, which ran in *Rockford*'s time period for five weeks in the spring of 1978. Stephen J. Cannell had originally introduced Richie in *The Missing 24 Hours*, a 1976 TV-movie starring Dennis Dugan and Suzanne Pleshette.

In this episode, we also learn that Rockford's trailer is 50 feet long, and that it can be transported by a rig. The episode also tells us that Richie drives a red Ford Mustang.

Rockford Forebodings

"The House on Willis Avenue" concludes with a disclaimer attributed to an unnamed source who at the time was a member of the U.S. Privacy Protection Commission:

> Secret information centers building dossiers on individuals exist today. You have no legal right to know about them or sue for damages. Our liberty may well be the price we pay for permitting this to continue unchecked.

This message and the issues addressed in the episode were both eerily prescient of the many concerns over privacy that have since become prevalent in recent years.

Fifth Season: 1978–1979

Beginning in September 1978, reruns of the first four seasons of *The Rockford Files* aired Monday nights on CBS as part of *The CBS Late Movie*. In addition to generating more revenue for the studio, the late night reruns broadened the demographics of the series by introducing *Rockford* to a whole new audience. Throughout its first four years, *Rockford*'s primary audience consisted of older viewers. However, by the end of the 1978-1979 season, a survey conducted by the Nielsen Television Index indicated that the series was becoming increasingly popular among young adults as well—a development that did not surprise Roy Huggins. "*Rockford* gradually became strong with young adults because of its attitude," he said. "It had the *Maverick* attitude, which Steve understood beautifully. And I'm sure that Steve tried to keep that alive throughout the show."

Cannell did just that, not only by weaving elements of classic *Maverick* episodes into *Rockford* stories, but also by continuing to bring out facets of the Maverick character such as the reluctant hero and Maverick's basic concern with his own self-interest. With an Emmy Award under his belt, Cannell believed he could now take risks and experiment—just as his mentor Huggins had done years before during the peak of *Maverick*'s success. So it's fitting that the fifth season of *The Rockford Files* introduces one of the show's most memorable characters, Lance White, whom Cannell patterned after a character from one of the most famous *Maverick* episodes of all, "The Saga of Waco Williams."

"The Saga of Waco Williams" paired Maverick with gunslinger Waco Williams, an honorable, brave soul with a knack for landing in the middle of situations that the pragmatic Maverick would normally avoid at all costs. For instance, if Waco picked a fight, Maverick would tell him, "Waco, don't do that. They could *kill* you." Waco would say, "Well, what would you expect me to do? Run away?" And Maverick would say, "By all means, yes" … because, like Rockford, Maverick's philosophy is that "being brave doesn't get you anywhere but dead real fast."

However, by the end of the show, everything manages to work out for Waco: he becomes engaged to the daughter of a big rancher, and becomes such a hero in the eyes of the townspeople that they consider electing him sheriff. Even Maverick, who had been steadfastly warning Waco not to live so recklessly, can't help scratching his head. In fact, the episode ends with a dumbfounded

Maverick looking straight into the camera and asking the audience, "Could I be wrong?"

Similarly, "White on White and Nearly Perfect" pairs Rockford with fearless Lance White (Tom Selleck), "a guy who was sickeningly heroic … which was exactly what Waco Williams was," said Cannell. "The story for that show was different, but the concept of that character was absolutely out of 'Waco Williams.' I thought that was one of the funniest *Mavericks* of all. And it was also something that you couldn't do early in the show. It was definitely a Year Four or Five kind of show, where you've fed the audience fastball after fastball—in terms of, you've done *Rockford* and done *Rockford*, and the audience knows what the platform is. Then you can throw this changeup pitch."

Although Cannell didn't actually screen "The Saga of Waco Williams" prior to writing "White on White," he knew the concept of the character so well that he didn't really need to. Lance White behaves as if he's a character in a spy novel or an action movie. Just like those characters, Lance operates in a world of incredible coincidences, where you can go back to your office and find a clue waiting for you just when you need it most. Understanding Lance's world requires a willful suspension of disbelief.

Rockford, on the other hand, operates in perpetual disbelief. Not surprisingly, he spends most of the episode telling Lance that everything he's doing is "wrong," just as Maverick had done 20 years before with Waco Williams.

In "White on White," Rockford and Lance investigate the disappearance of the daughter of a wealthy industrialist named Teasdale. The trail runs aground midway through the story … until a voluptuous beauty named Belle Labelle suddenly shows up with an apparently vital clue! Because Lance, like Waco Williams, goes about his business oblivious to the possibility that he could get himself killed, he's ready to pounce on the lead immediately. However, the discriminating Rockford—who is always more concerned with staying alive than acting heroic—advises Lance not to move so fast:

ROCKFORD
It hasn't occurred to you that this is a trap?

LANCE
A trap? Come on, Jim, I doubt that.

ROCKFORD
You know, I can't explain why you're still walking around! It's not going to last long. You're näive, Lance. You really are. You have to be cynical. You have to question things. You can't trust someone named "Belle Labelle" on face value. What's her angle, huh? Whose payroll is

she on? You find out the answers to those things, and you start moving fast and crooked. You go through doorways sideways, and low, at all angles. You look for the big lie. You question everything.

Although Rockford is right—in the sense that as a matter of self-preservation, you have to be a little cynical and skeptical from time to time—he is ultimately proven wrong, just as Maverick was proven wrong in "The Saga of Waco Williams."

Although it is Rockford who risks his life to rescue Teasdale's daughter, it's Lance who reaps the reward. At the end of the story, he gets the girl (along with complete control of Teasdale's company), simply because Teasdale believes that Lance is more capable than Rockford of providing for his daughter in the way in which she was accustomed. Teasdale even admits the unfairness of it all to Rockford, and offers some kind of compensation to Jim in addition to his regular fee.

Rockford politely declines, knowing that under normal circumstances Teasdale would probably insist on giving him the bonus. However, this is the world of Lance White, where normal circumstances do not occur. Thus, Rockford is proven wrong once again when Teasdale promptly withdraws the gesture ("I just thought I'd offer"). This is one time where Jim would have been better off accepting Teasdale's offer at face value.

One of the real treats of "White and White" is watching James Garner's reactions to Lance's straight-out-of-a-spy-movie behavior. "Jim kept coming up to me and saying, 'You know, I just feel as if all I'm doing is mugging,'" said Cannell, who also directed the episode. "I kept telling him, 'Jim, you're doing great.' Because that was the point of the whole show: all the jokes were geared to Jim's reactions. And Jim was terrific."

Selleck would return to play Lance White once again in the sixth season. Other familiar guest stars in 1978-1979 included Hector Elizondo, Mary Frann, Abe Vigoda, Ed Harris, Janis Paige, James B. Sikking, Nicholas Coster, John Pleshette, Allan Arbus, Denny Miller, Kenneth McMillan, René Auberjonois, Erin Gray, Glenn Corbett, Marge Redmond, Patricia Crowley, Ted Shackelford, Mills Watson, Harold Gould, John Considine, Reni Santoni, Leo Gordon, Lane Smith, and Kim Hunter.

*   *   *

Meanwhile, as production began on the fifth season of *The Rockford Files*, Universal's hardball stance with regard to Gretchen Corbett resulted in the loss of one of the show's most popular characters.

Corbett was the only cast member of the series who was under contract to Universal Studios. As such, that meant that her salary was paid by the studio: in order to have her on *The Rockford Files*, Cherokee Productions had to pay Universal whatever fee the studio charged for the use of her services. The studio would then pay Corbett her salary out of that fee.

Corbett contributed a great deal to the success of *The Rockford Files*. Her character "Beth Davenport" was among the most popular of the entire series. Not surprisingly, the studio raised its fee on Corbett after each of the show's first three seasons.

"What happened with Gretchen was that Universal wanted more money from us in order to continue using her on the show," James Garner explained in an interview for this book. "But at the same time, they wanted us to cut the budget by reducing the sets and the like, yet they still jacked up the price on her. I forget how much it was, but it was outrageously high. We couldn't afford it, and so, unfortunately, we had to eliminate her character.

"It was a difficult decision to make, because Gretchen was one of the family. But we couldn't afford to pay what the studio wanted."

Corbett was not aware of the negotiations between Garner and Universal regarding the use of her services. However, she does recall experiencing her own frustrations with the studio. "By that time, I was going crazy being under contract," she said. "I felt that I was not a 'typical contract player,' in that I had a lot of stage background, particularly on the New York stage, and it was therefore hard for me being lumped in with all the other 'kids under contract.' And so, I had asked out of my contract."

Although Universal had initially refused to accommodate Corbett, the studio changed its mind—on one condition. "In order to get out of my contract, I had to agree not to do *Rockford*," she said. "I don't really know what went down between Jim and the studio. But, as far as I know, that's why I did not return to the show after the fourth year."

Fans of Beth Davenport can take comfort in this: it essentially took two characters to replace her. Bo Hopkins (*Walking Tall*) appeared in three episodes as disbarred attorney John Cooper, Rockford's new legal counsel, while Kathryn Harrold (*MacGruder and Loud*, *I'll Fly Away*, *The Larry Sanders Show*, *Desperate Housewives*) starred as Rockford's new love interest, blind psychologist Megan Dougherty.

Photograph courtesy of TV History Archive
© 1979 Universal City Studios, Inc.

Left to right: Kathryn Harrold, James Garner, David-James Carroll and Betty Kennedy in "Love is the Word," the second of two episodes featuring Harrold as blind psychologist Megan Dougherty.

The departure of Corbett was also reflected in a cosmetic change in the opening sequence of the fifth season episodes. The still of Garner and Corbett, which had been added only one year before, was eliminated. A solo still of Garner smiling and laughing (from the episode "A Good Clean Bust with Sequel Rights") was inserted in its place.

Stuart Margolin won an Emmy for Best Supporting Actor—the first of two successive seasons in which he would be so honored. Joe Santos and Noah Beery Jr. also received nominations for Supporting Actor. In addition, James Garner was nominated for Best Actor, and the series was nominated once again for Best Dramatic Series.

After maintaining steady audience figures during its third and fourth seasons, *The Rockford Files* suffered a decrease in audience of nearly 10% in its fifth year and dropped 13 notches in the overall Nielsen ratings. However, the drop in audience is directly attributable to the show's temporary move to Saturday nights in February 1979. Prior to the move, *Rockford* had been averaging a 17.5

rating and a 29.2 audience share in its regular Friday 9:00 p.m. time slot—slightly lower figures from what the show had averaged the year before, but still respectable. But when the series was moved to Saturdays at 10:00 p.m. (where it competed against ABC's top-rated *Fantasy Island* for seven weeks), the audience figures dropped dramatically: *Rockford* averaged a 26.7 share (8% lower than its Friday night figures) and a 14.8 rating (15% lower) during that period of time. (Interestingly enough, when *Rockford* was returned to its customary Friday night time slot in April, the show's audience figures increased by 10%.)

✷   ✷   ✷

In the fall of 1979, MCA/Universal distributed the first 107 episodes of *The Rockford Files* to independent television stations across the country. During *Rockford*'s first year in syndication, the reruns aired under the title *Jim Rockford, Private Investigator* because the series was still producing new episodes for NBC. However, in the fall of 1980, after the series had ended its network run, MCA added the 12 sixth-season episodes to the package, and the reruns reverted to their original *Rockford Files* title. As noted earlier, the 90-minute pilot film was re-edited and included in the rerun package as a two-part episode entitled "Backlash of the Hunter."

Courtesy of A&E Television Networks
© 1979 Universal City Studios, Inc.

The cover of the *Rockford Files* syndication kit, originally released by
MCA/Universal in 1979

Courtesy of A&E Television Networks
© 1979 Universal City Studios, Inc.

From the original *Rockford Files* syndication kit: episode titles from the first five seasons, listed in their order of production. The 12 shows from the sixth season were added to the package in September 1980. Some stations (including superstation WGN) air the episodes according to this sequence, as opposed to the order in which they were originally broadcast on NBC. As noted earlier, both the pilot (syndicated under the title "Backlash of the Hunter") and the first-season episode "This Case is Closed" were somehow inserted among the fourth-season shows when *Rockford* first went into reruns. Most stations, however, air these episodes in their proper sequences.

Episode Guide for the Fifth Season

88.   HEARTACHES OF A FOOL

Production Number: 51106
Original Air Date: September 22, 1978
Written by: Stephen J. Cannell
Directed by: William Wiard

"Good Hearted Woman"
Music and Lyrics by Waylon Jennings and Willie Nelson
"Heartaches of a Fool"
Music and Lyrics by Willie Nelson
Both Songs Performed by Willie Nelson

Guest Cast: Taylor Lacher (Charlie Strayhorn), Lynne Marta (Carrie Strayhorn), James Shigeta (Clement Chen), Norman Alden (Roland Eddy), Joe E. Tata (Norman Abbott Kline), Leo Gordon (Clark Streeter), Mark Roberts (Hillman Stewart), Robert Phillips (Mike Thomas), Donald "Red" Barry (Shorty McCall), Herb Armstrong (Union Official), James Jeter (Mel), John Davey (Deputy Farnsworth), Raymond O'Keefe (Jake Sand), George Kee Cheung (Harry Lee), Byron Chung (David), Ben Jeffrey (Deputy Patino), Jayson Caine (Howard Freeman), Fred J. Gordon (Mel Willis)

Say, I'm the one who hit your car at Ford City. I've got no insurance— I'm broke. But I really wanted you to know how sorry I am. If it makes you feel any better, I hurt my arm ...

Synopsis. *Country-western recording star Charlie Strayhorn is beset with finan- cial and personal problems: production on his new album has been delayed; he has tax troubles; and his marriage is ending. Apparently, the only thing Charlie*

287

has going for him is the popular brand of smoked sausages that bears his name—but even that's a fraud. Charlie doesn't realize that his unscrupulous business partner, Clement Chen, has been circumventing the FDA and the Teamsters by producing the sausages in Mexico and arranging for non-union transportation of the product into the United States. Rocky becomes victimized by Chen's operation after he innocently agrees to pick up a load of the sausages in San Diego. Rocky not only has his truck overturned and destroyed by two men, he also loses his drivers license and has his union pension and medical benefits suspended. After Rockford confronts Charlie with the truth about his sausage company, the singer helps the private eye investigate the matter.

The fifth-season opener features two numbers performed by Grammy Award-winner Willie Nelson, whose title track is used in a particularly effective manner. The somber lyrics of "Heartaches of a Fool" provide a poignant backdrop to the breathtaking aerial footage that closes the episode.

Rockford Facts

"Heartaches of a Fool" appears on *Willie Nelson's Greatest Hits [and Some That Will Be]*, a Top 30 album first released by Columbia Records in Fall 1981.

89.   ROSENDAHL AND GILDA STERN ARE DEAD

Production Number: 51103
Original Air Date: September 29, 1978
Written by: Juanita Bartlett
Directed by: William Wiard

Guest Cast: Rita Moreno (Rita Capkovic), Abe Vigoda (Phil Gabriel), Robert Loggia (Dr. Russell Nevitt), Sharon Acker (Edie Nevitt), Robin Gammell (Donald Pilmer), John Karlen (Leo), Ron Gilbert (Freddie), Jo Anne Meredith (Ceil), William Joyce (Dr. Neil Rosendahl), Jason Wingreen (Earl Stagen), George Planko (Sergeant Curcio), Rick Goldman (Attorney), Clint Young (Harry the Doorman), Rod Masterson (Oscar Weinberg)

Hello? Are you the guy who lost his wallet in the Park Theater? Well, I'm kind of, like, into leather, so I'll be returning the money—but I'm gonna keep the wallet.

Synopsis. *Rockford once again comes to the aid of Rita Capkovic, the prostitute he befriended in "The Paper Palace." Although Rita witnessed the murder of arthroscopic surgeon Neil Rosendahl, the police arrest her on circumstantial evidence (she escorted the doctor to a medical convention dinner). In fact, Rosendahl was killed by noted crime king Phil Gabriel, who became permanently disabled after an unsuccessful hip replacement operation which Dr. Rosendahl performed. Rockford tries to gather evidence that will link Gabriel and clear Rita.*

This is the first of two sequels to "The Paper Palace," the Emmy Award-winning episode that introduced Rita Capkovic (Rita Moreno). Since we last saw her, Rita has managed to spend nearly all of the $300,000 she had inherited from her neighbor on new clothes, a new apartment, a microwave oven, capped teeth for her friend Ceil, and hospital expenses for Ceil's mother. "But you could have paid for all that on the interest of $300,000," Rockford points out. "What happened to the principal?"

Finally, Rita finally admits that she spent the rest of her money on "this guy." Rockford is about to admonish Rita when she suddenly explains, "But, Jim … I had such a good time spending it!"

Moreno, who had previously co-starred with James Garner in the 1969 private eye film *Marlowe*, would return to *Rockford* in the sixth season episode "No-Fault Affair," as well as the 1999 reunion movie *If It Bleeds ... It Leads*.

hotograph courtesy of Photofest
© 1979 Universal City Studios, Inc.

Rita Moreno and Noah Beery Jr. in a scene from "Rosendahl and Gilda Stern Are Dead"

90.   THE JERSEY BOUNCE

Production Number: 51109
Original Air Date: October 6, 1978
Teleplay by: David Chase
Story by: Stephen J. Cannell & David Chase & Juanita Bartlett
Directed by: William Wiard

Guest Cast: Bo Hopkins (John Cooper), Sorrell Booke (Wade Ward), Greg Antonacci (Eugene Conigliaro), Eugene Davis (Mickey Long), Luke Andreas (Artie Nodzak), Elta Blake (Celeste), Jim Scott (D.A. Cowan), Doney Oatman (Dawn Nodzak), George Planko (Cop), Tony Brand (Judge Carmine Rossi), Walter Olkewicz (Mac Amodeus), Paul Teschke (Carl Gibbons)

Jimmy ... Angel. Here's the tip, but his handwriting's bad: Third Son in the fifth race at Bell Meadows. Wait a minute—could be Fifth Son in the third. Wait—this might be next week's race ...

Synopsis. *Rocky and his neighbors have been harassed by Eugene Conigliaro and Mickey Long, a pair of lowbrow hustlers who are anxious to ingratiate themselves with mob boss Artie Nodzak. Conigliaro and Long intimidate the community with their wild parties, loud music and overt drug dealings. Jim intercedes on behalf of his father and nearly gets into a fight with Conigliaro. Later, Rockford unwittingly becomes an integral part of Conigliaro and Long's plans to coax their way into the mob. When they discover that Nodzak's sister dates a man who beats her, Conigliaro and Long kill the boyfriend—and pin the murder on Rockford.*

Besides introducing Bo Hopkins as John Cooper (Rockford's new lawyer), this episode features character actor Sorrell Booke, who starred as the scheming Boss Hogg in *The Dukes of Hazzard*. One of the shows that helped launch CBS to the top of the Nielsens in the early 1980s, *The Dukes of Hazzard* was an immediate hit when it debuted in January 1979—directly opposite *The Rockford Files* on Friday nights at nine.

Other guest stars include Eugene Davis, whose brother Brad Davis won a Golden Globe Award for Best Motion Picture Acting Debut for his lead role in *Midnight Express* (1978).

91.   WHITE ON WHITE AND NEARLY PERFECT

Production Number: 51105
Original Air Date: October 20, 1978
Produced, Written and Directed by: Stephen J. Cannell

Guest Cast: Tom Selleck (Lance White), Jason Evers (Brad Davies), Frank R. Christy (Vincent), Peter Brocco (Meyer Ziegler), Bill Quinn (Armand Teasdale), Eddie Fontaine (Augusto DePalma), Raynold Gideon (Tuner Watson), Jay Rasumny (Manolo), Karen Austin (Veronica Teasdale), Carolyn Calcote (Angela), Julienne Welles (Belle Labelle), Freddye Chapman (Maggie)

Pacific View Lots: "Perpetual care by people who care," at an unbelievably low price. Call Monteith & Snell, the Full Service Mortuary. "We won't rest easy until you do."

Synopsis. *Millionaire industrialist Armand Teasdale hires Rockford to locate his daughter Veronica, who has apparently eloped with her boyfriend Joey Blackwood, a seedy nightclub owner. Veronica's disappearance soon becomes linked with the plight of Meyer Ziegler, a notorious criminal who has been exiled from Israel. Ziegler kidnaps Veronica and threatens to kill her unless Teasdale, an arms manufacturer on the verge of selling 25 defense missiles to the Israeli government, can arrange for Ziegler's naturalization and acceptance into his homeland. When neither the U.S. nor Israeli governments will interfere in the matter, Rockford becomes Teasdale's only hope of seeing Veronica alive. Meanwhile, Rockford must also contend with Lance White, a rival private eye whose intrepid yet oblivious approach to their profession nearly gets them both killed.*

While Lance White clearly has his origins in Waco Williams, he also has much in common with a character from another classic *Maverick* episode: Jack Vandergelt, the wealthy socialite played by Roger Moore in "The Rivals." Like Lance, Jack is totally oblivious to reality: he acts as if he's a character in a romance comedy, someone who is in love with the idea of committing suicide in order to win the heart of the woman he loves. Similarly, Lance White loves the idea that he's a private investigator in the middle of a caper, and has no concept of the fact that his impulsive reactions could very well get himself (and Rockford) killed. Lance's credo is "Things have a way of working out. They always do."

In both instances (as Bret Maverick in "The Rivals," and as Jim Rockford in "White on White"), James Garner's role is the same: the voice of reason, a reactor who steps back from the action and asks himself, "Am I really in the same room with this person?" In both instances, Garner plays this part superbly.

Coincidentally, at the time of "White on White" was filmed, Tom Selleck bore a striking resemblance to Wayde Preston, the actor who played Waco Williams on *Maverick*. "I think that, when they were casting Waco Williams, they were looking for an actor who looked like James Arness on *Gunsmoke*," said Stephen J. Cannell, who also directed this episode. "I didn't have a James Arness in mind. I just wanted someone who 'looked heroic.' We found Tom Selleck, who was the perfect guy for the part. He was terrific."

Rockford Facts

Within two years of this episode, Selleck began an eight-season run as Hawaii-based gumshoe Thomas Sullivan Magnum III in *Magnum, p.i.* (CBS, 1980-1988). Interestingly enough, Magnum as initially conceived by co-creator Glen Larson was closer in spirit to Lance White than the self-deprecating character that Selleck came to develop. "I didn't like the [original] *Magnum* pilot very much," Selleck told *Cigar Aficionado* in 1995. "He was a kind of perfect character, a womanizing James Bondish kind of guy. I knew my acting instrument by then, I knew my appetites, and I knew I wanted to be a little more goofy than that and make mistakes.

"I was a huge fan of *The Rockford Files* and James Garner. I had done two *Rockford*s as a character called Lance White. I knew I could never be Garner, that I could never be as good as he is—but I also knew I could work in that kind of arena. And something made me persist. It may have been either my upbringing or just the idea that I was comfortable taking risks, because at the time everybody, including Universal, was saying, '*Who the hell do you think you are? Don't mess with us; you can't turn us down.*' But finally we worked out a deal where I could look at three shows, one of which could be *Magnum*—but it had to be rewritten. They brought in Don Bellisario, who wrote a terrific two-hour pilot, which they then filmed."

Selleck went on to win an Emmy and a Golden Globe for his portrayal of Thomas Magnum. *Rockford* producer Charles Floyd Johnson executive produced *Magnum* along with Bellisario for the entire eight-season run.

92.   KILL THE MESSENGER

Production Number: 51110
Original Air Date: October 27, 1978
Written by: Juanita Bartlett
Directed by: Ivan Dixon

Guest Cast: W.K. Stratton (Lieutenant Frank Dusenberg), Byron Morrow (Chief Everett Towne), Pat Finley (Peggy Becker), Alex Colon ("Captain Crunch"), Ed Harris (Officer Rudy Kempner), Tony Crupi (Bandit), Don Diamond (Lieutenant Alverez), Lee Farr (Booking Suspect), Robert Cleaves (Leo Benbrook), Nancy Parsons (Miss Buettner), Frank McRae (Junior), Michael LaGuardia (Officer Shumway), Sterling Swanson (Store Manager), Bucklind Beery (Officer Mazursky), Tiger Williams (Little Den), Joey Miller (Scotty), Doris Donaldson (Maude), John Wheeler (Cliff), Edward Dogans (Guard)

Jim—Chet, returning your call. Sorry I missed you, but I appreciate your calling back. Now, if you call again and I'm not in, just leave me a message, and I'll get back to you.

Synopsis. *As a nervous Becker prepares to take the examination for lieutenant, he's assigned a departmental hot potato: the homicide of parole officer Eileen Towne, wife of Deputy Chief of Police Eugene Towne. When Jim decides to help Dennis by conducting a preliminary investigation, he inadvertently jeopardizes their friendship and nearly sabotages Becker's chances for promotion. Rockford's disclosure that Eileen Towne frequently cheated on her husband (she fooled around with both paroles and young police officers) provides Deputy Chief Towne with a motive for killing her. But it also puts Becker in the awkward position of interrogating the very same man who will preside over the examination proceedings.*

Dennis Becker (Joe Santos) has always been one of *Rockford's* most appealing characters. Although he usually maintains a laidback, calm disposition, Becker is not immune to stress—as we see in this episode, as well as in others (such as "The Becker Connection"), he will occasionally lose his temper. Becker certainly

Photograph from the collection of Robert Howe

Joe Santos with Rob Howe, a friend of the show

had to go through the wringer (not to mention three years of waiting) before making lieutenant, but he finally earns that promotion in this episode. Nice guys don't always finish last.

"Kill the Messenger" is reportedly Joe Santos' favorite episode.

Rockford Funnies

Becker apparently has a friend at Universal Studios, because Peggy asks Dennis in this episode if he could arrange a special tour of the studio for Bud and his son Den.

Rockford Familiar Faces

This episode features future Oscar winner Ed Harris (*Pollock, The Right Stuff, A Beautiful Mind*) in one of his first credited screen roles.

93.   THE EMPTY FRAME

Production Number: 51114
Original Air Date: November 3, 1978
Written by: Stephen J. Cannell
Directed by: Corey Allen

Guest Cast: Richard Seff (John St. Clair), Paul Carr (Jeffrey Levane), Jonathan Goldsmith (Yossi Hindel), Dale Robinette (David Jones), Milt Kogan (Aaron Kiel), Troas Hayes (Carolyn Corkhill), Marianne Bunch (Cynthia Daskin), Dennis Robertson (John Jefferies), Eddie Ryder (Cateye Wilson), Lee Delano (Captain Salducci), Michael J. London (Norman Deekus), Sonny Kline (Pritzer), Douglas Ryan (Finta)

Jim, directions to the party: Left on Saugersfield, see a rock; left, left again, right, another left—there's kind of a hill. Keep going … you'll probably see a bunch of cars.

Synopsis. *Rockford is among the guests at a high-profile soiree honoring the appointment of Aaron Kiel (Angel's brother-in-law) to the Los Angeles Police Commission. Despite a security force led by Lieutenant Chapman, political activists crash the party and steal a set of paintings worth $2 million. John St. Clair and Jeff Levane, the hosts of the party, hire Rockford to recover the paintings. Meanwhile, Chapman's inept handling of the embarrassing incident lands him in the doghouse with the chief of police. The lieutenant is so desperate to save face that he swallows his pride and asks Rockford for help.*

Mostly known for playing hard-ass cops or steely-eyed killers, James Luisi got a rare opportunity to showcase his comic skills in "The Empty Frame." Not surprisingly, the episode remained the actor's personal favorite for many years. Knowing that, Luisi's nephew Vinnie Luisi obtained a copy of the script in early 2001 as a surprise gift for his uncle's birthday. With the help of MaryAnn Rea, Vinnie was also able to get James Garner, Stephen J. Cannell (who wrote the episode), and other members of the *Rockford Files* cast and staff to sign the script as part of the surprise. "We all loved Jimmy," Rea recalled. "Everyone was happy to sign."

Vinnie Luisi presented the script to his uncle Jimmy in November 2001, when the actor turned 73.

Sadly, James Luisi died suddenly less than a year later. He suffered a massive cerebral hemorrhage on June 7, 2002 and never regained consciousness.

Rockford Facts

This episode marks the first and only time we see Aaron Kiel, Angel's often-mentioned but heretofore unseen brother-in-law, who publishes *The Los Angeles Tribune*. When Aaron suspects that Angel is somehow behind the robbery, he threatens to turn him over to the police. What Aaron doesn't realize is that Angel has him over a barrel: he knows all about the amorous night Aaron spent in Newport Beach with Cynthia Daskin, an associate editor at the paper. To keep Aaron in line, Angel strongarms Aaron into using his influence with the police commission to further his latest scheme (an escort service).

"That's blackmail!" balks Aaron.

Only Angel thinks that given the circumstances, "blackmail" is too strong a word. "When it's in the immediate family," he tells Aaron, "it's called 'family spirit.'"

Aaron Kiel is played by veteran character actor Milt Kogan, who had a memorable scene as the heavy who doesn't fall for Rockford's famous cigarette trick in the premiere episode, "The Kirkoff Case."

Rockford Fun

The character "John Jefferies" was presumably named after production designer John D. Jefferies, who worked on a number of shows produced by Stephen J. Cannell for Universal in the '70s and '80s, including *Baa Baa Black Sheep*, *The Greatest American Hero*, and *Hardcastle & McCormick*. Earlier in 1978, Jefferies was the production designer for *The New Maverick*, the made-for-TV movie in which James Garner reprised his classic role from the late 1950s. More recently, Jefferies was the set designer for the second Austin Powers movie, *Austin Powers: The Spy Who Shagged Me* (1999).

94.   A THREE-DAY AFFAIR WITH A THIRTY-DAY ESCROW

Production Number: 51101
Original Air Date: November 10, 1978
Written by: David Chase
Directed by: Ivan Dixon

Guest Cast: Janis Paige (Miriam), Richard Romanus (Sean Innes), Robert Alda (Cy Marguilles), Maria Grimm (Khedra Aziz), Gilbert Green (Talib), Joshua Bryant (Deputy Chief Gorman), Andrew Massett (Ahmad Ibshid), Maurice Sherbanee (Ishaak), Socorro Swan (Concepcion), Richard Moll (Ludes), James Gavin (Pilot)

Rockford? Alice, Phil's Plumbing. We're still jammed up on a job, so we won't be able to make your place. Use the bathroom at the restaurant one more night ...

Synopsis. *A sheik named Talib kidnaps Rockford and demands to know the whereabouts of his daughter, Khedra Aziz, a woman whom a gigolo named Sean Innes hired Rockford to find. After he manages to escape Talib's family, Jim locates Innes, and discovers a bizarre scheme designed by unscrupulous real estate broker Cy Marguilles to break up Khedra's marriage so that he could sell her home. Marguilles engaged women to seduce Khedra's husband Muhammed, but when he found that Khedra, a traditional Muslim woman, would never divorce Muhammed despite his infidelity, he contracted Innes to bed her. Later, Rockford discovers that Khedra's family intends to kill her because she cheated on her husband—an offense punishable by death under Muslim law. The complications increase when Rockford and Innes find Muhammed dead.*

Like James Garner, Janis Paige (Miriam) began her film career as a contract player with Warner Bros. in the 1950s. After winning critical acclaim for her roles opposite Fred Astaire in *Silk Stalkings* (1957) and Doris Day in *Please Don't Eat the Daisies* (1960), she became a steady fixture in both films and television for over three decades. Among her many roles, she co-starred with Art Carney in the series *Lanigan's Rabbi* (the pilot of which featured Stuart Margolin in the title role), and played Mandy Packer, owner of the saloon that Maverick wins in a poker game, in the pilot for Garner's 1981-1982 series, *Bret Maverick.*

Other guest stars include Richard Romanus, who plays Dr. Melfi's ex-husband in David Chase's *The Sopranos* (and who also appeared in the *Rockford* reunion movie *A Blessing in Disguise*); Robert Alda, father of *M*A*S*H* star Alan Alda; and Richard Moll (*Night Court*), who plays a brute whom Rockford manages to disarm by opening a bottle of champagne and nailing him in the eye with a well-timed flying cork.

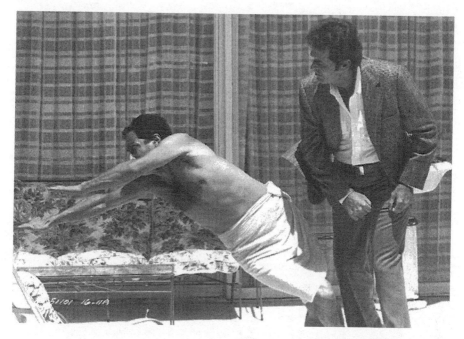

Photograph courtesy of TV History Archive
© 1978 Universal City Studios, Inc.

Sean Innes (Richard Romanus) learns the hard way that Jim Rockford (James Garner) is more than capable of landing a punch in "A Three-Day Affair with a Thirty-Day Escrow." Romanus also starred in the *Rockford Files* reunion movie *A Blessing in Disguise*.

95.   A GOOD CLEAN BUST WITH SEQUEL RIGHTS

Production Number: 51102
Original Air Date: November 17, 1978
Written by: Rudolph Borchert
Directed by: William Wiard

Guest Cast: Hector Elizondo (Frank Falcone), James B. Sikking (Jeff Seals), Nicholas Coster (Augie Augustine), James Murtaugh (Bob Parsons), Jerry Douglas (Walt Wexler), Louisa Moritz (Debbie), Patricia Donahue (Board President), Hank Brandt (Captain Gene Lindner), Joanna Lipari (Mrs. Stern), Jenny Sherman (Linda), Derek Murcott (Manny Ables), Marland Proctor (Clerk), Loni Ackerman (Brochure Girl)

Jim, I have to thank you for talking over my problems with me last Tuesday night. I love you for it, but can you have lunch tomorrow and talk about the divorce? I'm real bummed out.

Synopsis. *Jim becomes a temporary "babysitter" for Frank Falcone, a superstar cop from Chicago whose legendary exploits have spawned a best seller, a major motion picture, and a popular network TV series. Jeff Seals, the image-conscious PR man for a toy company planning to launch a line of Falcone-related merchandise at a sales convention, hires Rockford to keep tabs on his rambunctious client. Seals is concerned that Falcone, who became irate when his former police partner Walt Wexler wrote a book that criticized the Falcone legend, might go after Wexler—and generate the kind of publicity that could kill the toy campaign. Although Rockford blows the account when he allows Falcone to slip away, he still finds himself in a position to protect the celebrity when he learns that Falcone may be the target of a contract killer.*

The character Frank Falcone was loosely patterned after David Toma, the New Jersey undercover detective whose exploits provided the basis for both the *Toma* and *Baretta* series. Falcone is played by Emmy winner Hector Elizondo (*Chicago Hope*), who had previously guest starred in "Say Goodbye to Jennifer," and who would be reunited with James Garner in the spring of 2000 when Garner joined the cast of *Chicago Hope* for that show's final season.

96. BLACK MIRROR (Two-hour episode)

Production Number: 51191/51192
Original Air Date: November 24, 1978
Written by: David Chase
Directed by: Arnold Laven

Guest Cast: Kathryn Harrold (Dr. Megan Dougherty), John Pleshette (Jackie Tetuska), Carl Franklin (Roger Orloff), Allan Arbus (Myron Katzen), Denny Miller (Norman), Alan Manson (Dr. Carl Rainer), Leo Gordon (Charles Martell), John Howard (Mort), Peter Tomarken (Commercial Director), Thomas Ageas (Maitre D'), Julia Ann Benjamin (Bonnie), Wallace Earl (Myra), Melvin F. Allen (Mr. Engle)

Jim, I leave London four o'clock, arrive L.A. nine—I guess that's London time. Yeah, four to nine is five, minus twelve hours flying— no, plus twelve hours—ah, but then there's a time change ...

Rockford? Jake at the Sand Pebble. Sorry, old buddy, but there have been gun shots around your place once too often. The Neighborhood Association wants to have a talk with you.

Synopsis. *Megan Dougherty, a clinical psychologist who became permanently blinded in an accident ten years earlier, hires Rockford after she is menaced by a man in an elevator outside her office. Rockford suspects that one of Megan's patients is involved, but she won't compromise her professional ethics by allowing him to review their records. Megan does provide Jim with a writing sample of each client (in the form of canceled checks), which Jim is able to present to handwriting expert Myron Katzen, a former cellmate of Rockford's who has now gone straight. To Megan's absolute disbelief, Myron finds the potential for violent behavior in an apparently docile client she knows as "Danny Green." But Rockford later determines that "Green" is really professional killer Jackie Tetuska, who created the mild-mannered personality as part of an elaborate insurance policy in the event he is ever arrested (he could always plead insanity, and call on Megan as a witness to testify on his behalf). When Tetuska realizes that Rockford is onto his scheme, he tries to eliminate Jim and Megan.*

Although Rockford can certainly handle himself in a fistfight, that doesn't mean he has fists of granite: he gets hurt (sometimes very badly so) about as often as he inflicts pain. In fact, James Garner once estimated that he would "would get beaten up at least twice per show" on a typical episode of *Rockford*. "I don't know what it is about people, but they like to see me get whipped," the actor told Bob Costas in 1991. "And I don't understand that. I guess it's because they know I'm gonna come back later and get my licks in."

Later, when Costas asked Garner if he had ever been actually hit by another actor during the filming of a fistfight, the *Rockford* star shared an anecdote about Leo Gordon, his co-star on *Maverick* (and who plays Charles Martell in "Black Mirror"). "Leo is a big, burly guy," Garner said, "and we had this fight [scene early in the *Maverick* pilot], and he punched me in the gut. And I mean, he really nailed me. And I looked at him like, 'Whoa! What was that?' And I said, 'Okay.' But then the fight turns around, and I got to beat on him a little bit. And I buried my fist right up to his spine, and Leo looked at me and he kept trying to grin … We got along well after that. We understood each other. If you can give it, you gotta take it."

Rockford Facts

The Sand Pebble is an actual restaurant located at Paradise Cove and Pacific Coast Highway near the famous Malibu pier, where James Garner and Noah Beery were photographed fishing together as part of the opening title sequence for *The Rockford Files*. Now known as Bob Morris' Paradise Beach Café, the restaurant (as well as the surrounding Malibu Beach), remains a popular location for many films and television series.

For purposes of *The Rockford Files*, the restaurant was also known as The Sand Box in the sixth season (specifically, the episode "The Big Cheese"), as well as The Sand Castle in the reunion movies produced for CBS.

Rockford Familiar Faces

After his memorable turn as the weaselly Jay Rockfelt in "Dwarf in a Helium Hat," John Pleshette stretches his acting muscles in this episode by playing a dangerous man with a split personality. Both *Rockford* episodes in which Pleshette appeared were written by David Chase. "David entirely marches to the tune of his own drummer," Pleshette said in 2004 after filming an episode of *The Sopranos* for Chase and HBO. "Any one of the episodes he writes and produces for *The Sopranos* is better than anything else on televison."

"Black Mirror" also marks the first of Kathryn Harrold's two appearances as Megan Dougherty. Harrold would reprise the character in the sixth season episode "Love is the Word," as well as in the 1996 reunion movie *Punishment and Crime.*

97.   A FAST COUNT

Production Number: 51108
Original Air Date: December 1, 1978
Written by: Gordon Dawson
Directed by: Reza S. Badiyi

Guest Cast: Kenneth McMillan (Morrie Hawthorne), Mary Frann (Ruth Beetson-White), Rocky Echevarria (Jesus Hernandez), Lawrence Casey (Don White), Bert Kramer (Skip LaForce), Carl Anderson (Tony Malavida), Woody Eney (F.I. Blassette), Don Starr (Bernard Kaplan), John Kerry (Dixon), Frederic Franklyn (Priest), John Yates (Second FBI Agent), Tamara Eliot (Secretary), Lisa Marie Effler (Lucy), Rosa Turich (Mama Aguilar)

Jim, you give Peg the $200 for the painting. She owes me $70, and I owe you the $46 for the Christmas trees. Harry's still out $60 for the dinner, but at least it'll void that check.

Synopsis. *Rockford has a five-percent interest in the career of promising light-heavyweight boxer Jesus Hernandez, whose road to the title has hit a major stumbling block. Manager Morrie Hawthorne can't get Jesus a match on the popular Tuesday Night Fights TV program unless he sells car dealer "Right On" Ruth Beetson-White half-ownership of Jesus' contract in the event Jesus wins. (Ruth not only manages the leading contender, she's also the primary sponsor of the show.) When Morrie is suddenly besieged with problems—first, he's accused of bribing an immigration official; then, the Boxing Commission suspends his license; finally, he's accused of murder—Rockford suspects Ruth of putting the squeeze on Morrie in order to get him to sell.*

When he wasn't needed on the set, James Garner would often relax in his motor home by playing backgammon with Luis Delgado. "When backgammon was the thing to do, we used to play it all the time," said Delgado. "When Jim wasn't working in a scene or something, we'd be playing backgammon. When he wasn't working during the summer hiatus, sometimes we'd pack some sandwiches and take a ride to the beach, park the car near some tables, and play backgammon all day."

Original art © 2005 by Darin Bristow

James Garner and Luis Delgado playing backgammon

Garner and Delgado first learned the game from actress Melina Mercouri (Garner's co-star in *A Man Could Get Killed*) and her husband, director Jules Dassin.

98.   LOCAL MAN EATEN BY NEWSPAPER

Production Number: 51113
Original Air Date: December 8, 1978
Written by: Juanita Bartlett
Directed by: Meta Rosenberg

Guest Cast: Bo Hopkins (John Cooper), Scott Brady (Harold Witbeck), Kenneth Tigar (Jerry Simpson), Scott Marlowe (Augie Arnow), Rose Gregorrio (Natalie Arnow), Joseph Hindy (Leo Cotton), Gianni Russo (Johnny Bongard), Joe E. Tata (Sal), Pat Renella (Vincent), Harley McBride (Monica), Dallas Mitchell (Dr. Richard Hagans), Ed Crick (McNaughton), Bill Cross (Security Guard), Marland Proctor (Policeman)

Sonny, this message ain't for you—it's for me [Rocky]. I just want to remind myself to pick up the big ladder at the Paint Mart.

Synopsis. *Richard Hagans, the prominent Beverly Hills physician known as "the Doctor to the Stars," hires Rockford to infiltrate the tabloid newspaper* The National Investigator *after he suspects that someone at the paper broke into his office and raided his medical records. The Investigator recently reported that actor Johnny Bongard, one of Hagans' patients, was dying of cancer. Although Bongard is completely healthy (except for a minor case of skin cancer), the tabloid item could cause him irreparable damage: Bongard is also a prominent figure in the L.A. underworld, and he could lose control of his operation if his competitors perceive him as "weak." Bongard dispatches two men to check out Hagans' records. When Rockford and Hagans catch the goons breaking into the doctor's office, Hagans is shot. Complicating the matter further: when Harold Whitbeck, the editor of the tabloid, discovers that Rockford was spying on the paper, he retaliates by running a libelous story in the* Investigator. *When Bongard reads the article, he suspects Rockford of leaking the cancer story—and puts out a contract on the detective.*

Rockford certainly met his share of off-the-wall people over the years, but even the most outrageous character was still very believable—that is to say, they behaved in a way or possessed characteristics that most viewers could identify with. For example, the heavies in each episode had to be threatening, but at the same time "you have to remember that they don't think they're doing anything wrong," explained Juanita Bartlett. "They're protecting their territory, and they feel justified."

Think back to the scene in "Chicken Little is a Little Chicken" (written by Stephen J. Cannell) in which crime kingpin Chester Sierra refers to himself as an "urban horticulturalist" whose vast citywide "garden" was bestowed on him by another mobster. As such, Sierra believes that he cannot allow anyone else to conduct business in his territory—or as he puts it, sow anything in his "garden"—unless he reaps from it directly. While this doesn't necessarily justify attempted murder (Sierra orders two of his goons to execute Rockford and Angel, only Rockford engineers an escape), at least you can almost understand Sierra's rationale for taking such action by the time he finishes his speech.

Similarly, in "Local Man Eaten by Newspaper" (written by Bartlett), the ultra-Catholic Natalie Arnow lights votive candles and prays to St. Christopher for guidance in everything she does—even when it comes to commissioning murder. "If it's God's will for Hagans to die," she says in the episode, "so be it."

As vile as the villains may act on *Rockford*, almost all of them have a peculiar quirk that makes them interesting to watch. "None of the heavies walk around thinking, *'Gee, I wish I didn't have this black hat on,'*" added Bartlett. "We tried to give them characteristics that made them real."

The Rockford Files was also one of the first television series to feature characters that reflected some of the more colorful elements of the Southern California lifestyle without ever resorting to stereotypes. "We tried to show that there's a lot more to Los Angeles than sun worshippers and movie stars and the like," said Bartlett. "They're certainly a part of the makeup of L.A., but there's also a richness to the populace that goes beyond that. There is a variety. We tried not to stereotype anyone because you have to look at your characters as human beings."

For native and longtime Angelenos, the show is a particular treat because it captures the look of a Los Angeles that no longer exists. "*Rockford* was one of the last shows to really depict L.A. as it was before the era of skyscrapers and multiplexes," said writer and *Rockford* fan Frankie Montiforte. "That's something you really notice when you watch the show in reruns.

"In the last 20 years, for example, I've noticed that almost of all of the smaller locations used in various episodes—side streets, hot dog stands, restaurants, and so forth—have long since been torn down. One of the most noticeable is the winding road in back of Universal off of Forest Lawn Drive [used, among other instances, in the scene from 'Nice Guys Finish Dead' in which Rockford throws his Goodhue Award out the car window]. That road is now an outdoor parking complex for Warner Bros. Another example is the old Jack in the Box in Studio City where Rockford pulls up in 'The Girl in the Bay City Boys Club'—that was right down the block from Burbank's last great drive-in theatre, where Rockford tears it up pretty good in another episode. Alas, neither location exists anymore. The drive-in is now home to a huge shopping complex, while the Jack-in-the-Box was razed in order to build an office building.

"Now, I realize nothing lasts forever. But it was little, out-of-the-way, almost neighborhood-type places such as those that once gave this town a look of its own. So it's fun to see them again, at least in the world of Jim Rockford."

Rockford Facts

Twenty years after lampooning print tabloids in this episode, *The Rockford Files* would take on television journalism in the reunion movie *If It Bleeds ... It Leads*.

99. WITH THE FRENCH HEEL BACK, CAN THE NEHRU JACKET BE FAR BEHIND?

Production Number: 51115
Original Air Date: January 5, 1979
Written by: Rudolph Borchert
Directed by: Ivan Dixon

Guest Cast: René Auberjonois (Masters), Erin Gray (Alta Hatch), W.K. Stratton (Lieutenant Dusenberg), Marisa Pavon (Sophia), Howard Witt (Bancroft), Christopher DeRose (Luigi), Chris Palmer (Carrols), Jim B. Smith (Officer Kline), John Zenda (Security Chief), Albert Carrier (Monty Barucci), Margarite Rae (Margo), Michael Des Barres (Keith), Frederick Castellano (Pietro), Sandy DeBruin (Nurse), Suzanne Copeland (Girl), Paula Victor (First Buyer), Dolores Quinton (Second Buyer), John Furlong (Dr. Bosca)

Jim, it's Coop. I'm at the address you wrote down for the poker game tonight. This is a gas station, it's closed, there's no one around, and now my car is stalled. Now you gotta call me at 466-3—[phone clicks].

Synopsis. *Rockford probes the apparent suicide of his friend Carol Calcote, a high-fashion supermodel who was found dead on the same night an international jetsetter named Consuela Hooper was murdered. With the help of former model Alta Hatch, Rockford discovers a link between both deaths and internationally renowned couturier Masters, whose designs are on the cutting edge of the fashion industry, but whose financial troubles are so severe, he must borrow money from loan sharks to stay afloat—and even resort to murder to protect his reputation.*

"It can be difficult sometimes to come up with 20 or 24 different stories a year, particularly after you've been on the air for several years [as *Rockford* had been, at this point]," said producer Charles Floyd Johnson. "Once in a while, you might receive a script (or an idea for a story) from an outside writer [i.e., a writer who was not a regular member of the staff] that's similar to one you had done on an earlier show. If the writer puts a different spin on the 'old' idea, and you like the script, you might decide to do it."

That's the case with this episode, which (like "The Deep Blue Sleep" before it) takes place in the world of *haute couture*. Although both shows evolve around Rockford's investigation of the death of a top-rank model, the stories themselves are completely different.

Rockford Records

"With the French Heel Back, Can the Nehru Jacket Be Far Behind?" ties the record previously set by "Sticks and Stones May Break Your Bones, But Waterbury Will Bury You" for Longest Title of a *Rockford Files* Episode. Both episodes have 12 words in the title. The episode with the second-longest title (ten words) is "Never Send a Boy King to Do a Man's Job."

100. THE BATTLE-AX AND THE EXPLODING CIGAR

Production Number: 51104
Original Air Date: January 12, 1979
Teleplay by: Rogers Turrentine
Story by: Mann Rubin and Michael Wagner
Directed by: Ivan Dixon

Guest Cast: Marge Redmond (Eleanor Bateman), Sully Boyar (Bernie Petrankus), Lane Smith (NIA Agent Donnegan), Charles Weldon (NIA Agent Watkins), Lawrence Casey (Echo Two), Glenn Corbett (FBI Agent Spelling), Mitzi Hoag (Margaret), Dawson Mays (Treasury Agent Musia), Mary Nancy Burnett (Jill), Lindsay V. Jones (Susan), Antonie Becker (Stacy Hutchins), Roscoe Born (Taliaferro), James McAlpine (First Policeman), Dennis Holahan (Agent Kaiser), Joe Bratcher (Second Policeman), Bob O'Connell (Colonel Huxley), Kirk Mee (Agent Pearce), John Trujillo (Deputy)

Miss Hallroy, City Federal. Your lost check still hasn't arrived. It's impossible for us to lose checks, so unless we receive full payment by noon today, we'll foreclose.

Synopsis. *Down and out after a brutal gambling trip to Las Vegas, Rockford bums a ride back to L.A. from a man named Petrankus in exchange for doing most of the driving. But Jim's troubles only multiply: the Vegas police arrest Rockford and Petrankus on auto theft charges, then search the car and discover a horde of stolen weapons inside the trunk. The matter worsens in Los Angeles when Rockford discovers that not only has the FBI released Petrankus, apparently no record of Petrankus' arrest even exists. After he manages to post bail, Rockford sets out to clear himself—and eventually stumbles onto a bizarre government conspiracy to sell defective weapons to third world nations.*

Here's an example of six degrees of separation, *Rockford*-style. This episode features Marge Redmond, who had co-starred with James Garner several years earlier in "All in the Family," the famous final episode of *Nichols* in which Garner's character is gunned down at the top of the show by a villain played by

Anthony Zerbe. In that episode, which was written by Juanita Bartlett, Redmond played a character whose name also happened to be "Juanita."

Redmond is best-known role to TV audiences as Sister Jacqueline in *The Flying Nun* (ABC, 1967-1970). *The Flying Nun*, of course, starred Sally Field, who would co-star with James Garner in the Oscar-nominated *Murphy's Romance* (1985).

101. GUILT

Production Number: 51117
Original Air Date: January 19, 1979
Written by: Juanita Bartlett
Directed by: William Wiard

Guest Cast: Patricia Crowley (Valerie Pointer), Ted Shackelford (Eric Genther), Rita Gam (Cynthia Germaine), Robert Quarry (Joe Zakarian), Elisabeth Brookes (Jean Ludwig), Eldon Quick (Norman Singleton), Timothy Wayne (Allen Huff), James Lough (Brian Tage), Al Stevenson (L.J.), Ben Young (Mr. Goldstone)

Jimmy ... Angel. Listen, Eddie Taliaferro just gave me a hot tip on a class filly down in the eighth out at Hollypark. Only trouble is, I need twenty ...

Synopsis. *Bittersweet memories of a failed love affair and unresolved feelings of guilt come to the surface when Rockford receives a cry for help from Valerie Pointer, the woman he nearly married 20 years ago. Valerie attempted suicide after Rockford broke off their engagement—an incident for which Jim has never ceased blaming himself. In truth, however, Valerie is a master manipulator with an uncanny knack for pushing people's buttons. Despite the enormous emotional baggage that comes with dealing with Valerie, Rockford feels compelled to help her when he learns that someone is trying to kill her.*

The highlight of this episode is the excitingly-filmed action sequence in which Rockford and Eric Genther (Ted Shackelford of *Knots Landing*) are chased by a hit man flying a helicopter. The scene intercuts footage filmed from inside the cockpit of the chopper, which provides the viewer with some very effective P.O.V. shots.

"Guilt" also features Patricia Crowley, who had also played opposite James Garner in "The Rivals," another classic episode of *Maverick*.

102.   THE DEUCE

Production Number: 51118
Original Air Date: January 26, 1979
Written by: Gordon Dawson
Directed by: Bernard McEveety

Guest Cast: Mills Watson (George Bassett), Margaret Blye (Bonnie), Sharon Spelman (Karen Hathaway), Richard Kelton (Norman Wheeler), Patricia Hindy (Fran Bassett), Robert Sampson (Arthur Horvath), Edward Walsh (Van Sickle), Joe Maross (Al Corbett), James Karen (Martin Horvath), Michael O'Dwyer (Pete Johnson), Ed McCrady (Pete), Nancy Bond (Juror), Frank Downing (Jury Foreman)

Mr. Rockford? Arthur's Hi-Fi. Your stereo's ready, but since your warranty expired in the two months it was in our shop, you'll have to pay the $60 on the repair.

Synopsis. *Rockford is the lone juror who doesn't believe that George Bassett, a chronic drinker accused of vehicular manslaughter, was responsible for the victim's death despite overwhelming circumstantial evidence to the contrary. After receiving a temporary reprieve (the judge ordered a new trial as the result of a hung jury), Bassett hires Rockford to clear him of the murder charges. After determining that the accident could have been rigged, Rockford tries to determine who framed Bassett and why.*

Rockford admits that he took on George Bassett as a client primarily because he needed the money. He had to pull out of a case because of jury duty; by the time the trial ended, his client had already hired another investigator. However, his interest in the case grows, particularly after he examines the accident victim's car at the police impound and finds evidence indicating that the accident could have been manufactured.

Rockford then provides us with a detailed description of how the accident was rigged. It's fun to see the excitement build on his own face as he takes us through every step of the operation. "Usually detective work is not anywhere near this exciting," he explains. "It's usually just sitting outside of somebody's house. But every once in a while you get one of these physical layout things. That kind of recharges your battery."

Rockford Facts

A "deuce," in police lingo, refers to a person arrested for driving under the influence (DUI).

Rockford takes his civic duty seriously. He just doesn't like doing it, and would rather avoid it altogether (two characteristics that most viewers can identify with). He even tried to get his doctor to write a letter recommending that he be excused from jury duty because it would have been bad for his back, which Rockford injured during the Korean War.

The names of the baseball players Bassett mentions at the beginning of this episode (Cecil "Rabbit" Garriott, Wayne "Twig" Terwilliger, Dom DeLaSandro, Bill Schuster) all played for the Los Angeles Angels minor league baseball team in the late 1940s.

Finally, Jack Garner (Jim's older brother) also played pro baseball before he became an actor. Garner was a pitcher in the Pittsburgh Pirates organization.

103.   THE MAN WHO SAW THE ALLIGATORS
(90-minute episode)

Production Number: 51121
Original Air Date: February 10, 1979
Written by: David Chase
Directed by: Corey Allen

Guest Cast: George Loros ("Anthony Boy" Gagglio), Luke Andreas (Syl), Sharon Acker (Adriana Danielli), Joey Aresco (Richie Gagglio), Joseph Sirola (Joseph Minette), William Bronder (Buster Hutchins), Dehl Berti (Eddie Whitefeather), Penny Santon (Mrs. Gagglio), Joseph Perry (Murf Guellow), Howard Honig (IRS Auditor Berra), Noel Conlon (Congressman Hartschorn), Julie Parrish (Jeanie), Michael J. London (Chin Jake), Lavina Dawson (Conchetta), Marc Bentley (Ethan), Raymond O'Keefe (Jake Sand)

Mr. Rockford, do you know what to do if you are attacked and killed? Ask for Albert Kim See, and Grand Opening of Happy Dawn School of Secret Arts. Win free lessons!

Synopsis. *Rockford must contend with three kinds of trouble. First, he's just had his wisdom teeth pulled; then, he faces an audit from the IRS; finally, he learns that "Anthony Boy" Gagglio (the contract killer whom he'd last encountered in the episode "To Protect and Serve") has just been paroled from San Quentin. Gagglio wants revenge against Rockford, whom he blames not only for his arrest, but also for a chronic liver problem that resulted from a bullet wound he sustained in a shootout with Rockford. In the meantime, Joseph Minette, the New York kingpin who first hired Gagglio, wants Anthony Boy to come back to work. When Gagglio refuses, Minette dispatches two men to kill Gagglio—and Rockford. After barely evading Minette's goons, Jim flees to Lake Arrowhead, where he seeks refuge at a cabin owned by his accountant. Meanwhile, after Angel crashes Rockford's trailer, Gagglio arrives and forces Angel to reveal where Rockford is hiding.*

Because Rockford frequently resorts to phony names and occupations in order to coax information out of people in the course of an investigation, the writers of the show needed a steady arsenal of names that they could draw on at any time in writing a particular episode. More often than not, these names were borrowed from either actual street names in Los Angeles (as in "Jim

Slauson"), or from members of the *Rockford Files* staff and crew (such as "This is Mr. Bartlett, from Chase Food Services").

With that in mind, you may have noticed that the name "Minette" was frequently used in a similar manner in the course of the show (often, as in this episode, as the name of a prominent mob figure). In fact, the name "Minette" was even used in the same capacity in *I Still Love L.A.*, the first of the CBS *Rockford Files* movies. "Steve, Juanita and David really liked the sound of that name, so they often threw it in whenever they needed a name," said producer Charles Floyd Johnson. "And, because Rockford was always dealing with gangsters and two-bit mob people, 'Minette' sort of became this mythical criminal figure—which was the case with the two-hour show we did in 1994 [where the character was mentioned, but not actually seen]. 'Minette' was a name that they liked to use, but I don't believe it was named after anyone in particular."

Photograph by Robert Howe

James Garner (top row, fifth from the right) poses with his crew after wrapping up the last day of shooting on "The Man Who Saw the Alligators," the final episode filmed for *Rockford*'s fifth season. Although Garner intended to end *Rockford* after five years, NBC would renew the series for a sixth and final season.

```
                    SHOOTING CALL
            UNIVERSAL CITY STUDIOS, INC.
   Due to Extreme Fire Hazard, Please Be Careful Smoking, Use Butt Cans
                                                        E    Unit   1        Day of Shooting
        MAN WHO SAW THE ALLIGATORS          No.   51121  | Director        WM. WIARD

  Series      ROCKFORD FILES                 Date    FRI.1/26/79

  Art Director     BOB CRAWLEY              Shooting Call Time    Cond'tns of Call
                                                        830A
  Set Designer  &   BOB ZILLIOX                  REPORT TO LOCATION      BUS TO LOCATION
                    730A RPT TO BLL
```

PAGES	SET DESCRIPTION	SC. NO.	D/N	LOCATION
1-7/8	EXT. BACK OF A FRAME (ANGEL, ANTHONY, SYL)	40	D	LON CHANEY CABIN BACKLOT
1-5/8	INT. A FRAME (ROCKFORD, ADRIANNA)	29,43	D	
	MOVE TO STAGE 23			
3-2/8	INT. BECKER'S OFFICE (ROCKFORD,BECKER,MRS. LAFFERTY)	12,13	D	STAGE 23
5-4/8	INT. TRAILER (ROCKFORD,ANGEL,SERRA,WHITEFEATHER,HUTCHINS)	68A	D	

ADDED SCENES

CAST AND BITS	CHARACTERS			HAIRDRESS	MAKE UP	ON SET
JAMES GARNER	ROCKFORD	(NEW)(F)	RPT LOC		830A	9A
STU MARGOLIN	ANGEL	(NEW)	RPT	MU	730A	815A
GEORGE LOROS	ANTHONY	(NEW)	RPT	MU	730A	815A
LUKE ANDREAS	SYL	(NEW)	RPT	MU	730A	815A
SHARON ACER	ADRIANNA	(NEW)(F)	RPT	MU	730A	9A
JOE SANTOS	BECKER	(NEW)(F)	RPT	SS23	11A	1130A
	MRS. LAFFERTY	(NEW)(F)	RPT	MU	1030A	1130A
	SERRA	(NEW)(F)	RPT	SS23	2P	230P
	HUTCHINS	(NEW)(F)	RPT	SS23	2P	230P
ROYDON CLARK	STUNTOR	(NEW)(F)	RPT	PROD	730A	
	WHITEFEATHER	(NEW)(F)	RPT	SS23	2P	230P

ROCKFORD WRAP PARTY SUNDAY, JANUARY 28, 1979   6P-9P
AT EL CHIQUITO ACROSS FROM WARNER'S STUDIO.

ATMOSPHERE AND STANDINS		THRU GATE	REPORT	READY ON SET
5 STANDINS			BLL	730A

ADVANCE

```
MON. 1/29  EXT./INT. MUSEUM              L.A. COUNTY MUSEUM OF ART
PROD. #51122                             5905 WILSHIRE BLVD.

TUES. 1/30   EXT. LAKE                   FALLS LAKE (RETAKES)
PROD. #51121   INT. SYL CAR (MOVING)
               EXT. PHONE BOOTH
               INT. MINETTE'S OFFICE
```

From the collection of Robert Howe

Call sheet from "The Man Who Saw the Alligators"

While there was in fact no one named "Minette" on the *Rockford* staff or crew, Juanita Bartlett believes the name "Minette" may have been derived from a popular character actor who was under contract at Universal at the time. "It probably stemmed from actor Larry Minettei (*Magnum, p,i.*), who's a friend of ours," the producer said. "We often looked for names unlike Smith, or Jones, or Thompson—something that sounded unusual. But we couldn't use 'Minettei,' because it sounds obviously Italian, so we got rid of the 'i' and made it 'Minette.' But 'Minette' doesn't refer to anybody in particular on the show. It just became a name that was convenient to use."

Rockford Facts

While most of the action in "The Man Who Saw the Alligators" allegedly takes place at Lake Arrowhead (a popular mountain resort in Southern California), the episode was actually filmed on the back lot at Universal Studios. "The cabin they used in that show was the old 'Lon Chaney cabin' at Universal," said Rob Howe, a frequent visitor to the *Rockford* set during the show's fifth and sixth seasons. "Lon Chaney Sr., of course, was a huge film star at Universal back in the 1920s. The 'Chaney cabin' at Universal was a replica of the famous mountain hideaway that Chaney built in the Inyo National Forest in the Sierra Nevada—a cabin which, by the way, is a national monument today."

Though originally broadcast as a 90-minute episode, "The Man Who Saw the Alligators" was soon edited down to 60 minutes and included in the original *Rockford Files* syndication package that was released later in 1979.

104.   THE RETURN OF THE BLACK SHADOW

Production Number: 51119
Original Air Date: February 17, 1979
Written by: Stephen J. Cannell
Directed by: William Wiard

Guest Cast: Bo Hopkins (John Cooper), Paul Koslow (Whispering Willie Green), Dennis Burkley (Animal), Laurie Jefferson (Gail Cooper), Andy Jarrel (Phil Dankus), Jerry Ayres (Robert Gries), Ken A. Anderson (Harry), Noah Keen (Dr. Greenberg), Paul Mays (Festus), Sandra DeBruin (Nurse), Scott Walker (Hilliard)

Jim, this is Florence Boyle. You worked for my husband last month in Glendale. You were so helpful then, and—well, I have a problem of my own I'd like to discuss. Confidentially, of course.

Synopsis. *Rockford's excursion with Gail Cooper (John Cooper's sister) turns ugly when they find themselves harassed by a sadistic gang of bikers known as the Rattlers. While the rest of the Rattlers converge on Rockford, ringleader Whispering Willie abducts Gail, steals Rockford's car, drives her to a secluded area, and rapes her. With both Gail and Rockford hospitalized as a result of the ordeal, Coop undertakes the investigation himself. Drawing on his experience as a member of the old Black Shadow motorcycle gang, Coop infiltrates the Rattlers in order to bring down their operation—and avenge the brutal assault on his sister.*

William Wiard (pronounced "wired") was as close to being a regular director as *The Rockford Files* had: he helmed 26 of the show's 118 episodes, including this one. "Bill Wiard had been a film editor before he became a director, and that was reflected in his approach to directing," said Jack Garner. "When he was directing, he was always 'cutting' the film in his own mind. He always seemed to know exactly the shot he wanted when he filmed it, and because of that, he never needed to shoot a lot of unnecessary film. He was really efficient, and extremely effective as a director, and he was just marvelous to work for."

Rockford Facts

"The Return of the Black Shadow" is the last of the three episodes featuring Bo Hopkins as Rockford's attorney John Cooper. Hopkins had worked with several *Rockford* personnel prior to his stint on the show, including James Garner (on *Nichols*), Noah Beery Jr. (with whom he co-starred in the series *Doc Eliot*), Luis Delgado (who was a stunt driver on *The Getaway*), and Roy Huggins (producer of *The Invasion of Johnson County*, an acclaimed 1976 TV-movie featuring Hopkins).

Hopkins, a regular on *Dynasty* throughout the '80s, was also a fixture in Westerns, including *The Wild Bunch*, the classic 1969 film directed by Sam Peckinpah.

From the collection of Robert Howe

Call sheet from "A Material Difference."

105.   A MATERIAL DIFFERENCE

Production Number: 51116
Original Air Date: February 24, 1979
Written by: Rogers Turrentine
Directed by: William Wiard

Guest Cast: Michael McGuire (Robert Bernard), Joshua Bryant (Holt), David Tress (Brother Bert), Rod Browning (Brother Leonard), Michael Alldridge (Dobson), John Davey (Cramer), Donald Bishop (Brother Randolph), Phil Chambers (Old Man), Alex Rodine (First Man), Ari Barakar (Second Man), Ron McCabe (Patrolman), Vance Davis (Cop), Lydia Kristen (Woman), Cynthia Nye (Receptionist)

Jim—Joel Meyers of Crowell, Fitch & Merriweather. We're going to court tomorrow on that Penrose fraud case, but the steno misplaced your 200-page deposition. Could you come down tonight and give it again?

Synopsis. *Rockford becomes embroiled in Angel's latest, most bizarre get-rich-quick scheme yet. Advertising himself as a hit man named Jones, Angel figures he can make a fortune without ever killing anyone by simply collecting the front money. Though Angel thinks the plan is foolproof (his "clients" can't send the police after him without incriminating themselves), the operation hits a snag with the very first client: a Russian undercover agent who wants "Mr. Jones" to assassinate a Soviet defector believed to have a secret formula for denim. Rockford and Angel soon find themselves on the run from Russian agents (who want Angel for not killing the defector) and U.S. Naval Intelligence officials (who want the formula for use in making Navy dungarees). The matter becomes further convoluted when the man Angel was supposed to have killed turns up dead.*

Occasionally (as in this episode), Dennis Becker is put in a position where his personal friendship with Rockford becomes secondary to his duties as a police officer. Rockford telephones Becker for information, just as Chapman discovers that Rockford is wanted in connection with the shooting of Cramer. Chapman instructs Becker to stay on the line with Rockford long enough to have the call traced. However, Rockford senses what's going on, and he cuts the conversation short. Becker, a little defensively, tells Chapman he did the best he could—and we can certainly see that he did. Once again, Becker found himself in a no-win situation.

"We felt it would be realistic if we sometimes put Becker in those kinds of situations," said Juanita Bartlett. "He was Jim's friend, but he was also a police officer, and there were rules he had to follow. But you could understand why Becker did what he had to do in those circumstances, without losing respect for him."

Photograph by Robert Howe

James Garner shares a laugh with property master Bill Fannon (left) and assistant director Leonard R. Garner (right) during a break in the filming of "Never Send a Boy King to Do a Man's Job."

Rockford Facts

Part of the action in "A Material Difference" takes place on February 24, which was also the date this segment was first broadcast on in 1979. Also according to this episode, Angel's I.D. number in the police mug shot books is 608280.

106.   NEVER SEND A BOY KING TO DO A MAN'S JOB
(Two-hour episode)
(Originally Entitled: "The Return of Richie Brockelman")

Production Number: 51122
Original Air Date: March 3, 1979
Written by: Juanita Bartlett
Directed by: William Wiard

Guest Cast: Dennis Dugan (Richie Brockelman), Harold Gould (Mr. Brockelman), Kim Hunter (Mrs. Brockelman), Robert Webber (Harold "Jack" Coombs), Trisha Noble (Odette Lependeaux), Pepper Martin (Harry Stone), Gary Crosby (Larry Litrell), David Hooks (Frederick Doyle), Salt Walther (Drew), Stanley Brock (Cowboy Mickey), Jack Collins (Dr. Wetherford), Todd Martin (Robert Wendkos), Stephanie Hankinson (Toulie), Bob Basso (Auctioneer), Danny Ades (Egyptian Consul), Michele Hart (Maggie), Jennifer Holmes (Amy), John Wyche (Museum Guard), Robert Ward (Second Workman), Shirley Anthony (Receptionist)

Mr. Rockford? Miss Collins from the Bureau of Licenses. We got your renewal before the extended deadline, but not your check. I'm sorry, but at midnight you're no longer licensed as an investigator.

Jim—Denny, from Denny's Pest Blasters. I've a great deal for you. We'll rub out your rodents at a tremendously low cost, so call us. We're in the Yellow Pages, and we mean business.

Synopsis. *Ruthless sports promoter Harold "Jack" Coombs strongarms Richie Brockelman's father into selling the family printing plant, which he plans to turn into a race track. Coombs not only bought the family business for a fraction of its worth, he also soundly humiliated the elder Brockelman in the process—first by buying off the City Council and City Zoning Commission, then by bribing Brockelman's lawyer, and finally by having the old man brutally beaten. An angry Richie implores Rockford to intercede. Although initially reluctant to take on the powerful Coombs, Rockford decides to help the Brockelmans get their money back. With the help of Richie, Angel, and a cast of grade-A grifters, Rockford tries to* ensnare Coombs with a "big store" con designed around a bogus agreement with the Egyptian government and the Cairo Museum to arrange a second exhibit of the treasures of Tutankhamen.

Like "There's One in Every Port," "Never Send a Boy King to Do a Man's Job" is very similar to the classic *Maverick* episode "Shady Deal at Sunny Acres" in that Rockford employs several expert grifters as part of an elaborate sting operation designed to upend an unscrupulous opponent. The expanded two-hour length allows the episode to provide the viewer with a look at some of the preparation that goes into running such a con (including a sequence that finds Rockford holding a "casting call" for some of the grifters), which adds a sense of realism to the proceedings.

Photograph from the collection of Robert Howe

Rob Howe, a frequent visitor to the *Rockford* set during the fifth and sixth seasons, poses with Noah Beery Jr. during a break in filming on "Never Let a Boy King Do a Man's Job." "Pidge [Beery's longtime nickname] was very outgoing as Rocky, but off-camera he was really very shy," recalls Howe. "Many times between scenes, he would just sit quietly and smoke his pipe. But he was such a sweetheart. He and Jim had such great chemistry together, and their relationship as father and son really made the show complete."

Rockford Facts

"Never Send a Boy King" marks the third appearance of Jimmy Joe Meeker, Rockford's Oklahoma oilman alter ego. Rockford had previously brought back "Jimmy Joe" in "With the French Heel Back, Can the Nehru Jacket Be Far Behind?"

SHOOTING CALL
UNIVERSAL CITY STUDIOS, INC.
Due to Extreme Fire Hazard, Please Be Careful Smoking, Use Butt Cans.

Picture "BOY KING"	No. 51122	Unit 11 Director WIARD	Day of Shooting
Serial THE ROCKFORD FILES — 1 HR TV	Date MON. JAN. 29, 1979	
Art Director ROB CRAWLEY	Shooting Call Time 1030AM	Condition of Call
Set Dresser BOB ZILLIOX 9:00AM LV OLL	☐ REPORT TO LOCATION	☒ BUS TO LOCATION

PAGES	SET DESCRIPTION	SC. NO.	D/N	LOCATION
7/8	EXT. L.A. COUNTY MUSEUM (DOYLE,AMY,MAN,RICHIE,COOMBS,ATMOS.)	63A,63B	D	L.A. COUNTY MUSEUM OF ART
7/8	EXT. STREET MUSEUM (RICHIE,COOMBS,STONE,ATMOS.)	64	D	5905 WILSHIRE BL.
1-1/8	EXT. EGYPTIAN EMBASSY (COOMBS,STONE,AHMED,TOULIE,ATMOS.)	84,85,86	D	
2-6/8	INT. L.A. COUNTY MUSEUM (RICHIE,DOYLE,AMY,COOMBS,GUARD,ATMOS.)	63C,63D,63E	D	
1-7/8	INT. ALCOVE (RICHIE,DOYLE,COOMBS,AMY,ATMOS.)	63F	D	
5/8	EXT. EGYPTIAN EMBASSY (ROCKFORD,ODETTE,COOMBS,STONE,AHMED,ATMOS.)	65,66,67	N	

CAST AND BITS	CHARACTERS		HAIRDRESS	MAKE UP	ON SET
DENNIS DUGAN	RICHIE	(F)	RPT LOC	945A	1030A
ROBERT WEBBER	COOMBS	(F)	RPT LOC	945A	1030A
PEPPER MARTIN	STONE	(F)	RPT MU	900A	1030A
DAVID HOOKS	(NEW)DOYLE	(F)	RPT MU	900A	1030A
JENNIFER HOLMES	(NEW)AMY	(F)	RPT MU	830A	1030A
JACK GARNER	(NEW)MAN	(F)	RPT MU	900A	
ROYDON CLARK	STUNTOR	(F)	RPT MU	900A	1130A
DANNY ADES	(NEW)AHMED	(F)	RPT MU	900A	1130A
STEPHANIE HANKINSON	TOULIE	(F)	RPT MU	900A	1200N
JOHN WYCHE	(NEW)GUARD	(F)	RPT MU	900A	500P
TRISHA NOBLE	ODETTE	(F)	RPT MU	500P	

ATMOSPHERE AND STANDINS	THRU GATE	REPORT	READY ON SET
5 STANDINS	1000A	LOC	
15 ATMOS.	1000A	LOC	

ADVANCE

TUES. 1/30	
EXT. LAKE	FALLS LAKE
INT. SYL'S CAR	
EXT. PHONE BOOTH	
INT. MINETTE'S OFFICE	STAGE
WED. 1/31	
EXT. RACEWAY (2ND UNIT)	RIVERSIDE INTERNATIONAL RACEWAY

From the collection of Robert Howe

Call sheet from "Never Send a Boy King to Do a Man's Job."
This was for a location shoot at the Los Angeles County Museum of Art.

107. A DIFFERENT DRUMMER
(Originally Entitled: "A Chorus of Drummers")

Production Number: 51120
Original Air Date: April 13, 1979
Written by: Rudolph Borchert
Directed by: Reza S. Badiyi

Guest Cast: John Considine (Dr. Lee Yost), Jesse Welles (Sorel Henderson), Carmen Arganziano (Dumas), Walter Brooke (Dr. Bosca), Dave Cass (Casey), Reni Santoni (Perry), Harland Warde (Evan Grange), Fritzi Burr (Tax Assistant), Patrick Culleton (Patrolman), Sandy Freeman (Dr. Addison), Anne Bellamy (Nurse), Ray Stricklyn (Dr. Stark), Lesley Woods (Lucy Grange), Will Gill Jr. (Orderly), Glenn Robards (Father), Don Furneaux (Janitor)

Jim, this is Andrea, Todd's Food Mart. Listen, there's a guy down here by the name of Angel Martin who's charged $110 worth of groceries to your account. Is that okay with you?

Synopsis. *At a nearby VA hospital, where he receives treatment for injuries he sustained in a car accident, Rockford witnesses a transaction between Dr. Lee Yost, who runs a organ donor service in conjunction with the hospital, and the parents of a male patient who has just died. Yost receives authorization to remove the dead man's cornea. A short while later, while looking for a telephone, Rockford stumbles past the surgical room and catches a glimpse of Yost performing the operation. To Rockford's surprise, he sees movement in the fingers of the allegedly deceased body! Despite assurances that what he witnessed is not an unusual medical phenomenon, Jim becomes curious about Yost—particularly after the doctor goes out of his way to befriend him. With the help of a hospital trustee, Rockford discovers that Yost is an amoral character who "collects donors," then arranges for their deaths so that he sell their organs to his wealthy clientele.*

The initial premise of this episode once again brings to mind the tremendous physical toll that *The Rockford Files* ultimately had on its star, James Garner. "I know that Jim had knee surgery between the end of season two and the start of season three," said Rob Howe, a frequent visitor to the *Rockford* set while the show was originally in production. "But since the hiatus period between seasons is usually no more than three months, that's not enough time to recoup properly. Add in the fact that Jim was in 95% of the scenes and spent a great deal of time on his feet on the pavement, and he never really got a chance to recover from those surgeries."

In many ways, the injuries Garner sustained in the six years he made *Rockford* is yet another testament to the time and effort he puts into his craft. "I never once heard or saw Jim complain about having to put in the hours that were required to film *Rockford*," added Howe. "He was always ready to go, always accessible to crew and fans and people on the street who would come up to him to shake his hand or get an autograph. When [the show was on location] at Paradise Cove, Jim would have his chair in the sand and he would sit and sign autographs from a pad of paper that read 'From the Desk of Jim Rockford.' Little kids, who no doubt were sent by their mothers, would walk up soaking wet out of the surf and ask Jim for his signature. Jim was great with them, as he was with everyone. He would pose for pictures, no matter how exhausted he was. There was never any 'star' attitude with Jim."

That said, Garner has never been shy about discussing the various physical ailments he has sustained over the years. As often (and as matter-of-factly) as he mentions them in interviews, one gets the sense that he wears his injuries almost like a badge of honor. No doubt the actor's resilience from his injuries is part of his overall appeal. Like a Timex, a character played by James Garner may take a licking, but he'll somehow keep on ticking. "Jim was the same way on *Bret Maverick* after he got hurt when he got tossed off the mechanical bull while filming the pilot in 1981," added Howe. "He didn't complain. He just taped himself up and came straight back to work. The man is pure class."

Garner once gave a particularly memorable litany of his injuries when he appeared on *The Tonight Show with Johnny Carson* in 1986. "I'm always in pain, John," the actor said. "With all the injuries I've had, I'm always in pain. I've got nine incisions on my knee. I've broken 12 ribs at one time, about 16 or 17 altogether. I've broken bone on my spine, I've broken my tail bone, I've broken every [major] ligament and bone ... other than that, hey, I'm in good shape!"

"And you've only been married once," quipped Carson, a response that immediately broke Garner into laughter.

Rockford Familiar Faces

John Considine (Dr. Yost) co-starred with James Garner and Joanne Woodward in *Breathing Lessons*, a 1994 presentation of *The Hallmark Hall of Fame* based on the novel by Anne Tyler. A veteran of such daytime serials as *The Young and the Restless* and *Another World*, Considine is also the older brother of onetime Disney child star Tim Considine (*The Hardy Boys, Spin & Marty, My Three Sons*).

Appendix G
Christmas with Jim Rockford

Here are a few snapshots from the Christmas party that James Garner threw for the *Rockford Files* cast and crew on December 23, 1978, after production had wrapped on the episode "A Material Difference." The celebration took place on Stage 23 at Universal Studios, where interiors for the series were filmed.

My thanks to Rob Howe for sharing these informal shots and providing us with a rare peek at Garner relaxing with his professional family.

Photographs by Robert Howe

Left: James Garner plays Santa Claus as he chats with an unidentified crew member
Right: Garner presents a gift to his longtime stunt coordinator Roy Clark
(in leather jacket) as two members of the *Rockford* crew look on

Photograph by Robert Howe

Luis Delgado ("Officer Billings") happily clutches his Christmas present. Notice in the background the painting of Paradise Cove, which was used as a backdrop outside the trailer set on Stage 23.

Photograph by Robert Howe

Gaffer Gibby Germaine, whose association with James Garner dated back to the days of *Maverick*.

Sixth Season: 1979–1980

Sometime in the summer of 1979, an accountant at Universal Studios provided James Garner with a profit-and-loss statement for the first five seasons of *The Rockford Files*. The statement indicated that while the series grossed $52 million after the first five seasons, the production costs and other related expenditures amounted to over $61 million. In other words, the studio claimed that after five seasons, *The Rockford Files* was over $9 million in the red.

Garner was dumbfounded by the revelation, particularly since he had strived to produce the series on time and within budget every week. "It's pretty disheartening to know that you've done everything you could to bring a show in on schedule, and then find out it's all been a waste of time," he told *Playboy* in 1981. "We were no more than a total of seven days over on our shooting schedule [for the entire series]—and *nobody* had ever done that before. I also rented my company's semis and trucks and lights to the show for a lot less money than Universal would have charged in order to keep the show's costs down, to always keep it within our budget. I worked and scrimped and saved and pushed and cajoled and did everything I knew to make the show successful ... and then to find out it's all worthless, that'll punch a hole in your balloon."

The revelation about the show's apparent lack of profit was particularly shocking in light of the fact that Garner had amended his contract in 1976, taking a cut in his per-episode salary in exchange for a personal percentage of the show's profits. Those negotiations were based on good faith that there would indeed be profits to share by the time the series was completed.

The news literally added insult to injury. Garner had planned to end *The Rockford Files* after five seasons, partially because his 51-year-old body was beginning to wear down from the grueling physical demands of the show. By the end of the fifth season, the actor had undergone three knee operations, sustained a broken spinal bone, suffered two broken knee caps, and endured broken ribs, broken knuckles, a dislocated disk in his back and knee, and various other dislocations, sprains, torn ligaments and tendons since commencing production of the series in 1974. Although Garner's contract with Universal had one more year to run, the studio's contract with NBC with regard to *Rockford Files* had expired at the end of the fifth season. Garner figured that if the series ended after five years, he could finally give his body a rest. However,

PRIVATE INVESTIGATOR
"Charlie Harris
at Large"
today at 5 PM

While James Garner continued to film new segments of *The Rockford Files* for NBC, the episodes from the first five seasons were syndicated in the fall of 1979 under the title *Jim Rockford, Private Investigator*. This studio ad promoting the broadcast of the episode "Charlie Harris at Large" appeared in newspapers and television supplements throughout the country. The episodes from the sixth season were added to the syndication package in September 1980.

NBC head of programming Fred Silverman elected to renew *The Rockford Files* for a sixth season.

Garner understood the situation from the network's point of view. Coming off a season in which it finished last among the three major networks for the first time in its history, NBC really couldn't afford to cancel *The Rockford Files*, one of the few established shows the network had. After all, *Rockford* was still a Friday night staple: although its overall audience figures were 10% lower during its fifth season, that decrease was directly attributable to the show's temporary relocation to Saturday nights. For that reason, NBC decided to make *Rockford* the anchor of the network's Friday schedule. NBC president Mike Weinblatt explained the strategy to *Broadcasting Magazine* in September 1979: "We wanted to have every nine o'clock show on more solid structure—a returning show that had a built-in audience level—and let that show be the spine of the schedule. That's why we have *Rockford* back [at nine on Fridays]."

So Garner tried to tough it out. Indeed, he frequently visited the studio pharmacy for pain pills and muscle relaxants to keep him on his feet. However, one day in December 1979, "I was on the stage and I had such pains in my stomach and I didn't know what the trouble was," he told *Playboy* in 1981. "I just doubled up in pain, and I was bleeding rectally. I couldn't breathe because of one of my sinuses. It was not a wonderful moment. I said, 'Whoa, get me to a doctor,' so the studio doctor came out and discovered that my ulcer had come back with a vengeance."

For three days, Garner rehabilitated at the Scripps Medical Clinic in La Jolla, California, where his physicians advised him to take an immediate rest. As a result, Garner announced that *The Rockford Files* had shut down production for the year. Three weeks later, just before Christmas 1979, NBC announced that the series would leave the network's schedule following the January 10, 1980 telecast.

In the meantime, the series went out on a few high notes. NBC announced that a number of "big names" would guest star on *The Rockford Files* during the 1979-1980 season, including Lauren Bacall; Rita Moreno (in her third appearance as Rita Capkovic); country-western recording artist Barbara Mandrell; and Mariette Hartley, who had co-starred with Garner in an award-winning series of television commercials for Polaroid cameras that were tremendously popular in the late 1970s.

Another highlight was "The Hawaiian Headache," an episode filmed entirely in Honolulu. "Universal wanted us to do a show in Hawaii," recalled Luis Delgado. "But since there was nothing in Jim's contract addressing that, if they wanted to do a show out of state, they'd have to approach him first."

Garner agreed to make the special episode on one condition. "Jim said that he'd do the show in Hawaii, only if he could take his whole crew over there," Delgado continued. "Universal didn't want to do that because that would have made the show even more expensive—because in addition to paying everyone's salaries, they'd have to fly everyone over and back, and pay for rooming, and per diem, and all of that. Jim said, 'Well then, I'm not going over there. If my crew doesn't go, then I'm not going.'"

Eventually, the studio gave in and allowed Garner to take his entire staff and crew to Honolulu. While this may have been an exception as far as studio policy was concerned, there was nothing unusual about Garner's gesture. "Usually, when you go on location, the lowest man on the totem pole doesn't get to go any place," explained Delgado. "But, whenever we did *Rockford Files* out of state, the whole crew went. No one was left out—the cutters, the craftsmen, the stand-ins, the secretaries, everybody went. And then we stayed an extra day after we finished so we could have a party."

Photograph courtesy of Photofest
© 1979 Universal City Studios, Inc.

Noah Beery Jr. and James Garner in a promotional shot for "The Hawaiian Headache," one of the highlights of Rockford's sixth and final season on NBC

Stuart Margolin won his second consecutive Emmy for Best Supporting Actor in a Dramatic Series. *The Rockford Files* received several other nominations in its final year, including Best Dramatic Series, Best Dramatic Actor (James Garner), and Best Supporting Actor (Noah Beery Jr.). Lauren Bacall and Mariette Hartley also received Emmy nods for their guest appearances this season.

Photograph courtesy of Movieland Productions
© 1979 Universal City Studios, Inc.

Mariette Hartley and James Garner in a scene from "Paradise Cove," the episode that launched *Rockford*'s final season on NBC

Photograph by Robert Howe

Lauren Bacall and James Garner rehearsing a scene from "Lions, Tigers, Monkeys and Tigers," a two-hour *Rockford* from the sixth season

Episode Guide for the Sixth Season

108. PARADISE COVE

Production Number: 53801
Original Air Date: September 28, 1979
Produced, Written and Directed by: Stephen J. Cannell

Guest Cast: Mariette Hartley (Althea Morgan), Leif Ericson (Carl Colton "C.C." Calloway), Byron Morrow (Don McLinton), Frederick Herrick (Cliff Calloway), Christine Avila (Nurse), Peter Brocco (Roscoe Ragland), John Davey (Rudy), Raymond O'Keefe (Jake Sand), Branscomb Richmond (Frankie Revy), Jerry Sommers (McJerrow), Tony Brubaker (Kermit Wilson)

Jim, this is Cal from the Leave The Whales Alone Club. Our protest leaves from the pier Saturday at 3:00 a.m. The whales need you, Jim!

Synopsis. *Jim's latest nemesis is his neighbor C.C. Calloway, a retired Malibu County sheriff who has been trying to incite the other members of the Paradise Cove Trailer Colony into drumming Rockford out of the neighborhood. In addition, Calloway won a $35,000 judgment against Rockford for a ruptured vertebrae that allegedly resulted from a car accident which Rockford caused. Rockford thinks that Calloway feigned the injury, particularly after he spots the old man maneuvering a metal detector around the beach with no apparent difficulty. With Angel's help, Rockford discovers why his neighbor wants him out of the way. Calloway thinks there's a fortune in gold bouillon buried underneath Rockford's trailer.*

When Rockford determines why Calloway wants him out of Paradise Cove, he agrees to move his trailer if Calloway signs an affidavit waiving the judgment and declaring that his back injury was caused prior to the accident. Not only that, Calloway must give Rockford 10% of whatever he finds underneath the trailer.

What Calloway doesn't count on, of course, is Rockford using his own greed against him. Calloway overlooked the fact that the gold was stolen from a U.S. military vault—and thus belongs to the government. Which means that Rockford suckered Calloway into surrendering his judgment for nothing.

Rockford Facts

The actual Nashua trailer used on *The Rockford Files* was regularly transported to and from Paradise Cove in Malibu for the purpose of filming exterior shots such as the ones we see in this episode. The scenes inside the trailer, however, were always shot at the studio. "The interior shots for the trailer were filmed on Stage 23 at Universal," said Rob Howe, a regular visitor to the *Rockford* set during the fifth and sixth seasons. "It was a complete trailer with removable walls at the end by the couch [so that they could set up the camera to film scenes where Jim is standing in the kitchen] and behind Rockford's desk [so they could film people entering or exiting the trailer]. Stage 23 was also the soundstage where they filmed the squad room scenes at the police station, as well as the interior for Rocky's house, Becker's office, the interrogation room, and the hallway outside the squad room."

By the way, Officer Billings (Luis Delgado) must have received a promotion to plainclothes detective since his last appearance on the show. The character does not appear in uniform in this episode or in any of his other appearances this season.

Rockford Familiar Faces

Guest stars include Mariette Hartley, who at the time of this episode co-starred with James Garner in a popular series of television commercials for Polaroid cameras. The lighthearted banter between the two actors in those spots was so believable, many viewers were convinced that Garner and Hartley were actually married—which eventually prompted the actress to print a special T-shirt with the disclaimer "I am *not* Mrs. James Garner."

Though Garner and Hartley had obviously known each other for several years by the time she appeared on *Rockford*, it was not until filming began on the show that Garner first discovered a skill of Hartley's that immediately left an impression. "Mariette had this really great whistle—the kind you use in New York to hail a cab," said Rob Howe. "That's how loud it was. Once Jim realized how strong Mariette could whistle, he immediately put it to good use.

"Normally when we were on the soundstage, our sound man John Carter would ring the bell to signify *'Quiet on the set, we're ready to shoot.'* But John didn't have to have to do that on 'Paradise Cove.' Instead, Jim had Mariette do her whistle to get everyone's attention! That episode was a lot of fun, and it was great to see Mariette and Jim together."

Hartley received an Emmy nomination for Best Actress in a Dramatic Series for her performance in "Paradise Cove."

109.   LIONS, TIGERS, MONKEYS AND DOGS
(Two-hour episode)

Production Numbers: 53803/53804
Original Air Date: October 12, 1979
Produced and Written by: Juanita Bartlett
Directed by: William Wiard

Guest Cast: Lauren Bacall (Kendall Warren), Dana Wynter (Princess Irene Rachevsky), Ed Nelson (Blake Sternlight), Corinne Michaels (Linda Hassler), Michael Lombard (Gus Fairfield), Christopher Thomas (Freddie Danzig), Carmine Caridi (Tommy Minette), Leo Gordon (Charles Martell), Robert Dunlap (Repairman Crane), Jon Cedar (Peter Pantazzi), Roger Til (Henri Tayir), Abel Franco (Max Rocorro), Shirley Anthony (Gwen Bagley), Michael DesBarres (Gordon Flack), Charles Picerni (Richard Soderling), Douglas Ryan (Second Partygoer), Julie Parrish (Donna Soderling), Ivan Barrick (Maitre D'), Melody Thomas (Sherry), Nicholas Worth (First Partygoer), Wally Taylor (Policeman), Paul Marin (Attorney), T. Maratti (Paul Juliano Jr.), Harold Ayer (Minister), Alfred Dennis (Paul Juliano Sr.)

This is Betty Furnell. I don't know who to call, but I can't reach my Foodaholics partner. I'm at Vito's, on my second pizza with sausage and mushroom—Jim, come and get me!

Jim, this is Jenelle. I'm flying tonight, so I can't make our date—and I've got to find a safe place for Daffy. He loves you, Jim, and you'll see—Great Danes are no problem.

Synopsis. *A chance meeting at a posh Beverly Hills restaurant brings Rockford to the attention of the elegant Princess Irene Rachevsky, who wants to hire the private investigator to probe a series of attacks targeted at her close friend Kendall Warren. Rockford rescues Kendall from a knife-wielding assailant at a costume party, then tracks down the hit man at a nearby hotel. When the hit man takes a fatal leap off the hotel balcony after trying to escape, Rockford becomes accused of his murder, but Kendall and the Princess have the charges dropped. At first, Jim believes that fashion news reporter Gus Fairfield, whom the Princess is suing for* *libel, is behind the attacks. As a precaution, Kendall stays with Rocky until Rockford can resolve the matter. But after Kendall is assaulted once again, Rockford suspects the Princess herself—the only other person who knew where he was sheltering Kendall.*

Photograph courtesy of Photofest
© 1979 Universal City Studios, Inc.

Private eye Jim Rockford (James Garner) engages socialite Kendall Warren (Lauren Bacall) in conversation during a costume ball in the two-hour episode "Lions, Tigers, Monkeys and Dogs."

Photograph by Robert Howe

Lauren Bacall in a pensive moment between takes of "Lions, Tigers, Monkeys and Dogs"

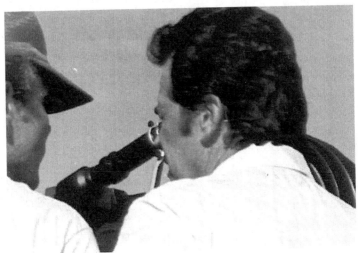

Photograph by Robert Howe

Officially, James Garner helmed just one episode of *The Rockford Files* ("The Girl in the Bay City Boys Club"), but he was often looked upon as an auxiliary director throughout the time the series was in production. Here we see him peering into the camera lens and consulting with cinematographer Steve Yaconelli before shooting a sequence on location at Paradise Cove for "Lions, Tigers, Monkeys and Dogs."

The dynamic onscreen rapport between James Garner and fellow screen legend Lauren Bacall highlights "Lions, Tigers, Monkeys and Dogs." It's fun to watch the two of them together, and it's clear that they both had fun filming the episode. "I didn't know Bacall before we worked together," said Garner in an interview for this book. "But we got along great. We understood each other, and I have such great admiration for her."

"That show was definitely a star turn," added Juanita Bartlett.

Photograph by Robert Howe

Noah Beery Jr. relaxes with his pipe in front of Rockford's trailer. Behind him from left to right: Stan (assistant property master), Bill Fannon (property master), an unidentified set photographer for Universal (back to the camera), and series star James Garner. This photo was taken during a break in filming on location at Paradise Cove for the episode "Lions, Tigers, Monkeys and Dogs."

"This photograph was taken the day I drove Pidge to his rental house up the road in Malibu," said Rob Howe, a friend of the *Rockford* set during the fifth and sixth seasons. "He was done shooting for the day, and for some reason none of the regular drivers were available to drive him home, so I told Bill Fannon I would be happy to give Pidge a lift. Bill said, 'Ask Pidge.' I did, and Pidge said, '*Are you sure? It's not out of your way?*' I said, 'Absolutely not.' So we went to my car. He was still in his wardrobe—which, I'm not mistaken, was mostly his own clothes. He looked inside my car and said, '*Oh, I can't get in that car with these dirty clothes on!*' I told him not to worry, that wouldn't be a problem at all. So he climbed inside, and I drove him home. It definitely was a memory that I cherish. He was a very sweet man."

Bacall, who received an Emmy nomination for this episode, later co-starred with Garner in *The Fan* (1981). Earlier in 1979, Garner and Bacall appeared together in *H.E.A.L.T.H.*, a feature film directed by Robert Altman.

Rockford Facts

This episode is available as part of MCA/Universal's *Rockford Files* home video series.

110./111. ONLY ROCK 'N' ROLL WILL NEVER DIE
(Two-Parter)

Production Numbers: 53802/53806
Original Air Dates: October 19 and 26, 1979
Written by: David Chase
Directed by: William Wiard

Guest Cast: Kristoffer Tabori (Tim Ritchie), Marcia Strassman (Whitney Cox), George Loros (Eddie), Lenny Baker (Ronny Martz), Stanley Brock (Bernie Seldon), Leigh Christian (Diane Bjornstrom), Jean Paul Vignon (Alain Florio), Fred Carney (Mitchell Robinson), Michael Champion (Dwight Deleau), Jan Marie Teague (Julie Immelman), Laurie Lea Schaefer (Linda Jones), Alan Chappius (Aonor Florio), Marion Yue (Chiyoko Takai), Jesse Dizon (Jerry Ito), Kathryn O'Neil (Secretary), Charles Rowe (Anchorman)

We're down at Hennesey's Bar, Jim,
*   having a drink or two!*
You'd better get down here quick, Jim,
*   or we'll probably take up your stool!*
[Drunken laughter ensues.]

Jimmy, this is Dora. I'm going to move in with the kids, but I'll sure miss you, dear. Thank you for taking out the garbage every week. I'll send you a card for your birthday.

Synopsis. *Pop music superstar Tim Ritchie, already facing a palimony lawsuit by his former live-in girlfriend Diane Bjornstrom, hires Rockford to locate his record producer and longtime friend Bryan Charles, who disappeared after they had a major dispute seven days earlier. Jim learns that Charles supplied Evergreen Management, a rival record label run by mobster Bernie Seldon, with bootlegged copies of Ritchie's latest LP* Renegade Lotion—*a move which has cost Ritchie's company $1.4 million in profits. The matter turns to murder when Rockford finds Charles buried in the back yard of his own home.*

Because of his chronic knee problems, James Garner was often required to wear knee pads while filming fight scenes and other action sequences. Though the pads provided the actor with some level of comfort and protection, for obvious reasons they could never completely absorb the kind of punishment Garner's knees often endured in the course of filming a fight.

Rob Howe, a frequent visitor to the *Rockford* set, recalls that Garner was in even greater pain than usual during the filming of this episode. "When Jim and George Loros are attacked at the trailer and Jim is 'shot,' he rolled over on the pavement and banged his knee pretty bad," he explained. "As the scene was originally written, Rockford was supposed to limp, anyway, after the shooting attempt—after all, he had just been 'shot.' But because of how badly Jim banged his knee during filming, they ended up attributing the limp in the show as a result of Rockford hurting his knee."

Once again, Garner somehow toughed it out and continued on despite the pain. "Jim worked through pain *all* the time," said Howe. "The man is a trooper. He soldiered on with ice packs and Tylenol and finished the scene ... I think Jim soldiered on more than anything else because he knew he had his 'family' to take care of—meaning, of course, his crew. Of all the celebrities I've met or worked for through the years, I have never found anyone more decent than Jim Garner."

Rockford Facts

George Loros was previously cast as the tightly wound mobster Anthony Boy in the episodes "To Protect and Serve" and "The Man Who Saw the Alligators," as well as the equally paranoid hit man Tommy Lorentz in "The Dog and Pony Show." This time, however, Loros plays a good guy: Eddie, a former stir mate of Rockford's who was hired as Ritchie's bodyguard.

"Only Rock 'n' Roll Will Never Die" also features Kristoffer Tabori, the son of distinguished film director Don Siegel (*Dirty Harry*) and a prominent actor/director in his own right. Among Tabori's early credits as an actor was "The One-Eyed Mule's Time Has Come," an episode of the short-lived James Garner series *Nichols*.

"Only Rock 'n' Roll" also marks the fourth and final appearance of Rockford's Oklahoma alias, Jimmy Joe Meeker.

Photograph courtesy of TV History Archive
© 1979 Universal City Studios, Inc.

Eddie (George Loros) quarrels with Whitney Cox (Marcia Strassman) while Rockford (James Garner) contemplates his next move in "Only Rock 'n' Roll Will Never Die."

Rockford Fun

Whitney Cox, the reporter from *Knickerbocker Magazine* who is writing a story on Tim Ritchie, tells Rockford that she thinks Ritchie is the most sensual rock star of his time. "It's my thesis that the 'macho man of action cowboy sex symbol' is not only over, it's history," she explains. "When you take Mick Jagger, Rod Stewart, even John Travolta, they've all proven that." The humor in that line, of course, comes from the fact that Whitney Cox is played by Marcia Strassman, who co-starred with Travolta earlier in the '70s on ABC-TV's *Welcome Back, Kotter*.

Strassman, who also starred with Rick Moranis in the *Honey, I Shrunk the Kids* movies, returned to the *Rockford* family in 1996. She played Dr. Trish George in *Friends and Foul Play*, the fifth in the series of eight *Rockford* telefilms produced for CBS.

Photograph courtesy of TV History Archive
© 1979 Universal City Studios, Inc.

James Garner and his brother Jack Garner in a scene from "Only Rock 'n' Roll Will Never Die."

112. LOVE IS THE WORD

Production Number: 53815
Original Air Date: November 9, 1979
Produced and Written by: David Chase
Directed by: John Patterson

Guest Cast: Kathryn Harrold (Megan Dougherty), David-James Carroll (Randy Smith), Anthony Herrera (Jeffrey Smith), Van Williams (Lieutenant Duane Kiefer), Richard Cox (Kevin Spector), Rick Goldman (Lou Metzer), David Cadiente (Keith Keoloha), Lisa Figus (Mrs. Dougherty), Betty Kennedy (Patty Sevarisi), Eduardo Ricard (Waiter)

This is Marie at Liberty Bail Bonds. Your client Todd Lehman skipped, and his bail is forfeited. That's the pink slip on your '79 Firebird, I believe. Sorry, Jim ... bring it on over.

Synopsis. *On his way home from a trip to Houston, Jim pays a surprise visit to Megan Dougherty (the blind psychologist with whom he began a "sometimes" love affair in "Black Mirror"), but the reunion becomes awkward when he learns that Megan has become engaged to architect Jeffrey Smith. However, after wrestling with his anger, hurt and disappointment, Rockford ultimately comes to Megan in a moment of need. When Smith mysteriously disappears, Jim volunteers his services (as "an early wedding present") to help her investigation. As they uncover a connection between Smith's departure, the architect's junkie brother, and the murder of a potential business partner, Rockford and Megan also discover that their feelings for each other are still very, very strong.*

Kathryn Harrold returns as Megan Dougherty in "Love is the Word," an episode filmed in early September 1979, following the production of "No-Fault Affair." "The scenes at Megan's house were shot at a house located just past Paradise Cove," said Rob Howe. "The building where Jim and Megan find the tape outline was an actual office building near Zuma Beach—in fact, Max Gail, who was starring in *Barney Miller* at the time we were shooting *Rockford*, happened to have an office in that building at the time we did that episode."

Interestingly enough, shortly after filming this episode Harrold would play Lauren Bacall—who, of course, had guest-starred earlier this season in "Lions, Tigers, Monkeys and Dogs"—in *Bogie* (1980), a made-for-TV biography about screen legend Humphrey Bogart. A decade later, Harrold would star as the ex-wife of talk show host Larry Sanders (Garry Shandling) on *The Larry Sanders Show* (HBO, 1992-1998).

Rockford Familiar Faces

This episode also features Van Williams, who (like James Garner) began his acting career as a contract player at Warner Bros. in the late 1950s. After co-starring with Troy Donahue in *Surfside Six* (one of several *77 Sunset Strip* clones produced by Warners in the early '60s), he went on to play the title role in *The Green Hornet* (ABC, 1966-1967), which despite its short-lived network run remains a cult classic. Williams' co-star on *The Green Hornet* was Bruce Lee, the martial arts superstar of the early '70s who made his feature film debut in a brief yet memorable sequence opposite James Garner in *Marlowe* (1969).

"Love is the Word" also features a cameo appearance by country-western recording star Barbara Mandrell ("If Loving You is Wrong, I Don't Wanna Be Right"), who later headlined her own variety series on NBC from 1980-1982.

113. NICE GUYS FINISH DEAD
(Originally Entitled: "The Goodhues")

Production Number: 53809
Original Air Date: November 16, 1979
Written by: Stephen J. Cannell
Directed by: John Patterson

Guest Cast: James Whitmore Jr. (Fred Beamer), Tom Selleck (Lance White), Simon Oakland (Vern St. Cloud), Larry Manetti (Larry St. Cloud), Erica Hagen (Brandy Alexander), Joseph Bernard (Carmine DeAngelo), Fritzi Burr (Mrs. DeAngelo), Roscoe Born (TV Commentator), Fred Lerner (Carl Richman), Steve Jones (Newsman), Al Berry (Ed Fuller), Gregory Norman Cruz (Attendant), Larry Dunn (Norm Cross), John Lombardo (Police Clerk)

Jim? Dwight. I put a new outlet in the kitchen. I laid in the cable, then the box, then I pulled the breaker just like you said—and both of my TV sets started burning. What do I do now?

Synopsis. *The United Association of Licensed Investigators honors Rockford with the coveted Goodhue Award for his work in a case that set precedent in the field of accident insurance. But the ceremony is cut short when the keynote speaker—a state senator whose legislation banning the use of surveillance devices could adversely affect the P.I. industry if passed—is found dead in the men's bathroom. When Fred Beamer, who discovered the body, panics and runs away, he becomes the leading suspect. Rockford tries to clear Beamer while also contending with his nemesis Lance White.*

Tom Selleck and the staff of *Magnum, p.i.* paid homage to *The Rockford Files* (and to this episode in particular) in "A.A.P.I.," a segment of *Magnum* that originally aired in October 1986. Not only is Magnum honored for his detective work in that episode, he keeps insisting (though not convincingly) that the award itself is not important. That, of course, is a gag lifted straight out of "Nice Guys Finish Dead."

According to Sylvia Stoddard (who wrote an excellent history of *Magnum* for the magazine *Television Chronicles*), Selleck and *Magnum* executive producer Charles Floyd Johnson both lobbied hard for James Garner to make a cameo appearance in "A.A.P.I." as Jim Rockford. At the time, though, Garner was embroiled in his lawsuit with Universal over his share of profits from *The Rockford*

Photograph courtesy of Photofest
© 1979 Universal City Studios, Inc.

Jim Rockford (James Garner) and Lance White (Tom Selleck) take in the latest developments at the Goodhue Awards dinner in the sixth-season episode "Nice Guys Finish Dead."

Files; for that reason, he politely declined. (Universal, of course, was the same studio that produced *Magnum*.)

Stephen J. Cannell, however, agreed to make a cameo appearance in "A.A.P.I." as hotel detective Ray Lemon. Cannell, of course, wrote "Nice Guys Finish Dead," as well as the episode that introduced Lance White, "White on White and Nearly Perfect."

One year later, *Magnum* again paid homage to *Rockford*—only this time, at the expense of Lance White—in the episode "Tigers Fan" (originally broadcast on November 4, 1987). "Tigers Fan" opens with three cops in the middle of a stakeout, with one of the cops discussing an episode of *The Rockford Files* that he'd seen the night before. "*Rockford* was great," says the cop. "Jim was being driven nuts by this pain-in-the-butt named Lance White. This guy's Mr. Perfect, right? He's finding all the clues, catching all the suspects …"

Interestingly enough, the guest stars in "Tigers Fan" included Joe Santos (in the role of police lieutenant Nolan Page, a character Santos played in four episodes of *Magnum*), as well as *Rockford* guest stars James Karen and Carlos Romero.

Rockford Feted

Jim Rockford may have lost the Goodhue to Lance White at the end of this episode, but he has certainly won his share of real honors in the years since. For one, the Rockford character ranked 17th among *The 100 Greatest TV Characters*, a special that aired on Bravo in November 2004. Prior to that, *TV Guide* named Rockford the Greatest Television Detective of All Time in a list of Top 25 gumshoes that appeared in the July 8, 2000 edition. Rockford was also named one of *TV Guide*'s 50 Greatest TV Characters Ever, a feature that appeared in the October 16, 1999 issue (Jimbo was No. 25).

Rockford Facts

We've talked before (in our discussion of "Just Another Polish Wedding") about the efficiency with which the *Rockford Files* cast and crew worked throughout the series. As with all other aspects of the production, that efficiency is a reflection of series lead James Garner. "I was working on something at Universal in 1979," said writer and *Rockford* fan Frankie Montiforte, "and I had a chance to sneak into one of the rooms where they ran the dailies. I was only 16 at the time, so I don't remember who else was inside, but there were three or four other people, and they were watching the dailies for what turned out to be the second episode with Tom Selleck ['Nice Guys Finish Dead']. They were running the dailies from the scene in which Larry Manetti is in a hospital bed. He has a bandage on his head, and says something like, 'Uncle Vern, get them out of here.' James Garner was in the scene, along with Selleck, and Simon Oakland. I remember Garner was running through his lines when suddenly he flubbed a line and said, 'I'm sorry, let's take it again.' So they pause, and this time Jim runs right through it: Boom, boom, boom, boom, boom. And then Selleck does his thing, and then the director says, 'Okay, let's shoot a reverse'—you know, where they run through the entire scene again, only with the camera on another actor.

"What I remember most—besides the fact that, being a huge *Rockford* fan, it was really cool just to be able to sit there and watch some of the dailies—was that they never had to shoot any of the scenes with Garner more than two or three times. I mean, he would nail it, they'd shoot a reverse, he'd nail it again, and they'd move on to the next scene. I was very impressed by that."

"Nice Guys Finish Dead" is available through MCA/Universal Home Video as part of its *Rockford Files* collection.

Rockford Familiar Faces

Manetti, Oakland, and James Whitmore Jr. all starred together on *Baa Baa Black Sheep* (NBC, 1976-1978), the World War II drama based on the exploits of legendary fighter pilot Greg "Pappy" Boyington. *Baa Baa Black Sheep* was produced by Stephen J. Cannell for Universal Television.

Manetti, of course, also co-starred with Selleck on *Magnum*, while Whitmore (the son of Tony Award-winning actor James Whitmore), has since become a prominent director in television. He has helmed episodes of such popular shows as *JAG, 24, Cold Case, NCIS, Dead Like Me, Dawson's Creek* and *Enterprise*. Whitmore also returned to *The Rockford Files* in 1994 when he directed the first reunion movie, *I Still Love L.A.*

114.   THE HAWAIIAN HEADACHE

Production Number: 53814
Original Air Date: November 23, 1979
Written by: Stephen J. Cannell
Directed by: William Wiard
Hotel Accommodations for this Episode: Ilikai Hotel, Hawaii

Guest Cast: Ken Swofford (Colonel John "Howling Mad" Smith), W.K. Stratton (Agent Dwight Whipple), James Murtaugh (Agent Gordon Lyle), Christopher Cary (Dutch Ingram), Daniel Kamekona (Sergeant Okamoto), Jimmy Borges (Marshal Mingus), Esmond Chung (Shawn Kimotto), Paul Dennis Martin (Doorman), Jay Hoopai (Benny Kimotto), Elyssa Dulce Hoopai (Waitress), Carmella Ledman (Desk Clerk), Julie Blisett (Mrs. Ingram)

Photograph courtesy of Photofest
© 1979 Universal City Studios, Inc.

Jim Rockford (James Garner) doesn't exactly welcome the presence of Angel Martin (Stuart Margolin) during his vacation in "The Hawaiian Headache."

Billings, L.A.P.D. You know, Thursday is Chapman's 20th year, and we're giving a little surprise party at the Captain's. I think you should come. By the way, we need five bucks for the present.

Synopsis. *Jim and Rocky think they've won an all-expenses-paid vacation to Honolulu from Mason's Department Store, unaware that the trip was actually arranged by "Howling Mad" Smith, the military commander who once saved Rockford's life during the Korean War. Now a national intelligence agent, Smith recruits Rockford for "Operation Net Serve," a covert operation that will lay the groundwork for sending a U.S. Ping Pong team to Vietnam. Smith wants Jim to transport a suitcase with $100,000 in American money in exchange for $100,000 in Vietnamese money. But the apparently simple assignment brings Rockford nothing but trouble, as he is drugged, kidnapped and framed for murder ... all in the same day.*

This episode was filmed entirely on location in Hawaii. "That show was really fun to make, because we had everybody over there, and it was just a marvelous, marvelous time," said Jack Garner. "We all enjoyed each other, and we worked well together. And it was directed by one of our favorite directors, Bill Wiard."

Garner had known Wiard since the days when the director was still a film editor. "One day, back when I first started acting, Bill told me that he had planned on becoming a director," Garner recalled. "So I said to him, 'When you become a director, use me.' And Bill said, 'Well, Jack, the first time I need a drunk blacksmith, you're it!' Some time later, my agent called me to see if I was available to do a segment of *Daniel Boone*—it was going to be directed by Bill Wiard, and he wanted me on the show.'"

Rockford Facts

According to this episode, Rocky has never been to Hawaii before; however, he had actually won a trip to the Islands a few years earlier in the episode "Dirty Money, Black Light."

115. NO-FAULT AFFAIR
(Originally Entitled: "One Heart in Three-Quarter Time")

Production Number: 53811
Original Air Date: November 30, 1979
Produced and Written by: Juanita Bartlett
Directed by: Corey Allen

Guest Cast: Rita Moreno (Rita Capkovic), Pat Finley (Peggy Becker), Jerry Douglas (Al Halusca), Corrine Michaels (Linda Hassler), Ignatius Wolfington (Silky), Gloria Calomee (Hildy), William Beckley (Mr. Norman), Sandy Freeman (Mrs. Kramer), Karen Bercovici (Carla), Julian Kessler (Lily Showalter), Mavis Neal Palmer (Mrs. Stelmitz), Gregory Michaels (Doug), Michael Barker (Perry)

Oh, I thought this was Dial-a-Joke. I'm going to a party, and I need some ice-breakers. But, uh, I guess that's that.

Synopsis. *After advising a young girl to get out of prostitution while she can, Rita Capkovic decided to practice what she preached: she completed beauty school, and now wants to begin a new career as a hairdresser. But her brutal pimp, Al Halusca, won't let go of her, and to get his point across, he knocks Rita around and threatens to continue beating her unless she returns to the streets. Fearing for her life, and with nowhere else to go, Rita turns to Rockford, who nurses her back to health. After two weeks, however, the situation becomes a little complicated when Rockford realizes that Rita has fallen in love with him. In the meantime, a determined Halusca tracks down Rita and threatens to kill Rockford unless she abandons her plans for a new life.*

Due to Extreme Fire Hazard, Please Be Careful Smoking. Use Butt Cans.		Unit 2	Day of Shooting
"TITLED" No. 53811		Director C. ALLEN	
ONE HEART IN THREE-QUARTER TIME	Date FRIDAY, 8/24/79		
Series ROCKFORD FILES - 1 HR.			
Art Director R. CRAWLEY	Shooting Call Time	Condition of Call	
	2PM		
Set Director R. ZILLIOX	☒ REPORT TO LOCATION	☐ BUS TO LOCATION	

PAGES	SET DESCRIPTION	SC. NO.	D/N	LOCATION
4-6/8	EXT. ROCKFORD TRAILER (ROCKFORD,JOSEPH,RITA,ATMOS.)	1,2	D	PARADISE COVE 28128 W. PACIFIC COAST HIGHWAY
1/8	EXT. ROCKFORD TRAILER (ATMOS.,PIDGEONS)	29	D	
1/8	EXT. ROCKFORD TRAILER (ROCKFORD,ATMOS.)	40	D	
4/8	EXT. ROCKFORD TRAILER (ROCKFORD,JOSEPH,RITA,LINDA,ATMOS.)	42	D	
1-4/8	EXT. ROCKFORD TRAILER/ROAD (ROCKFORD,JOSEPH,RITA,AL,ATMOS.)	46,47	N	
7/8	EXT. ROCKFORD TRAILER (ROCKFORD,RITA)	17,18	N	

NOTE: ALL CAST/CREW/ATMOSPHERE - MUST PARK AT BASEBALL FIELD!!!

CAST AND BITS	CHARACTERS	HAIRDRESS	MAKE UP	ON SET
JAMES GARNER	ROCKFORD	RPT/LOC	1P	130P
NOAH BERRY	JOSEPH ROCKFORD	RPT/LOC	1P	130P
STUART MARGOLIN	ANGEL	HOLD		
RITA MORENO	RITA	PICKUP @	1130A	130P
	AL	RPT/LOC	6P	7P
CORINEE MICHAELS	LINDA HASSLER (NEW)	RPT/LOC	230P	4P
ROY CLARK	OBL. ROCKFORD	RPT/LOC	1P	130P

ATMOSPHERE AND STANDINS	THRU GATE	REPORT	READY ON SET
4 SI'S (CARROLL,DELGADO,DELGADO,NELSON)	RPT/LOC W/CARS	1PM	
9 WOMEN (18-25) WEAR SWIM SUITS & BEACH CLOTHES	RPT/LOC	130P	
5 MEN (18-25) WEAR TRUNKS & BEACH CLOTHES	RPT/LOC	130P	

ADVANCE

MON. 8/27 EXT. SHOPPING MALL (DAY) SC 35,36,37	MALIBU CENTER, 3900 CROSS CREEK RD. MALIBU
INT. BEAUTY PARLOR (DAY) SC 3 THRU 6	EDWARD JONES HAIRSTYLIST MALIBU CENTER
EXT. ROCKFORD TRLR. (DAY) SC 20,21,34	PARADISE COVE

From the collection of Robert Howe

Call sheet from "No-Fault Affair." Note that while the episode was in production, the working title of the show was "One Heart in Three-Quarter Time."

Both Rita and Angel save Rockford's life in this episode. Just as Halusca is about to shoot Rockford, Rita leaps into the line of fire and takes the bullet meant for Rockford in the shoulder. Fortunately for Rita, she is not wounded seriously. Meanwhile, Angel grabs a chair, lunges into Halusca and knocks him out. Given all the times Rockford has bailed Angel out of trouble over the years, it's particularly nice to see Angel return the favor on occasion.

This is actually the second time Angel has come through in the clutch for Rockford: he threw his body into one of the two gunmen who accosted Rockford and Angel inside Jim's trailer (after Rockford dispatched of the other with the help of his freezer door) in "The Girl in the Bay City Boys Club."

Rockford Funnies

This episode includes another reference to "Fannon's boat," which is named after prop master Bill Fannon.

116.   THE BIG CHEESE
(Originally Entitled: "This Package is Extra Sharp")

Production Number: 53810
Original Air Date: December 7, 1979
Written by: Shel Willens
Directed by: Joseph Pevney

Guest Cast: Constance Towers (Sally Sternhagen), Alan Manson (Chuck Ryan), Ben Andrews (Stamps), Mark Lonow (Coco), George Pentecost (George Neff), Mary Jackson (Postal Supervisor), Hank Brandt (Sergeant Roy Floyd), Eldon Quick (Willis Hoad), Bill McLean (Fred Barlow), Jimmy Weldon (John Rockfield), Frank McCarthy (Eddie Hellinger), Brian J. Pevney (Allen Calder), Anne Churchill (Clerk), Marie Denn (Newspaperwoman)

This is the Baron. Angel Martin tells me you buy information. Okay, meet me at 1:00 a.m. behind the bus depot, bring $500, and come alone—I'm serious.

Synopsis. *Rockford's only clue linking the fatal stabbings of his longtime friend Eddie Hellinger and an accountant named Arnold Moe is a large parcel Eddie had mailed to Rockford just before he was killed. Eddie, a reporter for the Globe newspaper, had been working on an exposé of union czar Chuck Ryan. Upon discovering that Moe was Ryan's accountant, Jim deduces that Moe had been supplying Eddie with information incriminating Ryan—and that Ryan had both men murdered in order to protect himself. Jim believes that Eddie sent the evidence to him in the mail, but when the postal service inadvertently loses the package, the matter becomes a race between Rockford, Ryan and the police over who can retrieve it first. Meanwhile, a desperate Lieutenant Chapman tries to doctor his taxes after the IRS informs him of a pending audit.*

A well-paced, thoroughly entertaining caper, "The Big Cheese" features one of the best twists in the entire series—and a big laugh, at the expense of Lieutenant Chapman. First, when Rockford finally recovers the package, he finds that it contains nothing more than a block of his favorite cheddar cheese; the key to the puzzle was really in the wrapping paper. Jimbo's reaction when he opens the package is one of classic exasperation: "Oh, they're not gonna believe it. They're not gonna believe it, no matter what I tell them."

		SHOOTING SCHEDULE				
PROD. NO.	53810	THE ROCKFORD FILES	October 22, 1979			
TITLE	~~THE BIG CHEESE~~ THIS PACKAGE IS EXTRA SHARP		DIRECTOR	JOE PEVNEY		
START	10/24/79		ASST. DIR.	MIKE KANE		
CLOSE	11/1/79	CAMERA DAYS 7	UNIT MGR.	SAM FREEDLE		

CAMERA DAY AND DATE	DESCRIPTION OF SET OR LOCATION	ACTORS WORKING	SEQ	PAGE	VEHICLES LIVESTOCK PROPS	DAY OR NITE
1st Day Wednesday 10/24/79 BANK OF A. LEVY, 16926 SATICOY	INT. BANK Scs. 73, 74 Rockford meets Neff, offers lunch.	ROCKFORD GEORGE NEFF 4 Standins Miss Gerber (S.B.) 7 Women 5 Men 1 Guard	1-	5/8		D
16918 SATICOY (HEARTS)	EXT. HOT DOG STAND Sc. 65 Get address of other victim.	ROCKFORD BECKER 4 Standins Cook 4 Men	1-	4/8	CHILI DOG COFFEE SLIP OF PAPER ROCKFORD'S FIREBIRD BECKER'S CAR	D
9 ORESTA ST.	EXT. ROCKFIELD HOUSE Scs. 54, 55 Rockford learns package sent back. End of Act Two.	ROCKFORD IRA ROCKFIELD 4 Standins	1-	4/8	ROCKFORD'S FIREBIRD ROCKFIELD PICKUP	D
VAN NUYS STREET	EXT. PAY PHONE/STREET Scs. 71, 71-A pt. Talks to Sally about banks.	ROCKFORD SALLY (V.O.) 4 Standins		7/8	ROCKFORD'S FIREBIRD	D
18649 SATICOY (MONAHANS)	INT. BAR Scs. 75, 76 Rockford learns Moe was accountant.	ROCKFORD NEFF 4 Standins 6 Men 6 Women	2-	3/8	HAMBURGER FRIES	D
	END OF FIRST DAY	TOTAL PAGES: 8-1/8				

From the collection of Robert Howe

A breakdown of the shooting schedule for the first day of production of "The Big Cheese" (or as the show was known during the time of filming, "This Package is Extra Sharp").

Then, after spending most of the episode scrambling to collect receipts (even for expenditures he didn't make), Chapman is confident he can beat the system. "Those IRS guys are jerks—they never really check these things out," he assures his accountant in a phone conversation to which Rockford and Sally Sternhagen, the treasury agent who assisted our hero in this episode, are present.

At that point, Sally flashes her IRS identification badge. "You didn't give me a chance to introduce myself," she tells Chapman as she advises him to keep his mouth shut before he gets himself into even more trouble. The episode ends with a freeze-frame of Rockford enjoying a long-awaited last laugh at the expense of his longtime nemesis.

Rockford Facts

Like the first-season episode "Sleight of Hand," "The Big Cheese" also depicts a side to Rockford not often seen in the series. Rockford has far less patience than he ordinarily exhibits (especially with Angel), and his grief over Eddie's death is evident. The edginess further humanizes the character, and is an interesting change of pace.

Rockford Family

Director Joseph Pevney, who had previously directed James Garner in the 1959 film *Cash McCall*, cast his son Brian in a small role in this episode.

117.   JUST A COUPLA GUYS

Production Number: 53812
Original Air Date: December 14, 1979
Produced and Written by: David Chase
Directed by: Ivan Dixon

Guest Cast: Greg Antonacci (Gene Conigliaro), Gene Davis (Mickey Long), Simon Oakland (Beppy Conigliaro), Gilbert Green (Joe Lombard), Antony Ponzini (Tony Martine), Arch Johnson (Cardinal Finnerty), Lisa Donaldson (Renee Lombard), Robin Riker (Kathleen O'Meara), Cliff Carnell (Albert Constantine), Eric Sinclair (Butler), Doug Tobey (Anthony Martine), Vince Howard (Transit Cop), Joe Alfasa (Vito), Stephanie Hankinson (Car Rental Attendant), Jennifer Rhodes (Jean Martine), Ed Deemer (Delivery Man), Eric Taslitz (School Boy), Dean Wein (Detective), Frederick Rule (First Officer), Derek Thompson (Second Officer)

Mr. Rockford, this is Betty Jo Withers. I got four shirts of yours from the Bo-Peep Cleaners by mistake. I don't know why they gave me men's shirts, but they're going back!

Synopsis. *Renee Lombard flies Rockford to Newark, New Jersey to help her father Joe, a prominent member of the Catholic Church (and, unbeknownst to Rockford, a former mobster). Tony Martine, the lord of New Jersey crime, wants Joe to convince the Archdiocese to reverse its decision barring Martine's late brother Vincent from receiving a full Catholic burial. (The Church will not allow Vincent, an unrepentant murderer, to be buried on consecrated grounds.) Meanwhile, Gene Conigliaro and Mickey Long, two inept hustlers who will do anything to ingratiate themselves with the mob, set out to catch the vandal who has been torching Lombard's front lawn and littering it with animal carcasses. Instead they only exacerbate the situation—the vandal turns out to be the son of Tony Martine. An angry Martine first tries to kill Gene and Mickey, then later holds Renee captive unless the Church reverses its decision.*

"Just a Coupla Guys" was designed as a pilot for *The Jersey Bounce*, a possible *Rockford* spinoff series starring Greg Antonacci and Eugene Davis. The idea was not well received. "The show suffered a split personality," noted *Daily Variety*, "taking on the *Rockford* charm when Garner was on screen, lapsing into amateurish tedium when spinoff possibilities were being mined."

Perhaps this pilot fizzled because it confused the audience. "Just a Coupla Guys" asked the viewers to accept two characters who were essentially the same "coupla guys" who had harassed Rocky, killed a man (and framed Rockford for the murder), and then tried to bump off each other in a fifth-season episode that was also entitled "The Jersey Bounce." Other than their sudden transmogrification into heroes, the inept hustlers in "Just a Coupla Guys" are indistinguishable from the dim-witted bad guys in "The Jersey Bounce"—they have the same names (Gene Conigliaro and Mickey Long), are played by the same actors (Antonacci and Davis), hail from the same town (Newark), and have the same dubious aspirations (ingratiating themselves with the mob). They're also neither any more appealing than the first pair of characters, nor any less annoying.

Granted, there's nothing wrong with trying to put a new spin on an old character: after all, *The Rockford Files* is basically a reworking of *Maverick*. However, from the P.O.V. of the audience, it's hard to accept "Just a Coupla Guys" without any clue as to what motivates Conigliaro and Long to suddenly do good.

That said, time has been kind to "Just a Coupla Guys," at least in the sense that in some respects the episode provided the foundation for a far more successful venture. According to author Andrew Clark, who interviewed David Chase as part of a retrospective on *Rockford* published in the May 2004 issue of *Toro Magazine*, the origins of *The Sopranos* are partly rooted in this episode:

> Chase wrote and produced the *Rockford* episode "Just a Coupla Guys" in which two klutzy wannabe hoods try to get into the mafia by ingratiating themselves with a retired mob boss. Chase shopped the episode as a pilot but the networks were not interested in a show that mixed the mafia with comedy. It had not been the first time that Chase explored the mafia on *The Rockford Files*. His gangster character "Anthony Boy" Gagglio (played by George Loros) was a blueprint for the character of Tony Soprano. Like Tony, "Anthony Boy" is violent and ruthless but also emotionally traumatized by a troubled childhood and the criminal life he has chosen. (Loros now plays Raymond Curto on *The Sopranos*.) Chase has said that on both shows "character and character flaws drive the story."

Rockford Facts

Now known internationally for playing Ralphie Cifaretto (his Emmy Award-winning role on *The Sopranos*), Joe Pantoliano was a struggling young actor when he first met David Chase in 1979. No doubt Pantoliano made an impression, because Chase wanted to cast him in "Just a Coupla Guys."

"He was interested in me for this *Rockford Files* spin-off," Pantoliano told *Maxim Magazine* in 2002. "It didn't happen, but years later he approached me again about *The Sopranos*. I'd had some bad TV experiences and wasn't interested. Finally, he called me a year or so ago and said, 'Look, you're on a really short list of new characters for season three. This guy's charming and funny, but he's also a prick. Whaddaya think?' So after 20 years we finally got a chance to work together."

Rockford Fun

Blake Delgado, son of Luis Delgado, has a silent bit in the opening moments of this episode. Upon arriving at the Newark airport, Rockford rents a car and is about to pull out of the car rental port when he realizes the left turn indicator in the car doesn't work. Just as Rockford sticks his arm out to make the signal by hand, an opportunistic kid wearing a red knit cap and a blue and white high school jacket runs up to the car and plucks Rockford's watch right from his wrist! "I was the kid," said Blake. "At that point, a little foot chase happens until the kid finally loses Jim by jumping over a fence. [Like my dad] I also used to stand-in on *Rockford*."

118.   DEADLOCK IN PARMA
(Originally Entitled: "How the Trout Became a Lox")

Production Number: 53807
Original Air Date: January 10, 1980
Teleplay by: Donald L. Gold & Lester William Berke and Rudolph Borchert
Story by: Donald L. Gold & Lester William Berke
Directed by: Winrich Kolbe

Guest Cast: Sandra Kerns (Carrie Osgood), Henry Beckman (Sheriff Neal), Jerry Hardin (Mayor Sindell), Joseph Sirola (Henry Gersh), Ben Piazza (Stan Belding), Michael Cavanaugh (John Traynor), J. Edward McKinley (Lee Melvin), Virgil Frye (Perry), Gary Grubbs (Deputy Murray), David Clover (Officer Chet), Ken Letner (Hy Newman), Al Dunlap (Councilman), John Davey (Mechanic), Paul Larson (Waiter), Mary Munday (City Hall Clerk), Janice Carroll (Doctor), Jim Scott (State Trooper), Frederick J. Flynn (Virgil), Diana Hale (Councilwoman)

Because of where you live says so much about you, your home has been selected by Royal Imperial Roofing and Siding as our neighborhood showcase. A bonded representative will call on you.

Synopsis. *Jim vacations in nearby Parma with his friend John Traynor, a member of the city council who is about to vote on an initiative that would legalize gambling in Parma, as well as allow for the development of a natural wilderness area into a vast hotel and casino complex. Traynor, who must cast the deciding vote on the issue, feigns illness, then cons Rockford into acting as his proxy. What Rockford doesn't realize: Traynor sold himself out to both the land developers (who have gangland ties) and the town mayor (who was bought off by a Las Vegas corporation that wants the measure defeated in order to stifle any competition). The matter becomes even uglier when Rockford discovers Traynor dead in the woods.*

"Deadlock in Parma" was filmed partially on location in Wrightwood, California, a resort community about two hours northeast of Los Angeles. The *Rockford* cast and crew were in town for three days (November 19-21, 1979) to shoot various scenes for the episode. James Garner was in good form as he granted a brief interview to the local newspaper, *The Wrightwood Mountaineer-Progress.*

''Rockford'' has Village on ear

By Steve Hess

"Do you have a tape recorder? You'd better, because my comments are historical," announced

---

Stay tuned 'til next week for more photos, story

YES, THAT'S JAMES GARNER

James Garner, star of NBC's program the ''Rockford Files,'' who was in Wrightwood this week for the filming of an episode in that series.

Garner, a man of quick wit, outspoken but congenial and polite, granted a brief interview to the *Mountaineer-Progress* between the crowds that rushed for his picture. Several resident women wanted to be photographed arm-in-arm with the TV star.

"Everyone around here has Polaroids. Why is that?" Garner asked. "This is a town picture, and I've got a dirty shirt on."

The crew from Hollywood is shooting an episode entitled "How the Trout Became a Lox." They arrived Monday and left this morning. The crew works 10 to 12 hours a day while filming.

Garner said he liked Wrightwood because "it is a pretty little town. I might even be back in 10-12 years."

The Rockford Files has been on TV for six years, which is "too long," Garner quipped. But "it's a fun game to play."

"Say, you're from back East, aren't you?" the actor asked as he puffed on a cigarette. He was dressed in a ten-gallon hat and a ranch-style parka. I replied that I am from Kansas City.

"Well, that's close enough" to Oklahoma, where Garner is from.

Garner mentioned that he regrets not having anonymity as an actor. "You never know what anonymity is until you lose it." With a firm handshake and a smile, Garner then departed for the set.

Article and photograph © 1979 Wrightwood Mountaineer-Progress.
Reprinted with permission.

In addition to being the last original episode of *Rockford* to air on NBC, "Parma" was also the last episode filmed of the original series. "That show was filmed the week before Thanksgiving," said Rob Howe. "Everybody took the following week off for Thanksgiving vacation, then came back the first week of December to start filming on either 'Never Trust a Boxx Boy' or 'What Do You Want From Us?' [one of two shows slated for production in December 1979]. That was the point when Jim collapsed and production of the show shut down."

At the time of his collapse, Garner had completed only 12 of the 22 episodes scheduled for filming in the sixth season (the episode "Lions, Tigers, Monkeys and Dogs" was considered a two-parter, even though NBC originally telecast the show as a special two-hour segment). Well aware of how incensed Garner was over the studio's claim that *Rockford* had lost over $9 million through its first five years of production, Universal accused the star of faking his illness and shutting down the series midway through the season purely for reasons of spite. A look at the production schedule for the remainder of the season, however, clearly indicates that Garner intended to fulfill his obligation.

Furthermore, Garner was known throughout the industry as a conscientious actor who particularly looked after his staff and crew. Given that, it was not his style to capriciously pull the plug on any operation regardless of how he may have felt about Universal. As Rob Howe points out, Garner knew that ending production on *Rockford* mid-season would directly impact the livelihood of everyone who worked on the show. Therefore, he would never have made that decision lightly.

"There was a meeting in Jim's office just after he had been hospitalized," Howe recalled. "Luis Delgado [who by this time Garner had entrusted with more responsibility in the operation of Cherokee Productions] was there, as were Jim's assistant MaryAnn Rea and prop master Bill Fannon. It was an informal gathering, and at some point I popped in to say hello. Although I did not engage in the conversation other than to ask how Jim was doing, I do know that they discussed plans about resuming production once Jim got back from Scripps Medical Clinic in San Diego. What happened after that, I'm not sure, except to say that the show never resumed production. I saw MaryAnn a few more times, but by that point the doctor had already ordered Jim to shut down the show for good. It wasn't long after that that NBC canceled the show.

"I can't say for certain since I was not witness to it, but knowing James Garner as I had come to know him, it was *not* in his makeup to put 100 people out of work just because he had a dispute with the studio. If Jim had been well enough, he would have completed the sixth season of *Rockford* with its full schedule of episodes."

NBC replaced *Rockford* with *Skag*, a critically acclaimed drama starring Karl Malden as a fiery steel worker and union foreman who struggles to put his life back together after suffering a debilitating stroke. Heralded as Malden's return to television after *The Streets of San Francisco* (just as *Nichols* was lauded as Garner's first series since *Maverick*), *Skag* boasted a talented cast—including future Emmy winner Piper Laurie (*Promise*), future *O.C.* star Peter Gallagher, *Rockford* regular Tom Atkins, and *Rockford* guest stars M. Emmet Walsh, Frank Campanella, and George Voskovec—as well as stellar writing. *Skag* was created by Oscar winner Abby Mann (*Judgment at Nuremberg*), and also included playwright Marsha Norman (*'Night, Mother*) among its writers. But despite strong reviews and huge ratings for the three-hour pilot, *Skag* the series did not catch on with viewers and was gone from the schedule within a month's time.

Ironically, NBC ended up replacing *Skag* with none other than *The Rockford Files*. Repeats of the sixth-season episodes aired Thursdays at 10:00 p.m. until April 1980. Following a short hiatus, *Rockford* returned for the summer in its original Friday 9:00 p.m. slot before leaving NBC for good on July 25, 1980. Meanwhile, Garner's dispute with Universal regarding the profits of *The Rockford Files* would eventually make its way to court.

Photograph courtesy of TV History Archive
© 1979 Universal City Studios, Inc.

Noah Beery Jr. with his everpresent pipe

Rockford Facts

In addition to the location shooting in Wrightwood, some exteriors for "Deadlock in Parma" were filmed at historic Griffith Park in Los Angeles—a popular location for many movies and television series, including the climactic sequence of *Rebel Without a Cause* (1955), as well as multiple episodes of *Rockford*. According to Rob Howe, the shots of the bell that appear just before the opening credits of "Parma," as well as the establishing shot of Henry Gersh's trailer (to which Rockford is transported about ten minutes into the story) were filmed in Griffith Park.

Rockford Fun

Keep your eyes peeled on the bright blue wall of the Parma Pharmacy during the sequence with Belding and Sindell early in the third act of "Parma." As Belding walks up to Sindell after removing all copies of *Tempo* (the magazine with his picture on the cover) from the newsrack, you can see the shadow of the camera operator, as well as the reflection of one of the spotlights used to light this scene.

Appendix H
The Rockfords That Never Were

James Garner's sudden illness resulted in the premature conclusion of *Rockford's* sixth and final season after only 12 episodes. But as mentioned before, Garner had intended to complete the remaining ten episodes had he received medical clearance.

As is customary in television, the scripts for those ten shows had already been ordered by the time the sixth season began production in July 1979. At the time of Garner's illness, pre-production had just started on two of those final ten scripts ("Never Trust a Boxx Boy" and "What Do You Want From Us?"), and directors had already been secured for the remaining eight shows scheduled to be filmed between January and March 1980. Those plans, of course, all went out the window once *Rockford* shut down for good in December 1979.

In the interest of making this history as complete as possible, here is a list of four of those ten unproduced scripts for *Rockford's* sixth and final season. As you'll see from my summaries and notes that follow, the series would have gone in some interesting directions had these episodes indeed been made.

The scripts are listed in order of production number. My thanks to Rob Howe for making these scripts available.

HAPPY FATHER'S DAY
Production Number: 53813
Written by: Mark Griffiths

Synopsis. Rockford's world is rocked when 23-year-old singer Randy Benton shows up at the trailer—on Father's Day, no less—and announces that Jim is her biological dad. Rockford travels to Bakersfield, where Randy's mother lives, and learns that the news is apparently true. As much as Rockford resists the notion of parenthood, he finds himself protecting Randy anyway when he discovers the band members she has been bankrolling are really a band of thieves.

While "Happy Father's Day" takes a predictable path—a records search conducted by Dennis Becker eventually reveals the true identity of Randy's parents—there are some nice moments in which Rockford ponders what could have been had he ever started a family. In the hands of James Garner, those scenes would have worked well had the script in fact been filmed.

Much of the action in "Father's Day" is set in Bakersfield, the Southern California town where Rockford was raised as a kid—a fact that had previously been established in the second-season episode "The Aaron Ironwood School of Success." Besides renewing his acquaintance with old flame Mary Ann Benton (Randy's mom), Rockford attends his 25th high school reunion, where he ends up brawling with class bully Billy "Beefcake" Harris. Naturally, our hero tries to avoid trouble, but when Beefcake lunges after him Rockford lays him out. The script also tells us that Beefcake used to call Rockford "Rock-nurd" in high school, while everyone else in town called him "Jiminey."

"Happy Father's Day" was written by Mark Griffiths, best known for directing *Hardbodies* (1984), the sexed-up beach comedy considered by some to be the quintessential '80s movie. In an interesting coincidence, Griffiths, whose script for "Father's Day" includes a brief sequence with Angel Martin, would later write the screenplay for *Running Hot* (1984), a teen-aged take on *The Fugitive* that also featured Stuart Margolin. Griffiths also wrote for the *Hardy Boys/Nancy Drew Mysteries* series produced by Universal for ABC-TV in the late 1970s.

SOME PEOPLE ARE TROUBLE
Production Number: 53816
Written by: Shel Willens

Synopsis. *Convicted of murdering his wealthy wife Leona in 1957, Aubrey F. Spotwood was the center of the most sensational murder case in Los Angeles since the Black Dahlia. Released from prison after a 23-year sentence, Spotwood insists that his wife is alive and in hiding and wants Rockford to help him find her. (Leona left behind a multi-million-dollar estate upon her disappearance, but Spotwood can't touch it because of laws that prevent convicts from profiting from their crimes.) Though dubious at first, Rockford finds plenty of incentive to take on the case after Spotwood offers him the pink slip to his Cadillac as collateral— not to menion a finders fee equal to 1% of the value of the estate once Rockford locates Leona.*

"Some People are Trouble" was written by Shel Willens, the man who penned "The Big Cheese," the sixth-season episode that ranks among the very best *Rockfords* of all time. Like "The Big Cheese," the script for "Trouble" features a number of elements reminiscent of *film noir*, including extensive use of shadows, darkly lit scenes, and a trek into the seedy world of 1950s peep shows. Rockford also stumbles onto a vital clue while watching a rerun of *The Dick Cavett Show* in which Cavett interviews an adult film star turned gothic romance novelist named Sybil Trelawny.

Interestingly enough, the script for "Trouble" includes a reference to Beth Davenport, who was last seen in the fourth episode "The Queen of Peru." Though Beth does not appear in the script, Jim tells Rocky that he spent "about three hours in Beth's office getting a contract drawn up" reflecting the terms of his agreement with Spotwood. Given the hardball stance Universal had taken with James Garner and Cherokee Productions in 1978 regarding the use of Gretchen Corbett on future episodes of *Rockford*, it's unlikely that Corbett would have appeared in "Trouble" had the episode indeed been made.

In addition to *Rockford*, Shel Willens contributed scripts to several other series produced by Stephen J. Cannell, including *Baretta*, *The Greatest American Hero*, *Hardcastle and McCormick*, and *Renegade*, as well as episodes of *Police Story*, *Miami Vice*, *Spenser: For Hire* and *Walker, Texas Ranger*. In addition, Willens received story credit for "The Not So Magnificent Six," an episode of Garner's *Bret Maverick* series from 1981.

NEVER TRUST A BOXX BOY
(Originally Entitled: "Never Trust a Buss Boy")
Production Number: 53817
Written by: Stephen J. Cannell

Synopsis. *Angel's latest con has him masquerading as "Marty Martain," an up-and-coming agent in the employ of Hollywood talent mogul Marty Boxx. Though Angel believes he has found his true calling ("Where else do you get to dump all over people and still take ten percent of the gross?"), he ends up in over his head once again when he finds himself implicated in a defection scheme orchestrated by Boxx. Boxx wants to sign premier Russian ballet dancers Anton and Nina Kirov as clients, but the scheme backfires when the two stars are nearly killed by gun-toting KGB agents. Naturally, Angel uses the situation to his advantage, blackmailing Boxx into relinquishing control of the entire agency in exchange for his silence about Boxx's role in the defection. How does any of this concern Rockford? More than you can imagine. Having helped himself to Jim's car and trailer while our* *hero was out of town, Angel (1) was driving the Firebird when he helped the Kirovs flee the Russian agents, (2) was inside the trailer when the Kirovs were later abducted at gunpoint by two men, and (3) took off in the Firebird again to avoid getting killed himself. Before Rockford knows it, he finds himself facing a host of charges from the L.A.P.D., the F.B.I. and the Russian KGB.*

Stephen J. Cannell's script for "Never Trust a Boxx Boy" is reminiscent of "The No-Cut Contract," the second-season episode also written by Cannell, in two respects: not only is Rockford "hotter" than usual, he also exhibits a rare show of anger over the circumstances in which he has been cast. While Rockford in "Contract" was pursued by the cops, the feds, and the mob, in "Boxx Boy" he finds himself on the run from the cops, the feds, and Russian agents. And just as Rockford in "Contract" is genuinely steamed at King Sturtevant for throwing his life into turmoil (as Jim tells Beth in that episode, he does not lose his temper often), in "Boxx Boy" he becomes so exasperated at Angel that he actually hits him.

"Do you hate me?" Rockford asks Angel. "Have I done anything to make you hate me?"

"Naw, Jimmy, nothing like that," says Angel. "You wanna know the truth? You're a pigeon. Your sense of friendship is as easy to hit as a dump truck ... You shoulda hit me half-a-dozen times over the years, but you never do. You're a soft touch."

Eminently proud of himself, Angel smiles at Rockford ... at which point, Jim belts him so hard in the stomach that Angel doubles over. Needless to say, it's a moment that was a long time coming.

Angel also gets his just desserts in the tag at the end of the story, which takes place in Rockford's trailer. After Angel boasts about how easily he snagged a $5000 commission for booking country-western singer Mel Tillis at the Palomino Club (despite the fact that he doesn't actually represent Tillis), Jim tells him to be careful. "You just don't learn, do you, Angel?" says Rockford. "[What you're doing is] crooked. It'll catch up with you."

Naturally, Angel scoffs at the warning ("How's it gonna catch up with me?"). Sure enough, there's a knock on the trailer door. Angel opens the door and, wouldn't you know it, there stands Mel Tillis. With just one punch, Tillis knocks Angel clear across the room.

"Boxx Boy" was clearly intended as a star vehicle for Stuart Margolin— Rockford doesn't even make an appearance until 20 pages into the 60-page script. In this respect, "Boxx Boy" could be considered a sort of forerunner to Cannell's script for *A Blessing in Disguise*, the 1995 *Rockford* reunion movie that was also dominated by Angel.

"Boxx Boy," like *Blessing*, also pokes fun at the film industry, a world where seemingly every major player is named either "Jerry," "Marty" or both—hence, Angel adopts the name "Marty Martain" (then later, "Jerry Martin") as part of the ruse. Some of the other characters in Cannell's script for "Boxx Boy" include a producer named "Jerry Joseph," a writer named "Jerry Martinson," a director named "Marty Matz," and of course, a superagent named "Marty Boxx." Similarly, Cannell's script for *Blessing* includes a scene in which Rockford escorts Laura Dean to a meeting at a major talent agency. The scene takes place in a large conference room populated by ten men, "all named Jerry or Marty." Among the characters are agent "Jerry Michaels" and PR men "Marty Martinson" and "Jerry Jamison."

"Boxx Boy" also includes a reference to Eddie Whitefeather (Angel's con artist buddy, last seen in "The Man Who Saw the Alligators") and Solly Marshall, Rockford's bail bondsman (played by Joe E. Tata in "Profit and Loss," "A Portrait of Elizabeth" and "In Hazard"). Also according to "Boxx Boy," Rockford has a new lawyer: Jane Masselbinder. However, the script for yet another unproduced sixth-season episode, "Some People are Trouble," suggests that Rockford is once again working with Beth Davenport.

WHAT DO YOU WANT FROM US?
Production Number: 53818
Written by: Juanita Bartlett

Synopsis. *After a stint as technical advisor on the network TV series* Cops and Robbers, *Becker decides to write a book about his various police cases—including his current investigation of Bertram Avery, a Beverly Hills dentist whom Dennis arrested after witnessing the man assault his wife. As it happens, Avery also has Rockford as a patient. The matter becomes even more complicated after Avery is killed in his office while in the middle of an appointment with Jim. Hoping to add another juicy chapter to his book, Becker sets his sights on the most logical suspect, Avery's wife Sheila. But Rockford believes Sheila is innocent—especially after he saw a mysterious man dashing out of Avery's office within moments of the dentist's murder.*

"What Do You Want From Us?" gets its name from the title of Becker's book. While Dennis believes the title is perfect ("That title is something every cop in the world can identity with"), Rockford isn't so sure.

"What's wrong with that for a title?" asks Becker.

Rockford pulls no punches. "It whines a little."

Throughout the script the normally laidback Becker is tense and short-tempered, a depiction that calls to mind his surly characterization in the fifth-year show "Kill the Messenger" (which, like "What Do You Want From Us?," was also written by Juanita Bartlett). While Becker in "Messenger" was uptight because of his pending lieutenant exam, in "What Do You Want From Us?" we find him in the middle of a mid-life crisis. That, among other things, accounts for his decision to write a book despite the fact he has no real aptitude for writing—a realization he finally discovers (with a little help from Rockford) by the end of the story.

Part 3:
The Lawsuits

The REAL *Rockford* Files

In January 1980, Universal Studios filed a $1.5 million breach-of-contract lawsuit against James Garner, alleging that the actor had failed to meet his 22-episode obligation for the 1979-1980 season. Universal claimed that Garner feigned his illness and in effect quit the show in retaliation against the studio's claims that *The Rockford Files* had a net loss of over $9 million through the end of the first five seasons.

Garner has always maintained that he had become physically worn out after subjecting his body to the grueling pace of series television. Judging from the evidence (the episodes themselves), it's extremely difficult to dispute his claim. Garner was the consummate pro, having never missed a show in five-and-a-half years. He was onscreen 95% of the time, which meant that he was required to be on the set—or at least, on site—every day, regardless of how long the day went. And although he was 51 years old at the time the series ended, he continued to meet the physical demands of the show, particularly when it came to performing in action sequences.

But as far as Universal was concerned, while *The Rockford Files* may have ceased production in December 1979 after filming only 12 of the 22 shows scheduled for that season, the series was never officially axed by NBC. Indeed, while the network did announce later in December that it would remove *Rockford* from its regular lineup after January 10, 1980 (the date that "Deadlock in Parma," the 12th and at that point last unaired episode of the sixth season, was scheduled to be broadcast), the word "canceled" was never mentioned. Therefore, reasoned Universal, the studio still had a commitment to produce another ten episodes for NBC that season—and Garner was equally obligated to make those shows.

By all appearances, Garner was ready to deliver if necessary. As mentioned earlier, the actor had not only made arrangements to shoot two episodes in December 1979, he and his staff had also lined up directors for the remaining eight episodes of the season, which were scheduled for production between January and March of 1980.

Universal's argument, however, was dealt a major blow in early 1980, when NBC announced a pact between Garner, Warner Bros. and the network. Garner would star in and produce a new version of *Maverick* that would premiere on

Photograph courtesy of TV History Archive
© 1979 Universal City Studios, Inc.

James Garner

NBC in the fall of 1981—a development that effectively killed any chance Universal had of forcing Garner to resume production of *The Rockford Files*.

Simply put, NBC's deal with Warners now meant that *Rockford* actually *was* canceled. Not only did that sever the network's contract with Universal regarding *Rockford*, it also freed Garner from any remaining obligation he may have had to produce additional episodes for the studio.

"We thought it was a tremendous breach of ethics on NBC's part," recalled Frank Price, now the chairman of Price Entertainment, a major motion picture company. "Without telling us, NBC made a deal with Jim Garner, and in essence, canceled *Rockford Files*. The minute the network made that deal directly with Jim, we were no longer in the position where we could influence anything. Not only was *Rockford* canceled, but Jim already had his next series. It was a better deal for Jim, because he now had control over everything."

The focus of the dispute eventually shifted away from the breach of contract allegations against Garner and toward the matter of the profit participation. Garner believed that the studio failed to live up to its promise to provide him with his share of the *Rockford Files* profits. He also accused the studio of "creative bookkeeping"—that is to say, doctoring the books by including false expenditures (or by inflating the amount of actual expenditures), either to create the impression that no profits existed, or to understate the actual amount of profits available.

Garner was not the first in the film industry to challenge a major studio on the issue of creative bookkeeping. Actors Fess Parker, Robert Wagner and Natalie Wood and Universal Studios producer Harve Bennett had all filed similar lawsuits. In fact, the Bennett and Wagner/Wood litigations were settled shortly before Garner commenced his action against Universal. Garner's dispute, however, was one of the first to attract national attention, first in an item televised on *60 Minutes* in the fall of 1980, and later in an interview published in *Playboy* in early 1981.

Sidney Sheinberg, president of Universal's parent company MCA, also appeared on the *60 Minutes* segment. Sheinberg suggested that Garner had nothing to complain about because he'd already been "adequately compensated" for his work on the series (to the tune of $5 million total salary), then punctuated his remarks by calling the actor "worse than a crybaby." The studio's thinking: while the matter of profit participation may have been written into the contract, the matter of whether the series made any profit was not guaranteed. "I don't think your audience (those who are employed and those who are unemployed) are going to lose a great deal of sleep out of the fact that Jim Garner only is going to make $5-6 million out of *The Rockford Files*," Sheinberg told *60 Minutes*.

However, the issue didn't concern how much money Garner earned in salary. The issue concerned what happened to all the revenue generated from the phenomenal success of *The Rockford Files*. "If you work that hard," said Garner on *60 Minutes*, "and you do it right, and it is a tremendously successful series, you've got to believe that there's going to be profit at the end."

Given the "creative bookkeeping" charges, Garner anticipated that it would be a lengthy battle just to get a look at the studio's books. "It would be like trying to open the books at any major company," he acknowledged in the *Playboy* interview. "I'll be ten years in the courts trying to get a good look at their books, but that's all right. I'm not going anywhere."

On that point, Garner proved himself to be rather prescient. Nearly ten years would pass between the time the matter first surfaced in the summer of 1979 and the time it was finally settled on March 31, 1989.

According to the complaint Garner eventually filed in the Los Angeles Superior Court in 1983, Universal asked the actor on several occasions between June 1980 and July 1982 to refrain from taking any action against the studio in order to allow them the opportunity "to furnish complete accountings and complete financial information concerning the series and its profitability." At one point, the studio even stated in writing that it would provide such information to Garner no later than August 31, 1982. Although Garner agreed to wait and see, apparently the studio never provided him with any information throughout that two-year period.

In the meantime, Garner broached Roy Huggins about the possibility of joining him in his lawsuit against the studio. Although Huggins' contract with Universal entitled him to 25% of the profits of all seven series he created for the studio (*Run for Your Life, The Outsider, The Bold Ones: The Lawyers, Cool Million, Toma/Baretta, The Rockford Files, City of Angels*), he had yet to see a dime of profit from any of those series.

"Jim wanted me to join him—and, in fact, I probably should have," Huggins recalled. "But at the time I didn't want to, because I thought my case was different from Jim's. I felt that if I ever had to take Universal to court over the matter of profit participation, I would sue them over the profits for all seven series."

While Huggins may have felt his case was different than Garner's, the issues he faced were certainly similar. The complaint Huggins eventually filed in 1990 eloquently addressed one such obstacle that he and Garner would have to face:

> When and if any such profit participants are able to overcome the obstacles created by this conduct and demonstrate the computation of the overall profits is understated, and that they are consequently entitled to greater amounts than contended by defendants, defendants attempt to "negotiate" settlements which enable them to retain a portion of their wrongful gain as well as avoid paying interest for the use of the profit participants' money, upon the threat, expressed or implied, that otherwise the profit participants must face the prospect of a long, arduous and expensive litigation.

Garner had discussed the same problem in the *Playboy* interview. "We will try to go over their books, and then we will sue them," he said. "They will say, 'Well, let's not do it that way. Let's see if we can settle it amicably.' They'll offer to give me about ten cents on the dollar, but I won't take it."

In July 1983, Garner finally filed a $22.5 million breach-of-contract lawsuit against Universal, alleging that the studio failed "to properly account to Garner the true and correct accountings of the revenues, costs and other charges in connection with the series." The complaint also accused the studio of providing Garner with "substantially erroneous and deliberately improper statements of costs, income, revenues and profits" in order to create the impression "that no amounts were payable to Garner on account of his profit participation for the series."

To finance the lawsuit, Garner made a deal with NBC in which he sold back a portion of the profits he had earned from the network. Interestingly enough, NBC was originally going to partner with Garner in the lawsuit against the studio. Somewhere along the line, though, the network settled with Universal—without telling Garner. By that point, however, the actor felt his case was strong enough that he no longer needed NBC, and proceeded to sue Universal on his own.

In 1986, a court order consolidated Garner's action with the lawsuit Universal had previously filed against the actor in 1980. In the meantime, while the litigation took its natural course, *The Rockford Files* continued to generate revenue. In January 1988, Garner finally won the right to examine the studio's books. By that time, even though *Rockford* had generated over $119.3 million in profits, the studio still claimed that the show was $1.6 million in the red.

Garner conducted two separate audits: one examining the *Rockford* books through June 1980, the other through June 1985. The first audit estimated that the studio either overstated costs or underestimated revenue by approximately $10.9 million. The second audit raised even more questions. "The largest and most debatable charges raised by the auditors was a $7.9 million interest expense," reported *Barron's* in February 1989. "What Garner's suit claims, in short, is that Universal recorded expenses immediately, but deferred recording revenues and profits until cash was in hand. It would be as if you added up all your anticipated living expenses for the next ten years, and charged 6% interest against the amount, but at the same time, you added up your income only through yesterday, when you got paid. Of course, most businesses like to keep their books in exactly the opposite way—put off expenses as long as possible, and record income as quickly as possible."

From the time the action commenced through the present time, MCA/Universal has never commented on Garner's allegations. However, MCA president Sheinberg did reveal a key facet of Universal's defense during the *60 Minutes* interview telecast in 1980:

We all live by our contracts. When you are a big company called Cherokee Productions, and a big star called Jim Garner, and you've got big lawyers and big accountants, and big agents, you can't play the role of being the fella who just wandered in from Nashville.

In other words, Universal contended that Garner did not enter into any negotiations by himself: he had been well represented by parties who should have informed him of any loopholes or any other questionable conditions of the agreement. While that may have been true, it still doesn't address the issue of what happened to all the revenue.

The stress of the protracted legal battle would take its toll on Garner's health. The actor underwent two heart operations (including a quadruple bypass surgery) between April and June 1988. While Garner recuperated, Universal issued a new financial statement in late 1988 indicating for the first time that *The Rockford Files* had turned a profit after generating nearly $123 million in revenue to that point. According to *Barron's*, Garner received an initial payment of $243,313, plus additional payments totalling $363,687 over the next few months.

Meanwhile, Roy Huggins, who had been entitled to 25% of the show's profits under his contract, received a payment in the amount of $99,542.39 in December 1988. This development led Huggins to reevaluate his own situation with the studio. "I now had evidence that they were making a profit on *The Rockford Files*," he explained. "Although the amount that they paid me was by no means small, [my wife] Adele and I felt that it was nowhere near what they actually owed me. So at that point, I changed my line of thinking. I decided that if I had to, I would take them to court on *Rockford* alone."

Although the long-awaited trial between Garner and Universal was set to begin on March 15, 1989, the parties resumed settlement talks and reached a tentative agreement at the 11th hour. The matter finally ended two weeks later, when both sides signed the settlement agreement on March 31, 1989. The exact terms of the agreement remain confidential.

According to *Barron's*, Garner elected to settle rather than risk having the entire case thrown out of court, while Universal chose to settle in lieu of having to explain its accounting practices in open court. "Some entertainment lawyers questioned whether Garner's case would hold up in court, opining that Universal's accounting, fair or not, was nevertheless consistent with industry practices," *Barron's* reported in 1989. "[However], it was expected that Universal would likely have had to defend itself against charges of unfair practices as 'block booking,' whereby a distributor of television shows forces a TV station to buy a series it didn't want in order to acquire a popular show … If proved, block booking would have the effect of reducing syndication receipts from *The Rockford Files*, one way of postponing the point at which the series began making a profit and thus delaying the time at which Garner [and Huggins] were entitled to begin sharing in those profits."

A lawsuit is a long and incredibly draining process, particularly for the litigants. Not only had Garner gone through that experience before, he had also done so in the capacity of taking on another major studio. "I'm not litigious," he said on *Charlie Rose*, "but I left Warner Bros. in a lawsuit [in 1960] when I did *Maverick*. They laid me off when they didn't have a right to. They said, 'We can't [produce any more episodes] because there was a writer's strike.' Well, they had 15 writers writing under the table, which we got them to admit in court. So there went their lawsuit [out the window]."

Like his case against Universal, Garner's lawsuit with Warner Bros. showed him to be a man of principle, someone not afraid to put up a fight when he knows that he has been wronged. "I have always been that way," he said on *Charlie Rose*. "When you're right, you're right, and you have to stand up for that."

Garner's resolve in his case against Warner Bros. is even more remarkable considering how much the actor had to lose. The lawsuit against Warners, after all, took place very early in Garner's career. Had he lost in court, he faced the very real possibility of never working in the film industry again.

Obviously, the circumstances surrounding the *Rockford Files* lawsuit were considerably different. In 1980, Garner was an established star who had the resources to take on a major studio and withstand a long, arduous fight. "Fortunately, when I sued Universal, I had the money in the bank to do it," he said on *Charlie Rose*. "What they do is, they try to keep you out of court for as long as they can until you just give up. I spent $2.5 million in law fees—plus eight years of my life—just suing them. That's a long time. Most people can't afford to do that."

"These cases require an unusual plaintiff," said Michael R. White (Garner's attorney) in 1989. "He has to have a lot of money, but not be so flush that the outcome isn't important to him. Plus, he needs a property that's been successful and makes a lot of money. Few TV shows or movies ever achieve the success of *The Rockford Files*."

*　　　　　*　　　　　*

Although White had predicted at the time of the settlement that there wouldn't be the likes of *Universal v. Garner* for a long time, series co-creator Roy Huggins filed a $25 million breach-of-contract lawsuit of his own in July 1990. Although Huggins had been entitled to 25% of the net profits of all seven series he produced for Universal between 1965 and 1980, he concentrated his lawsuit on *The Rockford Files* because "I was afraid that I'd waited too long on the others," he said. "I was concerned that there may have been a statute of limitations problem that would have prohibited me from taking action on the other shows. And, also, the other shows hadn't gone that magic number of years [five years, or approximately 100 episodes] that guaranteed a profit. By the time Jim's suit was settled, I now had evidence that *Rockford* had turned a profit, so I decided to sue them on that show alone."

Huggins' matter was settled in far less time than Garner's lawsuit, due in part to a factor that wasn't present in the Garner case: Huggins' age. The writer/producer was 76 at the time the action commenced. Under California law, that entitled him to preference in getting a trial.

In March 1993, Huggins won the right to examine the *Rockford* books for the first time. Although Universal succeeded in having several of Huggins' allegations thrown out of the case two months later, the crux of Huggins' complaint—failure to provide Huggins with his rightful share of all profits, and failure to render a proper accounting of all expenses pertaining to the series—remained at issue. This, in turn, meant that had the matter proceeded to trial, Universal would have once again faced the likelihood of explaining its accounting practices. Rather than face that prospect, Universal elected to settle with Huggins in early 1994, just as the studio had previously done with Garner in 1989. The terms of the settlement with Huggins are also confidential.

Part 4:
The CBS Movies

The Reincarnation of Jim Rockford

It was only a matter of time before *The Rockford Files* came back—after all, the series ended just around the time when network television embarked on a wave of nostalgia. In the years since *Rockford* left NBC, over 100 popular shows of the '60s, '70s and '80s have been exhumed and revived as either "reunion specials," full-fledged series, or feature motion pictures. In fact, James Garner himself resurrected *Maverick* in *Bret Maverick* (NBC, 1981-1982), an updated series of adventures featuring the gentle grafter that first made him a star in the late 1950s. In some cases (such as *The Perry Mason Mysteries* and *Columbo*), the revivals have proven to be nearly as popular and as successful as the original series.

In the years following the settlement of his lawsuit with Universal, Garner had been approached on several occasions about reviving *The Rockford Files*. As much as he loved playing the character, Garner steadfastly refused as a matter of principle. After all, because Universal maintained majority ownership of the series, any revival of *Rockford* would have to be done through the studio. As far as Garner was concerned, too many bad memories lingered from the long, bitter legal battle, and it was too soon for the two sides to go back to work with each other.

Still, the talks persisted until finally, in the spring of 1994, the studio announced that Garner had agreed to produce and star in a series of six two-hour *Rockford* episodes that would air on CBS-TV over the course of the 1994-95 and 1995-96 seasons. Interestingly enough, the announcement of the new *Rockford*s was made shortly before the release of Garner's latest feature: a big screen version of *Maverick*.

"I finally thought, *Well, if I'm going to do it, now is the time*, as far as my availability and my health are concerned," Garner told *TV Guide* in 1994. "Four years from now, it's too late. And it's a marvelous character. It's a shame we haven't been doing it before, but I just couldn't bring myself to do it."

While Garner agreed to make the films for the studio, he made it very clear that he wouldn't shoot them *at* the studio. That would be asking too much. "I told this to the Universal people when we were negotiating: 'As soon as I got to that gate, it would be like sticking in a knife in my ribs and reminding me of a very bad circumstance before.' I could not do that to myself. It's too late in life to be miserable."

Interior footage for the CBS *Rockford* episodes were filmed at the Ren-Mar Studios, one of the oldest and most venerable film studios in Hollywood. Once home to the old Metro Studios (before that company merged into Metro-Goldwyn-Mayer in 1924), Ren-Mar was also the studio that originally housed Desilu Productions. *I Love Lucy* was filmed there, as was *Make Room for Daddy* and other classic shows from the '50s and early '60s. Now a major rental studio, Ren-Mar leases its lot and sound stages to film studios, television production companies, and independent filmmakers. In recent years, Ren-Mar has been the home base for such shows as *NewsRadio*, *Lizzie McGuire*, and *Monk*, as well as many series produced by David E. Kelley (including *Ally McBeal*, *Chicago Hope*, and *The Practice*).

James Garner served as co-executive producer of the new *Rockford Files* along with Juanita Bartlett and Charles Floyd Johnson, two of the producers from the original series. Also aboard: Stephen J. Cannell and David Chase, who (along with Bartlett) wrote the teleplays for the CBS movies; music composer Mike Post; executive assistants Luis Delgado and MaryAnn Rea; cast members Stuart Margolin, Joe Santos, Jack Garner, Gretchen Corbett, James Luisi, and Tom Atkins; and many of the original crew members, including assistant directors Cliff Coleman and Les Berke, cinematographer Steve Yaconelli, stunt coordinator Roydon Clark, and property masters Bill Fannon and Craig Binkley.

The first movie, *I Still Love L.A.*, brought *Rockford* up to date by showing how our hero contended with some of the major events that beset Los Angeles in the early 1990s: the riots following the Rodney King verdict in 1992; the fires in Malibu during the fall of 1993; and the Northridge earthquake of early 1994. Rockford still has his old Pontiac Firebird, although it's in repairs for most of the film. He also has a new trailer, a change that was borne out of necessity. The original Nashua trailer had been destroyed years before, although according to Garner there wasn't much left of it to begin with. "We'd have to tow the trailer from the studio to Paradise Cove and back again on the original show," the actor told CNN in 1994. "One night, they took it out on the Ventura freeway, and the trailer just fell in half! It fell right out and blocked four lanes of the freeway for hours."

Missing from the original cast was Noah Beery Jr. ("Rocky"), who had been in poor health since suffering a stroke in the mid-1980s. Beery died on November 1, 1994, less than a month before *I Still Love L.A.* premiered on CBS. The entire *Rockford* family paid tribute to the actor and the character in a heartfelt sequence that occurs near the end of the film. Following a phone conversation between Rockford and his father, the camera cuts to the photo of Rocky that Jim keeps on his desk. Rockford then picks up the photo and smiles warmly.

"That was filmed before Pidge [Beery] died," Garner explained in an interview for this book. "We knew that we wouldn't be able to have him on the show, so we put the picture on the table, and then I did that conversation on the phone. That was our little tribute to Pidge." The film also ends with the following dedication: *To Noah Beery Jr.: We love you and we miss you, Pidge.*

Photograph courtesy of CBS Productions
© 1994 CBS, Inc.

James Garner in a publicity photo for one of the *Rockford Files* reunion movies he produced for CBS

I Still Love L.A. was telecast on November 27, 1994, and benefited from three factors: (1) a built-in audience familiar with the show; (2) a widespread publicity campaign that included televised segments on *CNN Showbiz Today,* *CBS This Morning, Extra!, The Tonight Show,* and *CBS Sneak Peek,* as well as detailed features in *TV Guide* and *The Los Angeles Times;* and (3) a strategically placed time slot. The movie aired immediately following *Murder, She Wrote,* which at the time was the highest-rated show on CBS other than *60 Minutes.* "That was something that Jim and Universal negotiated with the network," said Charles Floyd Johnson. "Jim wanted a network that would appreciate the show, and a guarantee that the films would be shown in a good time slot. The first thing was easy: all three networks wanted *The Rockford Files,* so it wasn't a matter of having to sell the idea. All Universal had to do was say, 'We want to do *Rockford* again,' and they all came running.

"We went with CBS because they offered us Sunday night at nine, after *Murder, She Wrote.* Jim thought that was not only one of the best time slots in television, but also the best time slot for the show."

According to Johnson, ABC and NBC were apparently willing to rearrange their programming schedules in order to accommodate Garner. There was even talk that ABC might offer Garner a Wednesday night time slot (with *Roseanne* as a lead-in) or that NBC would air the TV-movies on Thursday nights (following *Seinfeld*). Because *Roseanne* and *Seinfeld* were also Top Ten shows at the time, a scenario with either of those shows as a lead-in would have also offered the prospect of a huge audience.

But Garner ultimately went with CBS partly because the network's demographics at the time were compatible with that of *Rockford*'s core audience. Whereas *Roseanne* and *Seinfeld* were both highly popular with "younger viewers" [ages 21-49], *Murder, She Wrote* was particularly strong among viewers who were 50 and older: the same age bracket from which *Rockford* has always drawn its greatest audience. In other words, Garner chose CBS because he believed Angela Lansbury's viewers were more likely to stay tuned to watch *Rockford* than Seinfeld's or Roseanne's.

That proved to be shrewd thinking on Garner's part. *I Still Love L.A.* was the No. 1 show on the West Coast that night, and finished fourth in the overall Nielsen ratings for that week. It scored an 18.5 rating, with a 28 share, acing out *Cagney & Lacey: The Return* as the highest-rated made-for-TV movie for the entire 1994-1995 season. An estimated 17,649,000 television households tuned in that night, an audience figure comparable to what the series was drawing at the peak of its popularity in 1975. The film scored particularly well with older viewers.

Strangely enough, in many respects *Rockford's* history on CBS would mirror its history on NBC. After a strong start, the series suffered a massive drop in audience with its second installment, *A Blessing in Disguise* (which originally aired in May 1995). On top of that, *Blessing* (as well as the third telefilm, *If the Frame Fits*) is plagued by some of the same problems that characterized the second season of the original show. Not only do both movies play Rockford for a sap, they make the mistake of allocating far too much screen time to the exasperating Angel Martin. As gifted as a performer as Stuart Margolin is, one imagines that even he might concede that the character he plays is one best taken in small doses.

Rockford's history with CBS does differ, however, in one important respect. While NBC stayed with the series through thick and thin, that wasn't always the case with CBS. Though the Eye Network would exercise its option with Garner and order another two movies (bringing the total number of reunion films to eight), it also seemed to lose interest in the franchise once the ratings began to slip. The most telling sign: after initially promising Garner that *Rockford* would air in the coveted Sunday 9:00 p.m. slot, CBS began scheduling the movies on nights that were traditionally the domain of other networks. The fifth installment (*Friends and Foul Play,* written by Stephen J. Cannell) was broadcast on a Thursday—a night that had belonged to NBC since 1984. Not surprisingly, *Rockford* was beaten soundly that night by *Seinfeld* and *Friends*. The sixth movie (*Punishment and Crime,* written and directed by David Chase) was banished to a Wednesday, a ratings Siberia for CBS for over 20 years. Competing against the top-rated *Grace Under Fire* and *The Drew Carey Show* on ABC (not to mention *Law and Order* on NBC), *Rockford* on that occasion finished a distant third.

Adding insult to injury: not only was CBS airing the movies in suicidal time slots, it exerted little if any effort to promote them. Or for that matter, even broadcast them. *Punishment and Crime* sat on the shelf for over a year before earning on a spot on the network schedule in September 1996. The eighth, and last, movie (*If It Bleeds … It Leads,* featuring Rita Moreno as Rita Capkovic) gathered dust for almost two years before CBS finally aired it, practically as an afterthought, in April 1999.

That was unfortunate, because for the most part the last few entries in the CBS series were actually quite good. Just as David Chase energized the original *Rockford* at the beginning of the third season, the CBS movies got a second wind with the help of a writer and a director who were both established in television but nonetheless "new" to the show.

One new such addition who immediately put his stamp on *Rockford* was producer/director Tony Wharmby (*The X Files, JAG, Without a Trace*), who directed two of the final four movies produced for CBS. "He really changed the look of the show," Garner said in 1996, "and it's just marvelous."

Production Credits: 1994–1999

NOTE. Most of the names on this list were obtained from the screen credits that appear at the end of each of the Rockford Files *movies produced for CBS. Some names, however, were obtained from additional sources, including The Internet Movie Database.*

Executive Producers: James Garner, Charles Floyd Johnson, Juanita Bartlett
Supervising Producers: Stephen J. Cannell, David Chase
Produced by: Mark Horowitz, David L. Beanes, Mark R. Schilz, Carey Smith-Ludwig
Created by: Roy Huggins and Stephen J. Cannell

Music by: Mike Post and Pete Carpenter
Film Editors: Pam Malouf-Cundy, Randy D. Wiles, Toni Morgan
Assistant Film Editors: Michael Carlich, Gregory Gontz, Timothy P. Joyce
Production Designers: Anthony Cowley, Sandy Getzler
Directors of Photography: Steve Yaconelli, Michael D. O'Shea
Aerial Director of Photography: Kurt E. Soderling
Additional Photography: Joseph D. Urbanczyk
Second Assistant Camera: Thom Willey
Dolly Grip: James D. Wickman
Associate Producer: Carey Smith-Ludwig
Unit Production Managers: David L. Beanes, Mark R. Schilz
First Assistant Directors: Cliff Coleman, Ron L. Wright, Concheta Rinaldo-Williams
Second Assistant Directors: Les Burke, Todd A. Covert
Second Second Assistant Directors: David L. D'Ovidio, Phil Cook, Todd Corman
Casting: David Giella, Eddie Dunlop, *Reuben Cannon & Associates*
Costume Designer: April Ferry
Art Directors: Sandy Getzler, Ann Harris, Kelly Hannafin, Beala B. Neel
Set Decorators: Robert L. Zilliox, Lynn Wolverton-Parker
Story Board Artist, Action Unit: Scott Duthie
Property Master: Bill Fannon
Makeup Artist: Charlene Roberson

Hair Stylists: Don Sheldon, Caron Codon-Tharp, Charlotte Harvey
Stunt Coordinator: Roydon Clark
Stunt Doubles: David LeBell, Michael J. Sarna
Special Effects Coordinators: Tom Love, M. Kam Cooney, Larry Fioritto
Sound Mixers: Darin Knight, Ron Collins, Sean Rush
Gaffer: Thomas Barone
Key Grips: Ron Stafford, Marlin E. Hall
Location Managers: Karlene Gallegly, David E. Berthiaume, Paul Brinkman, Murray Miller
Transportation Coordinator: Steve Hellerstein
Transportation Captains: Robert Benjamin, Lee Stepp, Marlo Hellerstein
Script Supervisors: Suzanne Gundlach, Gillian Murphy, Joanne Small, Billie L. Mayer
Production Assistant: David Mongan
Assistant to Executive Producer: Luis Delgado
Assistant to James Garner: MaryAnn Rea
Panaflex® Camera and Lenses by Panavision
Supervising Sound Editors: Ron Horwitz, Charlie Crutcher, Kevin Spears
Sound Editors: Ron Horwitz, Charlie Crutcher, Steve Burger, Rich Cusano, Andy Dawson, Michael Gollom, Tom Jaeger, Jeffrey Kaplan, Patty Morena, Stacey Nakasone, Robb Navrides, Cindy Rabideau, John O. Robinson III, Richard Webb, Kyle Wright, Lydian Tone
Music Editors: Patty McGettigan, Libby Pedersen
Dialogue Editor: Ron S. Herbes
Sound Effects Editor: Lydian Tone
Cable Person: Maurice Jacks Jr.
Post-Production Coordinator: Carey Smith-Ludwig

MGB Productions, Inc.
in association with
Universal City Studios, Inc.

Episode Guide for the CBS Movies

1.   I STILL LOVE L.A.
(Originally Entitled: "I Love L.A.")

Production Number: 82501
Original Air Date: November 27, 1994
Written by: Juanita Bartlett
Directed by: James Whitmore Jr.

Cast: James Garner (Jim Rockford), Joanna Cassidy (Halley "Kit" Kittredge), Joe Santos (Dennis Becker), Stuart Margolin (Angel Martin), Joseph Campanella (Mickey Ryder), Geoffrey Nauffts (Josh Lansing), Shannon Kenny (Dorie Lansing), Lawrence Pressman (Sidney Kornblum), Daniel Benzali (Dr. Ezo), Sherry Hursey (Maddie), David Purdham (Paco), Hoke Howell (Ed Emmenthaler), Lesley Woods (Myrna Emmenthaler), Sam Scarber (Lloyd Sanders), Lori Alan (Karen Kupfer), James A. Watson Jr. (Pete McCool), Jack Garner (Captain McEnroe), Eddie Mekka (Gus), Michael Bailey Smith (Philip Warsche), Bob Minor (Duty Officer), Shirley Anthony (Sally), Eliana Alexander (Officer No. 1), Diana Tanaka (Kornblum's Secretary), Jean Bartel (Lila Lansing)

Jim, it's Benny. I know your sewer's backed up, but I can't get out there today. Maybe your buyers won't notice ...

Synopsis. *As a favor to his ex-wife, attorney Halley "Kit" Kittredge, Rockford agrees to probe the murder of her friend, legendary film star Lila Lansing.*

I Still Love L.A. has much of the flavor of the original series, from colorful characters (including a Hollywood agent who is subpoenaed by the police while waiting outside Oliver Stone's office) to Angel's crazy antics (he plans to hawk stolen merchandise on the Home Shopping Network). One noticeable difference, though, is that there isn't as much "action" (car chases, fist fights, and the like) as one might expect from a typical *Rockford* story. Then again, considering James Garner's age at the time (66), it would have been a stretch to have the character be anywhere near as physical as he was in the original series. After all, even on its off-days *Rockford* was usually grounded in reality.

Photograph courtesy of CBS Productions
© 1994 CBS, Inc.

James Garner and Joanne Cassidy in a publicity still for *I Still Love L.A.*

Plus, given the particular story line for *I Still Love L.A.*, it made sense to have Rockford portrayed as more of a "reactor" in this case than perhaps he usually was. "For the most part, Rockford was up against natural disasters in that first show: earthquakes, fires, and the like," explained Juanita Bartlett, who wrote the teleplay. "There wasn't anybody who was actively trying to do him hard—other than, apparently, God. Now, you talk about your big time heavies ..."

The most inspired scene of the movie occurs in Act I, when Rockford watches live television footage of the looting caused by the riots in Los Angeles. The TV camera zooms in and catches Angel red-handed as he helps himself to merchandise from an electronics store. Then we cut to Rockford, whose look says it all. On the one hand, he can't believe what he is seeing—but on the other hand, he can, because nothing Angel does ever really surprises him. "Stuart came up with something when we first filmed that scene that made me laugh out loud," recalled Bartlett. "[Director] Jimmy Whitmore shot that sequence from a high angle, because it's supposed to be footage taken from a helicopter camera. Angel looks up, sees the camera, and panics. So he reaches out and takes a trash bag and puts it over his head ... only it's a see-through trash bag! Stuart does things like that all the time. He has all those wonderful, off-the-wall ideas that are just marvelous."

One item that the first movie did not address was the matter of Rockford's daily rate in 1994. "I would hope he'd get a little raise," Garner joked at the time. "There wasn't a scene in the first film where we got into that, but I'm sure we'll establish another price—probably around $350 a day."

The key, added Garner, is not to overprice him. "You want to underprice him," he said. "You don't want to go over, but it's okay to go a little under."

Garner earned a Screen Actors Guild Award nomination for Best Actor in a TV-Movie or Miniseries for his performance in *I Still Love L.A.*

Rockford Facts

Because the character Joanna Cassidy plays in *I Still Love L.A* looks like Beth Davenport and also happens to be an attorney, there was some speculation that she was essentially designed as a replacement for Beth in the new series of movies. According to Juanita Bartlett, however, that wasn't the case at all. "We figured that in the 15 years between the end of the old series and the start of the new series, Rockford would have probably have married," the writer/producer explained. "And that's who Joanna Cassidy is: somebody he married, and a character where you'd see why he would have married her, but also why they couldn't possibly have stayed together. But, no, she was not supposed to be a replacement for Beth."

One year prior to shooting *I Still Love L.A.*, Cassidy co-starred with James Garner in the HBO original movie *Barbarians at the Gate*, for which Garner won a Golden Globe Award in 1994. A decade earlier, Cassidy herself won a Golden Globe for playing Jo Jo, the long-suffering director and occasional girl-friend of irascible talk show host Bill Bittinger (Dabney Coleman) on *Buffalo Bill* (NBC, 1983-1984). Cassidy currently stars as Brenda's domineering mom on HBO's *Six Feet Under*.

Gretchen Corbett would eventually return to play Beth Davenport in three of the remaining seven *Rockford*s produced for CBS: *If the Frame Fits*, *Friends and Foul Play*, and *If It Bleeds ... It Leads*.

2. A BLESSING IN DISGUISE
(Originally Entitled: "Little Ezekial")

Production Number: 82502
Original Air Date: May 14, 1995
Written by: Stephen J. Cannell
Directed by: Jeannot Szwarc

Cast: James Garner (Jim Rockford), Stuart Margolin (Angel Martin), Joe Santos (Dennis Becker), Renee O'Connor (Laura Dean), Richard Romanus (Vincent Penguinetti), Aharon Ipale (Branka Decosta), Reuven Bar-Yotam (Milovan D'Sant), Eric Lutes (Danny Barkley), Morton Downey Jr. (Himself), Robert Desiderio (Jerry Michaels), Stuart Fratkin (Jerry Jamison), Mark Davenport (Marty Martinson), Vince Melocchi (Kyle Wendell), Bari K. Willerford (Zachery "Zack" Irons), Joel McKinnon Miller (Brian "Mackie" MacDonald), Niles Allen Stewart (Stevie), Elsa Raven (Sarah Lanka), Christine Romeo (Sister Eve), Carl Ciarfalio (Brother Bob), Shane Sweet (Little "Zeke" Ezekial), Joey Hamilton (Man #1), Sparkle (Woman #1), Merciful Angels Choir (Themselves)

Jim, it's Paul. Hey, I have been waiting two months for that invitation, buddy. Are you gonna get that new sports channel before the Rams leave L.A.?

Synopsis. *Angel's latest entrepreneurial scheme has him transformed into a tele-vangelist. Working in cahoots with Delphi Films (the producers of an ultra-low budget flick called* Little Ezekial*), Angel encourages his "flock" at the Temple of Holy Light to boycott the movie, knowing that the controversy will likely drive up the film's gross box office receipts. Rockford reluctantly becomes involved in the matter after the film's star Laura Dean receives death threats that appear to be tied to the boycott. Rockford agrees to protect Laura ... and soon discovers that Angel's partners at Delphi are closely tied to the mob.*

Given the stellar performance of the first *Rockford* reunion movie in November 1994—*I Still Love L.A.* not only won its time slot, it finished fourth among all shows that aired that week—CBS had high hopes for *A Blessing in Disguise*, especially given the favorable reviews from a number of television critics. "The movie is so whimsical, it's almost weightless," wrote David Hiltbrand in *People*. "But if Rockford did an infomercial on furniture shopping, I'd probably watch it."

John Carman of the *San Francisco Chronicle* went even further, calling *Blessing* "the most satisfying network movie I've seen in the last five years."

But *Blessing* also faced some of the most brutal competition any television program had ever seen. Scheduled for Mother's Day night 1995 (right in the heart of the annual May sweeps), the movie was pitted against not one, but two highly anticipated mini-series: *Stephen King's The Langoliers* on ABC, and *Naomi & Wynona: Love Can Build a Bridge*, an NBC mini-series based on the life of singer Naomi Judd.

Photograph courtesy of CBS Productions
© 1994 CBS, Inc.

Jim Rockford (James Garner) shows Laura Dean (Renee O'Connor of *Xena: Warrior Princess*) that chivalry isn't dead in this publicity still for the *Rockford Files* reunion movie, *A Blessing in Disguise*.

"It figures to be a big, bloody Sunday night, the most combative night of the sweeps," wrote Carman in the *San Francisco Chronicle*. "[But the choice] is not so hard. The best of the three is the new *Rockford Files* movie, with a sparkling script by Stephen J. Cannell and a chunky performance by Stuart Margolin as Angel Martin."

Unfortunately, it was *Rockford* that got bloodied that night, *Blessing* finishing a distant third behind King and the Judds. The movie scored an 11.0 rating and a 17 share—audience numbers that were 41% lower than those garnered by the first movie.

On the bright side, James Garner earned his second consecutive Screen Actors Guild Award nomination for Best Actor in a TV-Movie for his performance in *Blessing*.

Rockford Facts

Back in the second season of the original series (in the episode "Chicken Little is a Little Chicken"), we learned that Angel's real name is "Evelyn." But it isn't until the early moments of *A Blessing in Disguise* that we finally realize how Angel got his nickname in the first place. Rockford reminds Angel that he acquired the name during the time they were incarcerated together at San Quentin. "They called you Angel," says Jim, "because you were always on your knees, praying for hard cases not to kill you."

Production of *Blessing* was marred when a man was injured in a minor traffic mishap that occurred during filming of a routine driving sequence in downtown Los Angeles. According to an item published in the December 9, 1994 edition of the *Los Angeles Times*, James Garner was behind the wheel of Rockford's famous Pontiac Firebird when the man somehow slipped past the police officers who were escorting Garner and inexplicably darted in front of the car. Garner stopped the car immediately and offered his assistance to the victim. Despite sustaining a laceration to the head and a fractured foot, the man was not seriously injured and was released from the hospital the following day.

Rockford Family Reunion

Onetime *Rockford* supervising producer Jo Swerling paid a visit to the set during the filming of *A Blessing in Disguise* in December 1994. "They happened to be shooting down in the marina where I live," he explained. "On my way home, I dropped in (they were shooting at night), and I visited the guys on the set.

Photograph courtesy of CBS Productions
© 1994 CBS, Inc.

Jim Rockford (James Garner) has good reason to be dubious of Angel Martin's (Stuart Margolin) transformation from con man to holy man in the *Rockford Files* reunion movie, *A Blessing in Disguise.*

Nearly everybody from the old show was there: Joe Santos; Stu Margolin; Jimmy; Jimmy's stunt double, Roy Clark; the director of photography [Steve Yaconelli] was the camera operator on the old show; and the prop man [Bill Fannon] was the same on the old show. Charles Johnson did a remarkable job of gathering as many of the key people as he did. As a matter of fact, the guy who was the production manager on the original show [Les Berke] was back, only he was working as a second assistant director—*just to be on the show*. And the first assistant director, Cliff Coleman, was one of our first A.D.s on the original show. I also go back a long ways with the director [of the second movie], Jeannot Szwarc.

"It was an eerie feeling … it was almost as if I had stepped back in time, and it was old home week. But it was a lot of fun."

3.   IF THE FRAME FITS ...
(Originally Entitled: "Suitable for Framing")

Production Number: 82601
Original Air Date: January 14, 1996
Written by: Juanita Bartlett
Directed by: Jeannot Szwarc

Cast: James Garner (Jim Rockford), Dyan Cannon (Jess Wilding), Stuart Margolin (Angel Martin), Joe Santos (Dennis Becker), Gretchen Corbett (Beth Davenport Van Sant), James Luisi (Captain Douglas Chapman), Tom Atkins (Commander Alex Diehl), Jack Garner (Captain McEnroe), Carmen Argenziano (Hector Gustavo), Dyana Ortelli (Linda), Beverly Leech (Eleanor), Randy Oglesby (Stringer), Linden Chiles (Senator Aspall), Sal Lopez (Joselito), Michael Leopard (George), Herschel Sparger (Bud Monckton), James A. Watson Jr. (Pete McCool), Shirley Anthony (Sally), Xavier Montalvo (Officer Martinez), Perry Santos (Pete), Thomas Rosales (Ernesto), Leon Simmons (Desk Sergeant), Rolando Molina (Ramon), Terry Jackson (Agent Delamo), Jodi Baskerville (Commentator), Terry James (Officer #1), Robert Powell (Officer #2), Steve Eastin

Synopsis. *Falsely accused of murdering a rival detective, Rockford fights to clear his name despite a staggering circumstantial case against him and increasing animosity from his two longtime nemeses on the Los Angeles Police Department, Commander Alex Diehl and Captain Douglas Chapman. But our hero finds help from friends old and new, including Dennis Becker, former attorney (now best-selling novelist) Beth Davenport, and IRS agent Jess Wilding.*

While *If the Frame Fits* was the third of the new *Rockford* episodes to have aired on CBS, in many respects it was the first "true" reunion show. Besides James Garner, Stuart Margolin, Joe Santos and Jack Garner, the show brought back the three remaining members of the original cast: Gretchen Corbett (as Beth Davenport), James Luisi (as Lieutenant Chapman), and Tom Atkins (as Lieutenant Diehl). To illustrate the passage of time, the story establishes that Beth is now married and the author of the wildly successful novel *The Brief*, while Chapman and Diehl have moved up the ranks of the L.A.P.D. "Chappy" is now a police captain, while Diehl is now a commander.

Written by Juanita Bartlett, *Frame* is more in the spirit of the original *Rockford Files*. Not only is the pace faster, there's a little more action than we saw in the first two movies. There's even a traditional *Rockford* chase in the old

Pontiac Firebird, which Garner no doubt welcomed. "As much as Jim likes to do his own stunts, we didn't let him do any of them on these new shows," said Luis Delgado. "What he did do, however, was his own driving."

The movie also acknowledges the passing of Noah Beery Jr. with the help of guest star Dyan Cannon (*Heaven Can Wait, Bob & Carol & Ted & Alice*). Cannon plays Jess Wilding, an I.R.S. agent who was also an old acquaintance of Rocky's. Early in Act II, Jess tells Rockford that she was in Switzerland when Rocky died and that she "didn't hear about his death until I got home." She then asks Rockford to take her to Forest Lawn so that she can visit Rocky's grave. "I'd like to go there with you," she says. "I think Rocky would like that."

Though *Frame* was the third new *Rockford* to air on CBS, it was actually the fourth to be produced—and the second to refer to the death of Rocky. *Frame* was filmed in August 1995, four months after production had been completed on the third film, *Punishment and Crime* (written by David Chase), which CBS chose not to broadcast until September 1996. The shooting script for *Punishment and Crime* (dated April 7, 1995) also includes a line in which Rockford tells Megan Dougherty that "Rocky died late last year." This, of course, is a reference to Beery's death on November 1, 1994.

Frame was also the first of the CBS *Rockford* movies to part from the norm. Unlike the first two reunion movies (both of which begin with a traditional funny phone message on Jim's answering machine), *Frame* cuts right to the chase: a horde of squad cars pull up in front of Rockford's trailer in the middle of the night. Rockford is rousted from his sleep, arrested on suspicion of murder, and brought in to police headquarters for questioning.

As *Rockford* producers Charles Floyd Johnson and Juanita Bartlett previously explained, sometimes it wasn't easy for the original show to come up with a decent phone "tag" to begin each episode of the series. In that respect, it's not a complete surprise to find that the message tags were eventually dropped from the reunion movies. Like *Frame*, each of the remaining five shows produced for CBS start right in on the action.

If the Frame Fits also features veteran character actor Linden Chiles, whose last appearance on *Rockford* was back in the first season ("The Dark and Bloody Ground," Episode No. 2 of the original series), and Perry Santos, the son of Joe Santos.

 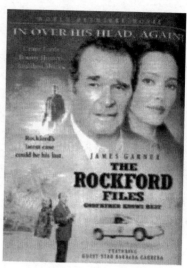

These ads for *If the Frame Fits …* (left) and *Godfather Knows Best* appeared in newspaper supplements as well as in *TV Guide*

Rockford Facts

Known for wearing her hair straight and long when she originally played Beth in the '70s, Gretchen Corbett has naturally curly hair in real life. She had her hair straightened regularly earlier in her career, but hasn't worn it that way in years. "I look different, so people don't approach me an awful lot unless I make my hair straight; then they recognize me a lot," she told David Martindale in 1996. "But my hair is actually curly and now I've just cut it all off. And they actually wrote all that into the screenplay! I couldn't believe it— you know, talking about my hair on national television. I mean, *oh my God …*"

Indeed, when Beth makes her first appearance in the early moments of Act II, Rockford can't help noticing that there's something different about her. Finally, it dawns on him, and he asks her: "What did you do to your hair?"

Rockford Fun

If the Frame Fits marks the second time in which the character played by Tom Atkins had his name altered. Throughout the original series, the character's last name was spelled D-I-E-L. However, for *Frame* (as well as all other reunion shows featuring Atkins), the spelling was somehow changed to D-I-E-H-L.

When Atkins first appeared on *Rockford* in 1974, his character's first name was originally "Alex," then changed to "Thomas" beginning in the second season. But in the promotional materials for the reunion movies, the character's first name was changed back to "Alex."

Rockford Finishes

Frame performed very well in the Nielsens, winning its time slot handily with a solid 13.0 rating and 20 share. While the numbers were nowhere near those of the first movie (*I Still Love L.A.*), they were certainly a marked improvement over those of the second (*A Blessing in Disguise*). Not only that, the audience numbers for *Frame* contined to increase over the course of the two-hour broadcast—always a good sign.

Overall, *Frame* finished in 22nd place that week (out of 111 shows), a full nine notches better than *Blessing*, which placed 31st place among 93 shows while finishing third in its time slot.

4. GODFATHER KNOWS BEST
(Originally Entitled: "Godfather 4, Cops 0")

Production Number: 82603
Original Air Date: February 18, 1996
Written by: David Chase
Directed by: Tony Wharmby

Cast: James Garner (Jim Rockford), Barbara Carrera (Elizabetta Fama), Stuart Margolin (Angel Martin), Joe Santos (Dennis Becker), Damian Chapa (Scotty Becker), Maxwell Caulfield (Ian Levin), Pat Finley (Peggy Becker), Jack Garner (Captain McEnroe), Edita Brychta (Katinka), Dan Lauria (Lieutenant Gencher), George Marshall Ruge (Sicilian Hit Man), Al Mancini (Don Gaetano), Dennis Fimple (Toothless Bob), Julian Reyes (Raimondo), Gerry Gibson (Critch), Jim O'Heir (Head Chef), Rick Worthy (Property Officer), Eve Brenner (Corky), Kim Oja (Young Woman), Joe Unger (Panhandler), Pat Lalama (Herself), Glen Chin (Master Jun), Gary Simpson (Santa Monica Policeman), Nicole Avant (Punch), Luis Contreras (Hispanic Man), Victor Aaron

Synopsis. *Rockford's godson Scotty Becker, the 30-year-old son of Dennis and Peggy Becker, is a wayward soul who somehow finds himself the prime suspect in the murder of fashion designer Elizabetta Fama.*

Once again, *Rockford* won its Sunday 9:00 p.m. time slot. *Godfather Knows Best* drew an 11.0 rating and an 18.8 share while finishing 25th out of 106 shows in the overall Nielsens that week. It was the third time in four outings that the reunion movies landed in the top 25—no mean feat, considering the indifference CBS seemed to exhibit when it came to promoting the film. Perhaps still smarting from its experience with *A Blessing in Disguise* (which despite an aggressive publicity campaign got clobbered in the ratings when it aired in May 1995), the Eye Network broadcast *Godfather* with barely a peep.

Though James Garner was troubled by the network's failure to promote *Godfather*, he was happy to see how well the film was received by the show's audience. The rapport between Garner and Damian Chapa (as Scotty Becker) is particularly strong.

There was, however, some initial concern about the Scotty Becker character. While Scotty was supposed to be rough around the edges, apparently he came across as a bit *too* rough and not particularly likeable in the first draft of David Chase's script. As much as Garner respects Chase (as he respects all his writers), he did ask him to pull back just a little on this particular occasion. "Jim felt it was important to make Scotty more appealing—otherwise, the audience might wonder why Rockford would get involved with him to the extent he did," said Garner's assistant MaryAnn Rea. "David understood Jim's concern and agreed to soften him a little."

Godfather also features Rick Worthy (*Murder One, Enterprise*), character actor Dennis Fimple (who previously guest-starred in the original series episode "The Competitive Edge") and onetime Los Angeles TV news anchor Pat Lalama, who is now the senior correspondent for the popular daily syndicated show *Celebrity Justice.*

Rockford Fun

Godfather begins with a shot of Rockford exiting a cinema multiplex. Jim has just finished seeing the movie version of Beth Davenport's bestselling novel *The Brief* when he bumps into Angel Martin.

"How was it?" asks Angel.

Rockford's response is also one of the best lines in the movie. "*The Brief* ... *The Firm* ... I'd like to know when one of these ex-lawyers is going to write a book called *The Fee.*"

5. FRIENDS AND FOUL PLAY
(Originally Entitled: "Field Trip to a Funeral")

Production Number: 82602
Original Air Date: April 25, 1996
Written by: Stephen J. Cannell
Directed by: Stuart Margolin

Cast: James Garner (Jim Rockford), Marcia Strassman (Dr. Trish George), Jason Bernard (Leon Martin), Stuart Margolin (Angel Martin), Joe Santos (Dennis Becker), Gretchen Corbett (Beth Davenport Van Sant), James Luisi (Captain Chapman), Jack Garner (Captain McEnroe), David Proval (Joseph "Happy" Cartello), Wendy Phillips (Babs Honeywell), Molly Hagan (Trudy Wise), Matt Gallini (Nicky Zeeno), Jonah Blechman (Tennison Keats), Kim Murphy (Melissa Fortner), Gerry Gibson (Critch), Charles Noland (Gumpy Cook), Kevin Sifuentes (Carlos Carilla), Dion Anderson (Carl Liggitt), Siena Goines (Candace Clark), Charlotte Stewart (Registrar), Rick Worthy (Policeman), Andy Kossin (Cole Matson), Donna Maria Moore (Dr. Cynthia Marsan), Suzan Byun (Dr. Smith), Dena Burton (Nurse Marylou), Lise Simms (Misty Rain), Pete Koch (Gary), Murray MacLeod (Minister), Robert Laretta (Ramone), Stefan Gierasch, Ivan Sergei

Synopsis. *Rockford tries to help his friend Babs Honeywell, a waitress at the Sand Castle, prove that her son was killed by mobster Happy Cartello. When Babs herself is murdered, Jim goes through her diary, hoping to find clues that could link the two deaths. Rockford is on the verge of cracking the case when Chapman orders him banned from the investigation. But when Rockford learns that Chapman is teaching a course on criminology—and that the captain has incorporated the Honeywell case into the curriculum—he immediately enrolls in the class himself so that he can study the matter first hand.*

Friends and Foul Play was the last of the six *Rockford Files* movies produced by James Garner as part of his original deal with CBS. Shooting wrapped in January 1996, after which time Garner suspended operations on *Rockford* pending word from the network on additional episodes.

Several weeks after *Friends and Foul Play* aired in April 1996, CBS informed Garner that it would exercise its option and order another two *Rockford* movies. Co-executive producer Juanita Bartlett, who had written two of the first six movies, would write the scripts for the additional two. However, because of Garner's other acting commitments (among other things, he traveled to Toronto in the fall of 1996 to shoot *Dead Silence*, a motion picture for HBO), production of the films would not begin in earnest until early 1997.

Still, Garner was pleased by the news, and was happy to hear that the network was satisfied with the ratings on the new shows. "CBS told us that they weren't expecting miracles, and that as long as we won our time slot, or at least held our own [as the new *Rockford*s had done at that point], that they'd be happy," said Garner associate MaryAnn Rea. "So far as CBS was concerned, Jim could continue to do *Rockford* for as long as he wanted."

Rockford Facts

Friends and Foul Play was originally broadcast on April 25, 1996, the first night of the annual four-week May television "sweeps" period. Unlike the first four CBS *Rockford*s (all of which aired on Sunday nights following *Murder, She Wrote*, pursuant to Garner's deal with the network), *Friends and Foul Play* aired in one of TV's toughest time slots: Thursday night at 8:00 p.m., the longtime domain of NBC and "Must See TV." *Rockford* ran against *Seinfeld* (the No. 1 show in television at the time) and *Friends* (a perennial Top Ten finisher). Not surprisingly, the movie finished a distant third that night, finishing 37th overall that week out of 102 shows.

On the bright side, the audience numbers for *Friends and Foul Play* (the movie scored a 9.5 rating) were the highest for a CBS show on Thursday night in over three months. As far as the network was concerned, *Rockford* continued to "hold its own."

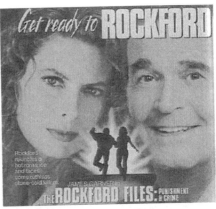

CBS ads for *Friends and Foul Play* (left) and *Punishment and Crime*

Rockford Familiar Faces

Friends and Foul Play features two actors who previously guest-starred on the original *Rockford Files*. Murray MacLeod appeared in the second-season episode "Where's Houston?" while Marcia Strassman starred in the sixth-season two-parter "Only Rock 'n' Roll Will Never Die."

6.   PUNISHMENT AND CRIME
(Originally Entitled: "Night Fishing")

Production Number: 82503
Original Air Date: September 18, 1996
Written and Directed by: David Chase

Cast: James Garner (Jim Rockford), Kathryn Harrold (Megan Dougherty Adams), Stuart Margolin (Angel Martin), Joe Santos (Dennis Becker), Richard Kiley (Frank Dougherty), Bryan Cranston (Patrick Dougherty), Ramy Zada (Festa), Ilia Voloxh (Boris), Elena DeBurdo (Ykaterina), Grace Una (Molly), Johnny Williams (Johnny Zeps), Jack Garner (Captain McEnroe), Lyndsay Riddell (Young Josie), John Christian Graas (Daniel), Heather Ehlers (Josie), Ruben Groove (Vacuum Man), Lilyan Chauvin (Ilovna Koblets), Charlene Simpson (Poker Woman), Natalia Lapina (Club Singer), Callan White (Sioban), Don Gettinger (Pete), Russell Young (Skateboarder #1), Stephen Berra (Skateboarder #2), Stacey Greene (Young Megan), Grinnell Morris (Young Patrick), Steve Monroe (Kravitz), Scott Denny (Tony), Vladmir Skormarovsky

Synopsis. *Rockford's renewed romance with old flame Megan Dougherty takes a treacherous turn when he learns that her arrogant playboy cousin Patrick is in over his head with deadly Russian mobsters.*

"This last installment of the six-pack of telefilms revisiting *The Rockford Files* is perhaps the group's best," wrote Adam Sandler in *Daily Variety.* "Scripter David Chase has crafted an interesting and intricate tale that shifts gears as often as a speeding Firebird in Malibu Canyon. In addition to mining dramatic gold from principals James Garner and Kathryn Harrold, the show crackles with nostalgia as Rockford rekindles a long-lost romance begun during the series' web run that by show's end is sure to foster warm and fuzzy feelings from viewers about the beachfront shamus.

"With Chase's steering of the able case into avoiding the typical *Rockford Files*-esque jocularity and letting it surface only infrequently—primarily through the antics of mainstay Angel Martin (Stuart Margolin)—the result is an exposition of a softer than usual Rockford, but one that is enjoyable nonetheless."

Ironically, *Punishment* had been gathering dust for over a year before it was finally aired. Originally completed in May 1995, the film was held back for broadcast by CBS because it was considered somber, slow and too much of a character piece—not exactly the kind of freewheeling fare that most viewers typically come to expect when they tune in to see Jim Rockford.

Then again, the beauty of *The Rockford Files*, as noted before, is that it often veered in interesting directions in the course of a given season. Chase in particular was known for his offbeat, thought-provoking stories that often explored the depths of Rockford's character. In that respect, *Punishment is* typical of the original *Rockford* because it's a "change of pace" story.

That said, from a network programming point of view, one can understand CBS' rationale for holding the movie back. Because *Punishment* is light on action and heavy on emotional drama, it does takes a while for the story to unfold. While those who stay with the movie for the entire two hours will no doubt be rewarded, there was concern that the pace of the show might cause some viewers to ultimately lose interest.

As it happens, the audience numbers bear that out. *Punishment's* viewership dropped a full ratings point during the second hour of the movie. No doubt the competition between 10:00 p.m. and 11:00 p.m may have had something to do with that: *Prime Time Live* on ABC (which ultimately won that hour), plus the season premiere of *Law and Order* on NBC. But given CBS' concerns about the pace of the film, it's hard to dismiss that as a possible contributing factor.

Rockford Facts

Unlike most of the first five reunion movies (four of which were broadcast during one of the three network "sweeps" periods), *Punishment and Crime* aired on September 18, 1996—right in the middle of "Premiere Week" for the new Fall 1996 season. In addition to facing the season premieres of *Prime Time Live* and *Law and Order* at 10:00 p.m., *Punishment* also ran against the season premieres of *Grace Under Fire* (a Top Five show heading into the season) and *The Drew Carey Show* between 9:00 p.m. and 10:00 p.m. Given that kind of competition, it's not surprising to report that the movie landed in third place that night (and 51st overall out of 112 shows that week), with a 9.0 rating and a 15 share.

But the news was not completely bad. As *Variety* noted, *Rockford's* performance "marked the third straight evening that [CBS] outrated last year's performance. For Wednesday [a night on which CBS has traditionally struggled], the Eye web was up 11% from last year."

Kathryn Harrold was one of the stars of *I'll Fly Away* (NBC, 1991-1993), a critically acclaimed but low-rated legal drama produced by David Chase. Shortly after *Punishment and Crime* aired, she began a two-year run as Dr. Karen Wilder on the CBS hospital drama *Chicago Hope*.

Rockford Familiar Faces

Richard Kiley (Frank) won a Tony Award as Don Quixote in *Man from La Mancha*, as well as Emmy Awards for his roles in *The Thorn Birds* and *A Year in the Life*. His film credits included *Blackboard Jungle*, *The Little Prince*, *Looking for Mr. Goodbar*, and *Jurassic Park*.

French actress Lilyan Chauvin (Ilovna) has been a fixture in films and television for over 50 years. Among her many roles, she appeared in "High Card Hangs," an episode of *Maverick* from 1958. Chauvin has more recently been seen in such popular shows as *Alias* and *ER*.

7.   MURDER AND MISDEMEANORS
(Originally Entitled: "Shootout at the Gold Pagoda")

Production Number: 82701
Original Air Date: November 21, 1997
Written by: Juanita Bartlett
Directed by: Tony Wharmby

Cast: James Garner (Jim Rockford), John Amos (Booker Hutch), Denise Nicholas (Leddy Hutch), Stuart Margolin (Angel Martin), Joe Santos (Dennis Becker), Conrad Janis (Harvey), Isabel Glasser (Brianne Lambert), Dan Lauria (Commander Gage), Shirley Anthony (Sally), Jack Garner (Captain McEnroe), Gerry Gibson (Critch), Glenn Morshower (Sergeant Cranston), Eugene Roche, Shashawnee Hall, Danny Quinn, Marco Rodrigues, Moira Walley

Synopsis. *Back from a long fishing trip, Rockford unwittingly takes on a heap of trouble when he takes over a case from his friend Booker Hutch—a less than scrupulous private eye who claims to be seriously ill. What Jim doesn't realize is that Booker is not only in perfect health, the case he has saddled him with is a highly-publicized hot potato involving alleged police misconduct that will once again get Rockford in Dutch with the L.A.P.D. As if that weren't enough, our hero must also contend with Angel's attempts to cash in on the controversy by selling a movie about Rockford's life.*

Preparations for *Murder and Misdemeanors* began the week of March 24, 1997. The original plan was to bring back Isaac Hayes as Gandolf Fitch, but that had to be scuttled once other commitments ultimately made Hayes unavailable. "That was really unfortunate, because Isaac wanted so much to come back and do Gandy," said executive producer Charles Floyd Johnson. "I would bump into him in New York occasionally at functions, and we'd always talk about it—you know, '*When are we gonna do this?*' But by the time we finally got the green light from CBS, Isaac's schedule had become so complicated that we just couldn't make it work. By then, of course, he was doing *South Park*, he was doing his radio show in New York, plus he was also shooting a movie. We had a three-week shooting schedule of our own to meet, and it would have been a lot to ask of him at the time. So we had to go in another direction."

Rather than recast Gandy with another actor, writer/producer Juanita Bartlett reworked the story to introduce a new character: Booker Hutch (played by John Amos), an ex-con turned private eye who looked a little like Gandy (at least, in the sense that Amos had taken to shaving his head those days)—and even had a pet nickname for Rockford, like Gandy ("Rocko," instead of "Rockfish")—but who was closer in spirit to Marcus Hayes, the fast-talking con man played by Lou Gossett in the original series.

"I think that was serendipitous," said Johnson, who originally created the Hayes character in the second season episode "Foul on the First Play." "I don't think it was by design. It wasn't as if either Juanita or I said, *'Remember the guy that Lou Gossett played ...?'* I think it was more a matter of, once we decided to go in a new direction, we tried to come up with a character that was more or less in the nature of the characters we had created in the past: someone who was always trying to fast-talk Jim and take advantage of him. Then once Juanita came up with the character [Booker Hutch], we tried to figure out who we could go with who could play off Jim Garner.

"I think it was Reuben Cannon [whose company Reuben Cannon & Associates helped cast the CBS movies] who suggested John Amos. So we sent the script to John, and he was intrigued by it. But I don't think we asked him to look at any of the previous shows. It was just an interesting happenstance, how John developed that character. And we had a great time doing that show. We weren't sure how it was going to work at first, given the fact that everybody kind of had Isaac Hayes in our heads at first. But Jim and John clicked from the start. They had a lot of fun together, and we had a lot of fun working on it."

Murder and Misdemeanors was marked by sadness, however, one week into pre-production. Longtime Garner company member Luis Delgado died of liver cancer on April 3, 1997. Besides playing Officer Billings and a host of other roles on the original *Rockford Files*, Delgado was James Garner's long-time stand-in, as well as one of the actor's oldest, closest, and dearest friends. According to Roy Huggins (Luie's brother-in-law), Garner tried to say a few words at the memorial service for Delgado, but was so overwhelmed with emotion that he broke down.

Later, however, Garner honored his friend in a special way. *Murder and Misdemeanors* was dedicated in memory of Luis Delgado.

Rockford Facts

Murder and Misdemeanors was broadcast on a Friday (November 21, 1997), the first time *Rockford* aired on its original night since July 1980. Airing between 8:00 p.m. and 10:00 p.m., the film once again faced tough competition, including *The X Files* in its first hour and *Dateline NBC* in the second. *Murder* started strong (and even won its time slot during the second half-hour) before finishing second overall. The film pulled an 8.7 rating and a 15 share—slightly lower figures than those of the previous two movies, but nonetheless respectable. For the week, *Murder* finished 48th overall out of 111 shows.

Rockford Fun

The scene at the Sand Castle in which Rockford talks to Harvey (played by Conrad Janis) also includes a clever example of product placement. The book Harvey is reading during this sequence is none other than *King Con*, the best-selling novel written by *Rockford* co-creator Stephen J. Cannell.

King Con was officially released in bookstores on June 1, 1997, just as *Murder* was completing production.

8.   IF IT BLEEDS ... IT LEADS

Production Number: 82702
Original Air Date: April 20, 1999
Production Consultant: Stephen J. Cannell
Teleplay by: Reuben Leder
Story by: Juanita Bartlett and Stephen J. Cannell
Directed by: Stuart Margolin

Cast: James Garner (Jim Rockford), Rita Moreno (Rita Capkovic Landale), Hal Linden (Ernie Landale), Stuart Margolin (Angel Martin), Joe Santos (Dennis Becker), Gretchen Corbett (Beth Davenport Van Sant), Tom Atkins (Commander Diehl), Jack Garner (Captain McEnroe), Christopher Bersh (Deputy), Loryn Locklin (Cindy Carteret), Stephanie Faracy (Selma Drown), Denise Crosby (Mrs. Muller), George Wyner (Gillespie), Gerry Gibson (Critch), James A. Watson Jr. (Reporter #2), Harvey Venton (Earl Janus), Luis Avalos (Alvin Sudakis), Shirley Anthony (Sally), Romy Rosemont (Mrs. Disarcina), Larry W. McCormick (Bob Kux), Pat Lalama (Wendy Aziz), Kevin Sifuentes (Carlos), William Kerr (Karros), Perry Santos (Reporter #1), Bob Tur (Captain Dave), Heather White (Allison), Ethan Glazer (Lily), Paige Tamada (Ronnie), Kirsten Storms (Laurie), Juanita Jennings

Synopsis. *Rita Capkovic turns to Rockford one last time when her husband Ernie Lansdale, a respected school teacher, is wrongfully suspected of being the West Side Rapist, the perpetrator of a series of brutal child molestations. When a police sketch of the rapist is leaked to the media, Ernie is immediately hounded by reporters because of his striking resemblance to the suspect depicted in the sketch. With Ernie's reputation in tatters, Rockford's only hope of restoring his friend's good name is to find the real culprit.*

The Rockford Files ended its run on CBS with a surprisingly strong finish, earning the second-highest household rating (10.3) and share (16.0) among all network programs that aired on April 20, 1999, the night it was originally broadcast. The movie drew 14,480,000 viewers, finishing a close second to the 14,540,000 viewers who tuned in to *Dateline NBC.* (*Dateline* that night devoted its entire hour to its coverage of the tragic shootings at Columbine High School in Denver, Colorado, which had taken place earlier that day.)

If It Bleeds ... also finished tied for 15th place in the overall Nielsens for the week. That marked the first time a *Rockford* reunion movie landed in the Top 20 since November 1994, when *I Still Love L.A.* placed fourth with a whopping

Photographs courtesy of CBS Productions
© 1997 CBS, Inc.

Publicity stills for the eighth and last *Rockford Files* movie, *If It Bleeds ... It Leads.*

28 share. *If It Bleeds ...* also delivered the best audience numbers for a *Rockford* movie since *Godfather Knows Best* posted an 11.0 rating and 18.8 share in February 1996. In addition, the numbers for *Bleeds* were 14% higher than the movie CBS aired in the same time slot one week before.

Needless to say, CBS was ecstatic. "They were thrilled and elated by the numbers," said Garner's assistant MaryAnn Rea. "Thank God the viewers didn't believe the critics."

Indeed, most of the advance reviews were less than kind. *USA Today*, for example, gave *If It Bleeds* only 1-½ out of a total of four stars. "The movie doesn't give Rockford much to do," wrote Robert Bianco. "There's no great mystery here for him to solve, and what little exists doesn't make a lot of sense.

"*Rockford* fans might have been willing to overlook the weak plot," Bianco continued. "After all, the show was always less interested in crime than in character. Incredible as it seems, however, *Bleeds* isn't even interested in Rockford. He's pushed aside so the movie can spend more time taking a sledgehammer to TV news. Never mind the rapist. The real villains here are electronic journalists."

CBS also had problems with the script, which may account for why the film sat on the shelf for nearly two years before the network finally broadcast it. "What's interesting," recalled executive producer Charles Floyd Johnson, "is not that the network thought it was a bad show, *per se*—they just thought it was too dark. They were particularly troubled by the scene in which Hal Linden's character takes his life by jumping off the roof. They read that and said, '*This isn't Rockford Files!*' And we said, 'Yes, it is. We do all kinds of stories on *Rockford*.'"

As Johnson alludes, the "problem" that CBS and critics alike had with *Bleeds*—if indeed, it can be called that—was more than anything else a matter of perception.

Though mostly remembered for its car chases, snappy dialogue and off-the-wall characters, *Rockford* was also a show with depth. In any given week (especially during the last four seasons of the original series), writers such as Juanita Bartlett or David Chase were liable to use the Rockford character as a vehicle to address the kind of social ills we see portrayed in *Bleeds*: invasion of privacy, "rush to judgment," our tendency as a country to try certain high-profile cases in the media, and other issues of fairness. After all, part of the charm of Jim Rockford—and by extension, James Garner—was that he was very much an Everyman. Charlie Rose, in fact, took that idea a step further when he called Garner the "quintessential American" during the actor's appearance on his PBS talk show in March 2002.

When a character like Rockford (or in the case of this movie, one of his friends) suddenly finds his rights violated or his life intruded upon by an overly aggressive media, it often makes us stop and think about the issue at hand perhaps more than we otherwise would have. After all, if it can happen to Jim Rockford … it can happen to anyone.

Nevertheless, although Garner and company wrapped production on *Bleeds* in the summer of 1997, nearly two years would pass before CBS finally scheduled it for broadcast. "And the irony about that, of course," adds Johnson, "is that once they ran it, the movie did very well."

Indeed, the audience numbers for *Bleeds* are even more remarkable considering the network's lack of interest. Even once it did get an air date, the movie came and went with very little fanfare.

"CBS hardly promoted it at all," said talk show host and *Rockford* aficionado Ronn Owens, who helped publicize *If It Bleeds … It Leads* on his top-rated morning talk show on KGO Radio in San Francisco. "It would have made sense if they put it on during sweeps, because both Garner and Rockford are still enough of an icon that they could have promoted the movie as 'an event.' Instead, they just tossed it out there in the middle of April, as if to say, 'Okay, here's the movie tonight. Go ahead and watch it if you want.'" *NOTE. In recent years, April has increasingly become known as a "dead" month in the television season. For the most part, the four major networks (ABC, NBC, CBS and Fox) use April as a month for reruns, holding off on airing any remaining new episodes, original movies and other "event" programming until May—when they can air them as part of the annual "sweeps" period that ends the television season.*

Rockford Facts

Juanita Bartlett was originally set to write *Bleeds*, but became unable to do so after she accidentally fell and broke her left wrist. To keep matters from falling behind schedule, Stephen J. Cannell helped Bartlett with the story, while Reuben Leder was brought in to write the teleplay.

Although Leder was new to *Rockford*, he was no stranger to co-executive producer Charles Floyd Johnson: Leder wrote 31 episodes of *Magnum, p.i.*, which Johnson produced and/or executive produced for eight seasons. Leder, whose sister Mimi Leder is the Emmy Award-winning producer of *ER* and *China Beach*, has also penned two episodes of *JAG*, on which Johnson has been co-executive producer since 1996.

Rockford Familiar Faces

If It Bleeds ... It Leads also reunites Rita Moreno with character actor Luis Avalos, who co-starred with Moreno (along with Morgan Freeman) in the acclaimed children's television series *The Electric Company* (PBS, 1971-1976). As fans of *The Electric Company* will remember, Moreno began each episode of the show (from the second season on) with the trademark yell, *"Heyyy-you-guyyyyys!!!"*

Courtesy of MGB Productions, Inc.

Logo for the *Rockford Files* production company formed by James Garner for the reunion movies. Garner had baseball caps and T-shirts sporting this logo specially made for the members of his crew.

Appendix I
The *Rockford* Novels

Covers of the hardcover editions of the *Rockford Files* novels written by Stuart Kaminisky: *The Green Bottle* (left, originally published in 1996) and *Devil On My Doorstep* (1998)

The successful revival of *Rockford* on CBS also led to the publication of two original *Rockford Files* novels: *The Green Bottle* and *Devil on My Doorstep*, both of which were penned by Edgar Award-winning mystery writer Stuart Kaminsky. "I was and am a big *Rockford Files* fan," Kaminsky told *January Magazine* in August 2002. "Tor Books [an imprint of St. Martin's Press] and the series' producers came to me to ask if I might be interested in writing original Rockford novels. They knew of my love for the series. We negotiated, I eagerly agreed and that was it."

Originally published in October 1996, *The Green Bottle* is a breezy whodunit that's bound to please even the most discriminating of *Rockford* philes. A simple matter of recovering a stolen collectible bottle for a wealthy orthopedic surgeon soon becomes far too complicated (not to mention dangerous) for Rockford's well-being. The search for the green bottle soon becomes a search for the doctor's missing teenaged niece, an aspiring but talentless actress sucked into the dangerous glitter of Hollywood.

Rockford in the novel is as mercenary as ever. Despite three attempts on his life (not to mention a pair of trumped-up murder charges), our man Jimbo can't quite walk away from the case—not after the doctor dangles a carrot in the form of an expensive reconstructive surgery that our sore-kneed hero otherwise can't afford. That, plus the prospect of a hefty paycheck, is enough to keep him motivated. Kaminsky clearly understands what makes Rockford tick.

Like a typical *Rockford* teleplay, *The Green Bottle* features a colorful array of offbeat characters (including a gay NFL middle linebacker), as well as three of the show's principal supporting players: Dennis Becker, Rockford's only friend on the L.A.P.D.; Beth Davenport, his lawyer and ex-girlfriend; and Angel Martin, "Jimmy's" former prison cellmate and permanent cross to bear. There's even a "B" story for comic relief: Rockford dispatches Angel to locate the missing cat of an eccentric but wealthy Beverly Hills socialite.

The most noticeable departure from the series formula—Rockford as his own narrator—brings mixed results. Kaminsky's Rockford is more reflective and far more of an intellectual than his TV counterpart. As James Garner played him, Rockford was certainly intelligent, but he was also a straight-shooting, street-savvy guy with little tolerance for hot air. It's hard to imagine him alluding to Bergman films (as he does throughout the novel), or having any kind of appetite for talk radio.

Then again, the use of first-person narrative makes sense in light of what Kaminsky set out to do: "The one contribution I made—besides, I hope, my creativity and originality—was to depict an older, more resigned Jim Rockford in keeping with James Garner's age." The first-person narrative is also very appropos, given Rockford's literary ancestry. As mentioned before, *Rockford* co-creator Roy Huggins was a successful mystery novelist in the Chandler vein prior to his career in television.

The Green Bottle may not be Kaminsky's greatest work (the escapade with Angel is more silly than funny) but overall it's a solid tale worthy of the *Rockford Files* banner.

Kaminsky followed up *The Green Bottle* with *Devil on My Doorstep*, which was originally published in March 1998. Though both books sold well, the series did not continue beyond that. "I'm not sure why they didn't want me to do more," Kaminsky told *January Magazine* in August 2002. "I would have been happy to do so ... I think if it were possible for me to do more *Rockford* novels, [my editor] would find a way."

Epilogue

Say Goodbye to Jim Rockford
(or, "This Case is Closed")

The outstanding finish for *If It Bleeds … It Leads* fueled some speculation that CBS might bring back *Rockford* for at least one more film—especially after encore showings of the first three movies continued to do well in the ratings. The repeat broadcasts of *I Still Love L.A.* and *A Blessing in Disguise* (shown on the nights of December 26, 1996 and June 2, 1997, respectively) drew respectable audience numbers, while the rerun of *If the Frame Fits* (shown August 12, 1999) actually won its overall time slot.

The possibility of more *Rockford*s certainly seemed conceivable given the hot streak James Garner was enjoying at the time. After a year (1998) which saw him receive stellar reviews for his performances in *Twilight* and *Legalese*, Garner began 1999 as much in demand as ever. Among other things, he embarked on his first animated venture, providing the voice of God for the animated comedy series *God, the Devil and Bob* (which eventually aired on NBC in the spring of 2000). Later in the year, he would star with fellow screen legends Clint Eastwood, Donald Sutherland, and Tommy Lee Jones in the movie *Space Cowboys*, which was released in 2000.

Also in early 1999, the Peacock Network began production of an hour-long documentary on Garner's life and career that would eventually air in early 2000 as a segment of *Headliners & Legends*. (Later in 2000, a second documentary on Garner, "James Garner: Hollywood Maverick," was produced for the popular nightly series *A&E's Biography*. That program continues to air regularly on the Biography Channel.)

As it happened, though, any talk about additional *Rockford*s turned out to be academic. CBS never made an offer. Even if they had, in all likelihood Garner would have turned it down for a very practical reason.

"Jim was reluctant to continue," said Garner associate MaryAnn Rea. "Remember, we'd finished shooting that last picture in 1997. Had we gotten another order from CBS right then and there, I think that he would have gone ahead and done at least one more. But we never heard from the network one way or the other. By the time they finally scheduled the movie, it was 1999. Jim was a couple years older, and he no longer thought that anyone would believe in a 71-year-old private detective."

Rockford fans who would like to see Garner continue on in the role might point to the likes of Barnaby Jones (Buddy Ebsen) and Jessica Fletcher (the character played by Angela Lansbury on *Murder, She Wrote*), two characters who were not only in their 70s, but also the linchpins for enormously successful detective shows that aired on CBS. *Barnaby Jones* ran for eight seasons (1973-1980), while *Murder, She Wrote* ran for twelve (1984-1996).

Then again, compared to *The Rockford Files*, *Barnaby Jones* and *Murder, She Wrote* were completely different shows. For one, neither Barnaby nor Jessica ever had to throw a punch—nor were they ever expected to. Whereas for all its peculiar idiosyncrasies, *Rockford* was at heart an action/adventure show. As much as Jim Rockford hated to fight, his audience knew that he could handle himself (and hold his own) if he absolutely had to. Take away that physical element—as the CBS movies had to do out of necessity, given Garner's age—and the show is no longer *Rockford*.

That, coupled with the network's apparent disinterest in the series, made the decision a slam dunk. As far as Garner was concerned, *If It Bleeds ... It Leads* was Rockford's last case. The fact the movie finished as strong as it did was simply icing on the cake.

"What's really amazing is that those movies had a presence on CBS for almost seven years," said executive producer Charles Floyd Johnson. "That's longer than the run of the original show. We were on NBC from '74 to '80. We started on CBS in '94. Even though there were only eight *Rockford*s in that series of movies, CBS continued to show them until the summer of 2001. I've always gotten a kick out of that."

✳   ✳   ✳

The Rockford Files is one of the few series in the history of television that never really left the air. Since concluding its original network run in 1980, *Rockford* continues to play daily in syndication on independent stations throughout the world. In addition, the series has remained a popular fixture on cable television since 1992, often airing twice a day on such networks as A&E, the Goodlife Network, the Nashville Network, TV Land and superstation WGN.

Court TV acquired the cable rights to the eight CBS movies in December 2000, airing the first six on consecutive Friday nights through February 2001 and the remaining two later in the fall. The Hallmark Channel then purchased the rights to the *Rockford* movies in 2002, and have broadcast them on a regular basis ever since.

Original art © 2005 by Darin Bristow

Bibliography

Most of the information in this book was derived from personal interviews with the following: Juanita Bartlett, Howard Browne, Stephen J. Cannell, Gretchen Corbett, Luis Delgado, Jack Garner, James Garner, Rob Howe, Roy Huggins, Charles Floyd Johnson, Frankie Montiforte, Frank Price, MaryAnn Rea, Steve Reich, Jo Swerling, Jack Wilson, and Anthony Zerbe.

The books and resources listed below were also of tremendous value:

Books

Brooks, Tim, *The Complete Directory to Prime Time TV Stars, 1946-Present.* New York: Ballantine Books, 1987.

Brooks, Tim and Earle Marsh, *The Complete Directory to Prime Time Network TV Shows, 1946-Present.* New York: Ballantine Books, 1995. Sixth edition.

Broughton, Irv, *Producers on Producing: The Making of Film and Television.* Jefferson, N.C.: McFarland & Company, Inc., 1986.

Castleman, Harry, and Walter J. Podrizak, *Harry and Wally's Favorite TV Shows.* New York: Prentice Hall Press, 1989.

————. *Watching TV: Four Decades of American Television.* New York: McGraw-Hill Book Company, 1982.

Christensen, Mark, and Cameron Stauth, *The Sweeps: Behind the Scenes in Network TV.* New York: William Morrow and Company, Inc., 1984.

Curran, Barbara, *25 Years of Dallas: The Complete Story of the World's Favorite Prime Time Soap.* College Station, TX: Virtualbook.com Publishing, 2004.

Gianakos, Larry James, *Television Drama Series Programming: A Comprehensive Chronicle,* Vols. I-III, VI. Metuchen, NJ: The Scarecrow Press, Inc.

Hagman, Larry, with Todd Gold, *Hello Darlin': Tall (and Absolutely True) Tales About My Life.* New York: Simon & Schuster, 1991.

Kaminsky, Stuart M., with Jeffrey H. Mahan, *American Television Genres.* Chicago: Nelson-Hall, Inc., 1985.

Kaminsky, Stuart M., *The Rockford Files: The Green Bottle.* New York: St. Martin's Press, 1996.

Katz, Ephraim, *The Film Encyclopedia: The Most Comprehensive Encyclopedia of World Cinema in a Single Volume.* Revised by Fred Klein and Ronald Dean Nolen. New York: HarperPerennial, 1998. Second edition.

Levinson, Richard, and William Link, *Stay Tuned: An Inside Look at the Making of Prime Time Television*, New York: St. Martin's Press, 1981.

Marc, David, and Robert Thompson, *Prime Time, Prime Movers.* Boston: Little, Brown. 1992.

Marrill, Alvin. *Movies Made for Television: The Telefeature and the Mini-Series, 1964-1984.* New York: New York Zoetrope, 1984.

Martindale, David, *The Rockford Phile.* Las Vegas: Pioneer Books, Inc., 1991.

McNeil, Alex, *Total Television.* New York: Penguin Books, 1996. Fourth edition. First published in 1980.

Meyers, Ric, *Murder on the Air.* New York: Mysterious Press, 1989.

————. *TV Detectives*, San Diego: A.S. Barnes & Company, 1981.

Parish, James Robert and Vincent Terrace, *The Complete Actors' Television Credits, 1948-1988, Volume I: Actors.* Metuchen: The Scarecrow Press, Inc. 1989. Second edition.

Peer, Kurt, *TV Tie-Ins: A Bibliography of American TV Tie-In Paperbacks.* New York: TV Books, 1997.

Robertson, Ed, *Maverick: Legend of the West.* Los Angeles: Pomegranate Press, 1994.

Stempel, Tom, *Storytellers to the Nation: A History of American Television Writing.* New York: Continuum Publishing Company, 1992.

Strait, Raymond, *James Garner: A Biography.* New York: St. Martin's Press, 1985.

Terrace, Vincent, *Encyclopedia of Television: Series, Pilots and Specials. Volumes I, II and III.* New York: New York Zoetrope, 1986.

Variety Television Reviews, 1923-1988, in 15 volumes. New York: Garland Publishing Company, 1988.

Magazine and Newspaper Articles

Alt, Eric, "We Want Answers: Joe Pantoliano," *Maxim*, December 2002.

Amory, Cleveland, "Review: *The Rockford Files*," *TV Guide*, December 21, 1974.

"Annals of Law: Taking the Fifth," *The New Yorker*, April 1976.

Beck, Marilyn, "James Garner Never Fails to Thank His Lucky Star," Special Features/New York Times Syndicate, August 24, 1974.

Bennett, Ray, "Gentleman Jim: The Women in James Garner's Life Call Him Television's Original Liberated Male," *TV Guide*, August 25, 1979.

Benson, Ray, "Garner in *Rockford* is First Non-Western," *Columbia Record*, March 23, 1974.

Bianco, Robert, "File Tired *Rockford* Under 'Misguided,'" *USA Today*, April 20, 1999.

Boyer, Peter J., "Rockford Opens His Last File," Associated Press, January 10, 1980.

Bulgin, Russell, "Less Romance, More Money: James Garner and Jacques Villeneuve Reflect on Grand Prix Racing, Then and Now," *Autoweek*, January 3, 2000.

Carman, John, "James Garner to Reprise *Rockford*," *San Francisco Chronicle*, July 25, 1994.

———. "Place Your Sunday Bets on *Rockford Blessing*," *San Francisco Chronicle*, May 12, 1995.

Clark, Andrew, "Tough Guys Wear Plaid: Thirty Years Later, Jim Rockford is Still TV's Coolest Private Eye," *Toro*, May 2004.

Deeb, Gary, "Can Jim Work *Maverick* Magic Again?" *Dallas Times-Herald*, January 1980.

Durgin, Vance, "*Rockford Files* Was The Show to Beat," *Orange County Register*, November 25, 1994.

Dyer, Bob, "Man Behind the Badge Still Roams the Tube Next Season," *Phoenix Gazette*, July 27, 1974.

Evans, K.J., "Kirk Kerkorian: The Private Lion," *Las Vegas Review-Journal*, September 12, 1999.

Foster, Bob, "Jim Garner to Try TV Series Again," *San Mateo Times*, August 1, 1974.

Hano, Arnold, "The Incredible Shrinking Actor," *TV Guide*, February 1, 1975.

Hawkes, Ellen, "Gentle Heart, Tough Guy," *Parade*, July 12, 1992.

Hess, Steve, "*Rockford* Has Village on Ear," *Wrightwood Mountaineer-Progress*, November 21, 1979.

Hiltbrand, David, "Tube Picks and Pans: *The Rockford Files*: A Blessing in Disguise," *People*, May 15, 1995.

"Huggins Responds to His Critics," *Daily Variety*, September 1974.

"June Allyson and Peter Lawford Together Again … in *Bad News!*" Review of video release of *They Only Kill Their Masters*, posted June 1, 2003 at imdb.com.

Kaufman, Dave, "TV Series Talent Shortage: Huggins of *Rockford Files* Finds Personnel Hard to Get for the One-Hour Vidshow," *Daily Variety*, August 26, 1974.

King, Susan, "Reactivating *Rockford*: James Garner Gets Back in the P.I. Business with Movies for CBS," *Los Angeles Times*, November 27, 1994.

Lewis, Dan, "Garner Recalls *Maverick* Fondly," *San Diego Union*, November 10, 1974.

Linderman, Lawrence, "James Garner: A Candid Conversation with the Easygoing Star about *Maverick, Rockford*, Funny Commercials, His Bizarre Childhood, and Corruption in Hollywood," *Playboy*, March 1981.

Martindale, David, "Reruns," syndicated column for week of January 14-20, 1996.

McDonald, C.M., "Stephen J. Cannell: Hollywood Tough (an interview in two parts), Writers on Writing: Exclusive Interviews," www.modestyarbor.com/writers.html, 2003.

Moss, Morton, "Noah Beery Jr.: Long Career Recipe," *Los Angeles Herald-Examiner*, August 20, 1974.

"New Housewife Blues, The," *Time*, March 14, 1977.

O'Flaherty, Terence, "Oh, My Aching Back," *San Francisco Chronicle*, September 16, 1974.

Pierce, J. Kingston, "Stuart M. Kaminsky: Murder is His Businesss," *January Magazine*, August 2002.

Pond, Steve, "The Garner Files: Jim Garner's Back, with Plenty to Say About *Rockford* and the Ups and Downs of Life," *TV Guide*, November 26, 1994.

Prelutsky, Burt, "Q. What Strange Twists of Fortune Brought Joe Santos from Construction Work to His Role in *The Rockford Files*? A. He Failed at Everything Else," *TV Guide*, August 26, 1977.

Raddatz, Leslie, "Old Pidge," *TV Guide*, March 6, 1976.

Riordan, Paul A., "An Interview with Tom Atkins," *Images Journal: A Journal of Film and Popular Culture*, October 1997.

Robertson, Ed, "Closing Out *The Rockford Files*: The Original Must See TV," *TV Party*, April 1999.

———. "Run For Your Life," *Television Chronicles*, April 1998.

Roth, Arnold, "A *Rockford Files* Sketchbook," *TV Guide*, March 5, 1977.

Rothstein, Mervyn, "A Star Returns: After Years of Battling Rumors and Bad Scripts, Tom Selleck, the Former Star of *Magnum, p.i.*, Is Poised for a Comeback," *Cigar Aficionado*, Winter 1995/96.

Ryan, Barbara Haddad, "James Garner to Try Again in *The Rockford Files*," *Denver Post*, June 26, 1974.

Scholl, Jaye, "The *Rockford* File; or, James Garner Learns Accounting the Hollywood Style," *Barron's*, February 6, 1989.

————. "No *Rockford* Trials: MCA Unit Settles with James Garner," *Barron's*, April 3, 1989.

"Stephen J. Cannell: Thousand-Episode Producer," *Daily Variety*, August 17, 1995.

Stoddard, Sylvia, "Magnum, p.i.," *Television Chronicles*, April 1997.

Swertlow, Frank, "As We See It: Garner Expected to File Suit Against Universal," *TV Guide*, January 30, 1982.

————. "As We See It: Garner Sues to Collect *Rockford* Money," *TV Guide*, July 23, 1983.

Swift, Arthur, "Inside The Sopranos," www.arthurswift.com, April 24, 2004.

"Television Reviews: *The Rockford Files: I Still Love L.A.*," *Daily Variety*, November 23, 1994.

"Television Reviews: *The Rockford Files: Punishment and Crime*," *Daily Variety*, September 18, 1996.

Thomas, Bob, "James Garner: Alive and Well," Associated Press, November 14, 1974.

Torgerson, Ellen, "James Garner Believes in Good Coffee—and a Mean Punch," *TV Guide*, June 2, 1979.

Utterback, Betty, "Meta Rosenberg: How This Female TV Producer Got to the Top," *Rochester Democrat-Chronicle*, September 24, 1974.

Vallely, Jean, "The James Garner Files," *Esquire*, July 3-19, 1979.

Voorhees, John, "NBC Betting on Garner for *Files*," *Seattle Times*, August 30, 1974.

Walker, Wendy Heinz, "James Garner: Getting to the Heart of the Matter," *Vim & Vigor*, Summer 1992.

Weinstein, Steve, "James Garner: A Weight Off His Broad Shoulders," *Los Angeles Times*, April 3, 1989.

Witbeck, Charles, "Jim Garner's New Series," King Features Syndicate, August 14, 1974.

Zuanich, Barbra, "Joseph Cotten: Limitations Led to Stardom," *Los Angeles Herald-Examiner*, August 14, 1974.

Other Sources

"Jim Rockford, Private Investigator: Episode Titles and Numbers, Stars and Guest Stars, Log Lines for TV Listings, Cast and Credits." Program kit distributed by MCA-TV, 1979.

James Garner v. Universal City Studios, Inc., Los Angeles County Superior Court No. C-459-716. First Amended Complaint for Damages, filed October 11, 1983. (Action later consolidated with *Universal City Studios, Inc. v. James Garner,* Los Angeles County Superior Court No. C-310-140, originally filed January 1980.)

"Program Test Report: *The Rockford Files,*" NBC Program Research, March 1974.

Roy Huggins v. Universal City Studios, Inc., Los Angeles County Superior Court No. BC007038. Complaint for Damages, filed July 31, 1990.

NOTE: *All other documents pertaining to the above litigations cited in this text were obtained via the Los Angeles County Archives Center.*

Memoranda and other documents pertaining to the creation of *The Rockford Files* cited herein are from the personal collection of Roy Huggins.

Information from the various television interviews cited herein was culled from videotapes from the author's personal collection.

About the Author

Photograph by Chloe Rounsley

Ed Robertson has written extensively about popular culture since 1990. He has had five books published, including two on the career of James Garner: *Maverick: Legend of the West*, a history of Garner's classic Western from the 1950s, and *This is Jim Rockford: The Rockford Files*, which was originally published in 1995. Ed was also a consultant and onscreen commentator on two documentaries on Garner's life and career: "James Garner," an hour-long film produced by NBC, and "Hollywood Maverick," a segment produced for *A&E's Biography* that continues to air regularly on the Biography Channel. He also writes for *Media Life Magazine*, and has contributed to a variety of publications and media venues, including the liner notes for many titles currently available through Columbia House Video Library.

A recognized expert in pop culture, Ed Robertson is frequently contacted by journalists across the country for comments on topics related to film, music and television. He has been quoted in such newspapers and media outlets as

TV Guide, FoxNews.com, ABCNews.com, USA Today, The London Observer, The Toronto Star, The Christian Science Monitor, The Dallas Morning News, The Atlanta Journal-Constitution, The San Francisco Chronicle and *The Los Angeles Times.* He has also appeared on over 150 radio and TV programs, including *Showbiz Today, CNN Headline News, First Light* (Westwood One Radio Network), *Up All Night* (BBC Radio), *Talk to America* (Voice of America Radio Network), *The Todd Mundt Show* (National Public Radio), *The Mancow Muller Show, E! News Today, The High Price of Fame* and *Entertainment Tonight,* and is a regular guest on *The Ronn Owens Program* (KGO-AM, San Francisco), *Hot Talk with Tony Gill* (WAIC-FM, Springfield) and *The Tony Trupiano Show* (Michigan Talk Radio Network).

www.edrobertson.com

Index of Names and Episode Titles

0-595-34244-2